THE
COMPLETE
I CHING

"This translation, from a Taoist master, is the most extensive treatment of the subject I have ever encountered. . . . the quality of the work is so exceptional that it is hard to find fault with it. . . . if you wish to learn this system, this book will be an indispensable aid to your education. There is such a wealth of information contained in this book (each page contains the hexagram being discussed and the ideograph of the name, so there is no confusion) that it is hard to overstate the usefulness of this work. . . . This it is of use and benefit for both the novice and the more experienced user."

MIKE GLEASON, *WITCHGROVE*

"Huang succeeds, also, in producing a work that keeps opening up new vistas of understanding and inviting the reader to explore the many layers of discovery offered by the mathematical, visual and literary dimensions of the classic."

REG LITTLE, *NEW DAWN*

THE
COMPLETE
I CHING

The Definitive Translation
by
Taoist Master Alfred Huang

Inner Traditions
Rochester, Vermont • Toronto, Canada

Inner Traditions
One Park Street
Rochester, Vermont 05767
www.InnerTraditions.com

Library of Congress Cataloging-in-Publication Data
Yi jing. English.
  The complete I ching : the definitive translation / by the Taoist Master Alfred Huang. — [10th anniversary ed.}
    p. cm.
  Includes index.
  Summary: "This 10th anniversary edition offers a thorough introduction to the history of the I Ching, how to use it, and several new divination methods; in-depth and easy-to-reference translations of each hexagram name, description, and pictogram; and discussions of the interrelations between the hexagrams and the spiritual meaning of their sequence"— Provided by publisher.
  ISBN 978-1-59477-386-0 (pbk.) — ISBN 978-1-59477-385-3 (hardcover)
  I. Huang, Alfred. II. Title. PL2478.D43 2010
  299.5'1282—dc22
                                                                    2010026767
Printed and bound in India by Replika Press Pvt. Ltd.

20 19 18 17 16 15 14 13 12 11

Text design and layout by Kristin Camp
This book was typeset in Caslon with Papyrus as the display typeface

*During this great time of change this
book is dedicated to those who are
longing to change and ready to change
to a meaningful and successful life of
abundance and happiness.*

If some years
were added to my life,
I would dedicate fifty years
to study of the Book of I,
and then I might come
to be without great fault.

CONFUCIUS
AT AGE 70

Contents

THE UPPER CANON

THE LOWER CANON

Acknowledgments

I would like to express my deep gratitude to three most important persons; without their loving support and encouragement this book would not have been possible. First is my revered teacher, Master Yin; without his earnest teaching instruction, I would not have the knowledge to translate this book.

Second is my dear friend Bill Smith, who has made I Ching a daily practice since 1973 and kept daily notes continuously. After he read over the fifth revision of my manuscript he said, "Alfred, for the past fifty years Richard Wilhelm's translation of the I Ching has been the standard. I hope your book will be the standard for the next fifty years." I don't know whether my translation will become the standard for the next fifty years, but Bill's challenge and encouragement have been the motivating force for the constant improvement of the translation.

The third important person is Jon Graham, the Acquisitions Editor of Inner Traditions International. His enthusiastic effort in conferring with his company about publishing my book reminds me of an ancient tale.

> It is not rare to find horses able to cover a thousand li a day, but Ba-le is rare. In the later period of the Spring and Autumn Annals (770–476 B.C.), there was a man, Ba-le, who was adept in looking at a horse to judge its worth. Among a herd of horses he was able to point out the one that was able to cover a thousand li a day. (Li is a Chinese unit of length equivalent to half a kilometer.)

The story suggests that, without Ba-le, horses able to cover a thousand li a day often go unrecognized. Although my new translation of the I Ching is not a horse that covers a thousand li a day, without Jon Graham it would not be recognized.

I also wish to offer my heartfelt thanks to Steve Thomson and Linda Millar. During the time I was working on this translation, I stayed at the Zen Monastery at Akahi Farm in Haiku, Maui, where I met Steve. When he saw I was making a new translation of the I Ching, he told me it was a matter of great interest to him to read my manuscript. During the first three months he came to my home every night to read over my new translation and point out my English mistakes. After I made the fifth revision, Linda proofread the text.

I would like to express my gratitude to Marguerite Dinkins for the love she gave me. She spent all of her precious time being with me, reading over my manuscript, and polishing the English of my translation during her vacation on Maui. We enjoyed the beautiful scenery, the nice weather, the harmonious atmosphere, and our lovely like-mindedness.

During the time I worked on the seventh revision, Courtney Collins came into my life. Through her pureness of heart and sincerity in love I experienced the harmony of yin and yang, the dance of the souls, and the interplay between Heaven and Earth. The virtue of her femininity brought me to a new level of understanding the true significance of Qian and Kun, the first and second gua of the I Ching.

I would like to extend further thanks to Bill Smith for his appreciation of the Tao of I and his understanding of the importance of finding the most appropriate English words for the names of the gua. During my eighth revision, I found that my original manuscript was not absolutely objective. With the help of Bill, I checked my manuscript word for word against the Chinese text several times and in most places I followed the Chinese word order. Without Bill's help it would have been almost impossible for my final revision to reveal the true essence of the I Ching.

I would like to express my appreciation to Inner Traditions International for publishing this book, making a great contribution in presenting and carrying forward Chinese culture. My heartfelt appreciation, in particular, to Thomas Thamm, for designing the beautiful cover which truly captures the essence of the book, and to Kristin Camp, for designing the interior and preparing the ancient pictograph for each gua. I also express my deep gratitude to my editor Rowan Jacobsen and copyeditor Marcia Means for their patience, support, and suggestions in helping me turn one of the most profound and abstruse Chinese classics into a readable book.

Preface

I

I emigrated from China to the United States in 1980. After sixteen years in America I found that people in the Western world are interested in the I Ching: The Book of Change. But there was a different story in its native land.

From the time I was very young I heard that the I Ching was a Tian Shu, a Heavenly book; without the verbal instruction of a competent scholar, no one can understand it. After the Communists took over China in 1949, the I Ching was denounced as a book of feudalism and superstition. It was banished from the market, and reading it was not allowed. In the early 1960s, before the so-called Cultural Revolution, Dr. Ting Jihua, a most eminent Chinese physician in Shanghai; professor Liu Yenwen, a well-known professor of Chinese classical literature; and I attended the revered Master Yin's private gatherings, where he taught us the I Ching. It was absolutely an underground activity. At that time, all of us had been labeled as antirevolutionary right-wing advocates. If our meetings had been discovered by any Communist Party member or the police, we would no doubt have been imprisoned. Master Yin was more than eighty years old. He sensed that a calamity would soon befall China and he wished to pass his teachings on before he died. He offered on his own initiative to teach us the esoteric knowledge of the I Ching, which he had inherited from his own revered master. As we studied, the situation in China grew worse, and our hearts grew heavier and heavier. We realized that many families would be broken up and countless people would be persecuted.

Although we knew that after the long night there would come the dawn, the dawn did not come soon enough. In two years Master Yin and Dr. Ting passed away one after the other. Professor Liu lost his desire to live. He attempted suicide several times. Although I encouraged him to persevere, deep in my heart I knew that those who died were the blessed ones. They had ended their sufferings and were able to enjoy everlasting peace. Those who were still living had to face unimaginable suffering and strive for survival.

According to the I Ching, every country has its destiny and every person has his or her fate, but everyone still has freedom to make his own choices. Of the four scholars, I was the youngest. The others were of my father's generation. Being with them I realized that I had much to learn and experience. From the bottom of my heart I chose to live, to live as long as I could and see the destiny of China, no matter what hardships I might endure. In July 1957 I was forced to do manual labor every day, and in September 1966 I was put into jail. During nine years in jail, I was interrogated almost every day about my "counterrevolutionary" activities. Because I graduated from a missionary school and had been the principal of a Christian high school, my captors pressed me to confess that I was an American spy. On every occasion I denied the charges against me. At last they became desperate, and sentenced me to death. However, because I was a popular figure with the Chinese people, they did not dare to follow through with the death sentence immediately, although they repeatedly told me that I would be put to death.

During twenty-two years of confinement, even though I could not remember the sixty-four gua (hexagrams), I fully comprehended the Tao of I, the essence of the I Ching, which holds that when events proceed to their extremes they give birth to their opposites. Every day I read the official six-page newspaper as carefully as I could, not missing a single word. As I saw the situation of my country deteriorating, my heart became lighter. I knew after the long darkness there would be a dawn. When the darkness grew darker and darker, the dawn drew closer and closer.

II

The I Ching is a very ancient book. It existed more than two thousand years before Confucius (ca. 551–479 B.C.). In the beginning, the language of the I Ching was simple and easy to understand. Unfortunately, this ancient language became antiquated long, long ago. At that time, the number of Chinese characters was small. As a result, many characters had the same form but entirely different meanings. On the other hand, many characters had different forms but shared the same sound. Their usage was interchangeable. Thus the text is open to many interpretations. Moreover, the old Chinese written language had no punctuation. Depending on how one punctuates a clause or a sentence, different meanings appear. For this reason, even the Chinese are rarely able to truly and fully understand the I Ching without the verbal instruction of a competent teacher. When I came to the United States I was surprised that there were so many translations of the I Ching in English. I cannot imagine how these translators all found the I Ching scholars and did the decades of study necessary to truly learn the I Ching.

To the Chinese, the I Ching is like a Holy Bible written by the four most honored sages in history—Fu Xi, King Wen, the Duke of Zhou, and Confucius. The Chinese translation of Holy Bible is Sheng Ching. Sheng is equivalent to "holy," and Ching means "classic." Chinese understand that Ching is the Tao, the Truth, the holiest of the ancient books, and because they revere and respect the sacred writings of the Jews and the Christian church, they honor the Bible by calling it Ching. For this reason, Chinese translations of the Holy Bible never depart from the original text. On this ground, I think that any translation of the I Ching should not depart from the original text; otherwise, it is not the I Ching.

Among all the translations Richard Wilhelm's (published in English in 1950) and James Legge's (published in 1882) are the best. But all the translations, according to my Chinese point of view, are not absolutely true to the original Chinese I Ching; they are Westernized. To smooth out the English or to capture a concept, they have added their own understanding of the text in a way that limits possible interpretations of a work that is famously open-ended. The ideal translation should be English in form, but Chinese in essence. As a book of divination, Confucius's commentaries are crucial. The Chinese call Confucius's commentaries the Ten Wings. They believe that the I Ching depends on the Ten Wings to be able to fly. In other words, without Confucius's commentaries the I Ching cannot be understood. This is a typically Chinese orthodox point of view. Consequently, every time I read translations that show little concern for Confucius's wisdom, I feel that something is missing. Sometimes when I used English translations to divine, I was so depressed that I had no desire to do it again. When I use the Chinese text it is entirely different; there is always hope.

The I Ching is a truly profound book. It is the source of much of the Chinese culture. Originally, the I Ching was a handbook for divination. After Confucius and his students had written the commentaries, it became known as a book of ancient wisdom. It is a book that not only tells one who consults it about the present situation and future potential but also gives instruction about what to do and what not to do to obtain good fortune and to avoid misfortune. But one still retains free choice. The guidance is based upon comprehensive observations of natural laws by ancient sages and their profound experiences of the principle of cause and effect.

In 1979 the Chinese Supreme Court declared me innocent. I was released from prison weighing eighty pounds and barely able to walk. I decided to emigrate to the United States. During my sixteen years in America I have known people who have devoted their whole hearts and minds to consulting the I Ching, but they could not comprehend its authentic essence or embrace its ancient wisdom because an authentic translation was not available.

I waited for a translation that would truly reveal the essence of the book. My wish was not fulfilled. When I moved to Maui in July 1993 my plan was to write a series of seven books on Taoist Chi Kung. One morning early in July, during my meditation, a voice came to me, urging me to make a new translation of the I Ching. At first, I ignored it. I had never entertained such an idea, and I had doubts. I understood that to work on it one first had to translate the ancient dead language of the original pictographs and ideographs into contemporary Chinese, then translate it again into English. If I made the commitment, the task would be extremely arduous. Nevertheless, the voice grew louder and louder. I could not escape it. I felt I had no choice because the more I meditated the more I felt that I had an obligation to work out a translation of the I Ching based entirely on Chinese concepts. I began to realize that during his last years, Master Yin's proposal to teach me the I Ching was not accidental. There was a reason. I sense now that in this great time of change, when people are longing to transform and the situation is ripe, a new translation of the I Ching based upon ancient Chinese wisdom and experience would be helpful to those making their own choices in this dynamic world of changes.

III

After I accepted the challenge, the first thing I decided was to keep the book small—a small book is much easier to work with. Confucius said that the I Ching is a book one should keep close at hand. A small book is easier to carry. It is readily available for obtaining ancient wisdom as guidance in daily life. Obviously, I failed in this goal. The project grew beyond my expectation. As I made several revisions, the book became bigger and bigger. By the seventh revision, the book was larger than I could have imagined.

The original I Ching consists of only sixty-four Decisions made by King Wen and three hundred and eighty-six Yao Texts composed by the Duke of Zhou. The Decisions are brief summaries of the meaning of each gua, dense in symbolic meaning but succinct in style. The Yao Texts are analyses, employing parables and metaphors, of each of the six lines in a given gua, which correspond to the six stages of a particular situation. Altogether there are less than five thousand Chinese characters. Translated into English it is at most forty pages. However, this tiny book reveals an ancient Chinese cosmology of Heaven and human beings integrated into one union. And it further reveals the Tao of Change or, in Chinese terminology, the Tao of I. These two concepts have been the source of Chinese culture and have permeated Chinese thinking for thousands of years. To truly understand the original language and the spirit of the I Ching, one must realize that its structure is extremely well knit and its wording is absolutely strict. Most translations do not understand this linkage.

As I tried to share the unique features of the I Ching as clearly as I could, the book expanded. Finally I realized that a complete volume that unfolds the essence of the I Ching is preferable. Once readers have come to a true understanding of the symbols, names, texts, and interrelations of the I Ching, they can fly on their own wings, ignoring the commentaries and explanations.

Ten Contributions of This Translation

1. EXPOUNDING THE TAO OF I

Many Westerners know the I Ching, but they do not know the Tao of I. Of the numerous treasures in the I Ching, I value the Tao of I the most. The main theme of the I Ching is that everything is in a process of continuous change, rising and falling in a progressive evolutionary advancement. Although this is the main theme of the I Ching, it is never mentioned in the text. It is revealed only between the lines, and in particular is embodied in the succession of the names of the gua and the sequences and structures of the gua and the yao (lines).

The Tao of I also discloses that when situations proceed beyond their extremes, they alternate to their opposites. It is a reminder to accept necessary change and be ready to transform, warning that one should adjust one's efforts according to changes in time and situation. The Tao of I also says: In a favorable time and situation, never neglect the unfavorable potential. In an unfavorable time and situation, never act abruptly and blindly. And in adverse circumstances, never become depressed and despair.

2. UNDERSTANDING THE STRUCTURE AND MEANING

Originally, this book was known as the I of the Zhou dynasty (1122–221 B.C.). Before that time there were two other I, the I of the Xia dynasty (2005–1766 B.C.) and the I of the Shang dynasty (1766–1122 B.C.).

Unfortunately, only fragments of these two earlier books survive.

Following the work of Fu Xi, who originated the eight primary (three-line) gua, King Wen of the Zhou dynasty arranged the sixty-four gua and wrote the Decisions on the Gua, his son, the Duke of Zhou, composed the Yao Texts, and Confucius wrote the commentaries (the Ten Wings). The contributions of these three sages of the Zhou dynasty bestowed upon the I of the Zhou dynasty significant meanings. After Confucius's commentaries were written, the I of the Zhou dynasty became revered as the I Ching.

Since the I Ching is a very ancient book and its original language has become an artifact, without Confucius's commentaries it is most difficult to understand. After the commentaries were written, the way opened for more scholastic study of the I Ching. In the Han dynasty (206 B.C. to A.D. 220) there appeared a new edition of the I Ching with five of Confucius's ten commentaries printed beside the original text. In this way, the commentaries shed direct light on the text. People have relied upon this type of presentation for more than two thousand years. In this book, I follow the same form, as well as its practical purpose, by blending the text with the five commentaries, letting Confucius's original words explain the text. My contribution lies in explaining the names and the structures of the sixty-four gua and the significance of the gua and the yao.

3. THE SEQUENCE AND NAMES OF THE GUA

The Tao of I is embodied in the sequence and names of the gua. Legge had a good command of the old Chinese written language, but he did not believe in the I Ching. Wilhelm believed in the I Ching, yet his translation relied upon his teacher's verbal interpretation. Both of their books do not give a clear concept of how the sixty-four gua represent sixty-four different stages in a connected, rising and falling sequence of cyclic change.

I have spent much time meditating upon and contemplating the names of the gua to help find the right English equivalents. It is completely inappropriate to consider each name in isolation rather than in its sequence and context. The sequence of the sixty-four gua is well organized. The system of the Upper Canon is well matched to that of the Lower Canon. For instance, after the first and second gua, Qian and Kun, Wilhelm translates the name of the third gua as Difficulty at the Beginning. John Blofeld translates it as Difficulty. I am uncomfortable with the idea that after Qian, meaning the

Initiating, and Kun, signifying the Responding, comes Difficulty. It gives one the feeling that the Creation was not good. This is not the Chinese way of thinking. Confucius said, "After Heaven and Earth came into existence, myriad things were produced. These myriad things fill up the space between Heaven and Earth." Nothing about this feels negative.

In King Wen's Decision, there is no hint of "difficulty." On the contrary, he bestows the third gua with the four most auspicious attributes in the I Ching. These hold the promise of great good fortune. Thus my translation of the name of the third gua is Beginning.

4. ANCIENT CHINESE IDEOGRAPHS AS EXPLANATIONS OF THE NAMES OF THE GUA

To fully understand the meaning of the names of the gua, I employ ancient Chinese ideographs called jin wen. Jin wen were inscribed on bronze objects of the Zhou dynasty, especially on the sacrificial vessels called cauldrons. Employing the jin wen of the Zhou dynasty to explain the names of the sixty-four gua is the most appropriate way to discover their true meaning, because these ideographs are pictures, and pictures are vital to understanding the exact meanings of Chinese words. For instance, the ideograph of the Chinese character of the third gua, Zhun, shows a tiny new sprout just appearing above the ground. This young sprout indicates the creation, the birth of myriad beings. (The ideograph of Zhun is shown in the outer margin.) The best name of the third gua, therefore, is Beginning.

5. INSIGHTS FROM THE HISTORICAL BACKGROUND

Traditionally King Wen is credited as being the author of Zhou I (the shortened title of the book). At the beginning of this century, most Chinese scholars still held the belief that King Wen rearranged the sixty-four gua during the seven years of his imprisonment by the tyrant of the Shang dynasty (see A Brief History of the Zhou Dynasty in the appendix). I believe that during his imprisonment King Wen gained the insight to rearrange the sixty-four gua according to his philosophy of the unity of Heaven and humanity. After being released, I think that he made several revisions based upon his personal and political life experience.

During the 1960s I studied the history of the Zhou dynasty, familiarizing myself with the historical background of King Wen's activities that related to the gua. Later, when I made the seventh revision of this translation, I reviewed the history again in greater depth. At first I doubted that I could gain insight from the historical background of the Zhou dynasty about each gua from beginning to end. I was taken by surprise when I did. Many incidents of historical importance happened after King Wen's death, a finding that I did not expect. Based upon this reality, I have revised my thinking. After King Wen there must have been sages who amended the Zhou I again and again until it attained the present form.

These insights provide a truer picture of the background of the I Ching. According to these insights, the first and second gua, Initiating and Responding, serve as the introduction to King Wen's philosophy of the unity of Heaven and humanity. The first gua represents the function of Heaven and acts as the guideline of the Upper Canon; the second gua represents the function of humanity and acts as the guideline of the Lower Canon. The third gua, Beginning, represents the start of a new cycle of King Wen's achievements, and the fourth gua, Childhood, stands for the childhood of the people of Zhou, who began a new era of enlightenment under King Wen. The last two gua, Already Fulfilled and Not Yet Fulfilled, indicate that the achievements the Shang dynasty had been completed and the accomplishments of the Zhou dynasty had not yet been realized.

6. Unifying the Translations of the Judgments

The I Ching is a handbook for divination. Along with King Wen's Decisions and the Duke of Zhou's Yao Text, the judgment of good fortune and misfortune is decisive for diviners. There are over five hundred items of judgment distributed among the 386 yao. Every yao carries at least one item of judgment. These hundreds of items of judgment are strictly worded and specifically arranged in different degrees. Standardizing and unifying these judgments of good fortune and misfortune, as I have done in this translation, affords diviners a clearer and more appropriate view of the outcome of a divination.

7. Introducing Simpler Ways to Consult

The traditional way to consult the I Ching is through the use of fifty yarrow stalks. Manipulating the fifty yarrow stalks three times produces one yao. For six yao, one needs to manipulate the fifty yarrow stalks eighteen times. It takes at least half an hour to get a six-line gua. More than two thousand years after the I Ching was written, during the Tang dynasty (618–907), a simpler way, using three coins, was created. These are the two methods most commonly used in the Western world. However, in the course of Chinese history, many different methods have been employed. Using the yarrow stalks or three coins, in many cases more than one moving line will appear. The moving line represents the present stage of development in certain circumstances, so if several moving lines appear their texts may contradict one another, causing confusion. In this book I introduce ways to solve this problem. I also introduce several new ways of divining:

1. A simple version of yarrow stalk divination
2. Eight-coin magic
3. Eight-gemstone augur

In the first method one manipulates the fifty yarrow stalks three times so that a six-line gua and only one moving line will be obtained. The second method uses eight coins instead of three, so that by manipulating the coins three times a six-line gua and one moving line will result. An even simpler method that I devised uses eight gemstones or cards and a die. These methods are simple and timesaving. Within a few seconds, one can achieve what the yarrow stalk method accomplishes in half an hour. All these methods are explained in detail later in the book.

8. UNDERSTANDING THE SITUATION

In divination, one's present situation is revealed by the name and the structure of the gua, together with King Wen's Decisions, Confucius's Commentary on the Decision, and Confucius's Commentary on the Symbols. The six lines indicate the six stages of change. Therefore, for gaining good fortune or avoiding misfortune, understanding one's place within the situation is crucial. Confucius said, "The wise person, just by contemplating the decision of the gua, is capable of realizing most of the content." The Decision is the interpretation of the whole gua, the six lines taken together. According to Confucius, a true understanding of the symbol and its name and of King Wen's Decision on the gua is critical to gaining perspective on one's present situation. I have seen many people who, when consulting the I Ching, pay attention to the lines while neglecting the overall situation. In this way they merely see the trees and are blind to the forest. This is not the proper way to consult the I Ching. I translate the text as faithfully as I can so readers can understand the entire situation and their place in it. At the beginning of the text of every gua is a section called "Name and Structure." I explain the significance of the gua—its name, sequence, and structure—and trace the derivation of the name. At the end of the text there is a section called "Significance," which explains the importance and implications of the lines. These interpretations rely on the ideas of Confucius as well as traditional Chinese sayings.

9. Present Information about Future Potential

When people consult the I Ching, they want to know their future potential as well as their present circumstances. These two are closely related. We are living in a time of profound change. If we accept that every action we take is a cause that has an effect and every effect has a cause, we can more clearly see the results of our actions. The intention behind each action determines its effect. Our intentions and our actions affect not only ourselves but also others. If we believe that every intention and action evolves as we progress on our spiritual journey, then if we act consciously we evolve consciously, but if we act unconsciously we *evolve* unconsciously.

In this book, each interpretation of the yao is not limited to the present situation. It is associated with the "approached gua," which indicates the future potential or tendency. At the beginning of the interpretation of every line, there is information about where the line will lead if it changes.

10. Additional Reference Information for Each Gua

Advanced students of the I Ching tend to explore each situation from a holistic perspective. They are not content with just information concerning the present situation and the future potential. They want to understand the situation from different angles as well as to explore its essence. In this book, additional reference information is given at the end of each gua, as shown in the following example from the third gua, Beginning.

Image:	Water above, Thunder below
Recite as:	Cloud over Thunder, Beginning
Element:	Water
Structure:	Two yang with four yin
Month:	The twelfth month of the lunar year, or January
Host of the Gua:	Initial Nine
Opposite Gua:	Establishing the New (50)
Inverse Gua:	Childhood (4)
Mutual Gua:	Falling Away (23)

In this way advanced students are able to look at the situation from the point above as well as the point below, from the obverse view as well as the reverse view, from the outer as well as the inner, from the present as well as the future. Much of this information will be beyond the scope of beginning students of the I Ching, but as they use this book and become more and more aware of the infinitely interrelated nature of existence, they will find it more and more useful.

About the Translation

The I Ching is a book that speaks in images, not words. The ancient Chinese language was composed of pictographs—pictures. They do not connect in the same way that English speakers think of words as doing. There is no tense, gender, plural, article, preposition, or punctuation, and quite often no subject or object. The beauty of this ancient language, and of the I Ching, is that it merely presents pictures and lets the reader's own imagination resonate with the scene. Translating these "sentences" into proper English is impossible without seriously limiting the wealth of possible meanings. People consult the I Ching for guidance. Every word added or neglected by the translator can influence readers' actions. This places a huge moral responsibility on the translator to not lead readers unnecessarily.

The I Ching is a work of poetry, not prose. It has its own oracular language and conceals its meaning in metaphors, parables, and images. There is even a matching of word and word order, and sometimes sound, within the lines. To preserve these unique features of the I Ching in this translation, I have followed two Chinese principles. The first is "shu er bu zuo," which means "narrate, don't write." In other words, when trying to convey another writer's thoughts, simply narrate them, do not write any of your own. I spent three years making this translation understandable, and was very satisfied with it. But unconsciously I had added my own interpretations to it. The profundity of the I Ching is such that it sparks insights in all who read it, and it needs no help doing so. In my final revision I sought to eliminate all my interpretations and worked hard to restore the I Ching's pure nature.

The second principle is "ning xing bu da," which means "better to stick to the truth than make the translation smooth." This principle was originated by the Chinese literary giant Lu Xing, who translated many Japanese works into Chinese after Dr. Sun Yat-sen's Republic of China was established. The lines in this translation are not always smooth, but they are always true.

Once readers understand that reading the I Ching does not mean reading sentences that make sense, but rather creating their own personal understanding from archetypal, poetic images, I believe they will not be frustrated by the lack of proper English and, in fact, will come to value the I Ching as a great, open-ended storehouse of ancient wisdom, in the same manner that the Chinese always have.

How to Use This Book

The following four pages provide a key to understanding the elements that make up each chapter of this book. Refer to the glossary for more detailed explanations.

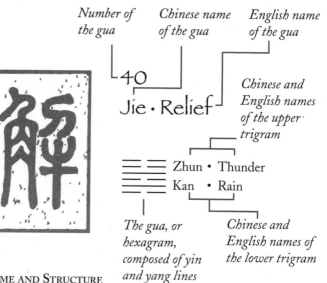

Number of the gua

Chinese name of the gua

English name of the gua

40

Jie · Relief

Chinese and English names of the upper trigram

Zhun · Thunder

Kan · Rain

The gua, or hexagram, composed of yin and yang lines

Chinese and English names of the lower trigram

Name and Structure
Examines the meanings implicit in the name of the gua, the image of the ideograph, and the structure of the hexagram

NAME AND STRUCTURE

Jie has many meanings. Originally it meant to separate or to remove and, later, to release or to relieve—especially to relieve pain or distress. In this gua, it signifies relief of the cause of hardship. Wilhelm translates Jie as Deliverance, and Blofeld translates it as Release. "Deliverance" and "release" both denote an act of allowing to go, setting free, or unfastening. Relief is closer in meaning to alleviation—lessening or ending pain, distress, or anxiety. Given the content of this gua, I adopt the name Relief.

Sequence of the Gua: *Things cannot remain in hardship without end. Thus, after Hardship, Relief follows.*

Sequence of the Gua
Confucius's explanation of the transition from one gua to the next

The ideograph of Jie pictures its original meaning, to separate or to remove. It consists of three parts. On the left, there is a horn, and at the bottom right, there is an ox. The image looks like the face of an ox with horns curved upward. Resting on the top of the ox, is a knife. Taken as a whole, the ideograph shows that a horn is separated and removed from the head of an ox by a knife.

The structure of the gua is Thunder ☳ above, Water ☵ below, signifying a thunderstorm with heavy rain. Thunder represents motion, and Water stands for darkness. One can imagine that the thunderstorm is wild and violent. When the tremendous strength of the storm has passed through the dark, the danger is relieved.

*Number of
the gua*

*Name of
the gua*

*Page
number*

└———— (40) Jie •329 ————┘

Decision

Relief.
Favorable in the southwest.
Nowhere to go,
Come back, return to normal. ————
Good fortune.
There is somewhere to go;
No delay: good fortune.

*Thumbnail
ideograph* ————

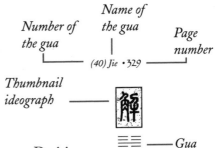

———— **Decision**

———— *Gua*

*King Wen's interspretation of
the meaning of the gua*

Commentary on the Decision

Relief.
Danger produces motion.
Through motion, danger is removed.
This is what relief means.

Relief.
Favorable in the southwest.
Going forward, win the multitude.
Returning back brings good fortune.
He obtains the central position.

———— **Commentary on the Decision**
*Confucius's elaboration of King
Wen's Decision. All Confucius's
commentaries are in italics.*

Commentary on the Symbol ————

Rolling Thunder with heavy Rain.
An image of Relief
In correspondence with this,
The superior person pardons mistakes
And deals gently with misdeeds.

———— **Commentary on the Symbol**
*Confucius's interpretation of the
significance of the juxtaposition of
the upper and lower trigrams.*

Yao Text ————

1. Initial Six
   No fault.

   Junction between yin and yang.
   There should be no fault.

2. Second Nine ————
   In the field

Yao Text
*The Duke of Zhou's
interpretation of each of
the six lines*

———— *"Nine" indicates a
solid, yang line*

330 • I Ching

Three foxes are caught.
Obtain a golden arrow.
Being steadfast and upright: good fortune.

Good fortune for the solid at the second place,
Due to the middle path.

Confucius's
interpretation
of each line

3. Third Six

Carrying a burden,
Riding in a carriage,
Tempting robbers to come.
Being steadfast: humiliation.

"Six" indicates a
broken, yin line.

Carrying a burden, riding in a carriage,
It is a shame.
When I myself tempt the robbers to draw near,
On whom shall I lay the blame?

Significance
An explanation
of the overall
meaning of the
gua

SIGNIFICANCE

This gua is the inverse of Hardship, the preceding one. Now, hardship is relieved. To relieve hardship, timing is important; if the time is not favorable, one must remain still. The Decision indicates that if there is nowhere to go, returning will be propitious. On the other hand, if there is somewhere to go, acting immediately will bring good fortune. Beside timing, harmony between people is absolutely important.

The gua has two hosts: the yielding line at the fifth place and the solid line at the second place. The yielding line at the fifth place represents a king who is humble and gentle. The solid line at the second place represents an official who is strong and firm. These two elements are complementary yin and yang. They mutually support each other. A wise leader is working with an able subordinate—they relieve hardship together. The yielding lines at the second, third, and sixth places use the fox, the robber, and the falcon, respectively, as images of potential dangers, suggesting that during a time when hardship is relieved, one should still be cautious.

An
explanation
of the
meaning of
each line

(1) Initial Six. Relief alternates to Marrying Maiden (54)

The bottom line denotes the transition between Hardship and Relief. It is a turning point. Thus the Commentary on the Yao Text says that there should be no fault. This line is a yin element at a yang place. The element is weak, and the position is low; therefore it is safe. When hardship begins to find relief, although there is not yet good fortune, at least there is no fault.

(2) Second Nine. Relief alternates to Delightful (16)

The second line is a yang element at a yin place. The position is not correct, but it is central. It corresponds to the yin element at the fifth place. One at this place is able to obtain support from the yin element at the king's place. Three foxes represent the other yin elements. Foxes are considered crafty and tricky. One at this place is firm and strong, able to banish those who try to trick the king.

The approached gua, formed if the line in question alternates from yang to yin or vice-versa

*(3) Third Six. Relief alternates to **Long Lasting** (32)* ⎯⎯⎯⎯⎯

The yielding line at the third position symbolizes a little fellow. It is a yin element at a yang place. Its placement is not correct, but it occupies the top position of the lower gua. Its status is not compatible with its position. In ancient times, only those with rank were allowed to ride in a carriage. This is a little fellow who is carrying a burden. While carrying a burden, one rides in a carriage, tempting robbers to draw near. However steadfast and upright, there will be regret.

Additional Reference Information for This Gua ⎯⎯⎯

Image:	Thunder above, Water below
Recite as:	Thunder above Rain, Relief
Element:	Wood
Structure:	Two yang with four yin
Month:	The second month of the lunar calendar, or March
Host of the Gua:	Second Nine
Opposite Gua:	Household (37)
Inverse Gua:	Hardship (39)
Mutual Gua:	Already Fulfilled (63)

Additional Reference
Additional information included for advanced study

Introduction

BETWEEN HEAVEN AND HUMANITY

It is believed that when the ancient sage Fu Xi drew the eight primary gua (eight trigrams), he laid out in embryonic form the Chinese written character. When King Wen developed the sixty-four accomplished gua (sixty-four hexagrams composed by combining two trigrams), he initiated the long stream of Chinese culture. These two sages, together with the Duke of Zhou and Confucius, formed the I Ching.

The literal meaning of *Ching* is Tao, Truth. It is the Truth of Heaven and Earth and the Truth of human life. A book that elucidates the Truth of Heaven and Earth is called Ching. The Chinese believe that the Truth of Heaven is also the Truth of humanity. This philosophical concept of the merging of Heaven and humanity into an organic whole is the foundation of traditional Chinese culture. It is also the source of all spheres of learning and thought in Chinese history. The earliest, most detailed and systematic book approaching this unity of Heaven and humanity is the I Ching.

The I Ching also expounds upon the truth of change, or the Tao of Change, which in Chinese terminology is called the Tao of I. It is a book based on the observation and experimentation of the sages. The ancient sages watched astronomical phenomena in the sky and topographical features on the earth, and studied the relationships among all beings. They realized that in Heaven and Earth there exists a universal principle that everything is in a continuous process of change. Change is absolute and certain; only the principle of change never changes. Through their experiences, the sages sensed that it was crucial for one to understand

1

the laws of change; only then could one respond and adapt to changes in the most suitable way. In the I Ching, The Book of Change, all this experience and knowledge is collected and recorded.

Over the past sixteen years, I have read numerous English translations of the I Ching. As a Chinese scholar, I dare to say that most English translations do not truly convey the spirit of the I Ching. All the English translations mention the concept of change, but they neglect its essence. The true spirit and the most authentic essence of the I Ching lies in the philosophical concept of the merging of Heaven and human life into an organic whole, which is the origin of Chinese cosmology.

Western readers have come to love the I Ching, and it is helpful to have many translations from which to choose. However, when the text of the book is mixed with the views of the writer or the translator, it is at most a comment, a treatise, an exegesis, or an explanation of the I Ching. It is not the I Ching itself. Any translation of a book should be made directly and faithfully from the original language and the original text. Otherwise, it is not a genuine translation. If the Western world accepts the idea that the I Ching is a sacred book, then it deserves reverence and respect and an appropriate translation, in the same way as the Holy Bible.

A BOOK OF DIVINATION, A BOOK OF WISDOM

At first, the I Ching was purely a handbook for divination. In ancient times, the Chinese related their fate directly to the spiritual power of Heaven and Earth. Before approaching any important event, they were bound to consult the will of Heaven and Earth through divination. The purpose of divination was to resolve doubts. An ancient historic record says that when people have doubts about great matters, they consult the tortoise shell and the yarrow stalks. The practice of divination far pre-dated the time of the I Ching, and there were many ways to consult an oracle. The court of the Shang dynasty (1766–1122 B.C.) divined with tortoise shells. In matters of grave import, such as seasonal sacrificial ceremonies, expeditions, royal enthronements, weddings, and hunts, and even weather, the augur would be asked to divine whether there would be good fortune or misfortune. The procedure of divining with tortoise shells was complicated. In most cases the belly surface of a shell was used. The shell would be prepared by drilling and chiseling with a tiny stylus; then the shell was heated until cracks appeared. By reading the patterns of the cracks, the augur interpreted the oracle.

During the time of the Zhou dynasty (1122–221 B.C.) divination with yarrow stalks was widely used. According to the *Book of Rites of the Zhou Dynasty*, a Grand Augur was employed in the royal court to take charge of divination by the three systems of I: Lian Shan I, Gui Cang I, and Zhou I. The first gua of the Lian Shan I is Gen: Mountain above, Mountain below. Lian means "to link together," Shan means "mountain"; Lian Shan indicates two mountains linked together. Gui Cang I begins with Kun: Earth above, Earth below. Gui means "to return"; Cang means "to store." The ancient sages believed that all things return to the earth and are stored within. Unfortunately, Lian Shan I and Gui Cang I were not passed down from antiquity.

The I Ching we use today is Zhou I—The I of the Zhou dynasty. Zhou I is the further evolution of the other two I. Through thousands of years it has gradually been developed to a high level. Zhou I is not a book used merely for telling fortunes. It gives advice as to what one should do and what one should not do. All through the ages, the Chinese have never consulted the I Ching lightly. People have always been instructed to adopt a correct attitude in divination. The purpose of divination is to resolve doubt and confusion. When one already knows what one should do according to common sense and moral principles, then one should not consult the I Ching. Divine only for important questions and events, never for mean purposes or with selfish motivations.

The Structure of the Book

At present, the I Ching is made up of two parts—the text and the explanation. The text is called Ching, the explanation is called Commentary.

The Ching

The original I Ching contains about 4,900 Chinese characters. The book is divided into sixty-four short chapters. Each chapter deals with a six-line symbol called a gua. Gua is generally translated as "hexagram." Originally, "gua" meant a symbol hung up for people to see. (In Chinese, a coat hanger is called yi gua, yi meaning "clothes" or "coat.") Each gua is composed of six horizontal lines, arranged one over the other. The Chinese call these lines yao. Most English translations call the yao "line." Originally, yao meant "crisscross"; it represented the intersecting of the yin and the yang. Because yao possesses the same sound as the word for imitation, yao has a hidden meaning: imitate the instructions given by the yao. There are two kinds of yao—the yin yao and the yang yao. Yin yao are represented by two broken lines (- -), yang yao by a solid line (—). The attributes of these two yao are exactly opposite. Yang yao symbolize the masculine, the firm, the strong, the odd numbers, as well as all active things. In Chinese thought, yang is a positive attribute; one example is the bright side of a mountain. Yin yao symbolize the feminine, the yielding, the weak, the even numbers, as well as all passive things. Yin, being the complement of yang, represents a negative attribute, in the sense of the shaded side of a mountain.

Each gua consists of six yao. The six yao are arranged from the bottom to the top, just as the bottom is the foundation and all things grow from the bottom upward. The Chinese call the bottom line the initial line and the uppermost line the top line. In Chinese, yang yao are represented by the number nine, yin yao by the number six. For instance, a solid line at the second place is called Second Nine. Likewise, a yielding line at the fourth place is called Fourth Six, and so on. The first line is called either Initial Nine or Initial Six. Likewise, the uppermost line is called either Top Nine or Top Six. Why Six and Nine? The yang element is associated with odd numbers, and the yin with even numbers. Yang refers to that which advances, and yin refers to that which retreats. It is considered a yang quality to be in the forefront. Thus, when we count the odd numbers from one to nine (advancing), the topmost number is nine. It is considered best for yin to maintain the central ground. When we count the even numbers from ten to two (retreating), the central number is six. This is why yang is named Nine and yin is named Six.

Each of the sixty-four six-line gua is divided into two parts—the upper and the lower. The first three lines from the bottom constitute the lower gua, and the top three lines constitute the upper gua. The lower gua is also known as the inner gua, and the upper gua is also called the outer gua. Fu Xi drew only eight gua—Qian and Kun (Heaven and Earth), Li and Kan (Fire and Water), Zhen and Xun (Thunder and Wind), and Gen and Dui (Mountain and Lake). Each of the eight gua consists of only three lines. Later, these eight gua were combined with one another and thereby a new system of sixty-four gua was obtained. From then on the eight gua were known as the primary gua and the sixty-four gua were known as the accomplished gua.

The sixty-four chapters of the I Ching consist of four parts each: the name of the symbol, the name, King Wen's Decision on the Gua, and the Duke of Zhou's Yao Texts. Each six-line gua has a name composed of one or two Chinese characters. The name is crucial, because it represents the whole situation. The symbol is made up of six lines representing the six stages of a specific situation. At the same time, each six-line gua is regarded as a combination of two three-line gua, representing the inner situation (lower gua) and the outer situation (upper gua). Thus, beneath the six-line symbol is a brief description usually composed of four words, such as Kun above, Qian below (Earth above, Heaven below), or Gen above, Dui below (Mountain above, Lake below). After the symbol and its brief interpretation comes the gua text, called the Decision. This is King Wen's own assessment of the situation together with moral advice. Following the Decision is the Duke of Zhou's Yao Text. The Yao Text gives a more detailed interpretation of each stage of the situation together with moral instructions.

The sixty-four chapters of the I Ching are divided into two parts, the Upper Canon and the Lower Canon. Generally speaking the Upper Canon represents the yang aspect and lays emphasis on the Tao of Heaven or natural phenomena. The Lower Canon represents the yin aspect and focuses on social phenomena and human affairs.

The Commentary

The Commentary comprises ten chapters, known as the Ten Wings. Wing means "to assist." The Ten Wings serves as a supplement to the text, helping people understand the I Ching. Traditionally, the authorship of the Ten Wings is attributed to Confucius. In later studies, they are said to have been written by different Confucian scholars at different times. The first and second wings are the Commentary on the Decision. The third and fourth wings are the Commentary on the Symbols. The fifth and sixth wings are known as the Great Treatise. The seventh wing is the Commentary on the Words of the Text. The eighth wing is the Discussion of the Gua. The ninth wing is the Sequence of the Gua. The tenth wing is the Miscellaneous Notes on the Gua.

Of all the commentaries on the I Ching, the Ten Wings is the best. I follow the most popular traditional editions by using the five wings considered to be the major commentaries to interpret the original text. In addition, I use the ninth wing to describe the sequence of the gua. All the commentaries from the Ten Wings are italicized.

Flying with the I Ching: Methods of Divination

CONSULTING THE ORACLE

Understand the Symbols

The I Ching is a book that deals with symbols. To understand the I Ching, one should first become familiar with the symbols. Each of the sixty-four primary symbols, or gua, represents a unique situation. To understand the gua, one has to know its specific place in the sequence and its significance as well as its structure, its image, and the things it represents. In teaching the I Ching, I always encourage students to make friends with these sixty-four gua. In this way, as soon as one sees the symbol, one is immediately able to recognize its name, its background, its character, and its significance, in the same way as one meets and recognizes one's friend. Each of these sixty-four friends can help resolve one's doubt or confusion in a specific situation. Twenty-eight gua each have an inverted form. These two forms have a close relationship, representing the two views of a thing—one from the front and the other from the back, or one from below, the other from above. Eight gua have no inverted form; when their original form is inverted, it is exactly the same. To understand the I Ching, therefore, one needs to make friends with only thirty-six gua.

Revere the Book

If one's intention is to divine, the I Ching should be used exclusively for divination. When not in use, the book and the yarrow stalks should be wrapped separately in silk or cloth. Most Chinese like to use rose silk, which is regarded as the most auspicious color and material. Both the wrapped book and stalks should be placed on a shelf at about eye level or somewhere clean and significant to you. Always wash the hands before divination, then unwrap the book and the stalks and spread the wrapper like a tablecloth on a table. Ideally the table sits in the center of the room, facing south. In ancient China only the imperial palace and temples were allowed to face directly south. In Chinese tradition, those in authority face south when granting an audience. During divination, the diviner should face north, listening to the instructions of the divine spirit. According to tradition, three sticks of incense are lit. An alternative way to choose the ideal direction for divination is to suppose that the door of the room faces south. If there is a table in the center of the room, the diviner's back should always face the door. In this way the divine spirit will be in the most revered position, in the center of the room and facing the entrance.

Frame the Inquiry

In every divination, ask only one question. The question should be simple and clear. Avoid vague and optional questions. It is better for a beginner not to ask for a prediction; the best inquiry is for advice.

METHODS OF DIVINATION

There are many ways to consult an oracle. The two most familiar methods in the West are the yarrow stalk oracle and the coin oracle.

The Yarrow Stalk Oracle

Originally, tortoise shells and animal bones were used for divination. The yarrow stalk oracle became popular in the Zhou dynasty, about three thousand years ago. Yarrow grew everywhere and was much easier to use than tortoise shells and animal bones. The stem of the yarrow was firm and tenacious and it remained unwithered for a long time. It was tall and straight, and could be prepared with little manual labor. Thus the ancients came to believe that yarrow was a divine gift bestowed upon humanity so that we could communicate with Heaven.

Traditionally, different lengths of yarrow stalk were relegated to people of different social strata. According to *The Book of Rites of the Zhou Dynasty*, the length of an emperor's yarrow stalk was nine chi (one chi equals approximately one foot); of a duke's or prince's, seven chi; of a high official's, five chi; and of a literate's, three chi. Literate was a social class between high officials and common people. Although the book does not mention how long the yarrow stalks should be for common people, it would be shorter than three chi. While it seems likely that the chi of the Zhou dynasty was shorter than today's measurement, five, seven, or nine chi was still not a short length by any definition. At that time divination was a social event, a ritual for seeking harmony between Heaven and humanity. People gathered to watch the diviner and his attendants. The yarrow stalks needed to be long enough to be seen by the audience. Subsequently divination became a personal affair, and the yarrow stalks became shorter. Today finding fifty yarrow stalks is no easy task, but we do not need to rely on them for divination. I feel very comfortable using fifty eight-inch bamboo skewers as a substitute.

The modern method of the yarrow stalk oracle is based on Confucius's descriptions in The Great Treatise, the fifth wing:

> *The number of the Great Expansion is fifty,*
> *Of which forty-nine are used.*
> *Divide them into two, symbolizing the two primary forces.*
> *Suspend one, symbolizing the three supreme powers.*
> *Manipulate by four, symbolizing the four seasons.*
> *Return the remainder, symbolizing the intercalary month.*
> *In five years there is another intercalation.*
> *Afterward the process is repeated.*
>
> *Therefore four operations produce a change,*
> *And eighteen changes yield a gua.*

The yarrow stalk oracle has been considered the classical way of consulting the I Ching. The process of operation is as follows:

1. *The number of Great Expansion is fifty.*
   Hold 50 yarrow stalks in your left hand.
2. *Of which forty-nine are used.*
   Put one aside on the table in front of you; it plays no further part

in the divination. This stalk symbolizes the commencement of Tai Chi ("ultimate beginning") from the void; it represents the state before Heaven and Earth were differentiated.

3. *Divide them into two, symbolizing the two primary forces.*
   Divide the remaining 49 stalks into two bundles at random, one in each hand. These bundles symbolize Heaven and Earth. The left bundle represents Heaven, the right represents Earth.

4. *Suspend one, symbolizing the three supreme powers.*
   Take one stalk from the right-hand bundle and put it between the ring finger and little finger of your left hand. This stalk symbolizes humanity. Heaven, Earth, and humanity are considered the three supreme powers in the universe.

5. *Manipulate by four, symbolizing the four seasons.*
   Take 4 stalks at a time from your left-hand bundle and put them aside until there are 4 or fewer stalks remaining in your hand. These 4-stalk bundles symbolize the four seasons.

6. *Return the remainders, symbolizing the intercalary month.*
   Place the remaining stalks between the ring finger and the middle finger of your left hand. This act symbolizes the intercalary month.

7. *In five years there is another intercalation.*
   Take 4 stalks at a time from your right-hand bundle and put them aside until there are 4 or fewer stalks remaining in your hand. Place the remaining stalks between the middle finger and the index finger of your left hand. Collect all the stalks between the fingers of your left hand. The sum should be either 5 or 9. Set these stalks aside.

   Now, after the four operations (putting one stalk aside, dividing the remaining stalks into two, removing 4 stalks at a time, and placing the remainders between fingers), the first process of change is completed. It takes three processes of change to get a yao, or line, therefore the process will be repeated two more times, as below.

8. *Afterward the process is repeated.*
   Leaving the result of the first process aside (either 5 or 9 stalks) repeat the four operations above with the remaining 40 or 44 stalks. This time the sum of the stalks remaining between the left fingers will be either 4 or 8. Set these aside. Now the second process of change is completed.

Repeat the four operations a third time, using the remaining stalks again, either 32, 36, or 40. After the final four operations, the sum of the remainder will again be either 4 or 8. Set these stalks aside.

Either 24, 28, 32, or 36 stalks will remain. Hold these in your hand and take away 4 at a time, counting how many groups of four there are—either six, seven, eight, or nine. Six and eight, even numbers, indicate yin yao. Seven and nine, odd numbers, indicate yang yao. In the system of the I Ching six is the symbol of Greater Yin, eight of Lesser Yin; nine is the symbol of Greater Yang; seven of Lesser Yang. Greater Yin and Greater Yang are pure, extreme; they tend to alternate to their opposite—yin to yang and yang to yin. These yao are called "moving lines." Lesser Yin and Lesser Yang are stable; they tend to remain in their original yin and yang qualities.

As each line is rendered, draw it. A gua is formed from bottom to top. If the result is six, draw a broken line with a cross in the middle, indicating a moving yin yao. If the result is nine, draw an unbroken line with a circle in the middle, indicating a moving yang yao. If the result is seven, simply draw an unbroken line, indicating a stable yang yao; and if it is eight, draw a broken line, indicating a stable yin yao.

9	Greater Yang	—————O—————	moving
8	Lesser Yin	——— ———	stable
7	Lesser Yang	—————————	stable
6	Greater Yin	———X———	moving

Consulting an oracle with yarrow stalks takes at least twenty to thirty minutes to obtain a six-line gua and thus provides a long period of time for the diviner to meditate. The repetition of separating, dividing, and counting the yarrow stalks requires a calm and unhurried approach, which actually helps to make the body, mind, and spirit work together. It induces a deeper level of awareness, where the divine and the diviner become closely connected.

The Three Coins Oracle

The three coins oracle is the most popular method used in the West. In China it first became popular during the Southern Sung Dynasty (1127–1279) after it was promoted by Shao Yun, the most eminent I Ching scholar of his time. This process involves throwing three coins six times; each throw obtains a yao. The whole process takes only a few minutes. Because there is less time to fall into the rhythms of the I Ching using this method, the diviner should meditate before and during the whole procedure. *The Correct Significance of Rites* of the Tang dynasty (618–907) says:

> Throw three coins.
> Two faces and one back equals Lesser Yang.   ——————
> Two backs and one face equals Lesser Yin. —— ——
> Three backs equals Greater Yang.   ——O——
> Three faces equals Greater Yin.   ——X——

Throw six times, from bottom to top, to obtain a gua.

A Simple Version of the Yarrow Stalk Oracle

My revered teacher, Master Yin, handed down several other ways of consulting the I Ching. The one that I favor and use all the time is a simple way of manipulating the fifty yarrow stalks, using bamboo sticks instead. The procedure is as follows:

1. Hold 50 bamboo sticks in your left hand.
2. Place one aside on the table in front of you, parallel to your body.
3. Randomly divide the remaining 49 sticks into two groups, one in your left hand and the other in your right.
4. Place these two groups on the table, one at your left side and the other at your right, with the ends of the sticks pointing in front of you.
5. Take one stick out from the right pile on the table. Put it between the ring finger and little finger of your left hand.
6. Pick up the right pile in your left hand. Using your right hand, take 4 sticks out of your left hand and put them on the table.
7. Using your right hand, take another 4 sticks out of your left hand. Put them on the table with the first 4, mixed together as a unit of 8.
8. Repeat steps 6 and 7 several times, taking 4 sticks plus 4 sticks each time to create a group of 8. Set each group aside.
9. At last there will be 7 or fewer sticks remaining in your left hand. Add the sticks remaining in your left hand to the one between your ring finger and little finger. The sum of these sticks is the number of your lower gua, as listed in Figure 1 (on page 12).

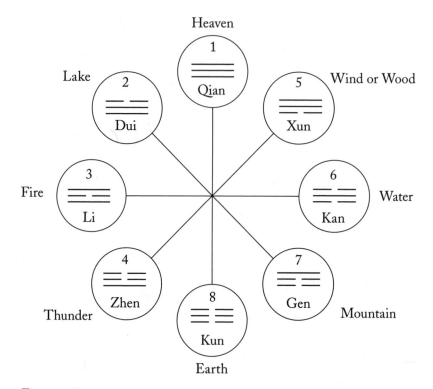

Figure 1. *The Earlier Heaven Sequence, based on Fu Xi's arrangement of the eight primary gua.*

10. Repeat procedures 1 to 9 to obtain the number of your upper gua.

After obtaining the lower gua and the upper gua, manipulate the fifty yarrow stalks again to obtain the moving line. The procedure is as follows:

1. Repeat procedures 1 to 5.
2. After picking up the left group in your left hand, with your right hand take 6 sticks instead of 4 out of your left hand and put them on the table.
3. Repeat procedure 2 several times, until there are 5 or fewer sticks remaining in your left hand. Then add the sticks remaining in your left hand to the one between your ring finger and little finger. The sum of these sticks is the number of your moving line, counted up from the bottom of the gua.

Eight Coin Magic

This is a simplified version of the coin oracle. When using the three-coin method, one throws three coins six times to obtain a six-line gua. By using eight-coin magic, one need only arrange the coins three times, and exactly one moving line will always appear.

1. Select eight coins of the same size, set aside exclusively for divination.
2. Put a dot in the middle of the tail side of one of the coins (a paint pen works well for this).
3. Mix the eight coins together with the tail sides face down.
4. Use the coins to cover each of the eight circles around the chart in Figure 1 (you can also use the chart at the end of the book for this purpose). Follow the numbers on the chart—from 1 to 4 counterclockwise, from 5 to 8 clockwise.
5. Turn the coins over in sequence, following the numbers shown on the chart. The dotted coin indicates the lower gua.
6. Repeat the procedure from 1 to 5 to obtain the upper gua.
7. Draw the lines of the two six-line gua on a piece of paper, beginning with the bottom line, with the upper gua over the lower gua.
8. Remove two of the unmarked coins and put them aside.
9. Mix the remaining six coins together with the tail sides face down.
10. Place the coins one above the other vertically, from bottom to top.
11. Turn the coins over one by one, beginning with the lowermost coin.
12. The dotted coin's place indicates the moving line.

Eight Gemstone Augur

For thousands of years the Chinese used yarrow stalks to consult the I Ching, until Shao Yun promoted the simpler coin method. It has been my experience that in this hectic age people desire a still simpler method of divination, so I created a method using eight gemstones and a die. I put the gemstones in a little velvet bag. I decide ahead of time which of the eight primary gua each gemstone represents. To divine, I just pick a gemstone from the bag to obtain my lower gua, then return the gemstone to the bag and draw again for my upper gua. Then I throw the die to obtain the moving line, counting up from the bottom. Within seconds I get the

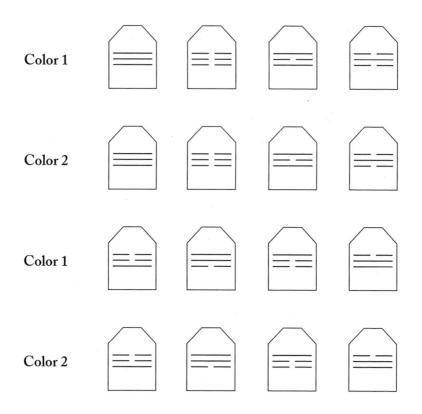

Color 1				
Color 2				
Color 1				
Color 2				

gua and also the line. I think this might be the method demanded for the twenty-first century. Besides gemstones, I have used ceramic tiles, wood blocks, bamboo chips, and cards. One can make one's own, personalized divining cards in the following manner:

1. Cut out sixteen cards of equal size, eight each of two different colors.
2. Cut off the two top corners of each card.
3. Draw each of the eight primary gua on each set of cards with cut corners at the top:

To divine:

1. Shuffle the sixteen cards and place them on the table in two rows of eight cards each of the same color, with the gua facing down. The upper row represents Fu Xi's arrangement. The lower row represents King Wen's arrangement.

2. Pick two cards, one from each row, and place them one over the other, with cut corners at the top.
3. Turn the two cards over to obtain a six-line gua.
4. Throw the die to obtain the moving line.

There are those who will feel that these faster methods do not capture the true tao, the soul of the I Ching, as successfully as do the more rhythmic, traditional methods. This is not necessarily true. The Chinese have a saying, "The type of vehicle does not matter, so long as it gets you to your destination." Any of these methods can get you to your destination, though some people will feel that the more ornate methods get them there in a better frame of mind while others will feel that the quick methods are the only ones that get them there fast enough.

GAINING INSIGHT FROM THE ORACLE

According to the Chinese, gaining insight from the I Ching is a technique as well as an art. As a technique, one should understand the eight primary gua and the sixty-four accomplished gua—the significance of their names, symbols, and structures—as well as the 386 yao—their positions, relationships, and meanings. One should also know the hidden principles of the changes and the symbology related to the gua and yao. As an art, one should cultivate an intuitive sense by studying the symbols to understand the divination. From a mathematical point of view, each symbol is the formula of a changing situation and its consequence. On this ground, as one I Ching scholar points out, one who really masters the I Ching does not necessarily consult the text. As for beginners, I recommend that they read the first and second chapters, Qian and Kun, very attentively. Even Confucius paid great attention to these two gua. According to his experience, they are the gateway to understanding the I Ching.

Before understanding all of this technical information, one can cultivate intuition to gain insight from the divination. One of the best ways to cultivate intuition is through meditation; however, the Chinese concept of meditation is opposite to the Western approach. In the West we think of meditation as deep thought about something, but when I was learning meditation, my masters always instructed me to think about nothing. Through many, many years of practicing meditation, I came to appreciate that to empty my mind is to align it with the will of the Divine. This concept, in the expression of Lao Tze, is "doing nothing"; to the Taoist, doing nothing is doing everything. In my experience, by emptying my mind and aligning it with the Divine, insight comes as spontaneously as floating clouds or running water. Sometimes this meditative mood lasts for several days. As time passes, insight will emerge—perhaps in mundane situations, when you are brushing your teeth or taking a bath.

After you have obtained the gua, read the name, King Wen's Decision, and Confucius's Commentary. Confucius's Commentary explains King Wen's Decision based upon the six lines as a whole. These texts will give you a general idea of your present situation. If you have some knowledge of the symbol and the lines, study them. Notice which two three-line primary gua constitute the six-line accomplished gua and their attributes, significance, and relationships. Confucius's Commentary on the Symbol explains the symbol of the accomplished gua and its significance in terms of the two primary gua.

Study the lines. Pay attention to their positions and relationships. Is each line's position "correct"? (Yang lines are correct in yang places— the bottom, third, and fifth. Yin lines are correct in the second, fourth, and top places.) Do they respond favorably with their corresponding lines? (The bottom, middle, and top of each trigram correspond, i.e., the first and fourth lines, second and fifth lines, and third and sixth lines, but they *correspond* only if they form a yin and yang pair. Two yin or yang lines do not correspond.) Is your moving line in the central place? (The middle of each trigram—the second and fifth places.) This bird's-eye view gives you a picture of the whole situation. Then you can pay special attention to your moving line, which is extremely important. It indicates the specific stage that you are in within the whole situation. If things are not moving, changes will not take place. Read the Duke of Zhou's Yao Text together with Confucius's Commentary on the Yao Text to gain insight about your particular stage. Do not ignore the more fundamental original gua, however; I have seen many Westerners give their attention to the instruction of the Yao Text and neglect the name, symbol, and decision, which is like taking the branch and discarding the root.

When using the classical yarrow stalk method or the three-coin method to divine, your result will sometimes have more than one moving line, and occasionally none. When there is no moving line, you need only consult the name, symbol, and decision of the gua. When you have exactly one moving line, you should pay special attention to the Yao Text for this line, and then you should consult the *approached gua*, the new hexagram that will result when the moving line changes from yang to yin or vice-versa. Read the name, symbol, decision, and commentary for the approached gua, which represents the outcome of your present situation. When there is more than one moving line, particularly when the Yao Texts of the moving lines conflict with each other, it becomes too complicated to get a clear answer. To solve this problem, I use the following method, also handed down by Master Yin.

1. If there are two moving lines—one yin and the other yang—consult only the yin moving line.
2. If the two moving lines are both yin or both yang, consult the lower one.
3. If there are three moving lines, consult only the middle one.
4. If there are four moving lines, consult only the upper of the two nonmoving lines.
5. If there are five moving lines, consult only the other, nonmoving line.
6. If six lines are all moving, consult the Decision of the new gua, the approached gua.
7. Since there is a seventh invisible line in the first and second gua, Qian and Kun, for these gua consult the seventh Yao Text, called All Nines or All Sixes.

If you want to know more about your present situation, you can get insight from the mutual gua, formed by the mutual interactions of the second, third, fourth, and fifth lines. The ancient sages considered these four lines to be the heart of any six-line gua. A mutual gua is formed by two trigrams. The second, third, and fourth lines of the original gua form the lower, or inner, mutual gua. The third, fourth, and fifth lines form the upper, or outer, mutual gua. Put the lower mutual gua and the upper mutual gua together and a six-line mutual gua is obtained. When you have the six-line mutual gua, read the name, symbol, King Wen's Decision, and Confucius's Commentary. The hidden meaning of any gua lies in its mutual gua; it should not be ignored.

THE
UPPER
CANON

The Upper Canon contains thirty gua, from Qian (Initiation) and Kun (Responding) to Kan (Darkness) and Li (Brightness). Qian represents the initiative power of Heaven, Kun represents the responsive power of Earth. Kan represents the darkness of the moon, Li represents the brightness of the sun. The canon begins with the interplay of Heaven and Earth; ends with the ceaseless cycle of darkness to brightness, as in sunset to sunrise; and sheds light upon the yang aspect of natural phenomena, the Tao of Heaven.

1

Qian • Initiating

≡ Qian • Heaven
≡ Qian • Heaven

NAME AND STRUCTURE

In Richard Wilhelm's book, Qian is translated as The Creative. In John Blofeld's translation, Qian is The Creative Principle. In this book, it is translated as Initiating. This gua is made up of two primary gua—Heaven ≡ above, Heaven ≡ below. All six yao are solid. Primary gua are described as "trigrams" in most English translations. The structure of six solid yao presents a picture of the perfect yang essence. It is the symbol of the firmest, healthiest, and purest yang energy in the universe.

The Chinese character Qian is an image of a rising sun radiating its light and energy—chi—and nourishing the whole world. The ancient Chinese ideograph of Qian, shown here, depicts a sun on the left side of the picture. Above the sun, there is a shoot of grass with two tiny leaves sprouting on the left and right. Underneath the sun, the root of the plant penetrates deeply into the ground. On the right side the chi disperses from the sun and spreads out under the sky. In Chinese, Qian The Initiating possesses the same sound as the word for health. It denotes health and vitality. In the process of the creation of the world, Qian took an active role as the initiator, providing the purest yang energy, the healthiest action, and the most powerful strength for Kun, the Responding, to receive.

In the I Ching, King Wen placed Qian as the initial gua and Kun as the second. Qian represents Heaven, and Kun represents Earth. It is worth mentioning that King Wen did not name the first gua Heaven; instead he named it Qian, Initiating. According to the ancient sage,

21

Heaven refers to celestial bodies or, to the Chinese, the divine deity, the Heavenly Elderly Father. The purpose of the I Ching is not to expose the nature of the celestial bodies or the divine deities but to offer guidance for favorable action in one's daily life and at the same time to avoid misconduct that invites misfortune. Thus, when Qian is named, its emphasis is upon function rather than an object.

Sequence of the Gua: *After Heaven and Earth have come into existence, myriad beings are produced. Qian and Kun are the origin, the source of Creation.*

Decision

> Initiating.
> Sublime and initiative.
> Prosperous and smooth.
> Favorable and beneficial.
> Steadfast and upright.

Qian, Initiating, represents the nature and function of Heaven. It is endowed with the four Chinese characters yuan, heng, li, and zhen, the four attributes of Heaven, symbolizing the virtues of an emperor, a leader, or a superior person. Yuan means sublime and initiative. Heng means prosperous and smooth. Li means favorable and beneficial. Zhen means steadfast and upright. Throughout the I Ching you will find these four phrases attributed to certain gua, though few are so auspicious as to have all four. These four Chinese characters also indicate the functions of the four seasons of a year: originating, developing, maturing, and declining, referring to spring, summer, autumn, and winter.

These are actually the viewpoints of the Confucian schools expressing the philosophical aspect of the I Ching. Their main purpose in studying the I Ching is to apply the philosophical instruction to life. They expound upon the meaning of the Decisions on the Gua, or the fastening text, to understand the relationships among Heaven, Earth, and human beings. They seek to follow the natural order and live in harmony with Nature. The fastening text, in the original Chinese, indicates the text that is attached to the gua to explain the significance of the symbol.

Originally, King Wen's Decision on Qian—yuan, heng, li, and zhen—had a different connotation. At the turn of the twentieth century, pieces of animal bone and tortoise shell with incised markings were discovered by a professor named Wang Kuo-wei (1877–1927) at herbal medicine stores in Beijing. Professor Wang recognized that these incised markings were inscriptions from the Shang dynasty. Searching for the origin of these bones and shells led him to the site of Yin, the ancient capital of the Shang dynasty on the plains of Hunan Province. Eventually, in 1899, a cache of oracle bones was uncovered, and, over time, one hundred thousand pieces of oracle bone were unearthed. These oracle bones were the royal records of divination of the Shang court. According to the ancient ideographs of these four characters, yuan denotes the origin, heng denotes the sacrificial offerings, li denotes the harvest of grains with a knife, and zhen denotes the divination.

From these pictographs we know that in ancient times, more than two thousand years before the time of Confucius, when people consulted divination, they first honored their origins. They comprehended that in looking forward to the future they had to look back as well. In divination, it was necessary to offer sacrifices to Heaven and Earth and to the ancestors. They cooked foods, burned incense, and offered flowers, allowing the divine spirits to enjoy the fragrance and aroma of their offerings. These acts, they believed, were beneficial to their divinatory consultations. Heng and zhen, the sacrificial offering and the divination, are key words in the I Ching. Heng appears forty-four times and zhen occurs 108 times within the sixty-four gua. From the ancient ideographs of yuan, heng, li, and zhen we comprehend that one needs to prepare for divination by aligning with the spirit of Heaven and Earth and presenting sincerity and reverence as sacrificial offerings; then one will reap the harvest of the divination to obtain guidance for favorable actions and to avoid misconduct that invites misfortune.

Commentary on the Decision

> *Vast indeed is the greatness of the Initiating.*
> *It is the source of all beings*
> *And regulates all creations under Heaven.*
>
> *Clouds flow and rain falls.*
> *All beings complete their forms.*
>
> *Greatly luminous, from beginning to end.*
> *Each of the six stages completes itself in its own time,*
> *As mounting on six dragons soaring in the sky.*

The way of the Initiating is change and transformation
So that each being obtains its true nature and destiny
And the union of great harmony is preserved.
This is what is favorable and upright.

The Initiating is high above all beings.
And thus all countries are united in peace.

Commentary on the Symbol

Heaven acts with vitality and persistence.
In correspondence with this
The superior person keeps himself vital without ceasing.

Yao Text

1. Initial Nine
   Dragon lying low.
   Do not use.

   Dragon lying low, do not use,
   For the yang is in the lowest place.

2. Second Nine
   Dragon becoming visible in the field.
   Favorable to see a great person.

   Dragon arising in the field.
   His virtue influences extensively.

3. Third Nine
   The superior person—
   All day long, initiating, initiating.
   At night, keeping alert.
   Adversity, no fault.

   All day long, initiating, initiating.
   One is on the proper way over and over again.

4. Fourth Nine
   Probably leaping from an abyss.
   No fault.

Probably leaping from an abyss,
In advance there will be no fault.

5. Fifth Nine
   Dragon flying in the sky,
   Favorable to see a great person.

   Dragon flying in the sky,
   There arises a great person to be a leader.

6. Top Nine
   Dragon becoming haughty.
   There is regret.

   Dragon becoming haughty, there is regret.
   A state of abundance cannot last long.

7. All Nines
   There appears a group of dragons without a chief.
   Good fortune.

   Following the virtue of Heaven,
   One should not appear as a chief.

SIGNIFICANCE

This accomplished gua is one of the eight that is constructed by doubling one of the primary gua. Here the accomplished gua is Qian ☰, Initiating; the primary gua is Heaven ☰. Qian expounds the nature of Nature, the principle of Creation. Qian, the Initiating, is the most sublime, the most firm, the most central, and the most upright. It possesses the attributes of initiation, prosperity, harmony, and steadfastness. It moves forward endlessly and inexhaustibly. It is an ideal model of human conduct. For this reason, Confucius did not tire of explaining it in minute detail. According to him, Qian and Kun are the gate of I, which means that if one intends to understand the I Ching one should first understand Qian and Kun; then the gate of I opens for understanding the rest of the gua.

King Wen's Decision gives yuan, heng, li, and zhen—the four attributes of Heaven. Translated into English, they also encompass the meanings of sprouting, growing, blooming, and bearing fruit. Each of these four attributes gives way to one another according to the change of the seasons, cycling around and starting again. The ancient Chinese believed that humans should follow the way of Heaven, understanding the nature of change and adjusting to the situation, knowing when to advance and when to retreat. When it is not favorable to advance, it is time to gather one's strength, hold one's faith, and stand steadfast waiting for the right time and proper situation. When the time is right to progress, one still should guard against arrogance and rashness, making no move without careful thought and always keeping in mind that things that go beyond their extremes will alternate to their opposites.

The significance of the gua is to explore the healthiest movement of Heaven. In ancient times, the Chinese believed that the Tao of Heaven was also the Tao of Humanity, especially for an emperor, who was regarded as the Son of Heaven and whose duty was to lead and educate his people to practice the Tao of Heaven. King Wen's father, Ji Li, was a nobleman of the Shang dynasty. He was granted the title of the West Lord and ruled the territory on the west side of the Shang empire. Ji Li manifested the Tao of Heaven; people from all around were drawn to him. The emperor of Shang felt threatened and killed Ji Li. King Wen carried on his father's magnanimous administration with great humility and circumspection for fifty years. He still could not escape the Tyrant of Shang's suspicion and jealousy, and eventually he was imprisoned. During his seven years of imprisonment King Wen worked with the I and pondered his future duties. He realized that every undertaking or revolutionary cause needed to pass through the four stages of yuan, heng, li, and zhen, or sprouting, growing, blooming, and bearing fruit. He visualized that his sublime initiation (yuan) would be prosperous and smooth (heng), favorable to the people and successful (li), and should be kept steadfast and upright (zhen). At that time he had already worked out an overall plan of how to rescue the people from the Tyrant of Shang's brutality. He was deeply attached to the Tao of Heaven and the law of natural development. He rearranged the sixty-four gua and put Qian at the very beginning to serve as the general guideline of the Upper Canon and as the polestar of his revolutionary course.

Heaven's movement is constant, persistent, and stable; it follows its orbit without deviation, still maintaining its equilibrium. (According to ancient Chinese cosmology, Earth was the center of the universe.)

Confucius said that "with vitality and endurance Heaven acts without ceasing! Heaven's motion is the healthiest." Greatly influenced by the significance of this gua, Confucius explored its truth in his Doctrine of the Golden Mean. The nature of Heaven is to follow the central path with no

excess and no insufficiency. Applied to human lives, all our actions should follow the way of Heaven, maintaining an equilibrium. In other words, every action should be in accord with the proper time and circumstances. When the time and situation are not suitable for one to move, one should have patience. On the other hand, when the time and circumstances are favorable for one to advance, one should not lose the opportunity. This is what the ancient sage meant: following the way of Nature. It is as simple as putting on more clothing when the weather gets cold. When your stomach feels empty, take something to eat. Likewise, the ancient sage encourages the diviner to follow the way of a superior person, always vitalizing and advancing oneself. In this way, one will obtain the four attributes of Heaven: initiation, prosperity, favorableness, and steadfastness.

Following the steps of his father, the Duke of Zhou used the image of six dragons to expound upon the six stages of change represented by the six yao. The dragon was the most revered animal in ancient China. It was believed that the dragon was able to swim in the ocean, walk on the ground, and fly in the sky. Its constantly changing actions were unpredictable, like changes in the weather.

The host of this gua is the solid line at the fifth place. Qian represents the Tao of Heaven; thus, the fifth place is the symbolic seat of Heaven. Qian also illustrates the Tao of an emperor, and in that regard the fifth place is also the symbolic seat for an emperor. This place possesses the four virtues of the yang aspect—firm, strong, central, and correct— and is thus the most suitable place for the host of this gua. Confucius's Commentary on the Decision says, "As mounting on six dragons soaring in the sky. . . . The Initiating is high above all beings." This is the Tao of the Initiating, the perfect time and position. Beyond this position, things begin to alternate to their opposites. In this yao, a yang element is at a yang place, indicating a perfect situation for a ruler or a leader. One in this position requires the qualities of a superior person: firm, strong, magnanimous, and energetic.

Qian is one of the twelve tidal gua, representing the fourth month of the Chinese lunar calendar. In the solar calendar, this month is May.

(1) Initial Nine. Qian alternates to Encountering (44) ☰

This line is represented by a dragon lying low. The dragon is in the low-est of the six lines, indicating an initial stage. The time is not suitable and the circumstances are not favorable for action. However, it is a time for preparation. This was exactly King Wen's situation when he was imprisoned by the tyrant of the Shang dynasty for seven years, but he conducted himself with remarkable patience and self-restraint.

(2) Second Nine. Qian alternates to Seeking Harmony (13) ☷

The second line is symbolized by a dragon arising in the field. This line is in the central place of the lower gua. It means that a great person is on the central path. The time is coming, and the situation is suitable; he is ready to take action, and his virtuous influence will spread extensively. But before a definite goal and direction have been established, it is advisable to seek guidance from someone who is great in virtue or experience. This was King Wen's situation when he was released after seven years of confinement.

(3) Third Nine. Qian alternates to Fulfillment (10) ☰

The third line represents a situation in which one has gone beyond the central place and reaches the top of the lower gua. This line is a yang element at a yang place—it is not good to become too yang, meaning self-willed and arrogant. One who is at this place should be watchful of not straying too far from the central path and thus creating an unfavorable situation. King Wen found himself in this position when he returned from prison to his own state and made determined efforts to prepare himself and influence his people to reestablish his kingdom. The Yao Text says, "The superior person—all day long, initiating, initiating. At night, keeping alert. Adversity, no fault." This describes King Wen's actions precisely.

(4) Fourth Nine. Qian alternates to Little Accumulation (9) ☴

The fourth line symbolizes a dragon getting ready to leap out of the abyss and fly into the sky. Since this is the first line of the upper gua, the time and the circumstance have reached a new level, but only at the initial stage. Before taking action, one should wait for the best timing. In both advancing and retreating, it is important to wait for favorable timing. It is worth mentioning that in this yao, the Duke of Zhou uses the word huo, meaning "if" or "probably." The dragon can either leap or take no action. One should be extremely cautious. The Duke of Zhou reminds us that in a difficult or dangerous situation one should act cautiously; then there will be "no fault." This yao is exemplified by the actions of King Wu, son of King Wen, who, under the instruction of King Wen, sent troops against the Shang dynasty and then retreated, making only an exploratory attack. He was testing his capability for success.

(5) Fifth Nine. Qian alternates to Great Harvest (14)

The fifth line is the central line of the upper gua. It is a yang element at a yang place—central, correct, and most auspicious. It indicates that the time and situation are ripe for taking action. The dragon is already flying—a man of great virtue is ready to be a leader. Everything is in its proper place. However, even in this context a wise leader still needs to seek assistance from worthy people. It is said that this gua represents how King Wu, under the instruction of his father, sent armed forces to suppress the tyrant of the Shang dynasty, gaining the love and esteem of the people.

(6) Top Nine. Qian alternates to Eliminating (43)

The sixth line is in the uppermost place. The haughty dragon reaches its limit. One in this place should be cautious of not going too far and afterward having regrets. The I Ching always reminds us that extreme joy begets sorrow. How can one expect a state of abundance to be everlasting? Always remember that one loses by pride and gains by modesty. The Yao Text says, "Dragon becoming haughty. There is regret." The haughty dragon represents the Tyrant of Shang. He had committed countless evil deeds and was heading for his doom.

(7) All Nines. Qian alternates to Responding (2)

All nines indicates that all yang lines alternate to yin lines. Among the sixty-four gua, only this one and Responding have an extra Yao Text applied to the situation when all six lines move. When all six lines change, one should read the Decision on the approached gua. The ancient Chinese believed that, although dragons were the strongest and most powerful creatures, they never fought for leadership. Only the most magnanimous and humble, the one who is able to manifest the will of Heaven and represent Heaven, would be selected by Heaven. Thus Confucius says in his commentary, "Following the virtue of Heaven, one should not appear as a chief." An emperor or a leader is an initiator, but at the same time he is responsive. He is responsive to the will of Heaven. Thus, the next gua, Responding, expounds the Tao of the Subordinate. In this way, Initiating and Responding, the yang and the yin, merge into one. This yao indicates that the subordinates of the Shang dynasty did not regard the tyrant as their leader. It was time for a true leader to be ordained by Heaven. Thus good fortune follows.

Additional Reference Information for This Gua:

Image:	Heaven above, Heaven below		
Recite as:	Qian represents Heaven		
Element:	Metal		
Structure:	Six yang		
Month:	The fourth month of the lunar year, or May		
Host of the Gua:	Fifth Nine		
Opposite Gua:	Kun	(2)	
Inverse Gua:	Qian	(1)	
Mutual Gua:	Qian	(1)	

WEN YEN
(Confucius's Commentary on the Words of the Text)

The Wen Yen makes up the seventh of the Ten Wings. It comments exclusively on the Decision and the Yao Text of the first and second gua; however, most of the comments are on the first gua. Confucius believed that Qian and Kun were the gateway of the I Ching, the rest of the gua being developed from them. He never tired of explaining them in detail. In this commentary Confucius went further, particularly emphasizing the moral content of the text of the I Ching. The authorship is traditionally credited to Confucius, but later studies indicate that it may have been written by scholars of various Confucian schools at different times.

This piece represents the ideological system of Confucianism and has profound influence in Chinese culture. It is worth mentioning that before the Jin dynasty (265–420) this commentary was only a part of the Ten Wings; it was not a part of the I Ching. Wang Pi, one of the most eminent I Ching scholars of the Jin dynasty, first published it, along with Qian and Kun, as an integral part of the I Ching. Almost all later editions of the I Ching followed his initiative.

The commentary is divided into six sections. The first section analyzes yuan, heng, li, and zhen, the four qualities and characteristics of Heaven, which is the Chinese concept of God. It indicates that the superior person should comprehend and exemplify the utmost goodness of humanity represented by these four virtues of Heaven: in so doing he is qualified to be a leader.

In the second, third, and fourth sections, Confucius gives detailed explanations of the texts of the six yao. The second section stresses how to advance virtue and improve one's social conduct. In the third section, emphasis is laid on the importance of doing the right thing, in the right position, at the right time. The central theme of the fourth section shifts to the principle of Heaven. In Chinese, it is called Tian Tao, the Tao of Heaven. The theme of the fifth section is still Tian Tao. Confucius, with his whole heart and mind, praises the magnificence of the principle and the qualities of Heaven, that is, yuan, heng, li, and zhen. Two lines in this section are considered key to studying the I Ching:

> *Alternations of the six yao unfold the truth;*
> *Transformations of the opposites bring forth the feeling.*

In the final section, Confucius summarizes his conclusions, based on the text of the six yao, on how to lead an ethical life.

1

Yuan, the sublime and initiative,
Is the first and chief quality of goodness.

Heng, the prosperous and smooth,
Is the accumulation of excellence.

Li, the favorable and beneficial,
Is the harmony of all that is just.

Zhen, the steadfast and upright,
Is the core of action.

Because the superior person embodies all that is human,
He is able to be the head of men.

Because he presents the assemblage of excellences,
He is able to unite people through courtesy.

Because he is favorable and beneficial to all beings,
He is able to bring them into harmony with justice.

Because he is steadfast and upright,
He is able to carry out all kinds of achievements.

The superior person applies these four virtues in actions,
Therefore, it is said: Qian is yuan, heng, li, and zhen.

2

Initial Nine says:
"Dragon lying low.
Do not use."

What does it mean?
The Master says:

The dragon holds virtue but conceals his light.
He makes no change with the influence of the world.
He acts on nothing to secure his fame.
Withdrawing from the world, he bears no regret.
Experiencing disapproval, he embraces no sadness.
Acts with joy if he is able to carry his principles into action.
Casts off sorrow if his time has not come.
Truly, no one can tear him from his roots.
This is the lying low dragon.

Second Nine says:
"Dragon arising in the field.
Favorable to see a great person."

What does it mean?
The Master says:

The dragon shows his virtue,
He is properly in the central place.
Truthful in his ordinary words,
And cautious in his usual conduct.
Guarding against degeneracy
And maintaining in his sincerity.
He dedicates himself to the world but without the least boasting,
And his virtue is extensively displayed, having great influence.
Thus the I says,
"Dragon arising in the field.
Favorable to see a great person."
This refers to the qualities of a superior person.

Third Nine says:
"The superior person—

All day long, initiating, initiating.
At night, keeping alert.
Adversity, no fault."

What does it mean?
The Master says:

The sage advances in virtue
And improves his deeds.

With true heart and good faith
He advances in virtue.
With attention to his words and stable sincerity
He improves in deeds.
Knowing the utmost point to be reached and reaching it,
He is able to grasp opportunity.
Knowing the end to be rested in, and resting in it,
He is able to comprehend appropriateness.
For this reason, he is able to not be proud in a superior position
And not distressed in a lowly one.
Thus, being active and creative as circumstances demand, and
watchful,
In this way, even in a situation of adversity,
He will not make any mistake.

Fourth Nine says:
"Probably leaping from an abyss.
No fault."

What does it mean?
The Master says:

Ascending or descending,
There is no constant rule
But not to commit evil.
Advancing or retreating,
There is no permanent measure
But not to desert others.
The superior person advances his virtue and improves his deeds
In order to seize the opportune time.
Thus, no fault can be made.

Fifth Nine says:
"Dragon flying in the sky.
Favorable to see a great person."

What does it mean?
The Master says:

Notes of the same key respond to one another;
Odors of the same nature merge together.
Water flows toward what is wet,
Fire rises toward what is dry.
Clouds follow dragons;
Winds follow tigers.
Whatever the superior person does, it can be perceived by all beings.
Those who draw their origin from Heaven move toward what is
*   above;*
Those who draw their origin from Earth cleave to what is below.
All beings follow their own kind.

Top Nine says:
"Dragon becoming haughty.
There is regret."

What does it mean?
The Master says:

Being noble, yet no corresponding position;
Dwelling high, yet no following of people.
A talented and virtuous person in the position below gives no support,
Should he move in such a situation, there will be no excuse for
*   regret.*

3

Dragon lying low, do not use.
Position is low.

Dragon arising in the field.
A time for action is arriving.

The superior person, all day long initiating, initiating.
Proceeding according to plan.

Probably leaping from an abyss.
Making a trial of his strength.

Dragon flying in the sky.
In a superior position leading and administering.

Dragon becoming haughty. There is regret.
Extremity brings calamity.

When all firms change to yielding,
Great order is achieved across the land.

4

Dragon lying low, do not use.
His energy is lying deeply low.

Dragon arising in the field.
All under Heaven is illuminated.

The superior person, all day long initiating, initiating.
He is acting, proceeding in harmony with good timing.

Probably leaping from an abyss.
The Tao of Qian is transforming.

Dragon flying in the sky.
Heavenly virtue is being bestowed on this position.

Dragon becoming haughty, there is regret.
Completion and ending correspond with timing.

When all firms change to yielding,
The model of Heaven is perceived.

5

What is Qian yuan?
It refers to Qian's initiation and heng.
And heng means that whatever he does and wherever he goes
He will find that things are prosperous and smooth.

What is li zhen?
It refers to Qian's nature and feeling.
Qian creates the world.

With his magnificent grace
He benefits all under Heaven,
But never mentions his effects.
How great he is!

How great is Qian?
Firm and strong, central and correct.
He is the purest and the most unadulterated.
Alternations of the six yao unfold the truth;
Transformations of the opposites bring forth the feeling.
Harnessing the six dragons on time,
Drive upon the principle of Heaven.
Clouds flowing and rain falling,
All under Heaven enjoy equality in peace.

6

The superior person acts for the completion of virtue;
His virtuous action may be seen in his daily course.
What is lying low?
It is withdrawing and not appearing,
Proceeding yet not completing.
This is not the time for the superior person to be active.

The superior person learns to accumulate knowledge.
He questions, to distinguish true from false.
Magnanimous in life,
Benevolent in action.
The I says, "Dragon arising in the field.
Favorable to see a great person."
It refers to the virtuous quality of a ruler.

Third Nine says:
Firmness is doubled and not central.
Above, it is not in the position referring to Heaven.
Below, it is not in the place relating to the ground.
Therefore, initiating and initiating as time demands
And still thoroughly keeping alert.
Then, despite the adversity, no fault.

Fourth Nine says:
Firmness is doubled and not central.
It is not in the position referring to Heaven above,
Nor at the place relating to the ground below,
Nor at the post associated with humans in the middle.
Then it is in perplexity.
And being so, it hesitates to make a decision.
No fault can be made.

The superior person is in harmony:
In virtue, with Heaven and Earth;
In brightness, with the sun and moon;
In orderly procedure, with the four seasons;
In good fortune and bad fortune, with the gods and spirits.
He may precede Heaven, but not oppose the principles of Heaven.
He may follow Heaven by aligning with the timing of Heaven.
If Heaven will not act in opposition to him,
How much less will men?
And how much less will gods and spirits?

The word haughty indicates
Knowing to advance but not to retreat,
Knowing to maintain existence but not to let perish,
And knowing to gain but not to lose.

It is only the holy person who knows
When to advance and when to retreat,
And how to maintain existence and how to let perish,
And does not lose appropriateness.
The holy person alone can do this!

2
Kun • Responding

≡≡ Kun • Earth
≡≡ Kun • Earth

NAME AND STRUCTURE

Kun means extension and submission. In Wilhelm's text, Kun is translated as The Receptive. Blofeld translates Kun as The Passive Principle. In this book, the term Responding is adopted. The ancient Chinese ideograph Kun is depicted here. The Chinese character tu—Earth—stands on the left side, and a powerful vertical stroke is placed on the right. The vertical stroke cuts through the middle of a field; it carries the sense of extension. In the I Ching, Kun represents the quality of Earth—submission. When these two meanings are put together, the ideograph represents the extension of submission.

In the I Ching, King Wen considered Qian to be the first of the sixty-four gua and Kun to be the second. Qian and Kun together act as an introduction to the whole book. Qian also operates as a guiding principle of the first thirty gua of the Upper Canon and Kun as a guiding principle of the next thirty-two gua in the Lower Canon.

The significance of Qian is to explore natural phenomena, the Tao of Heaven. The significance of Kun is to explore the social phenomena, the Tao of Humanity. The Tao of Heaven is initiation; the Tao of Humanity is submission and responding. As a human being, one has to be submissive to Heaven and be responsive to Heaven's will. Thus King Wen's Decision says "Sublimely prosperous and smooth. Favorable with a mare's steadfastness."

Creation and reception, initiation and responding, yang and yin, should unite into one and complement each other—this is the Tao of I.

Qian is the image of heat and light, yang energy, radiating from Heaven. Kun is the image of yin energy extending over Earth. Qian represents the function of Heaven, initiating the Creation of the world. Kun represents the function of Earth, submitting and responding to Qian. Kun acts harmoniously with Qian for the completion of Creation; thus, Kun is responsive to Qian's creative action. It is worth mentioning that King Wen did not name this gua Earth; instead he named it Kun. Earth refers to the celestial bodies and the Chinese deity Earth Mother. The purpose of the I Ching is not to expose the nature of the celestial bodies nor the divine deities but to offer guidance for favorable action in one's daily life and at the same time to avoid misconduct that invites misfortune. For this reason, King Wen named the second gua Kun. Kun is the yin energy, responsive to Qian's creative action. Responsiveness, flexibility, devotion, and humility are its feminine qualities. Kun is made up of two primary gua, both Earth ☷. The six yao are all yielding lines. This picture presents an image of the purest yin, the most responsive, flexible, devoted, and humble qualities.

Sequence of the Gua: *After Heaven and Earth have come into existence, myriad beings are produced.*

Kun takes the image of Earth. According to its nature, Kun can neither create nor develop. Although it has the potential, it cannot accomplish anything alone. Its accomplishment requires acceptance of the purest yang energy from Qian and action in accordance with perfect timing. Then it is able to produce myriad beings between heaven and earth. Qian sows the seeds; Kun brings them to birth—a perfect complement of Heaven and Earth.

The Decision in Kun begins just as the Decision in Qian does, except the steadfastness in Kun is "a mare's steadfastness." The ancient Chinese originated in northern China, close to the Yellow Ground Plateau. They lived a nomadic life and were familiar with horses, observing herds living together. Among hundreds of horses there was always a leader, and the leader was always a male. Wherever the leading horse went, the herd of horses, male and female, followed. During war, male horses always ran in the front, all female horses followed behind. The nature of the mare became representative of Kun's attributes.

Kun's attributes, however, cannot be beneficial in every situation. They are successful only when Kun is acting like a devoted and submissive female horse following the male horse who is running along the right path. Therefore, when acting in a predetermined manner, Kun loses; when following a well-chosen leader, Kun does well. It is favorable to have a master, but at the same time to be a master of one's own nature. In other words, Mother Earth should respond to the function of Heaven and still be true to herself; then she can grow and nourish myriad beings.

King Wen's Decision on the gua says, "Favorable in the southwest: finds friends. In the northeast: loses friends." The directions in the I Ching are based upon King Wen's circular arrangement of the eight primary gua. In King Wen's arrangement, the eight primary gua stand for eight directions. East, west, south, and north are represented, respectively, by Thunder, Lake, Fire, and Water; southwest is Earth, northeast is Mountain, southeast is Wind, and northwest is Heaven. Since southwest is the direction of Earth, there one will find friends. Northeast is the opposite direction, so there one loses friends.

Another interpretation points out that west is the position of Earth ☷ and Lake ☱ and south is the position of Wind ☴ and Fire ☲. These four gua carry the yin quality (a mother and three daughters). On the other hand, east is the position of Mountain ☶ and Thunder ☳, and north is the position of Heaven ☰ and Water ☵. These gua carry the yang quality (a father and three sons). Confucius's Commentary on the Words of the Text for Qian says:

> *Notes of the same key respond to one another;*
> *Odors of the same nature merge together.*
> *Water flows toward what is wet,*
> *Fire rises toward what is dry. . . .*
> *All beings follow their own kind.*

Like attracts like. Kun will find friends in the south and west but will lose friends in the north and east.

Kun is one of the twelve tidal gua, representing the tenth month of the Chinese lunar calendar. In the solar calendar, it is November.

Decision

Responding.
Sublimely prosperous and smooth.
Favorable with a mare's steadfastness.
Superior person has somewhere to go.
Predetermining, loses:

Following, obtains a master.
Favorable in the southwest:
Gets friends.
In the northeast:
Lose friends.
Be composed and content.
Being steadfast and upright: good fortune.

Commentary on the Decision

Perfect is Responding's greatness;
It brings birth to all beings
And accepts the source from Heaven.

Responding in its richness sustains all beings;
Its virtue is in harmony without limit.
Its capacity is wide, its brightness is great.
Through it, all beings attain their full development.

A mare is a creature of earthly kind.
Its moving on Earth is boundless,
Yielding and submissive, advantageous and steadfast.

The superior person comprehends her way of life:
Taking the lead brings confusion,
She loses the way.
Following and responsive,
She finds the normal course.

Find friends in the southwest,
Proceed with people of the same kind.

Lose friends in the northeast,
In the end congratulations will arrive.

Good fortune comes from resting in steadfastness.
It corresponds with the boundless capacity of Earth.

Commentary on the Symbol

Earth's nature is submissive.
In correspondence with this,

The superior person enriches her virtue
To sustain all beings.

Yao Text

1. Initial Six
   Treading on hoarfrost,
   Solid ice will come.

   Treading on hoarfrost—
   A token of solid ice coming—
   Yin energy is condensing.
   Following this natural sequence,
   Solid ice is at hand.

2. Second Six
   Straight, square, and great.
   That's how it is!
   Nothing is unfavorable.

   The movement of the second six is straight,
   Because of its uprightness.
   It is spontaneous, operating without effort;
   Nothing is unfavorable.
   The light of Earth is carrying forward.

3. Third Six
   Containing excellence,
   Appropriate to be steadfast and upright.
   Probably serving a king;
   Claim no credit,
   Carrying things through to the end.

   Hiding one's excellence, appropriate to be steadfast and upright.
   She will be discovered when the time is ripe.
   Probably serving the king,
   Great is the brilliance of this wisdom.

4. Fourth Six
   Tie up a bag.
   No fault, no praise.

Tie up a bag, no fault.
Through caution, there will be no harm.

5. Fifth Six
   A yellow lower garment.
   Supreme good fortune.

   A yellow lower garment, supreme good fortune.
   There is beauty within.

6. Top Six
   Dragons playing in the wilderness;
   Their blood is blue-yellow.

   Dragons making contact in the wilderness,
   Dead end is reached.

7. All Sixes
   Favorable to be perseveringly steadfast and upright.

   All six, perseveringly steadfast and upright.
   Great will be the end.

SIGNIFICANCE

This gua is one of the eight among the sixty-four accomplished gua that is made up by doubling one of the eight primary gua. Here, the accomplished gua is Kun ☷☷, Responding; the primary gua is Earth ☷. The I Ching describes the relationship of yin and yang, the two primary and fundamental forces in the universe. They are opposite but mutually complementary. The ancient Chinese believed that too much yang and too little yin is too hard, without elasticity and likely to be broken. Too much yin and too little yang is too soft, without spirit and likely to become inert. Yin and yang must coordinate and support each other. Qian represents the most yang; Kun represents the most yin. In the I Ching all sixty-four gua are derived from the principle of the mutual coordination and complementarity of yin and yang. One of the commentaries says,

> *Yin is the most gentle and submissive; when put in motion, it is strong*
> *and firm.*
> *Yin is the most quiet and still; when taking action, it is able to reach*
> *a definite goal.*

How can this be? Yin is gentle but not weak. It is submissive, without necessarily giving up its initiative. Yin receives yang qualities from nurturing the yang.

The host of the gua is the yielding line at the second place. Kun represents the Tao of Earth, the second place is the symbolic place for Earth. Kun illustrates the Tao of the subordinate, the second place is the symbolic place for subordinates. This place possesses the four virtues of the yin aspect—yielding, submissive, central, and correct. It is thus the most suitable as the host of this gua. The Decision advises that choosing one's own predetermined path will not work out well, but following another's wise lead will meet with success. It indicates the Tao of the subordinate or the responsive.

Generally, in the I Ching, the fifth place is the host of the gua. It is central to the upper gua and represents the position of a king or leader. The fourth place is directly underneath the king; it represents the position of a minister. The second place is also special, because it is central to the lower gua. Because it is far from the king, it is regarded as an official's position. If one takes this place, then one's role is as a servant to one's lord. In the lower gua, the second line is a yin element at a yin place, indicating a perfect situation for Responding. It represents all the yin aspects of a sage's quality by following the Tao of Heaven and establishing the Tao of Humanity.

(1) Initial Six. Kun alternates to Turning Back (24)

This line is a yin element at the bottom of the gua. Yin symbolizes cold; bottom symbolizes the ground. This gua represents the tenth month of the Chinese lunar calendar. In northern China, hoarfrost appears during this month. When people see hoarfrost on the ground, they know that winter is at hand. Thus the Duke of Zhou said, "Treading on hoarfrost, solid ice will come." The message is that from a small clue one should be aware of what is coming; then one can take preventive measures against possible trouble. This line indicates that King Wu followed the instructions of his father, King Wen, preparing to rescue the people from the brutality of the tyrant of the Shang dynasty. All the signs showed that the right time was at hand.

(2) Second Six. Kun alternates to Multitude (7)

The second line is a yin element at a yin place, central and correct. The ancient Chinese believed that Heaven is round while Earth is square.

The text suggests that Earth symbolizes a sage's virtue. Straightforward, square, and great are the features of Earth. In Chinese, square, when it is applied to morality, carries the connotation of upright. When one follows the way of Heaven as Earth does, one is great. Thus, a superior person should possess the virtues of straightness, uprightness, and submissiveness, like Earth responding to Heaven; then one is able to carry out the will of Heaven spontaneously, without effort. This line indicates that the Duke of Zhou assisted his brother, King Wu, in planning an expedition against the tyrant of the Shang dynasty. The Duke of Zhou advised King Wu to cultivate the virtue of Earth. Being straight and square, one would be great. Then the expedition could be conducted with no effort, and nothing would remain unfavorable.

(3) Third Six. Kun alternates to Humbleness (15) ☷☶

The third line, "Hiding excellence," suggests humility. When the yielding line at the third place changes into a solid line, this gua alternates to Humbleness. However, one's excellence cannot be hidden very long; sooner or later it will be discovered. According to this line, one who has talent should come forth to serve the people. When the right time presents itself, one should carry things through to the end and not hold any selfish motivation. This line indicates that the Duke of Zhou and King Wu were preparing an expedition against the tyrant of the Shang dynasty. Through the experience of having their grandfather killed by the Emperor of Shang, they realized the importance of hiding one's excellence and firmly maintaining it. Their strategy was to serve the tyrant with humility while bringing their plan to completion. Confucius praises their wisdom.

(4) Fourth Six. Kun alternates to Delight (16) ☷☳

The fourth line is a yin element at a yin place. It is at the bottom of the upper gua. Although the place is correct, it is not central. In the I Ching, Kun also represents cloth. Thus the text employs the image of a tied-up bag to explain an unfavorable situation. "Tie up a bag" vividly suggests that in an unfavorable situation one should restrain oneself. Be cautious in words and actions. Being cautious in an unfavorable situation, how can one be at fault? To be cautious is a preventive stance to avoid harm, but it is not productive. Therefore, there is no praise. This line indicates that in preparing an expedition against the Tyrant of Shang, the Duke of Zhou and King Wu not only humbled themselves but also were cautious in their words and actions, as if tying up a bag.

(5) Fifth Six. Kun alternates to Union (8) ☰☷

The fifth line is the central place of the upper gua; a yellow garment is used. In the I Ching, Qian represents the upper clothes, and Kun represents the lower garments. A lower garment symbolizes humility. In the Chinese system of the five elements, Earth is in the central place, and its color is yellow. For this reason the lower garment is yellow. A yellow garment symbolizes that one in this place is able to walk in the central path and be humble. It is extremely auspicious. In the class-based society of ancient times, the formal attire of a scholar was a black robe with a yellow lower garment. (Scholars were of the social stratum between senior officials and the common people.) The robe was long, and covered the yellow garment. Humility is of an inner beauty, like the beauty of the yellow garment covered by the black robe. Thus Confucius's commentary says, "There is beauty within." This line indicates that the time to send an expedition against the Tyrant of Shang was near. The Duke of Zhou and King Wu realized that humility should not be dealt with as a strategy. It should become one's nature.

There is a story relating to this line. There was a lord named Nan Gua who plotted to rebel against the king. He performed a divination and obtained this gua. He was very happy that the text said, "A yellow lower garment. Supreme good fortune." He was certain that he would meet with success. Nevertheless, a duke admonished him, "Dear Lord, it must be a faithful and truthful action to be auspicious. Otherwise it will fail." His explanation was based on the theory of the five elements. According to this theory, yellow, the color of Earth, represents the center, which guides one to act in accordance with the principle of Confucius's Golden Mean, that is, to act exactly right without excess or insufficiency. To rebel is to leave the central path; such an undertaking would be bound to fail.

(6) Top Six. Kun alternates to Falling Away (23) ☷☶

The top line reaches the extremity of the gua. In this gua all six lines are yin. The yin element approaches closer and closer; the yang element retreats again and again. The yang reaches its end point; it has no place to retreat, and so a struggle with the yin is unavoidable. It is a struggle between negative and positive, darkness and light. In Chinese tradition, the color of Heaven is blue. Two dragons—one yang and the other yin—are fighting. Consequently, the colors of their blood, blue (Heaven) and yellow (Earth), merge. The message of this yao is that when one approaches an extreme, the path comes to an end. If one is ready to change, this is a turning point. Otherwise, one will fall apart.

This line indicates that four years after King Wen had passed away, in the year 1066 B.C., King Wu followed his father's instruction, sending a punitive expedition against the tyrant of the Shang dynasty. At first, King Wu sent spies to Shang. It was reported that the rulers and administrators were dissipated and unashamed. King Wu thought that the time was not appropriate. Later, messages were sent back that all the righteous persons had been reproached and dismissed from their posts. King Wu believed that the time was still not mature. At last, the messenger came back and told how the people of Shang dared not speak. King Wu considered that the time was ready. At the same time there was a famine; people working in the fields preferred to go on an expedition. King Wu took three hundred chariots, forty-five thousand soldiers, and three thousand troops as a vanguard. Soldiers sang and danced, and morale was high. Eight different ethnic kingdoms came to join the rebellion. King Wu charged the tyrant with four indictments: that he was licentious and dissolute, indulging himself with concubines; that he did not offer sacrifices to Heaven and his ancestors; that he did not trust righteous persons, even his own relatives; and that he housed criminals of all kinds and harbored the escaped slaves of neighboring kingdoms. In a decisive battle, 170,000 troops of the Shang dynasty responded to King Wu's righteous movement and rose up against the tyrant. The cruel Shang dynasty was brought down.

(7) All Sixes. Kun alternates to Initiating (1)

All sixes indicates that all yin lines alternate to yang lines. As already mentioned, there are two extra Yao Texts with the first and second gua, Qian and Kun. Qian represents Heaven, pure yang, and Kun represents Earth, pure yin. When one's divination obtains this yao, one should use the full potential of the Earth quality; then "great will be the end," meaning that all six yin lines alternate to yang lines. In the I Ching, yang represents great, and yin represents little. When six yin lines alternate to six yang lines, that is great. The function of Earth is to respond. Earth responds to the action of Heaven. When one accepts the pure yang energy from Heaven and acts in accordance with perfect timing, then one is able to produce myriad beings between Heaven and Earth. This is a perfect complement of yin energy with yang energy. This line is a continuation of the preceding gua. King Wu fulfilled the will of his father, King Wen, who responded to the will of Heaven. The Tyrant of Shang was overthrown. All the yin energy turned to

yang. The Tao of Heaven was fulfilled, but there remained something not yet fulfilled. According to the Tao of Heaven, it was favorable to be steadfast and upright.

Additional Reference Information for This Gua

Image:	Earth above, Earth below	
Recite as:	Kun is Earth	
Element:	Earth	
Structure:	Six yin	
Month:	The tenth month of the lunar year, or November	
Host of the Gua:	Second Six	
Opposite Gua:	Qian	(1)
Inverse Gua:	Kun	(2)
Mutual Gua:	Kun	(2)

WEN YEN
(Confucius's Commentary on the Words of the Text)

1

Kun is most soft;
Yet in action it is firm.
It is most still,
Yet in nature, square.

Through following she obtains her lord,
Yet still maintains her nature and thus endures.
She contains all beings
And is brilliant in transforming.

This is the way of Kun—How docile it is,
Bearing Heaven and moving with time!

2

The family that heaps goodness upon goodness
Is sure to have an abundance of blessings.
The family that piles evil upon evil
Is sure to have an abundance of misery.

Murder of a ruler by his minister,
Or a father by his son,
Does not result from a single day and night.
Its causes have accumulated bit by bit
Through the absence of early discrimination.
The I says, "Treading on hoarfrost, solid ice will come."
It shows the natural sequence of cause and effect.

"Straight" indicates correctness.
"Square" indicates righteousness.
The superior person respects herself
In keeping her inner life straight.
And rectifies herself
In making her outer action square.
When respecting and rectifying are established,
Then fulfillment of virtue will be free from isolation.
"Straight, square, and great.
Not from learning.
Nothing is unfavorable."
It shows she has no doubt in what she does.

Although yin possesses beauty,
It is concealed.
Engaging in a king's service,
Claims no credit for oneself.
This is the Tao of Earth,
The Tao of a wife,
And the Tao of one who serves the king.
The Tao of Earth is to make no claim on its own,
But to bring everything to completion.

Changing and transforming of Heaven and Earth
Bring forth all plants flourishing.
If Heaven and Earth restrain their function,
Then an able person would withdraw from the light.
The I says, "Tie up a bag. No fault, no praise."
It counsels caution.

A superior person should hold the quality of Earth—
Yellow is central and moderate,
Understanding and considerate.

Correcting her position and perfecting her action,
Her beauty lies within.
It permeates her whole being
And manifests in all her doing.
This reveals the perfection of beauty.

When yin competes against yang,
A contest is certain.
Since no yang is considered,
Then a dragon is mentioned.
Since no category is changed,
Then blood—a yin symbol—is noted.
Blue and yellow is Heaven and Earth in fusion.
Heaven is blue, Earth yellow.

EXPLANATORY NOTE

The Commentary is divided into two sections. In the first section Confucius expounds further upon King Wen's Decision. In the second section he provides more detailed explanations of the Duke of Zhou's Yao Text. Both sections are based upon the moral principles of the Confucian school. All through the ages Confucian schools regarded Qian as a gua for the king and Kun as a gua for the queen. Qian reveals the truth of how to be a leader; Kun reveals the truth of how to be a follower. Confucian scholars consider that both leading and being led should be learned and practiced.

At the beginning of this section, Confucius gives an excellent example of the Chinese dialectical point of view. Kun is soft, yet still firm. It is still, yet also square. Soft and firm, still and square are entirely opposite, yet in the Chinese mind they can be united. Thus Confucius says, "Through following she obtains her lord, yet still maintains her nature." This is a typical Chinese dialectic—being submissive but not slavish, independent but not rebellious and, on the other hand, being a leader but not dictatorial.

This dialectical point of view—the merging of opposites—is deeply rooted in Chinese culture. The I Ching expounds first the Tian Tao, the Tao of Heaven, then Di Tao, the Tao of Earth. It instructs people that Heaven is the Initiator and that Earth should follow the Tao of Heaven, and humans should follow the Tao of Earth. Because King Wen had these ideas, he rearranged the sequence of the I Ching and put Qian in the first place and Kun in the second. Confucius highly admired the culture of the Zhou dynasty. He said, "How brilliant is the culture of Zhou. I prefer to follow Zhou."

Confucius expanded on this subject to explain the law of cause and effect. Through the influence of the I Ching, the idea of retribution was deeply impressed into Chinese culture. The Chinese people believe that the law of cause and effect operates not only within one generation but through at least three generations, affecting their ancestors, themselves, and their descendants. For this reason, the Chinese revered their ancestors after they passed away and emphasized their words and deeds and family education. In Chinese, the actual meaning of "abundance of blessings" and "abundance of misery" contains the sense of "remaining for a long time." In other words, the effect of good deeds and evil acts remain generation after generation. On this account, the Chinese believe that the effect of their deeds, whether good or bad, if not fulfilled in the present life, definitely come to fruition in the life of the next generation. Thus, they say, "care only for plowing and weeding, ask not for the harvest." Bearing this in mind, Liu Bei, the emperor of the Shu Han dynasty (A.D. 221–265), instructed his son on his deathbed, "Don't restrain your good deed because it is too tiny; don't perform your evil act because it is so little."

Commenting on the second yao, Confucius says, "When respecting and rectifying are established, then fulfillment of virtue will be free from isolation." "Respect" here means respect for oneself in keeping one's inner life straight. "Rectify" is to rectify oneself in making one's outer action square. In so doing, "fulfillment of virtue will be free from isolation." Confucius once told his students, "Virtue is not left to stand isolated. He who practices it will have neighbors." The idea of being free from isolation is based upon the principle of resonance. Confucius believed that the inner virtue and the outer actions of a king, a teacher, and a parent would influence people, students, and children. Likewise, their karmic deeds would influence their descendants for generations. Confucius believed that when one's words and deeds reach the level of straight, square, and great, then whatever one speaks and does, "nothing is unfavorable."

Confucius focuses on yin qualities in his commentary on the third yao. In the I Ching, Earth represents pure yin. It possesses beauty, yet is concealed; it engages in a king's service, yet claims no credit. This is the Tao of Earth.

Both Confucianism and Taoism originated from the philosophy of the I Ching. They both followed the Tao of Earth, but they diverged. For

instance, Confucius claimed that the Tao of Earth is taking no credit for success, but bringing everything to completion; yet this principle was carried out more thoroughly by the Taoists. In Chinese history, the greatest prime minister was a Taoist sage named Chang Liang. Chang Liang assisted the first emperor of the Han dynasty (206 B.C. to A.D. 220), Liu Pong, who overthrew the tyrant emperor of the Chin dynasty (221–206 B.C.). Chang Liang then withdrew from active life, becoming a hermit. Where did he go? No one knows. This is the true spirit of taking no credit for success, but bringing everything to completion. Chang Liang followed the instruction of this yao: After succeeding, resign. He embraced the Tao of I: When things reach the extreme, they alternate to the opposite. Chang Liang realized that with success his prestige was at its highest, just short of the emperor, but sooner or later he would fall. As he predicted, the emperor became suspicious and after a time had all the other ministers killed one by one. Chang Liang has come to be regarded as the wisest person ever known in China.

There was another well-known prime minister, Chu Ke Liang of the Shu Han dynasty. He also followed the spirit of this yao, but in a different way. Chu Ke Liang successfully assisted Emperor Liu Bei in establishing the empire in the province of Szechuan. He continued to assist the emperor by sending troops across Mount Gi six times. He captured the head of the southern nationality, Meng Huo, seven times and released him seven times. Consequently, Meng Huo conceded defeat and pledged allegiance to the emperor. After Emperor Liu Bei passed away, Chu Ke Liang honored his earnest request to continue assisting his son in ruling the country. His attitude was "Give one's all, till one's heart stops beating." This was Chu Ke Liang's understanding of the line "The Tao of Earth is to make no claim on its own, but to bring everything to completion." Although Chinese history considers Chu Ke Liang a Taoist, this is with regard to his military strategy and tactics. Concerning his way of serving the king, he was more Confucian.

In Confucius's commentary on the fourth yao, he says, "The I says, 'Tie up a bag. No fault, no praise.' It counsels caution." The spirit of "tie up a bag" was practiced more thoroughly by the Taoists than by the Confucians. The Taoist attitude is to be wise for personal survival and cautious during disorderly times. They tie the bag tight. This was exactly what Confucius said: "If Heaven and Earth restrain their function, then an able person would withdraw from the light." But most Confucian scholars could not follow this principle.

Let us go back to the story of Chu Ke Liang. In the beginning he lived life simply, in a Taoist way. At that time, he most cherished survival in a disorderly world. This is typically Taoist. But after Liu Bei visited his humble hut three times, he was so moved that he accepted Liu Bei's request to bring order to the disorderly world.

When Confucius was young, he was so determined to carry out the Zhou dynasty's brilliant social system in what was a disorderly era that even in his dreams he saw the Duke of Zhou. He encouraged his students by saying, "Having completed one's learning, one should apply oneself to being an officer." Once he told his students, "One's burden is heavy and one's course is long . . . only with death does the course stop—is it not long?" He visited the lords of six states, trying to persuade them to practice benevolent governing, like the Zhou system. After being rejected, he wept in grief. At that time, he did not understand that "If Heaven and Earth restrain their function, then an able person would withdraw from the light."

Confucius began to study the I Ching when he was fifty years old. He studied so hard that the leather thongs which bound the bamboo tablets of his I Ching wore out three times. At seventy years of age he said, "If some years were added to my life, I would dedicate fifty years to study of the Book of I, and then I might come to be without great fault." His attitude had changed entirely. He realized that in his early days he had made many mistakes.

Traditionally, the Chinese attribute the creation of Taoism to Lao Tze, a senior contemporary of Confucius. Confucius heard about Lao Tze and eventually had the opportunity to visit him. He asked for advice and was greatly impressed. Upon his return Confucius described Lao Tze to his students as a mysterious dragon. Quoting a few passages from the Tao Te Ching will demonstrate how their origin comes from the I Ching, a book that existed at least five hundred years before Lao Tze.

Man follows Earth,
Earth follows Heaven.
Heaven follows the Tao.
Yet the Tao follows Nature.

Tao produced one.
One produced two.
Two produced Three.
Three produced ten thousand beings.

Ten thousand beings carry yin and embrace yang;

By blending their energies they achieve harmony.
Therefore existence and nonexistence produce each other.
Difficulty and ease complement each other.
Long and short contrast with each other.
High and low rely on each other.
Sound and voice harmonize with each other.
Front and back follow each other.

The Tao fulfills its purpose quietly and makes no claim.
When success is achieved, withdrawing.

The highest good is like water.
Water benefits ten thousand beings,
Yet it does not contend.
Nothing under Heaven is as soft and yielding as water.
Yet in attacking the firm and strong,
Nothing is better than water.

It is believed that the concept of the Doctrine of the Mean, one of the four classics of the Confucian school, written by Tze Si, Confucius's grandson, came from the fifth yao. In Chinese, the Doctrine of the Mean is "Chung Yung." Chung means central; yung means permanent. Being without inclination to either side is remaining central. Admitting of no change is permanent. In other words, the golden principle of the Doctrine of the Mean is unchangeable; thus it is permanent.

In the last part of the commentary, Confucius explores the negative aspect of the yin quality. The entire I Ching is concerned with the relationship between yin and yang. Yin and yang represent two aspects. In the yang aspect, there are yin features and yang features. Likewise, there are yin features and yang features in a yin aspect. In the yang aspect, yang represents what is firm, and yin represents what is yielding. In the yin aspect, yang represents the good, and yin represents evil. When the firm yang corresponds with the yielding yin, there is perfect opposition because the yin functions harmoniously with the yang. Yin is a positive complement. On the other hand, when yin competes against yang, it reveals the yin aspect; then yin represents evil instead of yielding. When yang is without yin, it is too firm. It is defeated because it is too easily broken. When yin is without yang, it becomes vicious and leaves a legacy of trouble.

The I Ching demonstrates the opposing relationship of yin and yang. The quality of yin is positive—yielding, responding, and cooperating. The relationship between yin and yang should be harmonious, creative, and productive. In studying the I Ching, one should keep in mind that

> *When yin competes against yang,*
> *A contest is certain. . . .*
> *Since no category is changed,*
> *Then blood—a yin symbol—is noted.*
> *Blue and yellow is Heaven and Earth in fusion.*
> *Heaven is blue, Earth yellow.*

This is the Tao of Heaven and the Tao of Earth.

3
Zhun • Beginning

Kan • Cloud
Zhen • Thunder

NAME AND STRUCTURE

Wilhelm translates Zhun as Difficulty at the Beginning. Blofeld translates it as Difficulty. In this book it is called Beginning. The character for the name of the gua has two meanings and is pronounced in two different ways. In most cases it is pronounced tun, carrying the meaning of gathering, assembling, and filling up with abundance. In ancient China, a warehouse was called tun. In the I Ching, and only in the I Ching, this character bears the meaning of beginning. In this case, it is pronounced zhun.

The ancient Chinese pictograph of this character is a picture of Zhun, which might be the word's original meaning. The pictograph of Zhun looks like a tiny blade of newly sprouted grass with a root that deeply penetrates the ground. The horizontal line lying across the upper third of the pictograph represents the surface of the ground. Above the ground a tiny sprout is just coming up, and underneath a root penetrates the soil. This picture symbolizes new life. The structure of the gua presents another picture. The lower gua is Thunder. Two yielding lines mount a firm line. The yang element is stuck under the two yin elements. The upper gua is Water. A firm line lies between two yielding lines. The yang element is bogged down between two yin elements. This picture suggests a rough situation for a newly born being. Nevertheless, the newly born being possesses a strong and healthy root, gathering an abundance of life force for its growth.

Most people think of sprouts growing only in spring, but the ancient Chinese realized that there was a life force latent in seed form the whole winter. In addition, the ancients perceived the difficulties of a plant emerging from the ground. The little plant must overcome the pressure of the soil. There must be a wholehearted willingness to grow. Thus, this gua is bestowed with the four outstanding qualities of yuan, heng, li, and zhen, as are Qian and Kun, the first and second gua. Only six gua in The I Ching possess these four qualities.

According to the layout of the book, the first two gua outline the general principle of the sixty-four gua, and the last two gua serve as the conclusion. The third gua, then, is actually the first (the beginning) of the remaining sixty gua. King Wen recalled how his father had been killed by the emperor of the Shang dynasty and he himself was defeated and became a subject, at last being imprisoned. Summing up this historical experience and looking forward to the future, he gave the following Decision as a guideline for his sons. The Zhou dynasty at the beginning was like a tiny sprout. Supreme and smooth prosperity would prevail, but it was favorable only by being steadfast and upright. Nothing should be taken lightly. The principal achievement of King Wen was to establish feudal lords and to lay the foundation for his sons to overthrow the Shang dynasty. Through establishing feudalism, he gradually came into possession of two-thirds of the region of the Shang dynasty and became its greatest lord.

Sequence of the Gua: *After Heaven and Earth have come into existence, myriad beings are produced. These myriad beings fill up the space between Heaven and Earth. Thus, Beginning follows.*

After the interaction of Heaven and Earth (Qian and Kun), myriad beings are generated. For this reason, after Qian and Kun, the third gua is Zhun, the beginning of all beings.

Decision

The beginning of a tiny sprout.
Sublimely prosperous and smooth.
Favorable to be steadfast and upright.
Do not act lightly.
There is somewhere to go.
Favorable to establish feudal lords.

Commentary on the Decision

Beginning.
The firm and the yielding united at the very beginning;
Difficulties come into being.

Movement in the midst of danger,
Great prosperity and smoothness comes through steadfastness and
*   uprightness.*

The action of thunder and rain
Filled things up everywhere.
At the beginning of creation,
There was irregularity and disorder.
It was favorable to establish feudal lords,
But unstable conditions still might arise.

Commentary on the Symbol

Clouds and thunder fill up.
In correspondence with this,
The superior person plans and sets things in order.

Yao Text

1. Initial Nine
   Lingering and considering,
   Favorable to abide in being steadfast and upright.
   Favorable to establish feudal lords.

   Although lingering and considering,
   Upright intention still remains.
   The superior, respecting the inferior,
   Wins the hearts of all.

2. Second Six
   Difficulty in advancing, hard to proceed.
   Mounting on horses, still not going forward.
   Not invading, seeking a marriage.
   The maiden is chaste, marries not.
   After ten years, she marries.

Hardship of the Second Six
Mounting on the firm.
Married after ten years,
Hardship ends; a normal cycle returns.

3. Third Six
   Chasing deer, no guide
   In the midst of woods.
   The superior person is alert:
   Give up!
   Going forward: humiliation.

   Chasing deer, no guide.
   Let flee like a bird.
   The superior person gives up.
   By going on, humiliation will follow;
   There is no way out.

4. Fourth Six
   Mounting on horses, still not going forward.
   Seeking a union.
   Going forward: good fortune.
   Nothing is unfavorable.

   Seeking what you want. Go ahead.
   There is light.

5. Fifth Nine
   Asembling one's abundance.
   Little things—
   Being steadfast and upright: good fortune.
   Great things—
   Being steadfast and upright: guide against misfortune.

   The beginning of one's abundance.
   One's brilliance is not yet recognized.

6. Top Six
   Mounting on horses,
   Still not going forward.
   Weeping grievously,
   Shedding tears as if bleeding.

Sheds tears as if bleeding.
How long can it endure?

SIGNIFICANCE

This is an auspicious gua. It expounds the truth that a newly established situation is full of the potential to develop. On the other hand, it also contains latent difficulties. "Clouds over Thunder symbolizes Beginning"—this is the Chinese way to remember the structure of the gua. The structure presents a vivid picture of a tremendous power of energy, represented by thunder, lying at the base of clouds. In the Commentary on the Decision, Confucius says, "The action of thunder and rain filled things up everywhere." In his Commentary on the Symbol he says, "Clouds and thunder fill up." In both cases Confucius employs the image of clouds or rain instead of water. Clouds and rain have the same essence as water.

Contemplating the symbol, Confucius says, "Clouds and thunder fill up," but he doesn't mention rain. The attribute of Thunder is action, but there is no action. However, the clouds do presage a storm. When dark clouds fill the sky, sooner or later rain will come. This gua holds the potential to create. Confucius advises that "the superior person plans and sets things in order." It is time to prepare to do something.

On the other hand, meditating on the comentary on King Wen's Decision, Confucius says, "The action of thunder and rain filled things up everywhere." Eventually the action comes—it is rain. Confucius then says, "At the beginning of creation, there was irregularity and disorder." When I study this gua, I visualize the Chinese concept of genesis. Before Heaven and Earth were created, they were without form, void. During Creation, there were clouds, rain, and thunder. At first, there was irregularity and disorder. After the world was brought into being (the beginning), regularity and order were gradually established. Based on the idea of the union of yin and yang, Chinese scholars came to employ clouds and rain to suggest the actions of lovemaking. I can see this union appearing in the upper gua ☵, which suggests clouds and rain. The fruit of this union is Thunder ☳, the lower gua; in the I Ching, Thunder represents the eldest son. It is significant that this Chinese pictograph was selected to express the beginning of the world. In this pictograph the root is inscribed as much longer than the sprout. Before sprouting, the root must penetrate deeply. The sages learned from nature that before effecting a plan, it is important to set things in order.

The host of the gua is the solid line on the bottom. King Wen's Decision on the Gua says, "The beginning of a tiny sprout. . . . Favorable to establish feudal lords." One in this position is able to establish feudal lords to provide security. On the other hand, the solid line on the bottom symbolizes a beginning. Although it is firm and strong, it is on the bottom and carries two yielding lines. This situation indicates that a latent power will sprout, but in a difficult situation. The yang element at the fifth place lies in a supreme position—firm, central, and correct—and corresponds to the yin element at the second place. Everything is in order for it to be the host; however, since the name of the gua comes from the solid line at the bottom, that line makes a more suitable host.

Examining the structure, the lower gua is Thunder, indicating action and power. The upper gua is Water, indicating trouble. Thunder confronting Water delivers the message that when one faces difficulty at an initial stage, no matter how powerful one is, nothing should be taken lightly. This is the main theme of the gua. In this gua, the Duke of Zhou reaffirmed King Wen's guiding principle that care should be taken at the beginning of an undertaking. The time is favorable only for persevering in naming feudal lords in order to accumulate strength and laying the foundation for a new dynasty. His strength needed to grow as strong as a rock and as firm as a tree.

In the I Ching, in most cases, marriage refers to a political alliance. The Duke of Zhou described the process of establishing feudal lords as difficult to advance, likening it to four horses drawing a cart at different paces. Three ferocious minority tribes came to him asking for an alliance. King Wen considered that the time was not auspicious and refused. The Duke of Zhou restated King Wen's instruction that, without first knowing the situation of the Shang dynasty, launching an expedition would be like chasing deer without a guide in the midst of woods.

With time, the process of establishing feudal lords became like mounting on a horse but still not moving forward. King Wen took the initiative to form an alliance with Shang. As a result King Yi of the Shang dynasty gave his younger sister to King Wen in marriage. The situation improved. Being in an alliance with the Shang dynasty, the energy of the Zhou was obstructed. It was favorable only for small undertakings. In this gua, the Duke of Zhou repeated "Mounting on

horses, still not going forward" three times. He grieved deeply, shedding tears as if bleeding.

(1) Initial Nine. Beginning alternates to Union (8)

Nine at the beginning is a solid line at the bottom of the lower gua, Thunder ☳. The structure reveals two things. First, this line is at the initial stage of a process. Second, from this place one has great potential to move forward as thunder does. However, this element responds to the yin element at the fourth place, which is at the bottom of the upper gua, Water ☵. Water has dark depths, suggesting difficulty. This place requires one to linger and consider. The timing is significant. Although there is difficulty ahead, it is a crucial time to start a new enterprise. In this situation, persevering is critical.

The English translation of the Yao Text says, "Lingering and considering." In Chinese, the words for lingering and considering are *pan huan*. Pan is a huge rock, and huan is a big tree. When the Duke of Zhou saw a big tree growing on a huge rock, he realized that if there was sufficient life force then nothing could prevent the tree from growing. In the structure of the gua, there are several yin lines above the yang line, like a huge rock sitting above a tree. However, the tree eventually grows and stands firm on the rock. In ancient Chinese literature, a single word usually represented several thoughts. Huan meant pillar, and was also the name of the "Ode of Zhou," one of the pieces in *The Book of Songs*, a classic collection of folk songs compiled by Confucius. This ode praises the efforts of King Wu when he launched his expedition and eventually conquered the Tyrant of Shang. Later on, pan huan came to have the sense of lingering and considering. "Favorable to establish feudal lords" is an ancient Chinese expression equivalent to seeking support. If one plans to do something great, seeking support is a necessity.

(2) Second Six. Beginning alternates to Restricting (60)

Here the Duke of Zhou uses the image of the gua to tell a story. There are two yang elements and four yin elements. Six at the second place is a yin element symbolizing a maiden. She is enchanting two men. The one at the fifth place is her true lover; these two have a common interest and mutual affection. Unfortunately, they are not close together. Another man, Nine at the beginning, is her close neighbor. He woos her. Two men woo one woman; the woman has to make a decision. Her decision is to stay faithful to her true love, to remain steadfast. Finally she marries the man she has truly loved.

The story derived from the structure of the gua. Six at the second place is a yin element at a yin place, central and correct. It corresponds to the yang element at the fifth place. These two elements, yin and yang, are a perfect match. But another yang element, at the bottom place, carries the second line. This yang element is a close neighbor. This situation makes it difficult for the yin element at the second place to advance. The yang element at the bottom is at a yang place, dominant and tyrannical. He would force the maiden to marry him. The maiden is in a central place; she prefers to walk the middle path. She acts exactly in accordance with the main theme of the gua, that nothing should be taken lightly. She remains firm in her will, patiently waiting. Eventually she obtains what she wants.

(3) Third Six. Beginning alternates to Already Fulfilled (63) ☵

Here again, the Duke of Zhou tells a story. A group of people going hunting found a deer and chased it. The deer ran into the forest. Without the guidance of a forester, the wise man decided to give up; he let the deer flee like a bird. He knew that by going on, regret would follow. The Yao Text gives advice to one at the third place—at the top of the lower gua. The upper gua is Water, symbolizing a difficult situation. We have here a yin element at a yang place, neither central nor correct. If one at this place does not remain content and intends to proceed, there will be difficulty ahead. Furthermore, the yin element at this place does not correspond to the yin element at the uppermost place—they are both yin. If one at this place proceeds lightly, she will fall into dark depths. The text uses "chasing deer, no guide" as an analogy. Proceeding blindly with no guidance, one becomes lost. The message of this yao is that one should be wise enough, by knowing the situation, to make a proper choice of what to accept and what to avoid. Never act blindly.

(4) Fourth Six. Beginning alternates to Following (17) ☵

Here the story of the marrying maiden continues. In this gua the position of the maiden shifts from the second to the fourth place—she is much closer to her true love. The situation is favorable and the time is right. The Duke of Zhou says, "Seeking a union. Going forward: good fortune. Nothing is unfavorable." But the maiden still hesitates. The problem is that she corresponds to the yang element on the bottom.

On the other hand, she is much closer to the yang element at the fifth place. It is understandable that when two yang approach one yin, the yin becomes confused. In this situation Confucius encourages the maiden, "Go ahead. There is light." This decision is based on the structure of the gua. If one at this place proceeds, there is a yang element waiting. If she retreats, there are two yin elements behind. When one makes a decision, one should consider the most favorable position. The Chinese say, "A waterfront pavilion gets the moonlight first." The message of this yao is that when one is in a situation where it is difficult to decide between advancing or retreating, one should adopt a positive attitude in approaching the light.

(5) Fifth Nine. Beginning alternates to Turning Back (24) ☷☳

To understand the significance of this yao, we must examine the structure first. The structure usually sheds light on a situation. In general terms, a yang element at the fifth place is usually auspicious because its place is central and correct and in a supreme position. But in this gua, the yang element at this place is lying in the middle of the upper gua, Water ☵, the dark depths. Thus, Confucius says, "One's brilliance is not yet recognized." Accordingly, it is only favorable for small endeavors. Furthermore, the structure shows that the yang element at this place is surrounded by several yin elements. For this reason, the Yao Text recommended "being steadfast and upright," even in little ways. In the I Ching, where there is an auspicious omen, being steadfast and upright is often a prerequisite.

The structure also shows that the yang element at this place corresponds to the yin element at the second place. However, the yin element at the second place is being cut off and is too weak to give support, because two yin elements lie between. These two yin elements leave the yang element stuck in an isolated position. In this situation, one should retreat and preserve one's energy, waiting for the right time.

(6) Top Six. Beginning alternates to Increasing (42) ☳☷

In this gua, "mounting on horses" appears three times. Here, however, the rider is weeping. Her grief is so deep that shedding tears is like bleeding. What is this story based upon? The yielding line on the top has ascended to the uppermost position. It is as if the sun has set beyond the western hills. The day is waning, and the road is ending. There is no way to go forward. In addition, this line does not correspond to the yin element at the third place, indicating that there is no way to turn back. In the I Ching, the primary gua Water also signifies blood. The message of this gua is that, since one has already reached the uppermost position, one should not feel sorry about being unable to go forward or turn back. One must realize that when things reach an extreme they will alternate to the opposite. For this reason, the I Ching always calls for restraint before going too far.

Additional Reference Information for This Gua

Image:	Water above, Thunder below
Recite as:	Cloud over Thunder, Beginning
Element:	Water
Structure:	Two yang with four yin
Month:	The twelfth month of the lunar year, or January
Host of the Gua:	Initial Nine
Opposite Gua:	Establishing the New (50)
Inverse Gua:	Childhood (4)
Mutual Gua:	Falling Away (23)

4
Meng · Childhood

Gen • Mountain
Kan • Stream

NAME AND STRUCTURE

Wilhelm translates Meng as Youthful Folly. Blofeld translates it as Immaturity. In this book, the term Childhood is used. Meng is the inverse of the preceding gua, Zhun, Beginning ䷂. They are inverse in position but complementary to each other. Meng has different meanings. Originally, it was the name of a twining plant known as dodder, which grows easily and spreads everywhere. The ancients saw dodder growing and spreading on the roofs of huts and so created the ideograph of Meng to show grasses on the roof of a house. Later on, Meng came to mean covering, because dodder grows and covers roofs everywhere.

By the time King Wen wrote the Decision, the meaning of Meng was extended to include wisdom. The ancient Chinese believed that the nature of a child is like uncarved jade; its brilliance is hidden. At that time, an uneducated child was called tong meng. Tong means child, and tong meng indicates that the wisdom of a child is concealed or not yet uncovered. To educate a child was called qi meng. Literally, qi meng is to lift the cover or to uncover what is concealed. For this reason, in ancient times the place for a child to begin his education was called Meng Hall. Thus, Meng symbolizes the ignorant, the innocent, or the child, because wisdom is not yet uncovered.

The themes of Meng are highly regarded in Chinese culture—following the beginning of a life, uncovering the hidden brilliance of a child. The image of Meng is Water ☵ underneath Mountain ☶. Water flowing out from a mountain becomes a spring, pure and transparent, symbolizing the pureness of a child's innocent mind. After the spring flows out of the mountain, it accumulates sediment over time. The ancients realized from observing this phenomenon that the ignorant should be educated and enlightened.

Sequence of the Gua: *Zhun denotes what has just been born. What has just been born is in its childhood. Thus, after Beginning, Childhood follows.*

Decision

Childhood.
Prosperous and smooth.
It is not I who seek the ignorant,
The ignorant seeks me.
On the first divination, I give light.
Repeating again is contemptuous.
Being contemptuous, I give no more instruction.
Favorable to be steadfast and upright.

Commentary on the Decision

Unenlightened ignorant.
At the foot of a mountain lies difficulty;
Difficulty makes him stand still.
It is ignorant behavior.

The ignorant can be prosperous and smooth
If he acts in accordance with the proper time
And follows the principle of the central way.
It is not I who seeks the ignorant.
The ignorant seeks me.
His will responds to mine.

On the first divination, I give light.
He was firm and in a central position.

Repeating again is contemptuous.
Being contemptuous, no more instruction.
Showing contempt causes ignorance.

Uncovering the covered is to nourish the correct nature.
It is a holy task.

Commentary on the Symbol

A spring flows out of a mountain.
The symbol of an unenlightened ignorant.
In correspondence with this,
The superior person makes every effort
To cultivate virtue with resolute deeds.

Yao Text

1. Initial Six
   Enlightening an ignorant.
   Favorable to set examples.
   Operating with shackles,
   Going forward: humiliation.

   Favorable to set examples,
   It is to set up a norm.

2. Second Nine
   Being magnanimous to an ignorant:
   Good fortune.
   Taking a maiden as wife:
   Good fortune.
   The son is able to sustain the family.

   The son is able to sustain the family,
   The firm and the yielding interact.

3. Third Six
   Do not engage in taking this woman.
   Catching sight of a handsome man,
   Losing herself.
   Nothing is favorable.

   Do not engage in taking this woman.
   Her behavior is not prudent.

4. Fourth Six
   Confining an ignorant:
   Humiliation.

   The humiliation of confining an ignorant
   Far from the solid.

5. Fifth Six
   An ignorant is being enlightened.
   Good fortune.

   Good fortune to the enlightened.
   She corresponds to humbleness.

6. Top Nine
   Disciplining an ignorant.
   Not favorable to treat like a foe.
   Favorable to prevent further mischief.

   Preventing further mischief.
   Upper and lower go well.

SIGNIFICANCE

The image of the gua is a spring flowing out of a mountain and becoming a murmuring stream. Afterward, the stream grows into a great river, nurturing myriad beings. However, as the river flows over the ground it becomes dirty. This gua takes this image to expound upon the importance of enlightening and educating the ignorant while in the infant stage.

The host of the gua is the yang element at the second place. It is central and firm, able to revere the teacher and therefore to teach others. The yin element at the fifth place corresponds to this yang element. Two analogies are employed to expound upon the gua. One is about education; the other is about marriage. The yang element at the second place is a firm line at the central place of the lower gua. In the I Ching, the lower gua stands in a position inferior to the upper gua. Here, the yang element at the second place plays a major role. It represents a teacher who is enlightening and educating the ignorant. Because it is a firm line in the lower gua, it symbolizes the quality of magnanimity. There are four yielding lines surrounding it, one below and three above. Symbolically, these yielding lines are the ignorant who are to be enlightened. The Chinese believed

that every ignorant person is different. According to the ancient Chinese tradition, they should be taught in accordance with their aptitudes. The unenlightened should be humble and devout and take the initial step to seek enlightenment. In other words, they should be ready and willing to accept education. On the other hand, one acting as a source of enlightenment should also be patient and forgiving.

The image of this gua is Mountain above Water. In the I Ching, Mountain symbolizes a family, and Water represents the middle son. The four yin lines around a yang line can be viewed as four women approaching a man and intending to marry him. The solid line at the second place is a yang element, a man. The yielding line at the fifth place is a yin element, a woman. They correspond to each other, because both of them are in a central place and they are yin and yang, a perfect match.

King Wen arranged this gua as a continuation of the preceding one. The preceding gua pertained to establishing feudal lords; it was a question of foreign affairs. This gua was meant to educate his own people; it had to do with internal affairs. King Wen realized the importance of education in abolishing the old system and establishing a new one. His policy was to start with those who were humble and devout and willing to accept education. In ancient China, divination was part of the social fabric bringing people together. Through divination the king promulgated decrees. In accepting an elder's instruction, one should be as devout as when accepting the instruction of a divination.

In the Yao Text, the Duke of Zhou gives specific social advice; education, for example, should be used to lead the ignorant to the right path. Punishment should not be employed. A norm of proper behavior should be set up. It is important to be maganimous to docile minority tribes and to educate them in the way to establish harmonious families and help their descendants sustain their families. It is better not to form alliances with half-hearted tribes, because they are not ready. And for isolated minority tribes, it is necessary to help them come into contact with other people.

(1) Initial Six. Childhood alternates to Decreasing (41) ☷

The yin element at the bottom place is at a yang place, symbolizing the initial stage of enlightening one who is ignorant. Enlightening cures incorrectness. It is important and beneficial to start at the very beginning. The correction should be serious but not harsh; the purpose is to lead the ignorant one's way to the right path. Correction should not employ punishment as shackles that restrict the ignorant one's normal development; it is meant to establish a norm. Punishment will lead to regret and sorrow. According to the Confucian schools, the best moral education is achieved through setting examples. Confucius was named as a Teacher of Exemplary Virtue through all Ages. He advocated "education without words," believing that the most powerful influence of teachers, leaders, and parents is their own words, deeds, and discretion.

(2) Second Nine. Childhood alternates to Falling Away (23)

The solid line at the second place is a yang element at a yin place—firm, strong, central. It is the only firm element in the lower gua and is responsible for enlightening and educating all the yin elements in the gua. However, there are several yin elements in this gua, and each has a different aptitude. One in this place should be magnanimous. The central place dictates that the potential to be magnanimous is there. There is good fortune. On the other hand, the solid line at the second place corresponds to the yielding line at the fifth place. They are complementary yin and yang, suitable to be husband and wife. If the husband is kind and gentle to his wife, there is good fortune. Applying the gua to a family, the yang element in the second place represents a son; the yin element at the fifth place is the mother. The mother in the fifth place is weak (a yin element); she is not able to carry the burden of the family. However, the son is strong and firm and magnanimous. He is able to establish a home where the family flourishes. The message of this line is that dealing with different persons or situations requires different ways of responding.

(3) Third Six. Childhood alternates to Remedying (18)

The yin element at the third place is at a yang place, neither central nor correct. It matches the yang element at the top, indicating a possible marriage. This yin element is also attracted to the yang element at the second place—they are much closer together. As soon as one at this place sees the handsome man at the top, she loses herself. The text indicates that she should be prudent in making a choice. It is not advisable to change one's mind the moment one sees something new. Here the Yao Text employs marriage to explain the importance of establishing a correct attitude in dealing with different persons or situations. The upper gua, Mountain, also symbolizes gold and husband, and represents the youngest son.

The Chinese text says, literally, "Do not engage in taking this woman, catching sight of a golden man. Loses herself." Most English versions

translate "golden man" as "wealthy man." But according to the Book of Songs, one of the Confucian five classics, "golden man" means "handsome man." The Book of Songs was China's earliest collection of folk songs, most belonging to the Zhou dynasty.

(4) Fourth Six. Childhood alternates to Not Yet Fulfilled (64)

The Yao Text says, "Confining an ignorant: humiliation." The yang element at the second place is surrounded by two yin elements, one above and the other below. This fourth line is a yin element at a yin place, correct but not central. It responds with the yin element on the bottom, but they do not correspond to each other. They are both yin, so there is no help. The yang element at the second place asks this line to help, but it is not close enough. There is another yang element at the top, unfortunately, he is retired. He has no intention of helping. One at this place is totally isolated, surrounded by yin elements. He has neither teacher nor friends. He is overwhelmed with ignorance and suffers humiliation. Confucius's Commentary on the Yao Text says, "The humiliation of confining an ignorant far from the solid." The "solid" refers to the solid line at the second place. Solid in Chinese can also mean reality. In this sense, isolation is caused either by cutting oneself off from people or by losing touch with reality.

(5) Fifth Six. Childhood alternates to Dispersing (59)

The yin element at the fifth place is central and at the supreme place. It is close to the yang element at the top and corresponds to the yang element at the second place. In this situation, one can get help from above and below. It is a favorable condition for one who is about to undergo change. After this line moves and alternates to a solid line, then the approached gua will be Wind over Water, Dispersing (59). Then Wind and Rain will work together harmoniously, resulting in propitious weather and good fortune. Confucius's Commentary on the Yao Text says, "Good fortune to the enlightened. She corresponds to humbleness." In the I Ching, Sun is the Chinese character for Wind. After this line moves, the upper gua, Mountain, alternates to Wind. In the I Ching, the character Sun also represents humbleness.

(6) Top Nine. Childhood alternates to Multitude (7)

The yang element at the top is at the uppermost place. In this place one reaches the extreme and becomes self-willed and opinionated. The one responsible for enlightening and teaching the ignorants is too firm and

fiery tempered. The upper gua is Mountain. In the I Ching, the character for Mountain also represents hands; thus the Duke of Zhou refers to
punishing an unenlightened child. The ancient way of correcting a child
rarely employed punishment. Only when there was no alternative was
punishment employed. This gua gives warning that one should not treat
the ignorant as a foe. The purpose of punishment is to prevent further
mischief. This gua expounds upon a way of correcting mischief. The
attitude should be firm, but the means should be gentle. Even punishment should contain gentleness within and express firmness without. The
commentary says, "Preventing further mischief. Upper and lower go well."
The upper is the teacher, the lower is the student. The student should be
humble and open-minded and the teacher should be patient and forgiving.
Then, upper and lower, teacher and student, will do well.

Additional Reference Information for This Gua

Image:	Mountain above, Water below
Recite as:	Stream flows out of a Mountain, Childhood
Element:	Earth
Structure:	Two yang with four yin
Month:	The first month of the lunar year, or February
Host of the Gua:	Second Nine
Opposite Gua:	Abolishing the Old (49)
Inverse Gua:	Beginning (3)
Mutual Gua:	Turning Back (24)

5
Xü • Needing

Kan • Cloud
Qian • Heaven

NAME AND STRUCTURE

Wilhelm translates Xü as Waiting. Blofeld uses the term Calculated Inaction. I use Needing.

Sequence of the Gua: *When things are in their childhood, they should not be neglected without nourishing. Thus, after Childhood, Needing follows. Xü is the Tao of eating and drinking.*

The Tao indicates that we need food to nourish the body and spirit. The primary concern of the earliest agricultural societies was growing crops. Peasants did not worry about the sunshine, the air, and the soil; these were always abundant. Their major concern was water. The water they relied on depended largely upon rainfall. Without rain, they would have nothing to eat and drink.

The ancient ideograph of Xü shows this need for rain. There are two ways to interpret the picture. The first interpretation is that it is simply a picture of rain. The ideograph shows raindrops descending from clouds. The horizontal line at the top symbolizes Heaven. Two vertical lines on the left and the right indicate the boundary of the clouds. There are four raindrops within the clouds. The vertical line in the middle and four curved lines in the lower part of the ideograph represent the downward motion of the raindrops. This image reminded ancient people that the primary need of the Tao of eating and drinking is rain.

The second interpretation is that this is a picture of a man praying and waiting for rain. The upper part of the ideograph represents rain within the clouds not yet falling. The lower part symbolizes a man. Four curved vertical lines represent the mustache and beard of an elderly man, who might be the priest of the tribe, praying for rain.

When one needs something and cannot acquire it immediately, waiting is necessary. In this way, the meaning of needing extends to waiting. It is really the need for waiting. But "waiting" is not the primary meaning of Xü. The symbol of this gua shows that clouds are gathering in the sky, but the rain has not yet come down. This situation demands patience. When the symbol is placed on a horizontal plane, then its meaning becomes clear. On the vertical plane, the image is Rain above Heaven; however, on the horizontal plane the symbol is Heaven confronting Water. The attribute of Heaven is strength, and that of Water is danger. When strength is obstructed, then patience is demanded. If one has faith and remains steadfast, one's future will be bright.

Decision

Needing.
Being sincere and faithful,
Brilliantly prosperous and smooth.
Being steadfast and upright: good fortune.
Favorable to cross great rivers.

Commentary on the Decision

Needing:
Requiring faith and confidence to wait;
Danger lies ahead.

Being firm and strong,
One does not allow oneself to be involved in danger.
The conduct is right;
One will not fall into straits.

Needing, being sincere and faithful.
There will be brilliant success.
Be steadfast and upright.
Good fortune.

Being in the place assigned by Heaven;
It is central and correct.
Favorable to cross great rivers.
Going forward, your work will be accomplished.

Commentary on the Symbol

Clouds ascending in the sky.
An image of Needing.
In correspondence with this,
The superior person eats and drinks, feasting with joy.

Yao Text

1. Initial Nine
   One in need waits on the outskirts.
   Favorable to engage in perseverance.
   No fault.

   One in need waits in the outskirts.
   Do not take risks and enhance trouble.
   Maintaining perseverance is beneficial.
   No fault.
   Doing nothing abnormal, as usual.

2. Second Nine
   One in need waits on the sand.
   A little gossip
   Ends in good fortune.

   One in need waits on the sand;
   A stream extends between.
   Although there is a little gossip,
   In the end it turns to good fortune.

3. Third Nine
   One in need waits in the mud.
   Result: great trouble to come.

   One in need waits in the mud.
   Misfortune is outside.

It is you yourself causing the invader to come.
Be cautious; you will not be beaten.

4. Fourth Six
   One in need waits in the ditch.
   Get out of the pit.

   One in need waits in the ditch.
   Following the principle of yielding,
   Accommodate the situation.

5. Fifth Nine
   One in need waits with wine and food.
   Being steadfast and upright: good fortune.

   One in need waits with wine and food.
   The position is central and correct.

6. Top Six
   Falling into a pit.
   There are three unexpected guests coming.
   Showing respect
   Ends in good fortune.

   Unexpected guests are coming;
   Showing respect brings good fortune.
   Although the position is not proper,
   No great loss.

SIGNIFICANCE

Needing, coming after Beginning and Childhood, represents an initial stage of achievement. In an initial and uncertain stage, Needing calls for patience. Before taking action, nourish the body and accumulate strength. In this situation, waiting is absolutely demanded, yet it does not mean giving up. Wait for the proper time to accomplish the things one has planned. During the period of waiting, it is necessary to cultivate self-confidence, steadfastness, and uprightness and to be cautious in every step; then the outcome will bring good fortune.

The symbol of this gua is Water ☵ ahead of Heaven ☰. Heaven symbolizes strength; Water symbolizes danger. The picture is of strength confronting danger. In ancient times crossing a river was difficult and dangerous work. For this reason, Water symbolizes danger. However, Heaven is the purest yang energy, full of strength and power. As long as one's confidence remains strong, success awaits. The message of this gua is that faithfulness and steadfastness bring good fortune. Needing, together with Beginning and Childhood, are constituted of Water; that is, one of their primary gua is Water. Because Water symbolizes danger or difficulties, these gua all call for patience, confidence, faithfulness, and steadfastness, but they also have great potential for success. They are all auspicious gua.

There are four solid lines in this gua. The solid line at the fifth place is the host. Confucius's Commentary on the Decision says, "Being in the place assigned by Heaven; it is central and correct." This commentary refers to the fifth line. The solid line at the fifth place is firm and strong in the center of the upper gua. It symbolizes that a right person is in a correct position, but he is in the midst of Water, an unfavorable circumstance. He is waiting for the support of the three solid lines in the lower gua. The three solid lines in the lower gua are strong and energetic, yet they confront the upper gua, Water, a difficult situation. They are waiting for the guidance and support of the host who is central in the upper gua.

This gua suggests that under tyrannical administration people need a change, but the situation does not allow action. King Wen said that needing requires faith and confidence to achieve brilliant success. The Duke of Zhou gave examples of this need traced back to as early as when his grandfather was looking for a suitable place to establish the capital. In the Yao Text, the Duke of Zhou listed different possible places. In some places, there were troubles such as gossips. In other places they were confronted by invasions of the Rong and Di tribes. Eventually King Wen chose Feng, a name meaning "safe place," where they were able to wait with wine and food in a calm and unhurried manner until the time was right to overthrow the Shang. King Wen was made an official at the court. He opposed the Tyrant of Shang's brutal system of punishment and was imprisoned. During his imprisonment, three former officials of the Shang dynasty came to Zhou for shelter and were greatly respected. They offered suggestions to rescue King Wen and became his advisers.

(1) Initial Nine. Needing alternates to Replenishing (48)

The bottom line is the farthest line from the upper gua; it represents the outskirts, a place at a distance. There is danger, but not too near. This line is a yang element at a yang place. In this situation one should not take any risks to cause any further difficulty. The key is to persevere, to do normal things as usual. Doing otherwise might result in trouble. This line sends a warning that when a situation demands waiting, one must keep one's distance from the danger.

(2) Second Nine. Needing alternates to Already Fulfilled (63)

The second line moves closer to the upper gua, Danger. There is trouble, but only a little gossip. The second line is a yang element in a central place. One in this place is able to wait at ease. Although there is a little gossip, one must deal with it calmly and with equanimity. It is like a narrow strip of water extending on the sand that will shortly disappear. Patience is necessary; the end will be good.

(3) Third Nine. Needing alternates to Restricting (60)

The third line moves closer to the upper gua, beyond the central line. The situation is worsening. When the third line changes from yang to yin, the lower gua changes from Heaven to Lake. One becomes stuck in the mud and cannot walk easily. The discussion of the gua says that water symbolizes a robber or invader. Three yang elements in the lower gua are headstrong; they move closer and closer to the dangerous situation. Confucius's Commentary on the Yao Text says, "Misfortune is outside. It is you yourself causing the invader to come. Be cautious; you will not be beaten." This line warns that when one moves closer to a dangerous situation, extra caution should be exercised.

(4) Fourth Six. Needing alternates to Eliminating (43)

The fourth line is positioned in the upper gua. The situation is difficult, even dangerous. It is possible to get hurt. The Decision of the gua says that water is related to blood, a symbol of being hurt. Most English translations follow the Chinese text literally and translate the Chinese character xue as blood. However, there is another opinion that a component of the character representing water was left out on the left side of the Chinese character xue. With this radical, the character is pronounced xü, a ditch eight feet wide and deep. Here my translation conforms to the second meaning of "ditch," matching the situation suggested by the other three lines, that one approaches the sand from the outskirts, the mud from the sand, and the ditch from the mud. The situation keeps getting worse. The fourth line is a yin element at a yin place, a correct position. One in this place may not act lightly. The commentary advises, "Following the principle of yielding, accommodate the situation." In so doing, one will climb out of the ditch.

(5) Fifth Nine. Needing alternates to Advance (11)

The fifth line is the host of the gua. It is a yang element at a yang place, correct and also central and supreme. One in this situation is most safe. For this reason, he is able to wait with wine and food. Waiting with wine and food symbolizes self-confidence, waiting in a calm and unhurried manner. This is the best attitude with which to deal with unfavorable situations. This line tells us that even in the safest situation, one should still hold on to the principle of the Golden Mean, that is, walking the central path.

(6) Top Six. Needing alternates to Little Accumulation (9)

The uppermost line is a yin element at a yin place. Doubling the yin symbolizes weakness. This place is the height of difficulty. There is no way to wait. Eventually one falls into the pit. However, the yielding line on the top corresponds to the solid line at the third place. Three yang elements in the lower gua represent three unexpected guests. They have waited for a long time without a chance to advance. Now, at the last minute, they have the chance to rush forward with indomitable spirit. When they reach the end, the one at the uppermost place honors them. At last, all of them receive good fortune. This gua suggests that with a positive attitude there is no problem that cannot be solved, and the end will always be good.

Additional Reference Information for This Gua

Image:	Water above, Heaven below
Recite as:	Clouds ascend to Heaven, Needing
Element:	Water
Structure:	Four yang with two yin
Month:	The second month of the lunar year, or March
Host of the Gua:	Fifth Nine
Opposite Gua:	Proceeding Forward (35)
Inverse Gua:	Contention (6)
Mutual Gua:	Diversity (38)

6
Song · Contention

☰ Qian • Heaven
☵ Kan • Water

NAME AND STRUCTURE

In Chinese, Song means to dispute, to demand justice, or to bring a case to the court because there is contention. Both Wilhelm and Blofeld translate Song as Conflict. In this book it is termed Contention. This gua is the inverse of the preceding gua, Needing.

Sequence of the Gua: *Needing, scrambling for food, contention is certain to arise. Thus, after Needing, Contention follows.*

The ideograph of Song is a unification of two characters, speech and public. The left side of the ideograph is a picture of a person's face with an open mouth at the bottom, representing the act of speaking bluntly. The right side consists of two parts. The upper part is made up of two strokes—one to the left and the other to the right—presenting a picture of going in opposite directions and being equally divided. The lower part of the ideograph is the ancient character for self. When the upper part and the lower part are put together, the symbol represents the act of opposing selfishness and being fair. Joining the parts of the ideograph creates a vivid picture of someone bringing a case to a public place and speaking out bluntly, asking for justice.

The upper gua is Heaven, air ascending upward; the lower gua is Water, liquid flowing downward. The image is of conflict and contention. Water symbolizes dangerous and mean intention, and Heaven symbolizes a strong and firm character.

81

A person with these two characteristics inevitably will become involved in conflict and contention with other people. For these reasons, Contention is adopted as the name of the gua. The intention of the ancients was not to encourage contention, but rather to settle disputes with compromise. According to their experience, no perfectly satisfying result could be obtained at the end of any contention. Thus the Decision says, "Midpoint: good fortune. End: misfortune." The middle ground is the key for settling contention.

Decision

> Contention.
> Be sincere and truthful,
> Truth is blocked.
> Be cautious.
> Midpoint: good fortune.
> End: misfortune.
> Favorable to see a great person,
> Unfavorable to cross great rivers.

Commentary on the Decision

> *Contention.*
> *Strength is above, danger below.*
> *Danger with strength produces contention.*
>
> *Facing contention*
> *Be faithful and confident.*
>
> *Truth is blocked. Be cautious.*
> *Midpoint: good fortune.*
> *The firm comes and attains the central place.*
>
> *End: misfortune.*
> *It is better not to let contention happen.*
>
> *Favorable to see a great person;*
> *The central and correct is honored.*
> *Unfavorable to cross great rivers;*
> *This would lead one to the abyss.*

Commentary on the Symbol

Heaven and Water move in opposite directions.
There is contention.
In correspondence with this,
The superior person begins to make plans
Before he takes action.

Yao Text

1. Initial Six
   Do not persist in the case.
   A little dispute
   Ends in good fortune.

   Do not persist in the case.
   Contention should not be long.
   A little dispute;
   True or false will be distinguished.

2. Second Nine
   Unable to contend.
   Return and escape.
   His county of three hundred households:
   No trouble.

   Unable to contend.
   Retreat and hide.
   In an inferior position, contending against a superior one
   Causes your own trouble.

3. Third Six
   Living off ancestors' inheritance.
   Being steadfast: adversity;
   Ends in good fortune.
   Probably serving a king,
   Claim no credit.

   Living off ancestors' inheritance.
   Following the one at the top brings good fortune.

4. Fourth Nine
Unable to contend.
Turn back; submit to the truth.
Changing one's opinion:
Peace.
Being steadfast and upright: good fortune.

Turn back; submit to the truth.
Brings peace.
Be content with the truth;
One will not lose.

5. Fifth Nine
Dealing with contention.
Supreme good fortune.

Dealing with contention; supreme good fortune.
One is in the central and correct position.

6. Top Nine
Probably a leather belt is given with honor.
By the end of the morning—
Thrice taken away.

To obtain distinction through contention
Is not worthy of respect.

SIGNIFICANCE

The theme of the gua expounds the truth of avoiding contention. In human life conflict between differing opinions or interests arises everywhere. According to the ancient Chinese, contention, whether one wins or loses, is not enjoyable. It is better to solve the problem rather than let it develop to the point of contention. If one knows how to stop a fight before it goes too far, one would be able to remain in a trouble-free position in any situation. Generally, dispute arises from one's mean intention and overly self-willed conduct—lacking flexibility in considering other people's situations. The ancient sages advocate seeking common ground, not voicing differences. This is the way to avoid contention.

The host of the gua is the solid line at the fifth place, representing an arbitrator appointed by two parties to settle a dispute. The fifth line is

solid, firm, and strong and also in the central place of the upper gua. It indicates that an honest person is in a position to be honored and is able to maintain a neutral stand in solving the problem. The other five lines, either yielding or solid, represent persons involved in the disagreement. Confucius's Commentary on the Decision here says, "Favorable to see a great person; the central and correct is honored."

This gua tells us that, as the strength and population of the state of Zhou grew respectively stronger and larger, contentions arose among the people. King Wen gave instructions that in facing contention one should remain sincere and faithful. When truth is blocked, one should be cautious. Solving the dispute at the midpoint would bring good fortune. Holding on to the contention through to the end would invite bad fortune. In the Yao Text, the Duke of Zhou wrote about the struggle between King Wen and the Tyrant of Shang. King Wen served at the court of Shang but was greatly dissatisfied with the tyrannical administration of the Shang dynasty. He pleaded with the tyrant to stop the cruel punishment of the people, but his pleas went unheeded. King Wen pleaded again. This time he upset the tyrant and stirred up trouble. He retreated and hid without trouble in his little state of only three hundred households. Later on, King Wen was asked to serve at the court again, but he could still do nothing to stop the tyrant's brutality. Making peace with the reality of the situation, he kept quiet while accumulating his strength and preparing to overthrow the tyrant. In this way he brought peace and gained supreme good fortune. At last, a leather belt was given to him with honor, but the Tyrant of Shang was still suspicious of King Wen, changed his mind, and took the honor away three times.

(1) Initial Six. Contention alternates to Fulfillment (10) ☷

The first line is a yin element at a yang place—incorrect and on the bottom. The one in this position is weak. Although the line corresponds to the yang element at the fourth place, there is another yang element at the second place lying between and, fortunately, blocking them. They are not able to support each other to solve the problem. The one at the fourth place is firm and strong, willing to support from beginning to end. The advice is to lay low. Then, with a little assertion at the right time, the end will be good.

(2) Second Nine. Contention alternates to Hindrance (12) ☷

The second line is solid and firm. Being in the midst of the lower gua, Water (which symbolizes danger), it hints that the one in this place is

self-willed and fond of contention. Although the line is firm and central, it is in the lower gua, an inferior condition. While this yang element represents the principal force of the conflict, it is surrounded by yin elements above and below. This is a troublesome situation (in the midst of Water) and not conducive to winning the dispute. Thus, Confucius says, "Retreat and hide." The superior one is the yang element at the fifth place, who is firm and strong, central and correct. A self-willed person cannot win the fight against a central and correct person in a superior position.

(3) Third Six. Contention alternates to Encountering (44)

The third line is a yin element at a yang place, neither central nor correct. It lies between two solid lines suggesting there is no way to win a dispute in this situation. It is better to bear the situation with patience and rely for one's living on the place gained and handed down by one's ancestors owing to their virtue and merit. In ancient times, a high official obtained a manor from the court. The manor was a hereditary property. In the I Ching, the third line sometimes symbolizes one of the three dukes of ancient times who acted as a cabinet of advisers to the king. The Yao Text thus says, "Living off ancestors' inheritance." There is also a chance to serve the king.

(4) Fourth Nine. Contention alternates to Dispersing (59)

The fourth line is a yang element at a yin place, the bottom of the upper gua. Its place is neither central nor correct. At this place, it is not favorable to be involved in contention. Because this yang element is at a yin place, it is able to neutralize its usually firm and strong attributes. There is the potential to turn back and change one's original opinion. So doing will bring peace.

(5) Fifth Nine. Contention alternates to Not Yet Fulfilled (64)

The fifth line is in the superior place. It is a yang element at a yang place, central and correct. In the I Ching, a central place represents a position of impartiality and justice. One at this place bears the qualities of fairness, justice, and reasonableness, qualities that are crucially important in dealing with contention. Consequently, these qualities bring supreme good fortune.

(6) Top Nine. Contention alternates to Exhausting (47)

The uppermost line of the upper gua, Qian, represents Heaven. The ancient Chinese believed Heaven to be round; thus, Qian is at times represented by a circle. The Yao Text says, "Probably a leather belt [circle] is given with honor. By the end of the morning—thrice taken away." "By the end of the morning" derives from the lower mutual gua, Fire, which symbolizes the time of day from morning till noon. This line responds to the third line, "Probably serving a king, claim no credit."

A possible explanation of "thrice" derives from the upper mutual gua, Li. According to Fu Xi's arrangement of the eight primary gua, Li is in the third position, after Qian and Dui, thus "thrice" is used. On the other hand, the yang element at this place has already approached the extreme. If one at this place thinks he is firm and strong and forgets the present situation, he will win the contention with skill, but it cannot last long. The main theme of the gua is to explore the disadvantage of contention. Most of the lines show that a dispute should be carried out only if it is worthwhile. If one is fond of contention, evil awaits.

Additional Reference Information for This Gua

Image:	Heaven above, Water below
Recite as:	Heaven and Water oppose, Contention
Element:	Metal
Structure:	Four yang with two yin
Month:	The third month of the lunar year, or April
Host of the Gua:	Fifth Nine
Opposite Gua:	Brilliance Injured (36)
Inverse Gua:	Needing (5)
Mutual Gua:	Household (37)

7

Shi · Multitude

☷ Kun • Earth
☵ Kan • Water

NAME AND STRUCTURE

Originally Shi meant multitude. At present, it means teacher as well as troops or army. Both Wilhelm and Blofeld translate Shi as the Army. In this book, I follow the character's original meaning of Multitude.

Sequence of the Gua: *Where there is contention, a multitude is sure to arise. Thus, after Contention, Multitude follows.*

The ideograph of this gua consists of two parts. On the left is dui, signifying a multitude or pile. The right part is za, which denotes a circle or can mean "to go around." When the two parts join together, a new character is formed, presenting the picture of a multitude of people gathered together and circling a pivot. When the pivot is emphasized, shi indicates a teacher, a master or a person who deserves respect from society. When the multitude is emphasized, it means a multitude of people, not a military force. In ancient dictionaries shi denotes a group of 2,500 people.

In ancient China there was no special group of people maintained as an army, nor a specific class called soldiers. At that time, peasants and soldiers were combined into one group. In ordinary times, peasants worked the fields, and in the slack farming season they were given military training. Only during wartime were they called to defend their country. The ancients thought that keeping an army would cause trouble. An army carried the potential of danger; like running water, sometimes it could rage out of control. Peasants were docile, as stable as the ground. Thus, water under earth is the symbol of this gua, indicating that military strength should not be stored in the army but in the multitude of people, as water is stored in the earth. To the ancients, war was evil. It should not be undertaken lightly, but only when absolutely necessary. And the purpose of military affairs should be righteous. Only a person of noble character and high prestige could take charge of military affairs.

Decision

> Multitude.
> Be steadfast and upright.
> For a person of noble spirit,
> Good fortune.
> No fault.

Commentary on the Decision

> *Shi is a multitude.*
> *Persistence is for righteousness.*
>
> *One who is able to lead the multitude*
> *To persist for righteousness*
> *Is able to bring peace to the world.*
>
> *Firm and central,*
> *He obtains a response.*
> *Taking the risk of dangerous action,*
> *He confronts no hindrance.*
> *Relying on this,*
> *He maintains public order,*
> *And people follow him.*
> *Good fortune.*
> *What mistake should there be?*

Commentary on the Symbol

> *Water contained under Earth.*
> *An image of Multitude.*
> *In correspondence with this,*

The superior person embraces people
And cares for the multitude.

Yao Text

1. Initial Six
   Sending out a multitude,
   It should be kept under control.
   Otherwise, no good:
   Misfortune.

   Sending out a multitude,
   It should be kept under control.
   Losing control brings disaster.

2. Second Nine
   In the midst of the multitude,
   Good fortune.
   No fault.
   The king bestows thrice.

   In the midst of the multitude, good fortune,
   Grace from Heaven.
   The king bestows thrice,
   Thinking of all countries.

3. Third Six
   The multitude perhaps takes charge:
   Misfortune.

   The multitude perhaps takes charge,
   They crave greatness and success.
   No merit.

4. Fourth Six
   The multitude retreats.
   No fault.

   The multitude retreats.
   It does not deviate from the normal course.

5. Fifth Six
   In the field there are birds

Favorable for capture.
No fault.
The elder should command the multitude.
The followers taking charge,
Being steadfast: misfortune.

The elder should command the multitude;
He is walking in the central path.
The followers taking charge,
The appointment is not handled properly.

6. Top Six
   The great prince issues commands:
   Establish states and hereditary families;
   Inferior persons should not be employed.

   The great prince issues commands;
   It is to bestow merit properly.
   Inferior persons should not be employed.
   They are certain to cause trouble to the country.

SIGNIFICANCE

Most English translations call this gua the Army. However, in ancient China, soldiers were not differentiated from peasants; there was no specific class termed an army. For this reason, I adopt the original meaning, Multitude. The gua does not encourage military actions. To the contrary, it indicates that if contention is not resolved properly, it might lead to the use of force. The ancients considered that using force was evil and taught that involvement in military affairs should be approached with caution and that the purpose of war should be righteous. In their opinion only two kinds of war could be considered righteous: overthrowing a tyrant or protecting the country from invasion.

The host of the gua is the solid line at the second place; it is the only solid line in this gua and occupies the central position of the lower gua. Thus, it becomes the host of the multitude. The Duke of Zhou says, "In the midst of the multitude, good fortune. No fault." Normally the host of the gua lies at the fifth place, central within the upper gua. It is a superior position for a king. The king is usually the person who takes charge of a general, but not of the multitude. Thus, he cannot be the host of this gua, Multitude. On the other hand, the solid line at the second place is surrounded by five yielding lines symbolizing the multitude. They are harmoniously acting with one accord. The second line is firm and solid in the lower gua; he is the right person to take charge of the multitude.

This gua is a continuation of the preceding one, the fourth line of which says, "Unable to contend. Turn back; submit to the truth. Changing one's opinion: Peace. Being steadfast and upright: Good fortune." King Wen saw that he could not win a dispute with the tyrant. He changed his tactics, realizing that the only way to rescue the people from the abyss of suffering was to overthrow the tyrant. He was preparing for war, but he held fast that military action should move forward in a righteous course. There was no fault if a person of noble spirit led the multitude. The Duke of Zhou described King Wen's military action, carried out for the tyrant against minorities such as the Mi clan and the Shu clan. King Wen's policy was to meet them with goodwill, educating rather than punishing them. Before launching the multitude on a path of war, he kept them under strict control and expected that no disaster would result. Because King Wen insisted that only a person of noble spirit should take charge of military affairs, the tyrant acknowledged his leadership. King Wen created a strategic deployment, then explained to the Mi and Shu that his military action was only defensive, because they had invaded Shang's territory like birds trespassing on a field. He told them only the elders should lead the multitude. If the followers took control, disaster would follow. He instructed the leaders of the Mi and Shu clans that inferior persons should never be employed in positions of authority.

(1) Initial Six. Multitude alternates to Approaching (19) ☷☳

The bottom line denotes the beginning of a military engagement. The multitude is setting out; it should be kept under control. The text offers a warning that at the very beginning of any situation caution and discipline should not be neglected.

(2) Second Nine. Multitude alternates to Responding (2) ☷☷

The second line is a yang element in the central place of the lower gua; it represents the host of the multitude. A yang element at a yin place is firm and strong. As part of the lower gua, he is not reckless, but kind. The yang element at the second place corresponds to the yin element at the fifth place. The relationship symbolizes that the commander gains confidence from the commander in chief. Because the host of the multitude is responsive to his superior, the king bestows thrice. According to the rituals of the Zhou dynasty, the first bestowing was a post; the second, a garment; and the third, a title. The color of the garment matched the post and the title.

(3) Third Six. Multitude alternates to Growing Upward (46)

The third line is a yin element at a yang place. The place is not correct, symbolizing that one at this place is self-willed and opinionated. Failure certainly lies in wait. According to the structure, the lower gua is Water, representing corpses. The lower mutual gua is Thunder, representing a wagon. Thus, the Yao Text might be interpreted as "The multitude returns with wagonloads of corpses." However, in ancient times the character for wagon—yu—also meant multitude. Likewise, the character for corpse—shi—also meant to take charge of. By following the ancient meaning, the text is translated as "The multitude perhaps takes charge: misfortune." Misfortune is the consequence of improper people taking charge of serious matters.

(4) Fourth Six. Multitude alternates to Relief (40)

The yielding line at the fourth place is not central. To be yielding and not central indicates a situation where there is no chance of winning a conflict. The yin element at a yin place also suggests that one at this place knows her own limitation. She leads the multitude in retreat. When one knows that a conflict cannot be won, retreat is the wisest strategy. It conserves strength for a final victory. Confucius's commentary says, "The multitude retreats. It does not deviate from the normal course."

(5) Fifth Six. Multitude alternates to Darkness (29)

The Yao Text consists of two parts. The first part indicates that the yin element at the fifth place represents a true leader. The yin attribute and central position gives the element a noble quality. In dealing with a conflict she is not aggressive. She takes only defensive action. The Duke of Zhou uses the analogy of birds trespassing on a field to indicate that someone has invaded her territory. Her defensive action has a just ground. There is no fault. The second part of the Yao Text says that the one who is experienced and senior should lead the multitude. If the multitude takes control, the consequence would be misfortune.

(6) Top Six. Multitude alternates to Childhood (4) ☷

The top line denotes the end of a conflict by using forces; victory is obtained. The king dispenses rewards and honors according to merit. The text warns that inferior persons should never be employed in any position in the government. Their meanness is sure to cause trouble to the country. Of course, since there is no actual military conflict in our daily lives, this gua is a metaphor. We should search for the ancient wisdom between the lines and beyond the words.

Additional Reference Information for This Gua

Image:	Earth above, Water below		
Recite as:	Water contained under Earth, Multitude		
Element:	Earth		
Structure:	One yang with five yin		
Month:	The fourth month of the lunar year, or May		
Host of the Gua:	Second Nine		
Opposite Gua:	Seeking Harmony	(13)	☲
Inverse Gua:	Union	(8)	☵
Mutual Gua:	Turning Back	(24)	☷

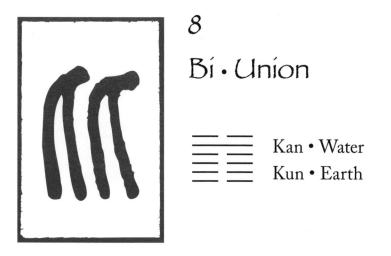

8

Bi • Union

☵ Kan • Water
☷ Kun • Earth

NAME AND STRUCTURE

Bi is the inverse of the preceding gua, Shi, Multitude. Bi suggests intimacy and closeness. People living together should love and care about each other; then they will become intimate and close. Wilhelm translates this gua as Holding Together (Union); Blofeld as Unity, Coordination. In this book, Bi is called Union.

Sequence of the Gua: *In a multitude, there must be a bond of union. Thus, after Multitude, Union follows.*

In ancient times, Bi was the fundamental unit of the Chinese household registry system. Every five households formed one unit, called Bi. In every Bi a head was appointed, to take care of the neighborhood. Thus, Bi also means neighborhood and symbolizes a close bond of the people in a community. The ancient ideograph of Bi is simple; it shows two persons standing close together. The structure of the gua is Water above, Earth below. When earth contains water, it becomes soft. When water is on the earth, it flows. The ancient king gained insight from the close relationship between water and earth; he established numerous states and maintained a close relationship with his subordinate lords.

Decision

Seeking union.
Good fortune.

Examine the divination:
Sublimely persevering, steadfast and upright.
No fault.
Restless factions just coming.
Lagging behind: misfortune.

Commentary on the Decision

Seeking union. Good fortune.
It is for mutual help.
The lower follows the upper.
Examine the divination:
Sublimely persevering, steadfast and upright.
No fault.
Due to its firmness and central position.
Restless factions just coming.
The upper and the lower correspond.
Lagging behind: misfortune.
There is no way out.

Commentary on the Symbol

On the Earth, there is Water
Flowing together, an image of Union.
In correspondence with this,
The ancient king established myriad states
And kept a close relationship with the lords.

Yao Text

1. Initial Six
   With sincerity and truthfulness, seeking union.
   No fault.
   Be sincere and truthful,
   As an earthen vessel that is full.
   End coming, there is something.
   Good fortune.

   Initial Six of Seeking Union
   Encounters unexpected good fortune.

2. Second Six
   Seeking union from within.
   Being steadfast and upright: good fortune.

   Seeking union from within,
   One would not fail.

3. Third Six
   Seeking union with wrong people.

   Seeking union with wrong people.
   How can it not be hurtful?

4. Fourth Six
   From without, seeking union.
   Being steadfast and upright: good fortune.

   From without, seeking union.
   Follow the one above.

5. Fifth Nine
   An illustration of seeking union:
   The king drives game on three sides,
   Loses those running out the front.
   Citizens need no admonition.
   Good fortune.

   Good fortune of an illustration of seeking union,
   Due to its correct central position.
   Discard those who are adverse;
   Accept those who are submissive.
   Lose those running out the front.
   Citizens need no admonition,
   The one above makes them central and harmonious.

6. Top Six
   Seeking union.
   Those not having taken the first step:
   Misfortune.

   Seeking union with those not having taken the first step.
   Nothing can be completed.

SIGNIFICANCE

This gua expounds the importance of loving and caring in a union. People living close together must love and care about each other. In our daily lives, nothing is more harmful than successive conflict, and nothing is more auspicious than the harmonious relationships between people. In this gua, Union, most lines are auspicious. The structure of the gua is Water above Earth. Here Water symbolizes a restless mind; thus, King Wen's Decision says, "Restless factions just coming." Confucius's Commentary on the Decision says, "The upper and the lower correspond." The "upper" refers to the upper gua and the "lower" to the lower gua. In the I Ching, the uppermost line symbolizes the end of a cycle. In this gua, the upper-most line is yin, and the fifth line is yang. A yin line mounting a yang line symbolizes an adverse attitude. Thus King Wen's Decision says, "Lagging behind: misfortune."

The solid line at the fifth place is the only solid line in this gua. It is the host of the gua. Its quality is firm and strong, and its place is central and correct. It symbolizes a right person in a right place who is sure to have great influence upon his surroundings. There are five yielding lines. All yielding lines submit to the solid line at the fifth place, except the yielding line at the top. This line represents one who goes beyond the proper limit.

King Wen's Decision says, "Seeking union. Good fortune. Examine the divination: sublimely persevering, steadfast and upright. No fault." To examine the oracle, in Chinese, is yuan shi. Yuan originally meant the source of a river. Later on, the character also came to mean "to examine" and "a beginning." Shi means to divine with yarrow stalks. Some translations skip this line. Others say "inquire further," "further consultation," or "inquire again." In ancient times, only in rare cases did yuan mean "again." Considering the Decision as a whole, there is no need to inquire of the oracle once again. It is more appropriate to translate yuan shi as "examine the divination." "Sublimely persevering, steadfast and upright" indicate the quality of the host of the gua, the solid line at the fifth position.

This gua tells us that King Wen was successful in an expedition. He brought goodwill to the minority clans, and they became allies. King Wen claims that it was auspicious to seek union. Only those whose minds were restless and who had just arrived or lagged behind might bring misfortune. The Duke of Zhou told how King Wen sought union with sincerity. He was as full of sincerity as an earthen well bucket filled with water. He began by seeking union within his own clan and then extended it to other clans. He sought union with wrong persons, but he followed in the steps of King Tang, a brilliant king of the Shang dynasty, driving game on three sides. Those who were willing to come, he welcomed. Those who did not want to join, he let go. Later on, those minority clans joined King Wen's revolution against the Tyrant of Shang.

(1) Initial Six. Union alternates to Beginning (3)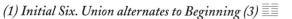

This line indicates that seeking union in a community should start with sincerity. Be close to people. Pour your sincerity into the community as when filling an empty vessel with wine or a well bucket with water. People will join the union. The lower gua is Earth ☷, here taken to be an earthen container.

(2) Second Six. Union alternates to Darkness (29) ☷

The second line is a yin element at a yin place, in the middle of the lower gua. Its place is central and correct. In the I Ching, the lower gua is also known as the inner gua; it represents one's inner world. In other words, sincerity should come from one's heart. Thus the Yao Text says, "Seeking union from within. Being steadfast and upright: good fortune." The yin element at this place responds and corresponds to the yang element at the fifth place. These two lines echo and correspond to each other. They are loving, caring, coordinating, and supportive. Their inner sincerity creates a very auspicious situation.

(3) Third Six. Union alternates to Hardship (39) ☷

The yin element at the third place is neither central nor correct. It is a yin element at a yang place. Above and below are more yin elements. And its correspondent line at the very top is yin as well. The situation shows that no one is ready for union. Thus Confucius's Commentary on the Yao Text says, "Seeking union with wrong people. How can it not be hurtful?"

(4) Fourth Six. Union alternates to Bringing Together (45) ☷

This line lies at the fourth position, responding but not corresponding to the bottom line. However, the elements in these two places are both yin. They cannot echo from afar; they cannot seek a union. For this reason, one in this position approaches the yang element at the fifth place, which is firm and upright. They are complementary yin and yang and are able to work in concert with each other. Being steadfast and upright brings

good fortune. Confucius's Commentary on the Yao Text says, "From without, seeking union. Follow the one above. " "Without" refers to the upper gua or outer gua. "Above" indicates the fifth line; it is positioned outward and above the fourth line.

(5) Fifth Nine. Union alternates to Responding (2) ☷

The fifth line is the host of the gua. It is a yang element at a yang place— firm, strong, central, and correct. It is the only yang element in this gua and is also located in the supreme position. For this reason, all the yin elements cling to the yang influence and seek union.

Once when King Tang of the Shang dynasty was hunting, he heard people spreading nets all around the wood and praying, "May the game of four directions enter into my nets!" King Tang considered this and said, "In this way, would not all the game be killed without any being left?" He ordered the people to take away the nets in three directions, leaving only the one in the front. Then he prayed: "May those that want to go to the left, go left; those that want to go to the right, go right. Only those that are willing to be my game, come and enter my net." Later on, a system of hunting was established that required that when the king hunts, nets could be spread only on one side in the woods. In this way the strongest and the fastest animals were able to escape and reproduce. This system was known as "driving game on three sides."

In this gua, the Yao Text says that the king orders the game keepers to drive game on three sides and let the game run off in the front. Thus he welcomed those who came and did not chase those who ran off. It shows the magnanimity of the king. Seeking union by using force never works. Only with sincerity, with love and caring, will people come around of their own volition.

(6) Top Six. Union alternates to Watching (20) ☷

The yielding line at the top has reached the extremity. According to its attribute and position, one at this place is not qualified to be a leader. On the other hand, she refuses to seek union with the influential person who is at the fifth place. In the end there is danger. In the I Ching, Water, the upper gua, also represents a leader. The leader is at the fifth place. The one at the top has gone beyond the fifth place. Thus the Yao Text says, "Seeking union. Those not having taken the first step: misfortune." In this position nothing can be completed.

Additional Reference Information for This Gua

Image:	Water above, Earth below
Recite as:	Water above Earth, Union
Element:	Water
Structure:	One yang with five yin
Month:	The fourth month of the lunar year, or May
Host of the Gua:	Fifth Nine
Opposite Gua:	Great Harvest (14)
Inverse Gua:	Multitude (7)
Mutual Gua:	Falling Away (23)

9
Xiao Xü • Little Accumulation

≡≡ Xun • Wind
≡≡ Qian • Heaven

NAME AND STRUCTURE

Wilhelm translates Xiao Xü as the Taming Power of the Small; Blofeld calls it the Lesser Nourisher. In this book it is termed Little Accumulation. The name of this gua consists of two Chinese characters. The first character, xiao, means little. The second character means to raise livestock or to store up something. Xü can be applied to storing up nourishment, strength, or even virtue.

There are two ideographs that demonstrate the meaning of this gua. The first ideograph denotes "little." It is made up of three strokes, one to the left and one to the right, with the third vertical stroke going all the way from top to bottom between the left and right strokes. This character symbolizes an act of dividing. To the ancient sages, things become little after division. The second ideograph consists of two parts. The lower one represents a field, and the upper part represents two piles of grass stored one upon the other with a cover on the top. The whole ideograph is a picture of storing up or accumulating.

Sequence of the Gua: *Multitude in a harmonious union surely results in something to be stored up. Thus, after Union, Little Accumulation follows.*

The structure of the gua is Wind ≡≡ above, Heaven ≡ below. There is only one yin line with five yang lines. Obviously, the yang element is stronger than the yin. King Wen saw a storm gathering and clouding over the western sky, yet no rain came down. He realized that the moisture in the cloud was

not abundant enough to form rain. There was only a little accumulation. Sooner or later rain would fall. He also realized that when five yang lines rely on one yin for nourishment, it becomes difficult for the yin. The yin needs time to accumulate energy and strength. When one's energy and strength are not adequate to a task, one should take a break to gather one's forces for further accomplishment. The break should be temporary, yet the achievement is continuous. This is the main theme of the gua.

In the I Ching, among the sixty-four gua there are two representing accumulation. One is Little Accumulation ☰ (9), and the other is Great Accumulation ☰ (26). Little Accumulation emphasizes the accumulation of nourishment; Great Accumulation emphasizes the accumulation of virtues.

Decision

> Little Accumulation.
> Prosperous and smooth.
> Clouds condense, yet no rain
> At my west side.

Commentary on the Decision

> *Little Accumulation.*
> *The little obtains the ruling position.*
> *Those above and those below respond to it.*
> *This is called Little Accumulation.*
>
> *Strong and gentle.*
> *The firm are in the central places;*
> *In the end their will will be fulfilled.*
> *Therefore, smooth and favorable.*
>
> *Clouds condense, yet no rain.*
> *They are still moving forward*
> *At my west side.*
> *His aspiration has not yet been obtained.*

Commentary on the Symbol

> *Wind blows in the sky.*

An image of accumulating nourishment by the little.
In correspondence with this,
The superior person polishes and beautifies his cultured qualities.

Yao Text

1. Initial Nine
   Return to one's proper way.
   How could that be faulty?
   Good fortune.

   Return to one's proper way.
   It is appropriate for good fortune.

2. Second Nine
   Hand in hand, return.
   Good fortune.

   Hand in hand, return in the central way.
   He does not lose himself.

3. Third Nine
   Spokes fall off the cart wheels.
   Husband and wife fall out.

   Husband and wife fall out.
   He is unable to take good care of his wife.

4. Fourth Six
   Being sincere and truthful,
   Anxiety goes away;
   Fear gives out.
   No fault.

   Be sincere and truthful,
   Anxiety goes away.
   Those above agree with you.

5. Fifth Nine
   Be sincere and truthful.
   Arm in arm, build relationships.
   Establish prosperity with neighbors.

Be sincere and truthful.
Arm in arm, build relationships.
It is not good to be wealthy alone.

6. Top Nine
    Rain falls. Rain stops.
    Regard the virtue fully accumulated.
    Woman
    Being steadfast: adversity.
    The moon is almost full.
    Superior person keeps going forward:
    Misfortune.

    Rain falls. Rain stops.
    Regard the virtue fully accumulated.
    Superior person keeps going forward:
    Worry about being hurt.

SIGNIFICANCE

This gua employs "Clouds condense, yet no rain" as an image to express the situation when the accumulation of one's latent energy and strength is not enough. A little break is required. It is not the time for one to carry out his purpose. During the process of development, progress frequently comes to a standstill. There might be a little obstruction owing to one's lack of experience or insufficiency of strength. In this situation, one should store up energy, preparing for the next move. The main teaching of the gua is to be sincere and truthful. This is the key to nurturing the multitude with little.

The structure of the gua is a yielding line at the fourth place surrounded by five solid lines. The fourth position is at the bottom of the upper gua, Wind. It gives us a picture that the yielding line has strength to stir up the clouds, yet it is not able to bring the rain. It obtains support from all the solid lines. Thus Confucius's Commentary on the Decision says, "Clouds condense, yet no rain. They are still moving forward." And he says, "The little obtains the ruling position. Those above and those below respond to it."

First there should be an accumulation, and then bestowal is possible. Accumulation means to store up, and bestowal is to pass over smoothly. The fact that the clouds condense, yet the rain does not come, displays a twofold truth. On the one hand, before helping others one must store up one's own knowledge, strength, and virtue. On the other hand, in order to help and support each other, people must be sincere and truthful. The ancients taught that "working together with one heart and one mind, grains of sand piled up will make a pagoda."

The host of the gua is the yielding line at the fourth place. It is a yin element at a yin place, which is correct. There are five yang elements that echo the yin, but it is not the right time for the yin to advance owing to its weakness as a yin element. In the I Ching, as has been mentioned, the first, third, and fifth places are yang, and the second, fourth, and sixth are yin. When a yang element is at a yang place or a yin element at a yin place, they are correctly positioned. When an element is in a correct place, it symbolizes that the right person is in the right place. In this gua the yin element in the fourth place is correct.

This gua tell us that King Wen returned to his homeland after seven years of imprisonment. He began to accumulate his strength, preparing to overthrow the Tyrant of Shang. He understood that in the meantime accumulation little by little would be favorable. King Wen's homeland, Zhou, was to the west of Shang; thus, the Decision says, "Clouds condense, yet no rain at my west side." The Duke of Zhou recalls how King Wen accumulated the strength of the Zhou. At first King Wen returned to his usual path, as before his imprisonment. Then he began to work hand in hand with those who were willing to accumulate strength with him. There were differing opinions, represented by spokes falling off the wheels of a cart and the husband and wife falling out. King Wen reminded his people that only by gathering strength little by little could they avoid a tragedy like that of his father, who was killed by the Shang. With sincerity and truthfulness, King Wen built union arm in arm with his people as well as his neighboring clans. At last, rain fell and then stopped. The moon was almost full. King Wen gave warning that overacting would cause misfortune.

(1) Initial Nine. Little Accumulation alternates to Proceeding Humbly (57) ☰

Nine at the beginning is at the bottom of the lower gua, Heaven. The proper place of Heaven is at the top. Thus the Yao Text says, "Return to one's proper way. How could that be faulty?" The proper way can be interpreted as the Tao of Heaven. The bottom line is a yang element at a yang place; its place is correct. It also responds to the yin element at the fourth place. There is no problem in returning to one's proper way. Therefore, things look auspicious.

(2) Second Nine. Little Accumulation alternates to Household (37)

The second line is central in the lower gua. One in this place has the same goal of returning to the proper path. The Yao Text says, "Hand in hand, return." In Chinese it is qian fu. Fu means to return and qian means to pull. Thus, in some translations qian fu is given as "allowing oneself to be drawn into returning" or "compelling oneself to go back." However, qian also means hand in hand. It indicates that to do something with someone sharing a common goal brings good fortune. According to the Yao Text, there is no negative sense, as in being pulled back, drawn back, or compelled to return. There is the positive connotation of returning hand in hand.

(3) Third Nine. Little Accumulation alternates to Innermost Sincerity (61)

The solid line at the third place represents a person with a firm and strong character. He has made a decision to return. However, he has already formed a union with the yin element at the fourth place as husband and wife. In the I Ching, Heaven also represents the husband, and Wind represents the eldest daughter or sometimes the wife. According to the ancients, husband and wife were united together as spokes on a wheel; they formed one unit. Meanwhile, one at the third place is stubborn and self-willed—a yang line at a yang place. He cannot take good care of his wife and obtain her support. He insists upon returning by himself. The result is obvious: the husband and wife will fall out of the cart and the house will not be kept in order. The line indicates that in a process of growing and developing, it is better to have a companion of the same mind and with similar goals.

(4) Fourth Six. Little Accumulation alternates to Initiating (1)

Six at the fourth place is the only yin element in this gua. In general terms, a yin element might be an obstruction to the advancement of the yang elements. In this gua the yin element is at yin place, which is correct. One in this place is able to be humble and is willing to accept support from the two yang elements on the top. Thus, the Yao Text says, "Anxiety goes away; fear gives out," which in Chinese is xue qu ti chu. Literally, it means "blood vanishes; fear leaves." The yielding line at the fourth place

together with the solid line at the third place and the solid line at the fifth place form the upper mutual gua, Water. Water symbolizes blood; thus Wilhelm translates it as "Blood vanishes and fear gives way," and Blofeld as "Bloody and terrible deeds are avoided." However, in ancient times, xue, blood, was a simple form of xü, anxiety. On this ground, the proper understanding is that anxiety vanishes, and fear gives way.

(5) Fifth Nine. Little Accumulation alternates to Great Accumulation (26)

The fifth place is the place for a king or a place of superiority and prosperity. In this gua it is a yang element at a yang place, central and correct. Generally, this line should be the host of the gua. However, the one at this place has innermost sincerity; he is willing to build a relationship with the yin element at the fourth place. They are corresponding yin and yang elements and are able to be harmonious. The solid line at the fifth place is a yang element in an auspicious place. He has already accumulated some wealth. He comprehends the Tao of Heaven, that is, that one who helps others in the end helps himself. So he is willing to establish prosperity with his neighbors. This is the key to success. Confucius's Commentary on the Yao Text says, "It is not good to be wealthy alone." Sharing wealth with others will bring more wealth to oneself. It is the Tao of Heaven.

(6) Top Nine. Little Accumulation alternates to Needing (5)

The uppermost line indicates that Little Accumulation has already reached the limit. The rain has fallen; one should be content. Wealth has been accumulated as the moon waxes full. It is time for one to rest and give serious attention to accumulating virtue. Normally, the yin element should be submissive to the yang. In this gua, the yin has already nourished the five yang; it is better to stop before going too far. Otherwise, if one keeps advancing without break, there will be misfortune.

Additional Reference Information for This Gua

Image:	Wind above, Heaven below
Recite as:	Storm wind darkens the sky, Little Accumulation
Element:	Wood
Structure:	Five yang with one yin
Month:	The fourth month of the lunar year, or May
Host of the Gua:	Fourth Six
Opposite Gua:	Delightful (16)
Inverse Gua:	Fulfillment (10)
Mutual Gua:	Diversity (38)

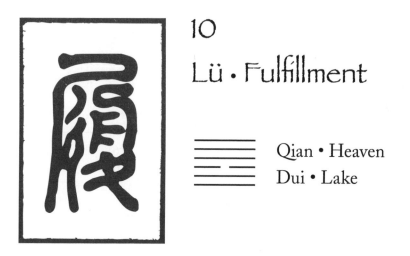

10
Lü · Fulfillment

Qian • Heaven
Dui • Lake

NAME AND STRUCTURE

Lü is the inverse of the preceding gua, Little Accumulation, which indicates a situation where it is better for one to take a break during a course of advancement. This gua, fulfillment, represents carrying out one's duty. The ideograph of Lü is a complicated, four-part picture of a person walking in shoes. At the top of the ideograph, there is one horizontal line that extends from left to right and then from right to left and all the way down to the bottom of the left side. The curved horizontal line represents the head of a person, while the long vertical stroke represents a human body standing upright. The rest of the ideograph is divided into two parts. On the left there are three curved strokes, symbolizing the footprints of three small steps. At the top right, there is a picture of a shoe. Underneath the shoe, there is another ideograph symbolizing the action of walking.

The original meaning of Lü is a pair of shoes. From shoes, the meaning was extended to include treading upon something and then carrying out one's duty or fulfilling one's agreement. In Chinese, fulfillment is made of two characters: lü xing. Literally, lü means shoes, and xing means walking. To the Chinese, walking with shoes symbolizes moving forward with firm steps, advancing to fulfillment. Both Wilhelm and Blofeld translate Lü as Treading, Conduct. In this book, it is translated as Fulfillment.

Sequence of the Gua: *After things have been accumulated, courtesy and righteousness should be fulfilled. Thus, after Little Accumulation, Fulfillment follows.*

An ancient saying goes, "Courtesy is the obedience of principle to what is proper. Righteousness is the accordance of actions with what is right." Courtesy and righteousness are duties everyone should fulfill.

The structure of the gua is Heaven ☰ above, Lake ☱ below. The attributes of Heaven are strength and energy; the attributes of Lake are meekness and gentleness. This image gave King Wen the inspiration that a cautious person handles a dangerous situation as if treading upon a tiger's tail. This was exactly the situation King Wen found himself in when he was fulfilling his obligation of rescuing people from suffering under the tyrannical administration of the Shang dynasty. He treaded upon the tyrant's trusted minister instead of upon the tyrant. This gua, Fulfillment, establishes the foundation of moral conduct. The main theme is that a wise man fulfills his duty as cautiously as he would tread upon a tiger's tail; then good fortune can be expected.

Decision

> Treading upon a tiger's tail,
> Does not bite.
> Prosperous and smooth.

Commentary on the Decision

> *Fulfill one's duty.*
> *The yielding treads upon the firm.*
> *Gentle and joyous*
> *Corresponds with Qian.*
> *Thereupon treading upon a tiger's tail,*
> *The tiger does not bite.*
> *Prosperous and smooth.*
> *The firm is central and correct;*
> *Fulfill one's duty in the place of a ruler and feel no guilt.*
> *His brilliance shines.*

Commentary on the Symbol

> *Above is Heaven; below is Lake.*
> *An image of Fulfillment.*
> *In correspondence with this,*

The superior person discriminates as to duty between high and low,
And sets people's minds at rest.

Yao Text

1. Initial Nine
   Plainly fulfill one's duty.
   Going forward: no fault.

   Plainly fulfill one's duty.
   Going forward alone is to carry out one's ideal.

2. Second Nine
   Fulfill one's duty,
   The path is smooth, smooth.
   The recluse,
   Being steadfast and upright: good fortune.

   Being steadfast and upright
   Brings good fortune to the recluse;
   He is walking on the central path and is not confused.

3. Third Six
   One-eyed person is still able to see,
   Lame person is still able to walk.
   Treading upon a tiger's tail,
   Risking a tiger bite.
   Misfortune.
   The warrior works for the great king.

   A one-eyed person is still able to see,
   But not with enough clarity.
   A lame person is still able to walk,
   But not fast enough as to walk with others.
   The misfortune of being bitten
   Is due to an inappropriate place.
   Like a warrior works for the great king,
   Because of his firm and strong will.

4. Fourth Nine
   Treading upon a tiger's tail
   With heed, heed,

Ends in good fortune.

Heed, heed, ends in good fortune;
One keeps on fulfilling one's will.

5. Fifth Nine
   Decisively fulfill one's duty.
   Being steadfast: adversity.

   Decisively fulfill one's duty.
   Being steadfast: adversity,
   Owing to his correct and appropriate position.

6. Top Nine
   Review the past.
   Summarize the journey.
   Everything is fulfilled.
   Supreme good fortune.

   Supreme good fortune at the topmost position.
   One deserves great congratulations.

SIGNIFICANCE

This gua expounds upon the principle of carrying out one's ideal, or fulfilling one's duty, in a difficult situation. One should act appropriately according to what is suitable in that situation. The image of treading upon a tiger's tail is meant to advise one to take precautions beforehand and guard against the latent difficulty and danger. The host of this gua is the yielding line at the third place. It is the only yielding line in this gua. A yielding line treading upon two solid lines gives a stable image of one stepping on solid ground. However, the yielding line is in the midst of five solid lines, which suggests a tough situation. Psychologically, one in this place would be very uncomfortable. On the other hand, because of the yielding quality, she is able to overcome the firm and the solid. The idea that the soft can overcome the firm is part of the wisdom permeating the I Ching and permeating Chinese culture as well.

In ancient times, the Chinese characters for "fulfillment" and "courtesy" shared the same sound. Thus, Confucius interprets Lü as courtesy. In ancient feudal society, an ethical code was established to provide that people of different classes treated each other with proper manners. To

Confucian scholars, fulfilling the ethical code was everyone's moral duty. Thus, the Sequence of the Gua says, "After things have been accumulated, courtesy and righteousness should be fulfilled."

This gua tells us that after being successful in his expeditions and alliances with the neighboring minority clans, King Wen thought it was time to fulfill his duty to rescue the people from the tyrannical administration of the Shang dynasty. This time King Wen's policy was to tread upon the tail of the tiger, but not the tiger itself. In other words, he began by removing the trusted minister of the tyrant. In this way the tiger (tyrant) would not bite him, and the results were prosperous. The Duke of Zhou recounted how his father King Wen reviewed his past journey and treaded upon the tiger's tail with utmost heed. King Wen adopted a low-key approach, speaking and acting simply, like a recluse. In this way his path was smooth, and his plans prospered. The Duke of Zhou also narrated how his grandfather acted like a reckless, bold warrior and made decisions promptly but impetuously. Working with the tyrant in that way was to invite the tiger to bite. A warrior with reckless courage could neither see clearly, like a one-eyed person, nor act appropriately, like a lame man.

(1) Initial Nine. Fulfillment alternates to Contention (6) ☰

The bottom line is solid, symbolizing that one at this place is able and content to stay in the lower position. This is the initial stage of fulfilling one's duty. The yang element on the bottom does not correspond with the yang element at the fourth place, since both of them are yang. So he walks alone with a plain heart to carry out his ideal.

(2) Second Nine. Fulfillment alternates to Without Falsehood (25) ☰

The second line is a yang element in the central place of the lower gua. Its character is strong; its temper moderate. It does not correspond to the yang element at the fifth place, since they are both yang. The image of a recluse illustrates the situation here. He walks in the central path with a pure heart and is content and happy.

(3) Third Six. Fulfillment alternates to Initiating (1) ☰

The lower mutual gua is Li ☲, or Fire. The upper mutual gua is Xun ☴, or Wind. In the I Ching, Xun also represents leg and Li, eye, which is why the Yao Text of this line mentions legs and eyes. Because this line is neither central nor correct, the Yao Text refers to a "one-eyed person" and a "lame person." As a yin element, it confronts the most extreme yang situation, Initiating; like a one-eyed or lame person, she cannot see clearly or walk fast enough. Moreover, this line is on top of the lower gua, Dui, or Lake. The structure of Dui ☱ looks like an open mouth—one in this place may quite possibly be bitten by the tiger. Misfortune ensues. Confucius's commentary says, "The misfortune of being bitten is due to an inappropriate place." On the other hand, the yielding line corresponds with the solid line at the top. The upper gua, Heaven, represents a king. When the third line alternates from yin to yang, the lower gua becomes Heaven, symbolizing a warrior. Thus, Confucius's commentary says, "a warrior works for the great king, because of his firm and strong will."

(4) Fourth Nine. Fulfillment alternates to Innermost Sincerity (61) ☲

The fourth line is yang. A yang element at a yin place is not correct. However, a yang element at a yin place is better than a yin element at a yang place. One in this place is strong but able to be humble. So he treads upon a tiger's tail with utmost heed. This is the proper attitude to adopt when dealing with a troublesome situation. In this way the end will be turned from evil to good. On the other hand, a yin line at a yang place means that one is weak; the problem is that she likes to pose as strong, but lacks self-knowledge.

(5) Fifth Nine. Fulfillment alternates to Diversity (38) ☲

The fifth line is a yang element at a yang place. The place is correct and central and in the upper gua. Here one is able to make a prompt decision. Because he is in the most favorable position, all the favorable conditions can work together for the good. In the end, he will escape the adversity safely.

(6) Top Nine. Fulfillment alternates to Joyful (58) ☰

The uppermost line has reached the final stage of fulfilling one's duty. Whether one reaps good fortune or misfortune depends upon how one's work has been accomplished. If everything has been well done, there is good fortune. It is important to review the past and summarize the journey from time to time. This is the only way to accumulate one's wisdom and achieve success.

Additional Reference Information for This Gua

Image:	Heaven above, Lake below
Recite as:	Heaven above Lake, Fulfillment
Element:	Metal
Structure:	Five yang with one yin
Month:	The sixth month of the lunar year, or July
Host of the Gua:	Third Six
Opposite Gua:	Humbleness (15)
Inverse Gua:	Little Accumulation (9)
Mutual Gua:	Household (37)

11
Tai • Advance

Kun • Earth
Qian • Heaven

NAME AND STRUCTURE

Tai is one of the most auspicious words in the Chinese language. Originally it meant "more than" or "most." It generally indicates a condition of being more than great. Tai also means peace, safety, security, good health; or it suggests progression, proceeding, advancing. Both Wilhelm and Blofeld translate Tai as Peace. In this book, the word Advance is adopted.

The ideograph of Tai consists of two parts. The upper portion represents greatness. The ancient Chinese believed that Heaven and Earth were great, and that human beings were also great. Thus, the ideograph looks like a person standing with arms and legs wide open. Underneath the two legs, there is the ideograph of water, sui. It looks exactly like the primary gua Kan ☵, or Water, standing upright. This ideograph presents the picture of running water proceeding forward smoothly with great ease. This is the primary meaning of Tai in the I Ching.

Sequence of the Gua: *After fulfilling one's duty with composure, one feels peaceful and safe. Thus, after Fulfillment, Advance follows.*

Heaven is above and Earth below—that is the natural phenomenon we find in our daily life. However, in this gua, Qian (Heaven) descends to the lower gua, and Kun (Earth) ascends to the upper gua. The situation seems inappropriate. Naturally, Heaven stands above and moves downward, and Earth stands below and moves upward. Yet in Tai, Heaven and Earth are moving together in communion. In this way they fulfill their duality.

117

There is a mountain named Tai that stands on the eastern coast of China. Mount Tai was regarded as a sacred mountain that connected Heaven and Earth. Each spring, the emperor would climb the mountain peak, making offerings there with great reverence. The purpose was to ask for harmony between human beings and their natural surroundings. The Chinese believed that when harmony between people and their surroundings was established then, in peace, safety, security, and good health, they would progress, proceed, and advance with great ease. Thus the meaning of Tai embraces all these auspicious meanings. Through thousands of years, the Chinese have sought guo tai ming an—a prosperous country and people at peace.

Traditionally, this gua represents the first month of the Chinese lunar calendar. It carries the message that spring is coming round to Earth once again. Heaven and Earth bring peace and blessing to all living beings. Myriad beings will renew their lives and move forward again. This concept represents the actual meaning of Tai. It is an auspicious time of prosperity and peace. There is an ancient Chinese saying that out of the depth of misfortune comes bliss. This bliss is Tai.

King Wen's Decision on the Gua says, "The little is departing, the great is arriving." The little denotes Earth, which is the most yin. The great denotes Heaven, which is the most yang. In the I Ching, the inner gua (the lower gua) moving to the outer gua (the upper gua) represents departing. In the reversed movement, the outer gua alternating to the inner gua indicates arriving. "The little is departing" indicates that Earth moves upward from the lower gua to the upper gua. "The great is arriving" indicates that Heaven moves downward from the upper gua to the lower gua.

Decision

> Advance.
> The little is departing,
> The great is arriving.
> Good fortune.
> Prosperous and smooth.

Commentary on the Decision

> *Advance.*

The little is departing;
The great is arriving.
Good fortune.
Prosperous and smooth.

Heaven and Earth unite;
All beings come into union.
The upper and the lower link;
Their wills are the same.

The inner is the yang; the outer is the yin.
The inner is the strong; the outer is the gentle.
The inner is the superior; the outer is the inferior.

Thus,
The way of the superior is expanding;
The way of the inferior is shrinking.

Commentary on the Symbol

Heaven and Earth are moving together.
An image of Advance.
In correspondence with this,
The ruler gives full play to his ability and wisdom
To complete the Tao of Heaven and Earth,
And assists their suitable arrangement,
to influence people.

Yao Text

1. Initial Nine
   Pulling out a reed,
   Other roots come with it.
   Moving forward: good fortune.

   Pulling out a reed,
   Going forward, good fortune.
   His will is carried outward.

2. Second Nine
   Embracing great rivers.
   Fighting a tiger with bare hands.

Crossing a river with bare feet.
Abandon not the remote;
Cliques dissolve.
Obtain esteem by walking the central path.

Embracing all the wasteland,
Act in accordance with the central path.
He is shining with glorious and great radiance.

3. Third Nine
   No plain without undulation,
   No past without return.
   In hardship,
   Being steadfast and upright: no fault.
   Grieve not over your sincerity and truthfulness.
   In inheritance there is happiness.

   No past without return.
   It is the law of Heaven and Earth.

4. Fourth Six
   Fluttering, fluttering.
   Not affluent.
   With your neighbors,
   No admonishing,
   Be sincere and truthful.

   Fluttering, fluttering,
   Not affluence;
   Solidarity has been lost.

   No admonishing.
   Be sincere and truthful;
   Wishes come from the core of their hearts.

5. Fifth Six
   King Yi married off his younger sister.
   This brought blessing.
   Supreme good fortune.

   This brought blessing and supreme good fortune.
   He is in the central position,
   Being able to fulfill what he wishes.

6. Top Six
   Castle wall returns into the moat.
   Use no multitude.
   To your own county, make your self-blame known.
   Being steadfast: humiliation.

Castle wall returns into the moat
Signifies a disordered destiny.

SIGNIFICANCE

In this gua, the significance of the union of Heaven and Earth is employed to display the importance of union among people. When people communicate sincerely and truthfully, harmony is created, and things will be achieved easily and smoothly. In Chinese, this situation is called Tai, Advance. The Yao Text of this gua is extremely difficult to understand. Different scholars have varying ideas. To the Chinese, the opposite of Tai is Pi. To go from Tai (Advance) to Pi (Hindrance) or vice versa is a natural law, as is the waxing and waning of the moon. The wise prefer to live in harmony with the laws of Nature. Be content with one's fate, and never blame Heaven or others.

This gua also displays the wisdom of keeping a state of prosperity and preserving a period of bliss. In human society, starting any undertaking is difficult, but maintaining the achievement is even harder. One should not sleep on the accomplishment and feel complacent, but instead be aware that when the achievement reaches a climax, it begins to decline. The interconnection between Heaven and Earth sets the example for mutual communication between human beings. People with the same faith and goals should maintain their mutual love and care and support each other; then the blissful situation can last longer.

Two lines in this gua are qualified to be the host, either the yang at the second place or the yin at the fifth place. Because of its yang quality, the yang at the second place is more suitable to be the host. This gua gives the image of that which is above, Heaven, coming down and that which is below, Earth, rising up. They unite in great compassion. This yang element and the yin element at the fifth place respond and support each other, suggesting a blissful condition in the natural environment. It is also applicable to social life.

This gua tells us that King Wen was ready to overthrow the Tyrant of Shang. Before taking action, King Wen recalled the rising and declining of the Shang dynasty. In his Decision, he felt that the Shang dynasty had already grown small and was about to end and the Kingdom of Zhou had gradually become great and was about to arrive. The situation was auspicious; progress and success awaited. The Duke of Zhou summarized the process of the rise and fall of the Shang dynasty. Before King Tang, the originator of the Shang dynasty, overthrew the Xia dynasty in 1766 B.C., he launched eleven expeditions to exterminate the alliances of the Xia dynasty. It was like pulling out a reed—other roots came with it; their roots were connected. The ancestors of the Shang embraced the wasteland as if fighting a tiger with bare hands and crossing a river with bare feet. They feared not the remote time and places and they eliminated selfishness in relationships and acted in accordance with the central path. But the descendants of the Shang disregarded the course of history, suggested by no plain without undulation and no past without return. They acted lightly, as a bird flutters, and lost their solidarity. After the Kingdom of Zhou became strong, King Yi of the Shang married off his younger sister to King Wen. This brought blessing and supreme good fortune to Zhou. However, it did not help the Shang dynasty stop the castle wall from returning to the moat. Even while his self-blame was known to his people, the divination shows that the humiliation of the tyrant was close at hand. Advance is one of the twelve tidal gua, representing the first month of the Chinese lunar calendar. In the solar calendar, it is February.

(1) Initial Nine. Advance alternates to Growing Upward (46) ☰☰

The bottom line is the first line of the lower gua: ascending begins. When one starts an undertaking, it is better to have supportive coworkers. The three yang elements of the lower gua cherish the same ideals and follow the same path. Thus the Yao Text says, "Pulling out a reed, other roots come with it. Moving forward: good fortune."

(2) Second Nine. Advance alternates to Brilliance Injured (36) ☰☰

This line is the host of the gua. The Yao Text employs a classic allusion to demonstrate the quality of Advance that ends with good fortune. It says, "Fighting a tiger with bare hands. Crossing a river with bare feet." This allusion was so well known that it was adopted in the Book of Confucian Analects:

Once Confucius's disciple Zi-lu asked, "If Master had the conduct of the three armed services of a great state, whom would you have to act with you?"

Confucius said, "I would not have him act with me who will fight a tiger with his bare hands or cross a river with bare feet, dying without any regret. My associate must be the one who proceeds to action full of watchful attention, who is good in stratagems and then carries them into execution."

Advancing with watchful attention and stratagems is the true message of this line.

Concerning the structure, this line is central, but it is a yang element at a yin place. The yang quality gives one at this place the disposition to be resolute and steadfast. The yin place bestows temperament of kindness and generosity. In this way, one is capable of bearing with the uncultured and relying on great courage—to fight a tiger with bare hands, cross a river with bare feet, and advance without fear of remote places. One is able to eliminate selfishness in relationships and to act in accordance with the central way. He is the one who gives full play of his ability and wisdom to complete the Tao of Heaven and Earth.

(3) Third Nine. Advance alternates to Approaching (19)

The solid line at the third place has reached the uppermost position of the lower gua. According to the law of Nature, after things proceed to the upper limit they begin to decline. Thus the Yao Text gives warning that there is no plain without undulation, there is no past without returning. Be upright in hardship; prosperity comes through sustaining.

(4) Fourth Six. Advance alternates to Great Strength (34)

This line has already passed through the lower gua. It is a yin element at a correct yin place, and it corresponds to the yang element at the bottom place. Thus the Yao Text tells us that one at this place is able to be trustful and sincere with neighbors without being reminded. Furthermore, the yin element obtains the help and support of the yang element at the third place. The third line and the fourth line are the junction of the lower gua and the upper gua—Earth and Heaven. Their mutual relationship comes from the core of their hearts, because they are complementary yin and yang, reflecting the Tao of Heaven and Earth. In the I Ching, "not affluent" indicates a yielding line. Because a yielding line is a broken line, Confucius's commentary says, "solidarity has been lost." The fourth line together with the fifth and sixth lines form the upper mutual gua, which is Zhen, or Thunder. In certain cases Zhen symbolizes fluttering or means neighbor. The Yao Text thus says, "Fluttering, fluttering. . . . With your neighbors, no admonishing, be sincere and truthful." The message of this line warns that one who lives in a peaceful and safe situation still needs to be aware of an unfavorable potential. Always be kind and cooperative with neighbors and do not act lightly, as a fluttering bird.

(5) Fifth Six. Advance alternates to Needing (5) ☵☰

The theme of this line is that King Yi of the Shang dynasty married off his younger sister to King Wen. This theme also appears in the Yao Text of the fifth line of Marrying Maiden (54) ☳☱. Before King Wen's son King Wu overthrew the Tyrant of Shang, King Wen had been a duke of the Shang dynasty. The basis for "King Yi married off his younger sister" comes from the structure of this gua. This line is at the fifth place—a place for the king. It corresponds to the yang element at the second place—a place for a supportive subordinate. The yin quality of this line suggests a generous king who is gentle, kind, and humble. The corresponding yang element at the second place suggests a powerful and virtuous subordinate of the king. The upper mutual gua, Zhen (Thunder), represents an eldest son. The lower mutual gua, Dui (Lake), represents a youngest daughter. Because of the king's generosity and humbleness, he gives his youngest sister as a wife to his virtuous subordinate; from this act the blessing of supreme good fortune will come. "King Yi married off his younger sister" serves as a metaphor. The true message is that one should choose only able and virtuous persons with whom to work.

(6) Top Six. Advance alternates to Great Accumulation (26) ☶☰

The yielding line at the top reaches the final stage of Advance. A turning point from Advance to Hindrance is waiting ahead. The Yao text gives warning: the castle wall returned into the moat. It is the law of Nature: when things have proceeded to an extreme, they return to their opposite. It is wise for one to know one's predestined fate. One should not try to alter natural law by using force. Recognize the situation. In ancient times when there were serious calamities an emperor often issued a "self-blame decree," a mea culpa, to calm people's indignation. Through self-examination and by being central and steadfast, wait for another cycle from Hindrance to Advance. Out of the depths of misfortune comes bliss. Be patient; there is always hope.

Additional Reference Information for This Gua

Image:	Earth above, Heaven below
Recite as:	Earth and Heaven unite, Advance
Element:	Earth
Structure:	Three yang with three yin
Month:	The first month of the lunar year, or February
Host of the Gua:	Second Nine
Opposite Gua:	Hindrance (12)
Inverse Gua:	Hindrance (12)
Mutual Gua:	Marrying Maiden (54)

12
Pi • Hindrance

Qian • Heaven
Kun • Earth

NAME AND STRUCTURE

Pi is the inverse of the preceding gua, Tai. The Chinese say, "Out of the depths of misfortune comes bliss. Beyond the extreme, joy begets sorrow." Tai and Pi, good fortune and misfortune, complement each other, as the waxing and waning of the moon. This gua reflects the law of Nature.

Sequence of the Gua: *Tai is advance without hindrance, but this condition does not remain forever. Thus, after Advance, Hindrance follows.*

The Chinese character representing the name of this gua can be pronounced in two ways: fou and pi. When it is pronounced fou, it means no or not. When it is pronounced pi, it has many negative connotations, such as bad, wicked, evil, or mean. Fou was used in ancient written language to represent the expression "No!" In the I Ching, Pi is used exclusively to signify the Opposite of Tai. The ideograph of Pi consists of two parts. At the top of the upper portion there is a horizontal line representing Heaven. Underneath is a picture of a flying bird. The little semicircle represents the head of the bird, and the two curved lines connected to the head and stretching all the way down to the left and right represent two wings. The ancients took the image of a bird in the sky not flying down to signify the negative expression "no." Between the two wings, there is a little circle representing an open mouth, symbolizing a person speaking the word "No!"

To the Chinese, Pi and Tai, as a pair of opposites, are as important as Qian and Kun. Qian and Kun and Tai and Pi form the core of ancient

126

Chinese philosophy. Qian and Kun (Heaven and Earth) illustrate the Chinese view of cosmology, and Tai and Pi (Advance and Hindrance) epitomize the ancient view of human fate, as explored in the I Ching. In the course of Chinese history, even now, almost every Chinese person knows and follows the truth of *pi ji tai lai,* meaning,

> Out of the depth of misfortune comes bliss.
> At the end of Hindrance appears Advance.

For this reason, in this book Pi is translated as the opposite of Tai, Hindrance. Both Wilhelm and Blofeld take Tai to mean Peace. Pi in Wilhelm's translation is Standstill; in Blofeld's work it is Stagnation, Obstruction.

The structure of this gua is Heaven ☰ above, Earth ☷ below. When Heaven moves upward and Earth downward, they are unable to communicate and unite. When the creative power of Heaven and Earth move apart, Advance gives way to Hindrance. To the Chinese, when Heaven and Earth associate with each other in balance, it is Tai, Advance. Contrarily, when Heaven and Earth are moving in opposite directions, in a state of imbalance, it is Pi, Hindrance. Thus, Advance brings prosperity, and Hindrance leads to misfortune. The wisdom of the I Ching shows that when things proceed to their proper limit, they alternate to the reverse condition. One reason that Chinese history has continued for more than five thousand years is that the Chinese pursue this truth of the I Ching—pi ji tai lai. No matter how difficult the situation, to the Chinese there is always a point where it turns favorable. In this way, hope always lies ahead.

Decision

> Hindrance.
> No one can alter.
> Unfavorable to superior persons.
> The divination:
> The great is departing;
> The little is arriving.

Commentary on the Decision

> *Hindrance,*
> *No one can alter.*

Unfavorable to the superior person.
The divination:
The great is departing; the little is arriving.

Heaven and Earth do not unite;
All beings do not communicate;
The upper and the lower do not link;
There are no relations between states.

The inner is yin, the outer is yang.
The inner is yielding; the outer is firm.
The inner is inferior; the outer is superior.

Thus,
The way of the little is expanding,
The way of the great shrinking.

Commentary on the Symbol

Heaven and Earth do not communicate.
An image of Hindrance.
In correspondence with this,
The superior person restrains himself with virtue to avoid calamities.
He should not pursue high position and handsome payment.

Yao Text

1. Initial Six
   Pulling out a reed,
   Other roots come with it.
   Being steadfast and upright: good fortune.
   Prosperous and smooth.

   Pulling out a reed;
   Being steadfast and upright.
   Good fortune.
   Responds to the king.

2. Second Six
   Embrace flattery.
   Little fellow: good fortune.
   Great person: hindrance.

Prosperous and smooth.

For the great person,
Accepting the hindrance brings progress and success.
He does not entangle himself with the multitude.

3. Third Six
   Embrace the shame.

   Embracing the shame.
   The position is not appropriate.

4. Fourth Nine
   It is the will of Heaven,
   No fault.
   Like minds clinging together
   Share the blessing.

   It is the will of Heaven with no fault;
   His will is fulfilled.

5. Fifth Nine
   Cease the hindrance.
   Great person: good fortune.
   Forget not! Forget not!
   Tying up to the trunks of mulberry trees.

   To the superior person, good fortune.
   The position is appropriate.

6. Top Nine
   Overturn the hindrance.
   First hindrance,
   Afterward joy.

   Hindrance reaches its end;
   It would fall down.
   How could it last long?

SIGNIFICANCE

This gua represents a situation of Hindrance. It is the turning point after Advance reaches its extreme. The Yao Text of this gua is difficult

to understand, as is that of the previous gua, Tai. The ancient Chinese watched the cycles of the seasons; they comprehended that there also was a cycle of good times and bad times. When favorable situations came to their conclusion, unfavorable situations follow. During unfavorable times they did not blame Heaven or other people. They restrained themselves with virtue to avoid calamities. In other words, do not become attached to success. This is the key point of the gua.

King Wen's Decision on Advance says, "The little is departing, the great is arriving." The Decision on this gua, Hindrance, says, "The great is departing; the little is arriving." The "little" denotes Earth, the "great" denotes Heaven. In the I Ching, a line moving upward from the lower gua to the upper gua is called departing; the reverse is called arriving. Events cycle from departing to arriving and again from arriving to departing. It is the law of Nature.

The spirit of this gua lies in the solid line at the fifth place, which is the host of the gua. The fifth line is at the most favorable location. It indicates that hindrance will fade and advance emerge. Thus the Yao Text says, "Cease the hindrance." However, it advises, "Forget not! Forget not!" What should one not forget? In the Great Treatise, Confucius says,

> *What is danger?*
> *It arises when one is satisfied with his security and neglects danger.*
> *What is to perish?*
> *It arises when one is satisfied with his survival and neglects death.*
> *What is disorder?*
> *It arises when one is satisfied with things in order and neglects disorder.*
>
> *Therefore the superior person does not forget danger when he is in security,*
> *Nor does he forget death when he is well,*
> *Nor does he forget disorder when his affairs are in order.*
> *In this way he gains personal safety and is able to protect the empire.*
>
> *Thus, the I says, "Forget not! Forget not!*
> *Tying up to the trunks of mulberry trees."*

The spirit of the I Ching is twofold. When the situation is favorable and smooth, one should never forget about hard times. On the other hand, when the situation is unfavorable, one should always look forward to the good.

This gua is a continuation of the preceding one. King Wen understood that over the six hundred years of existence of the Shang dynasty, from its rising to its decline, there was a natural cycle that no one could alter. Everything happened as cause and effect, never by accident. During its decline, it was unfavorable for the superior person to work toward a resurgence of the Shang. The divination already showed that Shang, the great, was departing and Zhou, the small, was arriving. The Duke of Zhou pointed out that the main hindrance to an empire was appointing people by favoritism rather than by merit and ability. The worst thing was entrusting petty persons and accepting their slanders. When virtuous emperors of the Shang cleared away the petty persons from the court, there was progress and success. When the tyrannical emperor took charge, the great person needed to understand the situation, being patient. Only by accepting the situation and being patient would he find success. The will of Heaven had already been made clear, as shown by the divination. When like minds cling together, they share the blessing of a new era. Hindrance ceases; good fortune comes to the superior person. Hindrance is one of the twelve tidal gua, representing the seventh month of the Chinese lunar calendar, or August.

(1) Initial Six. Hindrance alternates to Without Falsehood (25) ☰

The Yao Text of this line is exactly the same as that of the first line of the preceding gua, Tai. The only difference is that the preceding gua says, "Moving forward: good fortune," while this gua says, "Being steadfast and upright: good fortune." The preceding gua is auspicious; advance is favorable. This gua is inauspicious—one must remain steadfast and upright, meaning that one should not be influenced by unfavorable surroundings and the negative opinions of others. The bottom line denotes the beginning of an unfavorable condition. One must seek support. The Yao Text says, "Pulling out a reed, other roots come with it." Because their roots are connected, sincerity and unity bring progress and success.

(2) Second Six. Hindrance alternates to Contention (6) ☰

The second line is a yin element in the central, correct place of the lower gua. One at this place is able to get through the time of hindrance. There are two possible ways to do this. The petty person's fortunes are rising, but the great person endures by not entangling himself with the multitude and keeping to his own principles. He understands the importance of enduring mistreatment from the multitude during the time favorable to petty persons. With this proper attitude, although there is hindrance, progress and success lie ahead.

(3) Third Six. Hindrance alternates to Retreat (33) ☰☰

The third line is a yin element at a yang place. The place is neither correct nor central. The situation is bad. It indicates that the negative energy and influence of the petty person has become obvious. One should beware. "Embrace the shame." Explore the true nature of the person. A great person should be unaware of shame and not need to conceal it.

(4) Fourth Nine. Hindrance alternates to Watching (20) ☰☰

This line is a yang element at the fourth place. The fourth line has moved upward from the lower gua to the upper gua. The upper gua is "great." The fourth line lies at the bottom of the upper gua. This line has already passed halfway through the hindering situation. The dawn is appearing, and the situation is improving. Thus the Yao Text says, "It is the will of Heaven, no fault." The line is neither central nor correct, showing that the yang element is willing to do something to overcome the unfavorable situation but still needs the support of other people. The Yao Text says that those of like mind clinging together share the blessing. If one at this place is able to work sincerely and truthfully with the two yang elements at the fifth and the uppermost places, blessing will result.

(5) Fifth Nine. Hindrance alternates to Proceeding Forward (35) ☰☰

The yang element at the fifth place is the host of the gua. It is central and correct, indicating that one at this place is strong and firm, able to turn the hindering situation to advancement. This is a task for a great person, and the time is right. Thus the Yao Text says, "Great person: good fortune." Yet changing a situation from hindrance to advancement is not an easy task and requires a period of time. So the text warns: "Forget not! Forget not! Tying up to the trunks of mulberry trees."

In ancient times, mulberry trees by custom were planted next to one's house for protection against the wind and the rain, because their roots were deep, their shade was wide, and they grew fast. Chinese scholars still like to employ a mulberry tree to symbolize one's native home, because it gave people a sense of security. "Forget not!" in Chinese is qi wang. Qi, in ancient literature, is an auxiliary verb used to give a command. Wang means to die or perish. But in ancient times, die, perish, and forget shared the same sound and were interchangeable in written language. This line is in a superior situation to end the hindrance. It is good fortune for the great person; there is no reason to introduce negative feelings. Thus, the sage says, "Forget not! Forget not!"

(6) Top Nine. Hindrance alternates to Bringing Together (45) ☷

The uppermost line represents the completion of the Hindrance. An alternation to a new situation will begin. This is the natural law. For thousands of years the Chinese have gained tremendous strength from the message of Confucius's interpretation of this line. "Hindrance reaches its end; it would fall down. How could it last long?" The message of this gua lies at the fifth and sixth lines. One should always think positively. Persevere, looking forward to the good.

Additional Reference Information for This Gua

Image:	Heaven above, Earth below
Recite as:	Heaven and Earth falling apart, Hindrance
Element:	Metal
Structure:	Three yin with three yang
Month:	The seventh month of the lunar year, or August
Host of the Gua:	Fifth Nine
Opposite Gua:	Advance (11) ☷
Inverse Gua:	Advance (11) ☷
Mutual Gua:	Developing Gradually (53) ☶

13
Tong Ren ·
Seeking Harmony

≡≡≡ Qian · Heaven
≡ ≡ Li · Fire

NAME AND STRUCTURE

Wilhelm translates Tong Ren as Fellowship with Men, and Blofeld translates it as Lovers, Beloved, Friends, Like-Minded Persons, Universal Brotherhood. In Chinese, tong means similar, alike, the same. Ren means person or people. When the two characters are put together as a unit, it means to treat people alike. In ancient China, tong ren also meant people with the same interests. Herein, Tong Ren is translated as Seeking Harmony. It has the connotation of forming alliances. To break through a tough situation, people need to work together in harmony, as in an alliance.

The ideograph of the first character, tong, consists of three parts. The first part looks like an upright rectangle without the bottom line, symbolizing a door frame or a house. Within the house, there is a single horizontal stroke representing the number one. Underneath this is a little square symbolizing a mouth. In ancient China, people were counted by mouths. For instance, if someone wanted to know how many people there were in your family, they would ask "How many mouths are there in your family?" The three parts of the ideograph come together to depict a group of people gathered together as a single unit. Here, the mouth indicates that they are thinking or speaking as one. The Chinese can *feel* the harmony in the group. The ideograph of the second character, ren, suggests a person standing.

Sequence of the gua: *Events cannot remain hindered; thus, after Hindrance, Seeking Harmony follows.*

The image of this gua is Heaven above, Fire below. Heaven suggests ascension. The flame of fire moves upward. Fire approaching Heaven gives an image of people with the same interests working together in harmony. There is only one yielding line, at the second place. The ancient sage saw this as a picture of harmony; the one at the second place treated the other five elements at different places equally, with the same attitude. An ancient Chinese maxim says, "People in the same boat help each other, sharing weal and woe."

According to the I Ching, however, there is no absolute sameness. The ancient sages passed on the secret of obtaining harmony, that is, seeking common ground on major issues while reserving differences on minor ones. Tong Ren teaches that the wise classify people according to their natures, not for the purpose of treating them differently, but to seek common ground. If there is common ground, each one is able to act in harmony with the others. The ancient Chinese dreamed day and night that the world would belong to the majority and the government would serve the common interest of its countrymen. This is Seeking Harmony.

Decision

> Seeking harmony among people,
> Prosperous and smooth.
> Favorable to cross great rivers.
> Favorable for the superior person
> To be steadfast and upright.

Commentary on the Decision

> *Seeking Harmony.*
> *The yielding obtains the proper place.*
> *It is central*
> *And corresponds with Qian, the Initiating.*
> *This is Seeking Harmony.*

> *Seeking Harmony says:*
> *Seeking harmony among people.*
> *Prosperous and smooth.*
> *Favorable to cross great rivers.*
> *It is because Qian, the Initiating,*
> *Is progressing and advancing.*

Brilliance with strength,
Central and corresponding.
This is the correct way for the superior person.
Only the superior person is able
To convey the wills of all under Heaven.

Commentary on the Symbol

Heaven with Fire.
An image of Seeking Harmony.
In correspondence with this,
The superior person makes classifications of people
According to their natures
And makes distinctions of things
In terms of their categories.

Yao Text

1. Initial Nine
    Seeking harmony out of the gate.
    No fault.

    Going out of the gate to seek harmony.
    Who would find fault with this?

2. Second Six
    Seeking harmony within a clan.
    Humiliation.

    Seeking harmony within a clan.
    It is selfish and stingy.

3. Third Nine
    Hiding fighters in the bushes
    Ascend to the high hills.
    Three years,
    Unable to go into action.

    Hiding fighters in the bushes.
    The opponent is too firm.
    Three years, unable to go into action.
    Be content with things as they are.

4. Fourth Nine
   Mounting on high city walls,
   Unable to attack.
   Good fortune.

   Mounting on the high walls.
   Unable to attack.
   Bind with morality and justice,
   Not insisting on attacking.
   Good fortune
   Due to return to the truth.

5. Fifth Nine
   Seeking harmony
   Begins with crying and weeping,
   Ends with laughing.
   The great multitude succeeds in meeting.

   The beginning of seeking harmony,
   Straight in hearts.
   After struggling they meet;
   Celebrate the victory.

6. Top Nine
   Seeking harmony in the countryside.
   No regret.

   Seeking harmony in the countryside.
   One's ambition is not yet fulfilled.

SIGNIFICANCE

The Decision says, "Seeking harmony among people." This is the main theme of the gua. Seeking harmony should be done with absolute unselfishness and among the majority. This was the ancient lofty ideal of a world of harmony. Seeking harmony among people, in Chinese, is tong ren yü ye. Tong ren means seeking harmony. Yü means at, in, or among. And ye is the place beyond the suburbs. Thus, most English translations give ye as "the open." However, ye also means the folk or the people, as contrasted with the government. Considering the theme of this gua, it is more suitable to employ people for ye. In this way, it brings more sense to the Decision: "Seeking harmony among people. Prosperous and smooth."

The outer gua is Qian (Heaven), symbolizing firmness and strength. With this quality, it is favorable for a person to cross great rivers, to overcome difficulties. The inner gua is Li (Fire), symbolizing a quality of inner brightness. In this situation, the host is the yielding line at the second place. It plays a leading role. It is a yin element at a yin place, central and correct. Thus, Confucius's Commentary on the Decision explains that the yielding obtains the proper place and corresponds with Qian. This yin line in the center of the lower gua indicates that one at this place possesses a high morality and is gentle and sincere, humble and modest, and willing to seek harmony with other people. It corresponds to the solid line at the fifth place, which is also central and correct. These two lines symbolize an ideal condition where the time is auspicious, the situation is favorable, and the people are in harmony. This ideal situation results from the circumstance of overcoming hindrance.

Tong Ren reveals the truth that if people deal with each other in a spirit of equality, then peace and advancement are possible. Otherwise, there will be conflict and obstruction. The first three lines of this gua represent the fact that from sameness differences originate. The next three lines tell us that sameness derives from differences. Thus, at the fifth line, people are at first weeping and full of regret and then laughing to celebrate the victory. In ancient times, people called the piping time of peace the Great Harmony.

This gua symbolizes the historical incident in which King Wen formed alliances with neighboring clans to battle the rebellious Rong clan. King Wen proclaimed that seeking harmony with people of other clans would be prosperous and smooth. The Duke of Zhou recounts how there was no hindrance in seeking alliances with different clans, yet seeking alliances exclusively within his own clan caused isolation and brought about unfavorable results. At the very beginning, the alliance took defensive action by placing troops on a high hill and hiding fighters in the bushes. For three years there was no trouble. Later, the alliance besieged Rong's city walls. After great struggles it was victorious. What began with weeping ended with laughing. At last, the alliance gathered in Zhou's countryside. There was no regret about the struggles that resulted in success.

(1) Initial Nine. Seeking harmony alternates to Retreat (33) ☰

The Yao Text of this line is "Seeking harmony out of the gate." When this line moves from yang to yin, then the lower gua alternates from Fire

to Mountain. In the I Ching, Mountain also represents a gate. This line indicates the beginning of seeking harmony. The yang element has a firm and strong character, but it does not correspond to the fourth line since they are both yang. Here it symbolizes a lack of personal consideration between them. Seeking Harmony out of the gate suggests action in public, not in secret. The acts are open and aboveboard. The ancient Chinese believed that seeking harmony in a closed place would be to act with selfish motives. Thus Confucius says, "Going out of the gate to seek harmony. Who would find fault with this?"

(2) Second Six. Seeking Harmony alternates to Initiating (1) ☰

This is the host of the gua, as indicated by Confucius when he says, "The yielding obtains the proper place. It is central and corresponds with Qian, the Initiating." The content of the Yao Text is very clear: seeking harmony within a clan is selfish and stingy; it brings about humiliation. The yielding line at the second place is central and correct; it corresponds to the yang element at the fifth place. Generally, this condition represents a perfect situation and is very auspicious. However, in this gua it is not that positive. Seeking harmony exclusively in a family shows one's selfishness. It focuses on a personal relationship. Acting out of selfishness and personal considerations, how can one seek harmony with the community?

(3) Third Nine. Seeking Harmony alternates to Without Falsehood (25) ☳

The third line is at the top of the lower gua, Li (Fire); it gives an image of ascending. This line is located within the inner gua, symbolizing hiding. Li also means weapon and fighter. When the third line moves from yang to yin, the lower gua alternates to Zhen (Thunder), which represents bushes. Thus the Yao Text says, "Hiding fighters in the bushes ascend to the high hills. Three years, unable to go into action." The three years derives from the fact that this is the third line. It does not mean exactly three years, but rather a long period of time.

This line is a yang element at a yang place—not central. One at this place has an irritable, bad temper. This yang element does not correspond with the yang element at the fifth place. It is close to the yin element at the second place, which has a good relationship with the yang element at the fifth place: they are complementary. The yang element at the fifth place is much more powerful than the yang element at the third place, owing to its central, correct, and superior location. One at the third place knows that there is no way to win a face-to-face fight with the one at

the fifth place. So he ascends to the high hills to assess the geographical situation and hides fighters in the bushes. The one at the fifth place is much stronger; thus, Confucius says, "The opponent is too firm. . . . Be content with things as they are."

(4) Fourth Nine. Seeking Harmony alternates to Household (37) ☲☴

The Yao Text says, "Mounting on high city walls." This line comes from the lower mutual gua, Xun (Wind), which also suggests the meaning of a high wall. The fourth line is on top of the lower mutual gua; it gives an image of mounting. The fourth line is a yang element at a yin place, neither central nor correct. It responds to the yang element of the bottom line but does not correspond—they are both yang. Thus, this yang is closer to the yin element at the second place, but the yang element at the third place stands between them like a high wall. One at the fourth place knows that during a time of seeking harmony it is not good to take controversial actions. Thus, Confucius says, "Bind with morality and justice. . . . Good fortune due to return to the truth."

(5) Fifth Nine. Seeking Harmony alternates to Brightness (30) ☲

The Yao Text of this line bears a significance to the second line of the third gua, Beginning ☵☳. In Beginning, the yin element at the second place wants to respond to the yang element at the fifth place, but they are blocked by two yin elements at the third and fourth places. Here, the yin element at the second place wants to correspond to the yang element at the fifth place, but they are blocked by two yang elements at the third and fourth places. This time the blockage is two yang elements; great struggles are necessary to overcome it. To explore the significance of this line, the text continues the story of the previous two lines.

The yang element at the fifth place is central and correct, corresponding to the yin element at the second place. They are complementary yin and yang. However, the third line is hiding fighters in the bushes, and the fourth line is mounting on the high walls. These two lines, both strong yang elements, create a blockage. The second line is a yin element, gentle and weak. Therefore, one at the fifth place needs to use extraordinary strength to overcome the obstruction caused by the third and the fourth lines.

The message of this line is that when two people resonate with each other, while they might be separated physically, their hearts are still united. People might be kept apart by different kinds of obstructions that cause them to weep. But when they remain truthful in spirit, nothing can really separate them. After they experience the difficulty of separation, they are able to appreciate the true joy of union.

Confucius once said,

> *Whether in charge of a government or being a hermit,*
> *Or keeping quiet or making comment,*
> *When two people become one in their hearts*
> *They are as sharp as a knife that is able to cut iron.*
> *They cherish the same idea and follow the same path;*
> *Their words are like the perfume and fragrance of orchids.*

(6) Top Nine. Seeking Harmony alternates to Abolishing the Old (49)

The uppermost line is at the edge of the outer gua. In the I Ching, Initiating also represents the countryside. Thus, the Yao Text says, "Seeking harmony in the countryside." In ancient times, there were few people in the countryside. The yang element at the uppermost place wants to seek harmony with others, but there is no one to respond. Being content with the reality, although one's will is not yet fulfilled, one has the patience to wait for the right time. There is no regret.

Additional Reference Information for This Gua

Image:	Heaven above, Fire below
Recite as:	Heaven above Fire, Seeking Harmony
Element:	Metal
Structure:	Five yang with one yin
Month:	The seventh month of the lunar year, or August
Host of the Gua:	Fifth Nine
Opposite Gua:	Multitude (7)
Inverse Gua:	Great Harvest (14)
Mutual Gua:	Encountering (44)

14
Da You •
Great Harvest

$$\begin{array}{c}\text{——— ———}\\\text{———————}\\\text{———————}\end{array}$$ Li • Fire
Qian • Heaven

NAME AND STRUCTURE

Great Harvest is the inverse of the preceding gua, Seeking Harmony.
Seeking harmony brings about a great harvest. On the other hand, a great
harvest lends wings to seeking harmony. Seeking Harmony and Great
Harvest are complementary to each other and help each other advance.

Sequence of the Gua: *After seeking harmony with people, things are sure to*
respond to you. Thus, after Seeking Harmony, Great Harvest follows.

In Chinese, *da* means great, and *you* means possession. Da You means
possession in great measure. Both Wilhelm and Blofeld translate Da You
as Great Possession. However, in ancient times *you* also meant harvest.
According to the spirit of this gua, there is no sense of possession, but
it does reveal the light of a harvest. Confucius's Commentary on the
Decision says,

> *His virtue is firm and strong and also brilliant.*
> *He corresponds with Heaven*
> *And acts in accordance with time.*
> *Thus there is supreme progress and success.*

To maintain virtue, it is not appropriate to take any action of possession.
Corresponding with Heaven and acting in accordance with time suggests
an act of harvesting.

There are two ideographs representing the name of this gua. The first

142

ideograph looks like a person standing upright with arms and legs wide open. The ancient sages believed that Heaven and Earth and human beings were great. Thus, they employed the image of a human being to represent great. The second ideograph consists of two parts. The upper part suggests the image of a hand with three fingers open as in the act of grasping something. Underneath the hand is the ideograph of a moon. The whole image presents a picture of a hand in the act of grasping a moon. It is interesting that early on, *you* meant "not appropriate to possess." The ancient Chinese knew that during a lunar eclipse the moon was taken away and the world fell into darkness. In this context they created the ideograph of *you*, reflecting the transitory nature of possession, and taught people that it was not right to appropriate other's possessions. Later on, people forgot about the instruction of the inappropriateness of possession and *you* came to simply mean "possess."

The structure of the gua is Fire above, Heaven below. It symbolizes the sun shining in the sky and giving light and heat to myriad beings on Earth—an image of prosperity and abundance. It is the time for great harvest. As an extension of the preceding gua, it shows that only in the spirit of seeking harmony with people can we promote peace in the world, manifest prosperity in our country, and create abundance for our families.

Decision

> Great Harvest.
> Sublimely prosperous and smooth.

Commentary on the Decision

> *Great Harvest.*
> *The yielding obtains the honored position,*
> *Great and central.*
> *The upper and the lower respond.*
> *So the name of Great Harvest comes.*
>
> *Her virtue is firm and strong and also brilliant,*
> *Corresponding with Heaven*
> *And acting in accordance with time.*
> *Thus there is supreme progress and success.*

Commentary on the Symbol

Fire is above Heaven.
An image of Great Harvest.
In correspondence with this,
The superior person represses evil and promotes good,
Carrying out the glorious virtue of Heaven.

Yao Text

1. Initial Nine
   No pride, no harm.
   Of course no fault.
   Being aware of hardship:
   No fault.

   Initial nine of Great Harvest,
   No pride and harm.

2. Second Nine
   A big wagon for loading.
   There is somewhere to go.
   No fault.

   A big wagon for loading,
   Store up in the middle.
   No failure.

3. Third Nine
   The prince is engaged
   In presenting offerings to the Son of Heaven.
   Petty fellows cannot do this.

   The prince is engaged in presenting offerings to the Son of Heaven.
   If petty fellows engage, they lead to disaster.

4. Fourth Nine
   Not inflated,
   No fault.

   Not inflated,
   No fault;
   He is bright, discriminating, and clear.

5. Fifth Six
   Sincere and truthful communication
   Makes dignity shine through.
   Good fortune.

   Sincere and truthful communication
   Kindles the will of others.
   The good fortune of her dignity
   Comes from her nature.
   It arises easily and spontaneously.

6. Top Nine
   From Heaven comes blessing.
   Good fortune.
   Nothing is unfavorable.

   Great Harvest, good fortune at the top.
   Blessing descends from Heaven.

SIGNIFICANCE

This gua (Fire ☲ above, Heaven ☰ below), Great Harvest, is the inverse of the preceding one, Seeking Harmony (Heaven ☰ above, Fire ☲ below). The attribute of both Fire and Heaven is ascending. When the sun ascends, it gives light and heat to myriad beings. The sun shining in the sky represents an extremely auspicious situation. This gua is more favorable than the preceding one because the host is in the most auspicious place.

The host of this gua is the yin element at the fifth place. It is the only yin element, and it is located in the supreme place of the gua. It looks like an ancient king, generous and humble, bearing the spirit of seeking harmony with his people and thus able to reap the great harvest. Here we are told the secret of success: one in a leading role should be humble and sincere, gentle and magnanimous, willing to seek harmony with people, then blessing will descend to him from Heaven.

Although the name of this gua is Great Harvest, it does not directly expose the secret of how to obtain a great harvest. Instead, it expounds the truth of not spilling over after becoming full. In other words, it warns one not to become proud after success. This gua takes the role of connecting link between the preceding gua and the following gua—Seeking Harmony and Humbleness, respectively. "One loses by pride and gains by modesty" is a classic aphorism of Chinese culture. This gua reminds people that one loses by being prideful; the next says that one gains by being humble.

The gua tells us that after victory over the rebellious Rong clan, King Wen received a great award from the Tyrant of Shang. King Wen considered the award the great harvest of his political and military course. It would bring him supreme progress and success. The Duke of Zhou recounted King Wen's humble attitude upon receiving the award from the tyrant. The award was big enough to fill a wagon, but King Wen was still aware of the hardship of his revolutionary course against the tyrant's brutality. When King Wen enjoyed food with the tyrant, he dared not take too much. His confidence and modesty shone through with his dignity. Owing to these virtues, blessing came from Heaven. These were signs of good fortune; nothing was unfavorable.

(1) Initial Nine. Great Harvest alternates to Establishing the New (50) ≡

The Yao Text of this line is difficult to understand. Wilhelm translates it as "No relationship with what is harmful." Blofeld gives it as "Having no contact with evil." In Chinese, the text starts with these three characters: wu jiao hai. Wu means no, jiao is to associate with, and hai is harm. Because there is no punctuation in ancient Chinese literature, wu jiao hai can be understood as either wu jiao hai (without a comma) or wu jiao, hai (with a comma). Wu jiao hai can be translated as no association and harm; or no relationship with what is harmful, as Wilhelm says; or having no contact with evil, as Blofeld says. However, if a translator believes that a comma is meant, then wu jiao, hai might be thought to be "no association, harm."

In ancient times jiao meaning both "associate with" and "pride" carried the same sound but in a different form. In written language they were interchangeable. Therefore, wu jiao hai can also be translated as "no pride and harm." Considering King Wen's arrangement of the sequence of the gua and the main theme of this gua, a more appropriate translation might be: "No pride, therefore no harm." Although the bottom line is solid, it is still at the bottom. One in this place is firm and able, yet not overly self-willed. It does not respond to the yang element at the fourth place; there is no support. According to King Wen's opinion, the most harmful thing in a great harvest is pride. Since one at this place is at a beginning stage of his career and in an isolated condition, he should not become proud. This way, there will be no harm and no fault.

(2) Second Nine. Great Harvest alternates to Brightness (30) ☲

The second line is a yang element in the middle of the lower gua. Owing to its central and humble position one at this place is able and strong and would not be opinionated. This line responds to the host, the yin element at the fifth place. He is entrusted with an important task by the host, like a big wagon about to be loaded. The lower gua is Qian, which can represent a circle. Here it symbolizes the wheel of a big wagon. This yang element is at the central place, indicating that there is a way to progress.

(3) Third Nine. Great Harvest alternates to Diversity (38) ☲

In the I Ching, the third line can represent a prince, because it is at the top of the lower gua. Here the third line is a yang element at a yang place; his merit matches his position. He deserves the honor of presenting offerings to the emperor. Petty people have no merit—they do not deserve the honor. The message of this gua is that one should honor those who have merit and should not blindly put trust in petty persons.

(4) Fourth Nine. Great Harvest alternates to Great Accumulation (26) ☶

The yang element at the fourth place represents a minister of a king. This yang element is at a yin place; one at this place is an able minister. The emperor is humble as a result of his yin quality. In the situation of Great Harvest, the fourth place can represent overabundance. He is mounting on three yang elements and is located next to the king. He has the opportunity to overstep the king. However, he is a yang element at a yin place. He is bright, discriminating, and clear, and he does not dare to exceed his position. Thus, there is no fault.

(5) Fifth Six. Great Harvest alternates to Initiating (1) ☰

This line is the host of the gua. It is the only yin element and it hosts the five yang elements. Its quality is yielding; its place is central. It represents a brilliant person who is able to take a leading position as a king. This element corresponds to the yang element at the second place. Their relationship is harmonious. Together, they are able to kindle the will of others.

(6) Top Nine. Great Harvest alternates to Great Strength (34) ☳

Generally, the topmost line represents the extreme—it is an unfavorable

place. However, this gua follows the principle of full, yet not spilling over. One in this place still remembers to be humble. Humility is one of the highest virtues of a superior person. In this way, blessing will come from Heaven. The line calls for good fortune; nothing is unfavorable.

Additional Reference Information for This Gua

Image:	Fire above, Heaven below
Recite as:	Sun above sky, Great Harvest
Element:	Fire
Structure:	Five yang with one yin
Month:	The fifth month of the lunar year, or June
Host of the Gua:	Fifth Six
Opposite Gua:	Union (8)
Inverse Gua:	Seeking Harmony (13)
Mutual Gua:	Eliminating (43)

15

Qian •
Humbleness

≡≡ Kun • Earth
≡≡ Gen • Mountain

NAME AND STRUCTURE

This gua is very special. To the Chinese, being humble always brings about a great harvest. Both Confucius and Lao Tze learned a great deal from this gua. What Confucius learned is fully expressed in his commentaries. What Lao Tze learned can be found in what he says in the Tao Te Ching:

> I have three treasures
> That I guard and hold dear:
> The first is love;
> The second is contentment;
> The third is humbleness.
> Only the loving are courageous;
> Only the content are magnanimous;
> Only the humble are capable of commanding.

From Seeking Harmony (13), through Great Harvest (14), going on to Humbleness (15), these "treasures" are fully expounded. By living with these treasures, the outcome will be Delight (16).

This Qian, meaning Humbleness, is entirely distinct from the Qian of the first gua, Initiating. They are two different characters. The Chinese often link the word humble with amiable and courteous. Qian-he is to be humble and amiable; qian-gong is to be humble and courteous. Both Wilhelm and Blofeld translate the name of this gua as Modesty. According to King Wen's sequence of the sixty-four gua, this one should have the sense of lack of pride and self-importance. Confucius's Commentary on the Decision fully expresses this sense. Thus, in this book, the term Humbleness is used.

The ideograph of this gua consists of two parts. The picture of a man's face with an open mouth forms the left portion of the ideograph, it represents an act of speaking. In the ideograph of the sixth gua, Contention, this image represents conflict. Here it suggests humility. On the right side of the ideograph there are two bundles of wheat standing side by side and a hand with three open fingers in the middle of the two bundles. This picture symbolizes the act of equally dividing something. As Confucius says in the Commentary on the Symbol, "The superior person decreases what is excessive and increases what is scarce. He weighs things and makes them balance."

This is the true meaning of Humbleness. When the two parts of the ideograph are combined, they indicate that the act of weighing things and making them balance should be expressed and manifested in one's daily life.

Sequence of the Gua: *After a great harvest, one should not be filled with satisfaction and become proud. Thus, after Great Harvest, Humbleness follows.*

The structure of this gua is Earth ☷ above, Mountain ☶ below. Normally mountains are high and the Earth is low. What makes a mountain a mountain is its standing high above the Earth. In this gua, the mountain stands underneath the Earth. This image represents a state of becoming humble. The inner gua, Mountain, has the attribute of standing still. The outer gua, Earth, has the quality of gentleness. If one is able to restrain one's ego and be gentle to others, then one will possess the quality of humility. To the ancient Chinese, being humble is one of the highest virtues. It takes a long time to cultivate. Thus the Decision says that humbleness leads to prosperity and success. A superior person carries this virtue to the end.

Decision

> Humbleness.
> Prosperous and smooth.
> For a superior person there is an end.

Commentary on the Decision

Humbleness,
Prosperous and smooth.

It is the Tao of Heaven to send its energy down
Shining upon all beings.
It is the Tao of Earth to send its energy up
Linking with Heaven.

It is the Tao of Heaven to decrease the full
And increase the humble.
It is the Tao of Earth to alternate the full
And make the full humble.

It is the Tao of spirit beings to harm the full
And bless the humble.
It is the Tao of humans to dislike the full
And love the humble.

The humble is honored to radiate its brilliance.
When the humble is in a lower position,
He does not lose his principle.
Thus the superior person is able to carry his principle through
*   to the end.*

Commentary on the Symbol

Within the Earth, there is Mountain.
An image of the humble.
In correspondence with this,
The superior person decreases what is excessive
And increases what is scarce.
He weighs things and makes them balance.

Yao Text

1. Initial Six
   Humbly, humbly, the superior person
   Engages in crossing great rivers.
   Good fortune.

Humbly, humbly, the superior person
Humbles herself
To cultivate humility.

2. Second Six
    Humbleness resonates.
    Being steadfast and upright: good fortune.

    Humbleness resonates.
    Being steadfast and upright leads to good fortune.
    Virtue comes from the core of the heart.

3. Third Nine
    Toiling humbly, the superior person
    Ends in good fortune.

    Toiling humbly, the superior person.
    The multitudes of people completely accept him.

4. Fourth Six
    Nothing is unfavorable.
    Give full play to humility.

    Nothing is unfavorable.
    Give full play to humility.
    It does not violate the principle.

5. Fifth Six
    Not being wealthy.
    Together with his neighbors
    Favorable to engage in subjugation.
    Nothing is unfavorable.

    Favorable to engage in subjugation.
    Conquer those who do not submit.

6. Top Six
    Resonating humbleness.
    Favorable to engage in mobilizing the multitude.
    Consolidate your own state.

    Resonating, humbleness.
    Her will is not yet obtained.
    One may take action.
    Consolidate one's own place first.

SIGNIFICANCE

Among the sixty-four gua, only in Humbleness are all lines auspicious. It is very special in the I Ching. One can see how much value was placed on the quality of humility by the ancients. To them, humbling oneself did not mean to act negatively by holding oneself back. Instead one should act positively by doing something with other people cooperatively and harmoniously. The key is to respect people and treat them equally. Only in this way can true peace and harmony be established in a community.

The host of this gua is unusual. It is at neither the fifth nor the second place but at the third. The third place is at the top of the lower gua. Normally this is not a favorable place. In this gua, it is the only solid line. It symbolizes a humble sage standing with all the yin elements around him. It is firm and strong, energetic and powerful, but humbly stays in the lower position. This is the true spirit of being humble. Humility is not an innate virtue; it must be cultivated over a long period of time. If a leader is able to be truly humble, then people will accept and follow him. This is the core spirit of the gua. This gua is an extension of the preceding one, Seeking Harmony, which is the key to a great harvest.

This gua tells us that after a great harvest King Wen's brilliance and radiance appeared. He sensed that in this situation extreme humility was necessary. A superior person should carry this virtue to the end. Otherwise the Tyrant of Shang would keep a wary eye on him. The Duke of Zhou recounted how King Wen exalted in and toiled at being humble. With this attitude he was able to overcome all difficulties, as if walking safely through great rivers. Even while he was not as wealthy as the Tyrant of Shang, King Wen still obtained love and esteem from his neighboring clans. Even in the act of subjugating, nothing was unfavorable, yet King Wen was still cautious and was not in a hurry to take action against the tyrant.

(1) Initial Six. Humbleness alternates to Brilliance Injured (36) ☷

The attribute of a yin element is yielding, which represents the quality of humility. The yin element in this gua is happy to stay at the bottom. It is another way to show one's humbleness. Thus the Yao Text says, "Humbly, humbly," indicating that one who wants to cultivate the quality of humility should first be humble at heart. With the quality of humility, one is able to deal with any kind of situation, no matter how difficult or dangerous. This is the true spirit of humility—not acting negatively by holding oneself back but acting positively by moving forward to do something productive. The three lines above the bottom line form the inner mutual gua, Water; thus the Yao Text says, "Humbly, humbly, the superior person engages in crossing great rivers."

(2) Second Six. Humbleness alternates to Growing Upward (46)

The yin element at the second place is central and correct. It symbolizes that the beautiful quality of humility is cherished in one's inner heart and blooms in one's outward conduct. Thus it arouses sympathetic resonance from the surroundings. When the second line moves from yin to yang, the lower gua alternates from Gen (Mountain) to Xun, which is Wind. Here Xun represents a cock. When one cock crows, other cocks follow: resonation.

(3) Third Nine. Humbleness alternates to Responding (2)

This line is the host of the gua. It is the only solid line, mounting on top of the lower gua and symbolizing a person shouldering an important task. Since it is a yang element at a yang place, firm and strong, the other five yin elements rely on it as their center. He is able to toil and still be humble; inevitably he will win the support of the people, and things will end in good fortune. Confucius says,

> *Working hard yet not showing off,*
> *Having great accomplishment yet not feeling complacent,*
> *Being honest and sincere to the utmost,*
> *Indicates the person who has merit but still remains humble.*

(4) Fourth Six. Humbleness alternates to Little Exceeding (62)

The fourth line is a yin element at a yin place. Its nature is gentle; its place is correct. It is content to be at the bottom of the upper gua, symbolizing its humbleness. Therefore, nothing is unfavorable. Although the position of the fourth line is higher than the third line, the fourth line is not as strong and firm as the third. Since it is aware of this fact, it gives full play to humility. Confucius tells us that it does not violate the principle of humbleness.

(5) Fifth Six. Humbleness alternates to Hardship (39)

The fifth line is a yielding line, which is not an image of wealth. As a yielding line situated at the supreme place of Humbleness, it is special. One at this place is honorable but still humble. She does not influence people by wealth but by virtue, and so, with the support of other people can still carry out great achievements. The Yao Text says, "Favorable to engage in subjugation. Nothing is unfavorable." This shows the power of being honorable and humble.

(6) Top Six. Humbleness alternates to Keeping Still (52) ☶

The sixth line is at the uppermost place; usually it represents a situation like the glow of a setting sun—something close to the end of one's career or life. However, the uppermost line of Humbleness is unusual. The sun is still shining and humility still has resonance. For the other gua, the text normally advises retiring and taking no action. Yet for Humbleness, the advice is, "Favorable to engage in mobilizing the multitude."

Once a disciple of Zhu Xi, one of the most eminent Confucian scholars of the southern Sung dynasty, asked, "Master, I question why in the Yao Text of Humbleness it approves taking military action in the fifth and sixth lines?" Zhu Xi replied, "The content of military strategy and tactics includes humility as well. It is to retreat in order to advance and thus bring about triumph." Lao Tze expresses a similar idea in the Tao Te Ching. He says,

> If a great country treats a smaller country with humility,
> It will gain the obedience of the smaller country.
> If a small country treats a great country with humility,
> It will obtain the magnanimity of the great country.
> Therefore one benefits by becoming humble;
> The other benefits by being humble.

Additional Reference Information for This Gua

Image:	Earth above, Mountain below
Recite as:	Mountain below Earth, Humbleness
Element:	Earth
Structure:	Five yin with one yang
Month:	The twelfth month of the lunar year, or January
Host of the Gua:	Third Nine
Opposite Gua:	Fulfillment (10) ䷌
Inverse Gua:	Delight (16) ䷏
Mutual Gua:	Relief (40) ䷧

16
Yü · Delight

Zhen • Thunder
Kun • Earth

NAME AND STRUCTURE

Yü originally meant delight: today it also means peace and happiness. Delight is the inverse of the preceding gua, Humbleness. Humbleness leads people to delight. Thus, Humbleness and Delight are complementary. Wilhelm translates Yü as Enthusiasm; Blofeld translates it as Repose. In this book I follow the original meaning, Delight.

Sequence of the Gua: *When one's harvest is great and one can still remain humble, there is sure to be an outburst of delight. Thus, after Humbleness, Delight follows.*

The ideograph of this gua is a very old form consisting of two parts. The left portion is an ideograph of yü, which means hand out or give something away. There are two hands at the top and a vertical straight line connected to the lower hand, representing the arm. Between the two hands there is a little object. Taken as a whole it is a picture of the act of giving and receiving. The right portion of the ideograph represents an elephant, xiang. The elephant is standing upright on two rear legs with the tail touching the ground. The two front legs are held up in the air. The head of the elephant is looking forward with the long trunk curling upward. In the past there were elephants in the southern part of China, though they no longer exist there. In southern China, elephants were trained to help workers carry heavy things, but in the north they were trained for the purpose of giving people pleasure and delight. People performed a kind of dance known as the elephant dance, which King Wu was fond of. The two parts of the ideograph together mean delight—enjoyed by oneself or given to others.

The structure of this gua is Thunder ☳ above, Earth ☷ below. Thunder represents action, and Earth submission. These two primary gua standing together symbolize the action of the yang element followed delightfully by all the yin elements. In ancient China, people believed that the power of thunder had influence for a distance of a hundred li (a Chinese unit of length designating about one third of a mile), equivalent to the realm of a feudal lord. For this reason, the Decision says, "Favorable to establish feudal lords and mobilize the multitude." Earth is the symbol of a multitude. And establishing feudal lords means gaining assistance.

Decision

Delight.
Favorable to establish feudal lords
And mobilize the multitude.

Commentary on the Decision

Delight.
The firm meets with response.
Its will is fulfilled.
Acting in accord with the time and moving forward;
This is Delight.

Delight.
Acting in accord with the time and moving forward;
It is following the way of Heaven and Earth.
How much more will it be so
In establishing feudal lords and mobilizing the multitude?

Heaven and Earth move in accordance with the time;
Therefore sun and moon do not deviate from their courses,
And the four seasons do not err.

The holy person moves in accordance with the time and situation;
Therefore punishments and penalties become just,
And people are genuinely convinced.
Great indeed are the time and significance of Delight!

Commentary on the Symbol

Thunder comes out of the Earth,
Rising and stirring:
An image of Delight.
In correspondence with this,
The ancient king composed music to honor virtue and merit;
With ardent eagerness, he offered it to God
And shared it with his ancestors.

Yao Text

1. Initial Six
   Singing out delight:
   Misfortune.

   Singing out delight:
   One's will comes to an end.

2. Second Six
   Firm as rock,
   Not merely for a whole day.
   Being steadfast and upright: good fortune.

   Not merely for a whole day.
   Being steadfast and upright: good fortune.
   It is central and correct.

3. Third Six
   Staring upward, wallowing in delight:
   Regret.
   Delaying:
   Regret again.

   Staring upward, wallowing in delight,
   There is regret.
   The place is not appropriate.

4. Fourth Nine
   Cause of delight;
   Great accumulation obtained.
   Be not suspicious.

Gather friends around you,
As a hair clasp holds hair together.

Cause of delight;
Great accumulation obtained.
One's will is bold enough to fulfill great aims.

5. Fifth Six
   Be steadfast and upright.
   Even sick,
   Still persist.
   Won't die.

   Be steadfast and upright, even sick,
   Resting upon a solid line.
   Still persistent; won't die.
   The central way averts death.

6. Top Six
   Dark delight.
   Make a change:
   No fault.

   Dark delight reaches the top.
   How could it last long?

SIGNIFICANCE

The name of this gua is Delight, but the Yao Text is not so delightful. The aim of this gua is to expound the principle of harmony and delight. When one has accomplished great achievements and still remains humble, people will be delighted to gather around. However, this gua does not describe a situation of harmony and delight, but gives warning against self-satisfaction. It is too easy for one to indulge in one's own pleasure and forget the delight of other people. To the Duke of Zhou, delight was not for one's own sake but for all. The key is humility and sincerity; these two qualities bring harmony. This is the true meaning of Delight.

The image of this gua is Thunder ☳ above, Earth ☷ below. Thunder is the sound of yang energy. Thus, Confucius says, "The ancient king composed music to honor virtue and merit; with ardent eagerness, he offered it to God." When thunder bursts above the Earth, myriad beings are nourished by its yang energy and become delighted and alive. It is a time of enthusiasm and delight. An enthusiastic and delighted mood is helpful to one's success, but overenthusiasm and too much delight cause self-satisfaction. And self-satisfaction can lead to misfortune. For this reason, all the lines in this gua portend misfortune, except the second line.

This gua echoes the third gua, Beginning, the start of King Wen's work. King Wen's Decision on Beginning says,

> The beginning of a tiny sprout.
> Sublimely prosperous and smooth.
> Favorable to be steadfast and upright.
> Do not act lightly.
> There is somewhere to go.
> Favorable to establish feudal lords.

King Wen's Decision on this gua says,

> Delight.
> Favorable to establish feudal lords
> And mobilize the multitude.

After years of cautious and hard work, through perseverance King Wen manifested the vision he had proclaimed at the very beginning. An alliance of feudal lords was established, and he obtained supreme success. This gua reveals King Wen's delight with his success. The morale of the multitude in his realm as well as among the allies was high enough to send a punitive expedition against the Tyrant of Shang. However, the Duke of Zhou narrates the brilliance of his father not taking reckless action. King Wen realized that smugness over delight would bring misfortune. Instead, he stood firm as a rock, not merely for a whole day, but steadfast and upright from beginning to end. He gathered feudal lords around him like a hair clasp holding hair together. He gave warning that wallowing in delight, instead of keeping a sober mind, would bring regret. The shadow of delight had passed; it was time to prepare the next step in mobilizing the multitude for the revolutionary course against the tyrant and establishing a magnanimous new dynasty.

The host of the gua is the solid line at the fourth place, the only solid line in this gua. It is delighted to stay at the bottom of the upper gua and corresponds to the yielding line at the bottom of the lower gua. Thus, the Commentary on the Decision says, "The firm meets with response. Its will is fulfilled."

(1) Initial Six. Delight alternates to Taking Action (51)

This line is a yin element at a yang place—not correct. It corresponds to the solid line at the fourth place. Because this element is the only one in this gua to obtain support from above, it becomes immensely proud and overexcited. Being overexcited and oversatisfied, especially at the very beginning, will bring misfortune.

(2) Second Six. Delight alternates to Relief (40)

This line is a yin element at the second place; the only one located in a central and correct place. In a situation full of delight, most people indulge in worldly pleasures and tend to live day to day. Only this line stands in the middle and walks along the central path; thus, the Yao Text says that she is as firm as a rock, not merely for a whole day, able to remain just and steadfast through prudent consideration in making a clear distinction between right and wrong. In this way, during a time of delight, one would not muddle along without a clear purpose and plan for one's life. Gaining insight from this line, The Great Learning, one of the Four Books of the Confucian school, says that the superior person settles himself first; then he is able to meditate. After he is able to meditate, then he is able to achieve.

Here, to meditate denotes making a clear distinction between right and wrong through prudent consideration and steadfastness. In so doing, one should first become inwardly as firm as a rock.

(3) Third Six. Delight alternates to Little Exceeding (62)

The third line is a yin element at a yang place, neither central nor correct. Because the place is not appropriate, one in this place expects to obtain pleasure and delight from people. The line at the fourth place, standing above, is the host of the gua. Thus, the one at the third place stares upward, wallowing in delight. The Duke of Zhou warns that delay in keeping a sober mind can bring regret. It is not a realistic perspective and is not the right way to obtain delight.

(4) Fourth Nine. Delight alternates to Responding (2)

This line is the host; it represents a minister's position and is the only solid line in this gua. One at this place harmonizes with all the yin elements, especially the one at the king's place, the fifth place. They are close and complementary yin and yang. One in this position obtains the king's trust and becomes the source of delight. Thus the Yao Text says that as a result

of delight, great accumulation will be obtained. But the text does not say that circumstances are auspicious. Instead the warning is "Be not suspicious." The true source of delight does not rely solely on one's position. One should gather friends around, as a hair clasp holds together hair, and care about others. This is the true source of delight.

(5) Fifth Six. Delight alternates to Bringing Together (45) ☷☵

This line is located at a supreme place, but the Yao Text does not suggest circumstances are supreme. During the time of delight, people easily become proud. Pride is one hindrance to success. As a yin element at a yang place, this line is weak and fragile. It tends to be overly comfortable, as in a cozy nest. One wants to be great but mounts on the solid line at the fourth place, feeling threatened. Psychologically the place is not tranquil and stable. Thus the author of the text advises: "Be steadfast and upright. Even sick, still persist. Won't die." Here is a warning that in facing an overly comfortable situation one should remain steadfast and upright and be on guard against conceit and impetuousness. Otherwise, death awaits.

There are different ways to interpret this line. The Yao Text in Chinese is zheng ji. Zheng can mean steadfast and upright, or divination. Ji means sickness. Wilhelm translates zheng ji as "persistently ill" and Blofeld as "illness is presaged." James Legge translates it as a chronic complaint. Another translation puts a colon between zheng and ji and translates the phrase as "The divination: sickness." Here the fifth line is considered a further stage of the fourth line. The situation of the fourth line is that, as a result of delight, great accumulation will be obtained. "Be not suspicious. Gather friends around you, as a hair clasp holds hair together." This element, representing a situation that comes out of the fourth line, should remain steadfast and upright, consistent with what the text has advised. Even when sick, one should persist in the principle of keeping delight alive. The upper mutual gua is Kan, or Water. Kan also represents sickness. The upper gua is Zhen, or Thunder. Zhen represents the state of being alive. Thus, the Yao Text says, "Won't die."

(6) Top Six. Delight alternates to Proceeding Forward (35) ☰☳

The yielding line at the uppermost place represents the climax of Delight. A Chinese adage says, "Extreme joy begets sorrow." Darkness arrives; sorrow is coming. Delight is over. How can a dissolute life last long? The upper gua, Thunder, represents motion. One at this place needs to take action to make a change; then there will be no fault. The problem of this line lies in not following the advice of the Yao Text of the fifth line. The Duke of Zhou advises the one in the fifth place to remain steadfast and upright. Even when sick, persist in humility and seek harmony. Make a change; proceed.

Additional Reference Information for This Gua

Image:	Thunder above, Earth below
Recite as:	Thunder above Earth, Delight
Element:	Wood
Structure:	Five yin with one yang
Month:	The third month of the lunar year, or April
Host of the Gua:	Fourth Nine
Opposite Gua:	Little Accumulation (9)
Inverse Gua:	Humbleness (15)
Mutual Gua:	Hardship (39)

17
Sui • Following

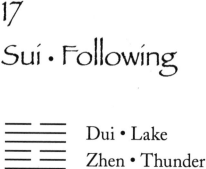

Dui • Lake
Zhen • Thunder

NAME AND STRUCTURE

Wilhelm translates Sui as Following. Blofeld translates it as Following, According With. In this book I adopt Following, which also carries the meaning of accompanying amiably.

Sequence of the Gu: *When one is humble and full of delight, surely people will come to follow. Thus, after Delight comes Following.*

The ideograph of the name of this gua is a beautiful picture consisting of three parts. On the left, there is an ancient ideograph of walking. At the top of it there are three strokes curling upward, representing three footprints. Underneath the footprints is an ideograph of the word stop, zhi. In the middle of the ideograph are three pennants with a tassel at the top of a pole, representing the standard of a king. On the right, a guard holds a weapon above his head, with one foot touching the ground and the other foot about to land—he is following the pennants. This is a picture of the procession of a commander-in-chief with guards accompanying and following. The structure of the gua is Lake ☱ above, Thunder ☳ below. The attribute of Lake is joy and of Thunder is movement. Thus, Following is moving forward with joy, or following. How can one influence people to follow?

The structure of the gua is Lake over Thunder. Two yang elements underneath a yin element form the image of Lake. One yang element underneath two yin elements forms the image of Thunder.

In both cases the yang are underneath the yin elements. Moreover, Lake represents the youngest daughter, and Thunder represents the eldest son. Lake over Thunder symbolizes that the elder complies with the younger. It demonstrates that the strong allows himself to follow the weak. Only by behaving humbly can one attract others to follow. If one wants to lead, one must first learn to be led. In this way, there will be progress and success. When the solid line at the second place of Exhausting (47) ☵ descends to the lowest place, and when the solid line at the uppermost place of Eradicating (21) ☳ descends to the fifth place, they each become Following. In other words, when the firm element descends to a place underneath the yielding, it represents Following.

This gua is very special, for it possesses the four virtues, as do the first and the second gua: yuan, heng, li, zhen. In ancient times, there was a noble woman who was offered marriage by a lord. She called in an augur to consult the I Ching. After manipulating the yarrow stalks, she obtained this gua. The augur said, "Congratulations. Sui is following. It possesses the four great virtues of yuan, heng, li, and zhen, as do Initiating and Responding. It is extremely auspicious for you to follow your husband and be married." Nevertheless, the woman said, "I have none of those four virtues. My situation is not compatible with the gua." She preferred to wait for another opportunity. The lady's decision exemplifies the way one should use the I Ching. It is not simply a matter of blindly following the oracle, but rather of understanding one's place within the situation.

Decision

> Following.
> Sublimely prosperous and smooth.
> Favorable to be steadfast and upright.
> No fault.

Commentary on the Decision

> *Following.*
> *The firm comes and places itself under the yielding.*
> *Moving with delight,*
> *It is Following.*

Great prosperity and smoothness,
As well as steadfastness and uprightness.
There is no fault.

All under Heaven follow the course of time.
Great indeed is the significance of timing!

Commentary on the Symbol

Thunder in the midst of Lake.*
An image of Following.
In correspondence with this,
The superior person withdraws for rest
When the sun goes down.

Yao Text

1. Initial Nine
   Situation has changed.
   Being steadfast and upright: good fortune.
   Going out to communicate,
   There is good effect.

   Situation has changed.
   Following what is correct leads to good fortune.
   Going out to communicate, there is good effect.
   One does not lose one's steadfastness.

2. Second Six
   Involved with little fellow,
   Loses great person.

   Involved with little fellow.
   One cannot be with both at the same time.

3. Third Six
   Involved with great person,

---

*According to King Wen's arrangement of the eight primary gua, Thunder symbol-
izes the sun rising in the east, and Lake the sun setting in the west. "Thunder in the
midst of Lake" symbolizes that sunrise will surely follow sunset, that time continues
in the proper order.

Loses little fellow.
Following, one gets what one seeks.
Favorable to abide in being steadfast and upright.

Involved with great person.
By the decision of his own will,
He abandons the one below.

4. Fourth Nine
Following obtains results.
Being steadfast: misfortune.
Be sincere and faithful,
Act in accord with the right way.
Make the purpose evident;
What error could there be?

Following obtains results.
There is misfortune.
Be sincere and faithful,
Act in accordance with the right way,
Which brings evidence of his deeds.

5. Fifth Nine
Being sincere and truthful
In an excellent situation:
Good fortune.

Being sincere and truthful,
In an excellent situation.
Good fortune.
His position is central and correct.

6. Top Six
Holding and involving.
Binding together.
The king is engaged
In presenting his offerings to the West Mountain.

Holding and involving,
It reaches the uppermost place, the extreme.

SIGNIFICANCE

This gua is very special; it expounds the way to influence people to follow. In human society, conflicts are unavoidable. Sometimes one has to give up one's own interest or ideas to chime in with others. This is the way to maintain harmony and delight in a community.

The host of the gua is the solid line at the bottom. It stands underneath two yielding lines, providing a picture of the strong humbling himself to the weak, maintaining harmony and delight. King Wen's Decision on the Gua expounds the principle of how to win people to follow; the Duke of Zhou's Yao Text explains how to follow others.

This gua tells us that King Wu followed his father's instruction in preparing to launch a punitive expedition against the Tyrant of Shang. King Wu called two gatherings to form the alliance at a place called Meng Jing. Over eight hundred lords came the first time. They asked King Wu to send a force against the tyrant. King Wu decided that the time was not ripe. Later, he called his armed forces together a second time. More minority clans came to join. When the armed forces arrived at Meng Jing, the eight hundred lords came again with their troops. As more followers joined, the alliance expanded. King Wen proclaimed that if people came together and followed, there would be progress and success. The Duke of Zhou records that going out to communicate with people brought about a good effect. It was wise to be involved with persons of great virtue and let the little fellows go. As more and more followers joined, opportunists and political speculators were unavoidably among them. It was important to act in accordance with the right way and have confidence in making the purpose of the alliance evident. To reach a common understanding and to coordinate action, King Wu held a ceremony.

(1) Initial Nine. Following alternates to Bringing Together (45) ☷☳

The bottom line of this gua is the principal line of the lower gua. In the I Ching, if one solid line is combined with two yielding lines in a primary gua, the solid line is the principal line. If there is one yielding line with two solid lines, then the yielding line is the principal line. The lower gua is Thunder—its attribute is motion. Only when one takes action can others follow. According to the structure, the yang element at the bottom place should take the leading role, letting others follow, but he humbles himself by staying at the bottom behind the two yin elements. Thus the Yao Text says, "Situation has changed." The Duke of Zhou encourages keeping steadfast and upright and predicts good fortune. Here, "situation has changed" indicates that the leading role becomes subordinate. Most people cannot accept such a change. The truth lies in going out to communicate with people. One who expects people to follow ought to know people first. Only following what is correct leads to good fortune.

(2) Second Six. Following alternates to Joyful (58)

The solid line at the bottom represents a little fellow; the solid line at the fifth place represents a great person. Confucius used to call his disciples little fellow, meaning young man. In comparison, a great person denotes a mature adult. The yin element at the second place corresponds to the yang element at the fifth place. They are a good match, but they are not close. So the yin element at the second place becomes involved with the yang element at the bottom; they are close together. It is human nature for most people to follow the nearest leader; this is what the yin element at the second place does. She is not cautious and cannot wait, and in so doing loses the great person. The message of this line is that when one intends to follow a leader, one should make the right choice.

(3) Third Six. Following alternates to Abolishing the Old (49)

Seeking relationships with the opposite sex is human nature. The second line is a yin element. There are two yang elements close by—one at the bottom and the other at the fourth place. Which is the right one? The yin element at this place does not correspond to the yin element at the uppermost place—they are both yin. In this case, the one at this place makes the right choice. She chooses the yang element at the fourth place rather than the yang element at the bottom. The yang element at the fourth place is not only closer but also mature. He is at a minister's place, better than the one at the bottom. So the Yao Text says, "Involved with great person, loses little fellow. Following, one gets what one seeks. Favorable to abide in being steadfast and upright." In the I Ching, the one at the upper place represents a great person, and the one at the lower place represents a little fellow.

(4) Fourth Nine. Following alternates to Beginning (3)

The yang element at the fourth place is firm and strong. It is close to the yang element at the fifth place, which is also firm and strong. The fifth place is a supreme place that represents a strong leader. A strong person following a strong leader should be extremely cautious. Even steadfast and upright, he might still be suspected. The best way is to be sincere and truthful, acting in accordance with the right path, so that all of one's deeds are self-evident. Making one's deeds self-evident is crucially important. This is the ancient wisdom of the Chinese.

(5) Fifth Nine. Following alternates to Taking Action (51)

The solid line at the fifth place is central and correct. It is a yang element at a yang place. One at this place should be a virtuous person. This element corresponds to the yin element at the second place, which is also central and correct. One at this place is also a virtuous person. In the I Ching, a central and correct firm line corresponding to a central and correct yielding line is extremely auspicious. This line symbolizes a virtuous person corresponding with another virtuous person. The situation is excellent and bodes well. The message of this line is that one should select the most suitable person to follow.

(6) Top Six. Following alternates to Without Falsehood (25)

The uppermost line of a gua has no further to go, no one to follow. Only the two yang elements behind follow closely. They join together and are difficult to separate. This kind of togetherness is a result of faithfulness and sincerity. The Duke of Zhou used the historical example of King Wu presenting his offerings to the West Mountain to indicate the importance of sincerity and faithfulness. Only through the sincerity and faithfulness of both parties can people join together without regret. In ancient China, presenting offerings to the mountain and river was a most important event. The Yao Text says, "The king is engaged in presenting his offerings to the West Mountain." The king refers to King Wu, son of King Wen, who was born on the West Mountain. Presenting offerings celebrated people's binding together.

Additional Reference Information for This Gua

Image:	Lake above, Thunder below
Recite as:	Lake above Thunder, Following
Element:	Metal
Structure:	Three yin with three yang
Month:	The second month of the lunar year, or March
Host of the Gua:	Initial Nine
Opposite Gua:	Remedying (18)
Inverse Gua:	Remedying (18)
Mutual Gua:	Developing Gradually (53)

18

Gu · Remedying

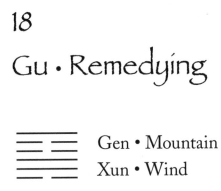

Gen • Mountain
Xun • Wind

NAME AND STRUCTURE

Literally, Gu means worm, particularly a parasite in the intestine. Wilhelm translates Gu as Work on What Has Been Spoiled; Blofeld translates it as Decay. Other translations use Poison, Destruction, or Corruption. In this book Gu is translated as Remedying.

Remedying is the inverse of the preceding gua, Following. According to the ancient sages' experience, one following others amiably may tend to go along with evil streams and become degenerate. In that case, one should turn over a new leaf and make a fresh start. Thus, the I Ching arranges Following and Remedying as an inverse pair because they are complementary. The pictograph of Gu shows three worms in a container. It indicates that in a container not used for a long time worms grow and develop, symbolizing a situation of ruin and decay and a need for remedying and innovating.

Sequence of the Gua: *Following others with pleasure and delight, surely something will happen. Thus, Remedying comes after Following.*

The structure of the gua is Mountain ☶ above, Wind ☴ below. Mountain represents the youngest son; it is a yang gua. Wind represents the eldest daughter; it is a yin gua. The attribute of Mountain is coming to a standstill; the attribute of Wind is following. Mountain over Wind presents a picture that the yin gua is willing to follow, but the yang gua is standing still. Thus the yin gua cannot move forward. Moreover, the yielding lines of both gua are lying under solid lines, symbolizing yin elements restrained by

171

yang elements and unable to do anything, just like the abandoned, unused containers where worms develop. This situation needs a remedy.

Although Gu, together with its ideograph, does not directly indicate that its meaning is remedying, considering the Sequence of the Gua and King Wen's Decision, it is appropriate to translate Gu as Remedying. King Wen's Decision says, "Sublimely prosperous and smooth. Favorable to cross great rivers." If Gu is "decay," "poison," "destruction," or "corruption," how can the gua deserve the most auspicious labels of prosperity and smoothness, and be favorable to cross great rivers? Confucius's Commentary on the Decision says, "The world will be regulated in good order. It is favorable to cross great rivers. It is time to go forward and do something. . . . It indicates a new beginning follows every ending. This is the course of Heaven." Obviously, Gu bears the meaning of turning over a new leaf and making a fresh start. On this ground, I adopt Remedying as the name of this gua.

Decision

Remedying.
Sublimely prosperous and smooth.
Favorable to cross great rivers.
Before starting, three days.
After starting, three days.

Commentary on the Decision

Remedying.
The firm is above and the yielding below.
Gentle and standing still.
This is Remedying.

Remedying.
Sublimely prosperous and smooth.
The world will be regulated in good order.

Favorable to cross great rivers.
It is time to go forward and do something.

Before starting, three days.
After starting, three days.

It indicates that every ending follows a new beginning.
This is the course of Heaven.

Commentary on the Symbol

Wind blows at the foot of the mountain.
An image of decaying and repairing.
In correspondence with this,
The superior person mobilizes people
And nurtures their virtue.

Yao Text

1. Initial Six
   Remedy for the father
   Is a son.
   The deceased father: no fault.
   Adversity
   Ends in good fortune.

   Remedying for the father.
   He succeeds in his father's will.

2. Second Nine
   Remedy for the mother.
   Not appropriate to be steadfast.

   Remedying for the mother.
   He finds the middle way.

3. Third Nine
   Remedy for the father.
   There is slight regret.
   No great fault.

   Remedying for the father.
   No fault in the end.

4. Fourth Six
   With ease, remedy for the father.
   Going forward,
   Humiliation appears.

With ease, remedy for the father.
Going forward, he will not succeed.

5. Fifth Six
   Remedy for the father
   Obtains a good reputation.

   Remedying for the father
   Obtaining a good reputation.
   He succeeds and manifests virtue.

6. Top Nine
   Not serving kings and lords;
   Highly elevates his own pursuit.

   By not serving kings and lords,
   He is concerned with his loftier spirit.

SIGNIFICANCE

The gua demonstrates the proper attitude to adopt in remedying a difficult situation. The ancient sages believed that no matter how difficult a situation was, there was always a way to work it out. The attitude of the one who deals with the matter is vitally important. Before starting, he should fully plan; after finishing, he must deeply reflect. During the course of action he should neither act with undue haste nor continue in the same old rut and be content with temporary success. Otherwise regret will come.

The name of the gua, Remedying, denotes a ruined and decayed situation caused by predecessors that needs a remedy. Thus, the Yao Text of five of the six lines mentions a father or mother, symbolizing the predecessors. The host of the gua is the yielding line at the fifth place. Although the line is yielding, it is at a superior place and gets the support of the solid line at the second place. Thus it obtains a good reputation.

This gua tells us that King Wen knew that the Shang dynasty was ruined and decayed. He considered that overthrowing the Shang dynasty was a remedy to the ruined and decayed situation. He proclaimed that remedy would bring progress and success to the people. But before starting, the remedy should be fully planned; after finishing, it should be fully reflected upon. King Wen regarded that taking over the decaying Shang dynasty

was to inherit the duty of caring for the people, as bestowed by Heaven. He regarded the ancestors of the Shang dynasty as his forefathers. Thus, after King Wu overthrew the tyrant he immediately presented offerings to King Tang, the originator of the Shang dynasty, as his ancestor. The Duke of Zhou records that the deceased ancestor (father) could be free of blame, and to remedy what happened to the subordinates of the Shang dynasty (mother) one should not be too severe. King Wu obtained a good reputation. He did not follow in the footsteps of the kings and lords by dividing the treasures and the spoils of war, but set a higher goal to establish a magnanimous empire.

(1) Initial Six. Remedying alternates to Great Accumulation (26)

The bottom line is the beginning of ruin and decay. The situation is not serious. The Duke of Zhou employed the image of a son who is dealing with the remedy for what happened to his father. The son is able; thus the father can be freed from blame. If the situation is perilous, the remedy should be hard work. In this way the end will be good. The message of this line is that in remedying an unfavorable situation one should not take an easy attitude and act carelessly.

(2) Second Nine. Remedying alternates to Keeping Still (52)

The yang element at the second place is central. It represents an able son, corresponding to the yin element at the fifth place. Since the fifth line is a yin element, a loving mother's image is employed. As a capable son with a firm character, but in a yielding place, he is able, in dealing with the remedy of what happened to a loving mother, to be considerate and not hurtful. The lower gua is Wind. So the Yao Text suggests, "Not appropriate to be steadfast." He should hold the principle of the middle path. Anything that goes beyond the middle path will hurt the loving mother. The message of this line is that in remedying something that has happened blaming the past is not helpful. One should hold the principle of the Golden Mean, walking in the central path and looking forward to the future.

(3) Third Nine. Remedying alternates to Childhood (4)

The third line is solid. It is a yang element at a yang place and beyond the central place, indicating an overly strong character. With this kind of character, in dealing with the remedy of what happened to the father, it would be difficult to avoid impetuosity. There will be regret. Since the yang element is at the top of the lower gua, Wind, and its place is correct, one in this place would be gentle to his father. There will be a little regret but no great fault.

(4) Fourth Six. Remedying alternates to Establishing the New (50) ☰

The fourth line is a yin element at a yin place, indicating that the character of the one in this place is weak, not able to deal with important matters. To deal with what happened to its predecessor, this character might procrastinate. It is too generous; if it continues in this way, it will not succeed and will bring regret in the end. The message of this line is that in applying a remedy one should cure the cause instead of dealing with the symptom.

(5) Fifth Six. Remedying alternates to Proceeding Humbly (57) ☰

The yin element at the fifth place denotes a gentle and generous character. This element is in the central place of the upper gua, a supreme place corresponding to the yang element at the second place, which represents the son. All these conditions show that he is in a favorable situation and obtains support from his capable son. In ancient times, King Tai-jia of the Yin dynasty and King Cheng of the Zhou dynasty, King Wu's son, were too gentle and generous, but they sincerely accepted the assistance of their respective capable prime ministers, Yin-yi and the Duke of Zhou. As a result, both of them had good reputations for managing the country well and assuring people peace and security. The message of this line is that in remedying a situation one should obtain the support of capable and virtuous persons.

(6) Top Nine. Remedying alternates to Growing Upward (46) ☰

The uppermost line usually represents a detached hermit of great wisdom. It illustrates a profound piece of ancient Chinese wisdom, that is, that one retires after achieving great success. Not everyone is able to do it. During the long course of Chinese history, only a few sages have been capable of carrying it out. Thus Confucius says, "By not serving kings and lords, he is concerned with his loftier spirit." This quotation was widely used by Taoist recluses.

Additional Reference Information for This Gua

Image:	Mountain above, Wind below
Recite as:	Mountain above Wind, Remedying
Element:	Earth
Structure:	Three yin with three yang
Month:	The third month of the lunar year, or April
Host of the Gua:	Fifth Six
Opposite Gua:	Following (17)
Inverse Gua:	Following (17)
Mutual Gua:	Marrying Maiden (54)

19
Lin · Approaching

☷ Kun · Earth
☱ Dui · Lake

NAME AND STRUCTURE

Lin expounds the principle of leadership. Both Wilhelm and Blofeld translate Lin as Approach. Other translations employ Leadership, Overseeing, Prevailing, and Arriving. In this book, Approaching is adopted.

Sequence of the Gua: *When many things have happened and been remedied, one can approach greatness. Thus, after Remedying, Approaching follows.*

When many things have happened, there are opportunities for one to achieve greatness. It is not beneficial to wait—one should respond positively and immediately. This is the essence of Lin.

The Chinese word Lin has a range of meanings. Originally, it meant "overlooking," in the sense of viewing from above. It implies occupying a height or a commanding position to lead, rule, and control. This concept derives from the structure of the gua, Earth ☷ above, Lake ☱ below. Earth above Lake suggests overlooking the Lake.

There are two solid lines at the bottom; they are approaching the four spaces occupied by the four yielding lines above. They are growing and expanding, suggesting a state where one is advancing, preparing oneself to be great, a leader. The ideograph of Lin hints that Lin denotes approaching and becoming great. The ideographs selected for this book come from inscriptions on bronze objects of the Zhou dynasty. It is quite possible that at that time Lin did carry the meaning of becoming great. The ideograph consists of three parts. At the top left is the ideograph

chen, which represents an official of a feudal ruler. A semicircle symbolizes a bending body, representing an official, bowing in deference to the ruler. On the top right is the ideograph ren, representing a person. It looks like a person standing. Usually it looks similar to the ideograph at the thirteenth gua, Tong Ren. Here, for artistic reasons, one leg is much longer than the other leg. Underneath the official and the great man there are three horseshoe shapes representing three mouths. In ancient China people were counted by mouths. These three mouths are arranged with one mouth leading the other two forward, symbolizimg a leader who is guiding a group of people or a multitude, moving forward, promoting, or becoming great. The connotation "great" derives from the ideographs for the official and the great man at the top.

The attribute of the lower gua, Lake, is joy. The attribute of the upper gua, Earth, is yielding. According to the ancients, yielding joyfully ensures one's progress and success. This gua is absolutely auspicious. According to the law of the waning and waxing of yin and yang, after six months, the yin will be prosperous and the yang will decline. This gua is one of the twelve message gua, each representing a month. This gua represents the twelfth month of the Chinese lunar calendar. The yang energy becomes prosperous in the eleventh month, so King Wen's Decision suggests that at the end of the eighth month there will be misfortune. A new cycle begins.

Decision

> Approaching.
> Sublimely prosperous and smooth.
> Favorable to be steadfast and upright.
> Ends in the eighth month;
> Misfortune comes.

Commentary on the Decision

> *Approaching,*
> *The firm is advancing and growing.*
>
> *Joyous and obedient.*
> *The firm is central and properly responded to.*
> *Great success along with his correctness.*
> *This is the Tao of Heaven.*

At the end of the eighth month,
There will be misfortune.
Recession is not too long in coming.

Commentary on the Symbol

Earth above Lake.
An image of Approaching.
In correspondence with this,
The superior person is willing to teach inexhaustibly
And, in his tolerance, protect the people without limit.

Yao text

1. Initial Nine
   Corresponsively approaching.
   Being steadfast and upright: good fortune.

   Corresponsively approaching.
   Being steadfast and upright: good fortune.
   His will is to act in the right way.

2. Second Nine
   Corresponsively approaching.
   Good fortune.
   Nothing is unfavorable.

   Corresponsively approaching.
   Good fortune.
   Nothing is unfavorable.
   Not everyone might be obedient.

3. Third Six
   Sweetly approaching.
   Nothing is favorable.
   Since worried,
   No fault.

   Sweetly approaching.
   The place is not appropriate.
   Since worried,
   Misfortune will not last long.

4. Fourth Six
   Closely approaching.
   No fault.

   Closely approaching, no fault.
   The place is appropriate.

5. Fifth Six
   Wisely approaching.
   Proper for a great prince.
   Good fortune.

   Proper for a great prince.
   He pursues the way of the middle.

6. Top Six
   Sincerely approaching.
   Good fortune.
   No fault.

   Good fortune sincerely approaching.
   The will is carrying on inwardly.

SIGNIFICANCE

This gua is very special. The four most auspicious virtues of yuan, heng, li, and zhen have been bestowed upon it. It expounds the principle of leadership. A leader should influence people with his noble character and conduct. The ancient Chinese believed that the king was the Son of Heaven. When the king arrived (lin) on Earth, he represented Heaven to protect and nurture his people. If the king acted in accordance with the will of Heaven, people from eight directions would come and follow him. The two solid lines at the bottom of the gua are qualified to be the host. They represent the advance of the firm. However, the firm element at the second position is central and properly corresponds to the yielding element at the fifth place; it is more suitable to be the host. Thus Confucius says, "Great success along with his correctness. This is the Tao of Heaven."

King Wen's Decision says, "Ends in the eighth month; misfortune comes." There are several possible interpretations. The basic idea rests upon the growth and advance of the yang energy. In a yearly cycle, yang energy emerges in the eleventh month of the lunar calendar. It is represented by the twenty-fourth gua, Turning Back ☷☳. The cycle of the waxing and waning of yin and yang is given in the following table.

eleventh month, December	Turning Back	(24)	☷☳
twelfth month, January	Approaching	(19)	☷☱
first month, February	Advance	(11)	☷☰
second month, March	Great Strength	(34)	☳☰
third month, April	Eliminating	(43)	☱☰
fourth month, May	Initiating	(1)	☰☰
fifth month, June	Encountering	(44)	☰☴
sixth month, July	Retreat	(33)	☰☶
seventh month, August	Hindrance	(12)	☰☷
eight month, September	Watching	(20)	☴☷
ninth month, October	Falling Away	(23)	☶☷
tenth month, November	Responding	(2)	☷☷

The eighth month, Watching ☴☷, is the inverse of Approaching ☷☱. At this time the yin is stronger than the yang. Thus, "Misfortune comes." Another interpretation is that the sixth month, Retreat ☰☶, is the opposite of Approaching ☷☱. From the eleventh month to the sixth month is exactly eight months.

This gua tells us that the time for establishing the Zhou dynasty was approaching. King Wen's Decision says yuan, heng, li, zhen. It also mentions that King Wu became sick in the eighth month. The Duke of Zhou narrates that as King Wu responded to the approaching situation, the divination augured good fortune and nothing unfavorable. But after he took over the Shang dynasty, there was no peace. The omen changed from nothing being unfavorable to nothing being favorable. King Wu was so occupied that he had no time to eat or sleep. He was a perfect leader—more wise, honest, and sincere than the tyrant. Approaching is one of the twelve tidal gua, representing the twelfth month of the Chinese lunar calendar. In the solar calendar, it is January.

(1) Initial Nine. Approaching alternates to Multitude (7) ☷☵

The first line is the beginning, symbolizing that the influence of a leader is becoming manifest. The yang element at the bottom corresponds to the yin element at the fourth place. They mutually influence each other with their noble characters. The bottom line is correct—a yang element at a yang place. His will is to act in the right way. Through steadfastness, there will be good fortune.

(2) Second Nine. Approaching alternates to Turning Back (24) ☷☱

This is the most auspicious line of this gua. A yang element at the second place is not correct, but it is central. It corresponds to the yin element at the fifth place. One is firm and strong; the other is gentle and docile. They are yin and yang mutually influencing each other with their noble characters. However, this yang element is close to four yin elements; there might be some obstruction. The commentary says that there is someone who is not truly obedient. Thus, one at this place should walk in the central path and exert influence with his firm and magnanimous character. In so doing, nothing is unfavorable.

(3) Third Six. Approaching alternates to Advance (11) ☷

All lines in this gua presage good fortune except the third one. "Sweetly approaching" is not inauspicious; the problem lies in neglecting the sense of proper timing and a favorable situation. One at this place should understand that her position is neither central nor correct. If one gives free reign to one's own will, the result will not be favorable. Instead, constraint is called for. Follow what Confucius advises: if one sees the error in one's self-centered behavior, then the misfortune will not last long. Advancing with joy, responding to the will of Heaven and the wishes of the people, will bring good fortune; then nothing will be unfavorable.

(4) Fourth Six. Approaching alternates to Marrying Maiden (54) ☳

The fourth line is at a correct place, a yin element at a yin place. It also responds to the yang element at the bottom. The fourth place is higher—it accords with the principle of Approaching. One at this place is at a commanding place, able to have a view from above and help people move forward. Thus the commentary on the Yao Text says, "Closely approaching, no fault. The place is appropriate." One at this place is in a perfect situation and is able to lead the one at the bottom by going forward with trust in harmony.

(5) Fifth Six. Approaching alternates to Restricting (60) ☵

The fifth line is at a king's place, a yin element in the central place corresponding to the yang element at the second place. It represents a brilliant and magnanimous, humble and wise leader who knows how to act in accordance with the principle of the Golden Mean. She is able to give full trust to subordinates to promote their talent and ability. This is the

wisest way to lead. Thus the Yao Text says, "Wisely approaching. Proper for a great prince."

(6) Top Six. Approaching alternates to Decreasing (41)

When Approaching is at the uppermost place, it reaches the climax. When things reach their extreme they alternate to the opposite. Generally, the top is not an auspicious place. However, in this gua it is an exception. Due to a gentle and docile nature, one at this place can kindly accept the two yin elements underneath approaching together. Not many leaders can do so; if one can, it presages good fortune for both the leader and the subordinates. To the ancient sages, when a leader was able to be gentle and humble, honest and sincere, there was always no fault and good fortune.

Additional Reference Information for This Gua

Image:	Earth above, Lake below
Recite as:	Earth above Lake, Approaching
Element:	Earth
Structure:	Two yang with four yin
Month:	The twelfth month of the lunar year, or January
Host of the Gua:	Second Nine
Opposite Gua:	Retreat (33)
Inverse Gua:	Watching (20)
Mutual Gua:	Turning Back (24)

20

Guan • Watching

Xun • Wind
Kun • Earth

NAME AND STRUCTURE

Guan means watching, observing, examining, contemplating. Wilhelm translates Guan as Contemplation and Blofeld as Looking Down. In this book, the term Watching is adopted. Guan is the inverse of the preceding gua, Lin (Approaching). Lin is looking downward from above. Guan is looking upward from below. Both indicate keeping a watch over, yet from different perspectives. They are complementary concepts.

The ideograph consists of two parts. On the left is a front view of a bird with two bright eyes wide open. The name of the bird is guan, which provides the sound for the name of the gua. At the top right is an image of an eye. Originally the pictograph was expressed exactly in the form of an eye. Later on, becoming part of a complicated ideograph, the horizontal eye was turned sideways to form a vertical oval. Later still, on inscriptions on bronze objects of the Sui dynasty (589–618), the oval-shaped eye was changed to a vertical rectangular form. Underneath the vertical eye is the ideograph ren, a person. The ideograph shows a bird and a human watching attentively with their eyes wide open.

Sequence of the Gua: *When things become great, they require careful attention. Thus, after Approaching, Watching follows.*

In China a Taoist temple is termed Tao Guan; literally it is "a place for watching the Tao." The esoteric secret of Taoist meditation is watching—watching the breath, or the flowing of energy, or nothing.

185

The purpose of watching is keeping alert. While chanting or reciting scriptures both Buddhist and Taoist monks beat wooden fish rhythmically. Because fish never close their eyes, the wooden fish remind one to stay alert. The Chinese name for Avalokiteshvara (an incarnation of the Buddha) is Guan-yin. Guan-yin means watching (guan) the sound (yin). To the Chinese, contemplation is watching; contemplative watching is focusing on one point and being attentive. During meditation, the sect that worships Guan-yin watches the sound either inside or outside the body. Watching the sound but not getting caught up in it, one is totally detached from the world. This gua not only sheds light on meditation but also expounds the truth that people should always keep their eyes open, watching the virtue of a leader. Thus a leader should always be sensitive to morality and justice and manifest these qualities to his people.

The structure of the gua is Wind ☰ above, Earth ☷ below, an image of Wind flowing over the Earth. In accordance with this image, the ancient kings toured various regions to observe people's lives and give instruction. This gua is an extension of the previous gua, Approaching ☳. In the previous gua two solid lines are at the bottom, moving upward. In this gua the two solid lines are at the top. Those who are at the top should exercise caution in their words and deeds because they are always watched by the people below.

The Decision employs the analogy of offering a sacrifice to show one's sincerity. In ancient China, before offering a sacrifice a person would wash his hands thoroughly. It was actually a process of meditation, focusing one's heart and mind on the offering. In this way, the offerer took the opportunity to kindle and radiate his reverence and sincerity while washing his hands. Then the reverence and sincerity from his inner being would spontaneously appear and resonate to the observers. This is the way the ruler set forth instruction to his people, by his own example.

Decision

> Watching.
> Hands are washed,
> Offerings are not yet presented.
> Being sincere and truthful,
> Reverence appears.

Commentary on the Decision

> *The great virtue to be watched is above,*
> *Gentle and obedient.*
> *In the central position and correct place,*
> *He exhibits his virtue to all under Heaven.*
>
> *Watching.*
> *Hands are washed.*
> *Offerings are not yet presented.*
> *Being sincere and truthful,*
> *Reverence appears.*
> *In this way,*
> *Those below observe him and are transformed.*
>
> *Watching the divine Tao of Heaven,*
> *The four seasons proceed without error.*
> *Thus the holy sage adopts the divine Tao to give instruction,*
> *All under Heaven submit to him.*

Commentary on the Symbol

> *The Wind flows over the Earth.*
> *An image of Watching.*
> *In correspondence with this,*
> *The ancient king examined various regions,*
> *To observe the people*
> *And set forth instruction.*

Yao Text

1. Initial Six
   With a lad's view, watching.
   Inferior person:
   No fault.
   Superior person:
   Humiliation.

   > *With a lad's view, watching.*
   > *It is the way of the inferior.*

2. Second Six
   Through a crack, watching.
   Favorable for the chastity of a woman.

   Through a crack, watching.
   It is chastity for a woman.
   It is ugly for a man.

3. Third Six
   Watching one's own life.
   To advance or to retreat?

   Watching one's own life.
   To advance or to retreat?
   One should not lose one's own way.

4. Fourth Six
   Watching the brilliance of the kingdom.
   Favorable to engage in being a guest of the king.

   Watching the brilliance of the kingdom.
   The king honors the guest.

5. Fifth Nine
   Watching one's own life.
   Superior person:
   No fault.

   Watching one's own life
   By watching others' lives.

6. Top Nine
   One's own life is watched.
   Superior person:
   No fault.

   One's own life is watched.
   His mind cannot get peace.

SIGNIFICANCE

The theme of the gua is to demonstrate the wisdom of watching. There are two aspects of watching, subjective and objective. Subjective watch-

ing deals with one's self; it is to examine one's inner motives. Objective watching deals with others; it is to watch others' reactions to one's conduct. The wisdom of watching is like looking at a mirror, checking one's original intention and outward conduct. The ancient sages believed that inner sincerity is always revealed through one's conduct.

The two solid lines at the top are both qualified to be the host. Both are looking downward from above. The solid line at the fifth place is central and correct—it is more appropriate to be the host. Confucius's Commentary on the Decision says: "In the central position and correct place, he exhibits his virtue to all under Heaven." "He" denotes the solid line at the fifth place. All the yielding lines of this gua are watching the solid line in the fifth place.

This gua indicates that after King Wu overthrew the Tyrant of Shang, he presented offerings to King Tang, the originator of the Shang dynasty. King Wen's Decision says, "Hands are washed, offerings are not yet presented. Being sincere and truthful, reverence appears." King Wen and King Wu exhibited their brilliance and virtue to all under Heaven. The Duke of Zhou tells about people of different walks of life watching the new leader from different viewpoints. A new leader should watch his own life because his life is being observed by all people. Watching is one of the twelve tidal gua, representing the eighth month of the Chinese lunar calendar. In the solar calendar, it is September.

(1) Initial Six. Watching alternates to Increasing (42) ☲

The bottom line is a yin element at a yang place, neither correct nor central. It symbolizes an immature child. It is far from the fifth line. Besides immaturity, being situated at the bottom, this person cannot stand tall and look far. In other words, the person cannot take a broad and long-term view. For such a shortsighted and uneducated person, there is no fault. For one who is mature, it is shameful.

(2) Second Six. Watching alternates to Dispersing (59) ☵

The yin element at the second place is much more mature than the one at the bottom. She watches with a narrow point of view. The line is a yin element in the middle of the inner gua—in darkness. When she watches, she does so as if from the dark; the brightness dazzles her. The text employs an ancient tradition to explain the situation. In ancient China, women were not allowed to see the outside world beyond their houses. What they could do was steal a glance by peeking through the crack of a door. This behavior was proper for a woman, because she was not allowed to go out before she married. For a man, however, it was inappropriate. One should watch with a broad view as well as an open mind. An old Chinese adage says, "For one who watches a person through a narrow crack, the person he sees becomes narrow." In other words, by watching with a narrow view, one cannot obtain the authentic reality.

(3) Third Six. Watching alternates to Developing Gradually (53) ☶☷

The third line is at the top of the lower gua. It is in the middle and can either advance or retreat. The yin element at this place corresponds to the yang element at the top and is closer to the yang element at the fifth place. This signifies an opportunity to progress. When this yielding line alternates to a solid line, this gua changes to Developing Gradually (53) ☶☷. Developing Gradually indicates that one has time to watch one's own condition and make a decision about advancing or retreating. The message of this gua is that one should not follow others blindly.

(4) Fourth Six. Watching alternates to Hindrance (12) ☰☷

The fourth line is an extension of the third line. The text advises the one at the third position to watch his own condition before deciding to advance or retreat. This line offers direction for selecting a good lord to serve. In ancient times the fondest wish of a scholar was to assist a virtuous king to carry out a policy of benevolence. By watching people's lives, a scholar was able to understand the administration of the kingdom and the virtue of the king. Then he could make a decision concerning advancing or retreating.

On the other hand, the king also looked for virtuous scholars to be his assistants. When the king learned of a virtuous scholar, he would summon him for an interview and treat him with honor. The fourth line is close to the fifth line. It symbolizes a virtuous scholar summoned by the king as an honorable guest. An ancient scholar believed that watching the lives of the people would help him to grasp the virtue of the king. Likewise, when he experienced how the king treated him, he would know how the king treated his people. Thus, the Duke of Zhou's Yao Text says, "Watching the brilliance of the kingdom. Favorable to engage in being a guest of the king." By knowing the king, the scholar could make the decision of whether to serve the king.

(5) Fifth Nine. Watching alternates to Falling Away (23)

The fifth line is the host of the gua. It is a yang element at a yang place—central, correct, and superior. It represents a king of high virtue. Four yin elements are watching him. As a leader, one should be introspective about one's own life, to assess whether it is a good example for others to follow. Watching people's responses to one's words and deeds is another form of self-examination. Ancient sages instructed that by watching social customs and people's lives, a ruler could evaluate whether what he had done was right or wrong. In ancient China, such watching and introspection concerning one's own words and deeds were regarded as one of the highest virtues of a ruler or a sage. The message of this gua is that by watching another's response, one can come to know oneself.

(6) Top Nine. Watching alternates to Union (8)

The line at the top is above the king's place. It represents a sage. Even when a sage has retreated from the world, his words and deeds are still watched by the people. Although having retreated from the world, one's introspection and self-examination should not cease. The fifth line and the top line are the two yang elements of this gua. The fifth line stresses self-examination, while the uppermost line places emphasis on being watched by others.

Additional Reference Information for This Gua

Image:	Wind above, Earth below
Recite as:	Wind flowing over the Earth, Watching
Element:	Wood
Structure:	Two yang with four yin
Month:	The eighth month of the lunar year, or September
Host of the Gua:	Fifth Nine
Opposite Gua:	Great Strength (34)
Inverse Gua:	Approaching (19)
Mutual Gua:	Falling Away (23)

21
Shi He •
Eradicating

Li • Fire
Zhen • Thunder

NAME AND STRUCTURE

Shi means to bite. He means to close and unite. Literally, Shi He is to close the mouth to bite. This gua indicates a situation where, after biting, the obstruction is eradicated. According to the literal meaning, the name of the gua should be close the mouth to bite. Based upon its content, Eradicating is the most accurate term. Wilhelm translates Shi He as Biting Through and Blofeld as Gnawing.

Sequence of the gua: *When things are worthy of careful attention, surely people will draw close together. Thus, after Watching, closing together follows.*

The ideograph of the first character, shi, consists of two parts. On the left, a small square represents an open mouth. On the right, there is an ideograph of shi, which provides only the sound to the character, with no implication as to the significance. However, the ideograph of shi is a beautiful picture of an act of divination. At the top two little plants represent yarrow stalks. In the lower portion, there are two people in a hall. The horizontal line above them represents the roof; the horizontal line below represents the floor. The vertical line between them symbolizes a post or a pillar. The two persons are kneeling on the floor face to face. One is the diviner, the other is the inquirer. When this character is combined with the mouth on the left, it means "biting."

The ideograph of the second character, he, also consists of two parts.

On the left there is another mouth. On the right is a container that looks exactly like a type of bronze utensil of the Zhou dynasty having four legs and a cover. The stroke in the middle represents an object within the container. There is a tiny space between the cover and the container that suggests that the cover is being put on; it is an act of closing. This action signifies the movement of bringing two parts together. When this picture unites with that of the mouth, it appears as an action of bringing the upper jaw and the lower jaw together, or closing the mouth to bite.

The structure of the hexagram looks like an open mouth with an obstruction. The yang lines on the top and the bottom are the lips. All the yin lines resemble teeth. The solid line at the fourth place represents an obstruction between the teeth—the mouth cannot close. The union of the lips and the teeth requires the eradication of the obstruction. This picture indicates an obstruction in one's daily life that would affect union and harmony among people. Only through eradicating the obstruction can the high and the low—people from all walks of life—come together in harmony and understanding.

Eradicating reveals the principle of administering justice by removing obstructions in a peaceful community. To administer justice, sometimes punishment is necessary; but the punishment should be appropriate. The Confucian Analects say that when punishments are not properly administered, people do not know what to do. The upper gua is Li, or Brightness, and the lower gua is Zhen, or Thunder. Together they symbolize that carrying out an eradication of evils with punishment is like the action of a thunderbolt with the brightness of lightning. It is vigorous and resolute, but also fair and just.

King Wen's Decision on the Gua says, "Eradicating. Prosperous and smooth. Favorable to administer justice." The main theme of the gua is to administer justice by eradicating an obstruction. After an obstruction is eradicated, justice can be established. After justice is established, progress and success prevail.

Decision

Eradicating.
Prosperous and smooth.
Favorable to administer justice.

Commentary on the Decision

There is something in the mouth.
It is called eradication.
Through eradication, prosperity and smoothness come.

The firm and the yielding are equally divided.
The movement and the brightness are clearly shown.
Thunder and lightning are united and manifest their brilliance.
The yielding is in the central place and rules in its high position.

Although the place is not appropriate,
It is still favorable to administer justice.

Commentary on the Symbol

Thunder and lightning.
An image of Eradicating.
In correspondence with this,
The ancient king clarified the penalties
And strengthened the law.

Yao Text

1. Initial Nine
   Feet in stocks.
   Toes hurt.
   No fault.

   Feet in the stocks.
   Toes hurt.
   One is unable to walk further.

2. Second Six
   Biting tender meat.
   Nose buried.
   No fault.

   Biting tender meat.
   Nose buried.
   The yielding rests upon the solid.

3. Third Six
   Biting cured meat.
   Strikes a thick piece.
   Slight humiliation.
   No fault.

   Strike on a thick piece.
   The position is not appropriate.

4. Fourth Nine
   Biting dried bony meat.
   Receives metal arrows.
   Favorable to work hard.
   Being steadfast and upright: good fortune.

   Favorable to work hard.
   Be steadfast and upright.
   Good fortune.
   His brightness has not yet been sufficiently shown.

5. Fifth Six
   Biting dried meat.
   Receives yellow gold.
   Being steadfast: adversity.
   No fault.

   Being steadfast: adversity.
   No fault
   Because of acting appropriately.

6. Top Nine
   Wearing a cangue.*
   Ears disappear.
   Misfortune.

   Wearing a cangue.
   Ears disappear.
   Honest advice jars on the ears.

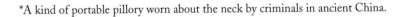

*A kind of portable pillory worn about the neck by criminals in ancient China.

SIGNIFICANCE

The gua displays the wisdom of administering justice. To administer justice, the executive should be clear in mind and firm in action. Removing obstructions by legal constraints should be as sharp as the act of biting through something. But the attitude should still be compassionate and the purpose educational. The aim is to prevent further mischief. Then there will surely be success. The host of the gua is the yielding line at the fifth place. It is in the central location of the upper gua. The Commentary on the Decision says, "The yielding is in the central place and rules in its high position." This refers to yielding line at the fifth place. Generally, the bottom line and the uppermost line represent persons with no social status. In this gua, they represent persons who receive punishment. The other four lines represent those administering the punishment.

This gua indicates how, after King Wu overthrew the tyrant of Shang, there was resistance and rebellion from the ruling class of the Shang. Counterattack was demanded. King Wen had instructed that eradicating the rebellion was crucial and would bring prosperity. But it should be based on justice. The Duke of Zhou records different punishments that were used in different cases. Although the legal constraints were sharp, they were carried out with a compassionate attitude and educational purpose.

(1) Initial Nine. Eradicating alternates to Proceeding Forward (35) ☷☳

The Yao Text says, "Feet in stocks. Toes hurt." This line refers to a person led astray by bad companions and caught by the trap. In terms of a human body, the bottom line represents the toes, while the top line represents the head. If one in this position is able to abandon bad behavior and adopt good conduct, there will be no fault. Confucius's Commentary on the Yao Text says, "One is unable to walk further," indicating an inability to do further evil.

(2) Second Six. Eradicating alternates to Diversity (38) ☲☲

The Yao Text says, "Biting tender meat. Nose buried." The second line represents an executive. It is a yin element at a yin place in the middle of the lower gua. Its position is central and correct, indicating that the executive is just and the punishment is appropriate. The Yao Text says shi fu mie bi. Shi is biting; fu usually means skin. In ancient times it also meant tender meat. Mie means destroy, and bi is nose. Here, mie bi should not be understood as cutting off the nose, which seems too severe a punishment. According to the opinion of most I Ching scholars, mie bi in this line means burying the nose. Nevertheless, here the criminal case is more serious than that represented by the bottom line. The executive's resolution is firm. The Yao Text shows a vivid picture, in the form of a story, of this firm resolution to abandon bad conduct, likening it to taking a forceful bite of tender meat, even burying his nose in it. Confucius's Commentary on the Yao Text says, "The yielding rests upon the solid." Therefore, the biting has to be forceful.

(3) Third Six. Eradicating alternates to Brightness (30)

The Yao Text says, "Biting cured meat. Strikes a thick piece." The third line is a yin element at a yang place, neither central nor correct. Its yielding attribute denotes that the executive is hesitant and irresolute. During the process of administering justice, there would be some hardship. It corresponds to the yang element at the uppermost place. One in that position is brutal. It is not an easy task to deal with brutality, as it is not easy to bite a thick piece of meat.

(4) Fourth Nine. Eradicating alternates to Nourishing (27)

The Yao Text says, "Biting dried bony meat. Receives metal arrows." Dried bony meat is harder than cured meat. The line suggests that the evil is more serious than that represented by the cured meat. The fourth place also denotes that the mischief has gone beyond the middle place. The case is serious and difficult to deal with, like biting bony meat. The executive is a yang element at a yin place, which signifies that he is sentimental. This element is at the bottom of the upper gua, Li (Brightness). His firmness and sentiment tend to be overresolute and decisive. One at this place should work hard on self-control and be upright. The Yao Text says, "Receives metal arrows," indicating that one should act as firm as metal and as straight as an arrow. This line is favorable but one in this place has to work hard and remain upright. Confucius says that his brightness is not yet sufficiently evident.

(5) Fifth Six. Eradicating alternates to Without Falsehood (25)

The Yao Text says, "Biting dried meat. Receives yellow gold." Dried meat is not as hard as dried bony meat. Because this line is at a supreme place, the case is less serious. A yielding line at the fifth place suggests that the executive is kind and gentle, because the line is central within of the upper gua. "Receiving yellow gold" is a Chinese idiom. In the system of the five elements, the color of Earth is yellow, representing a central place. Yellow symbolizes Confucius's principle of the Golden Mean, that is, to act appropriately without overdoing or insufficiency. To receive yellow gold also means to receive the assistance of the yang element at the fourth place. The purpose of punishment is educational, to prevent further mischievous conduct. For this reason, punishment should not be used lightly. Be steadfast. Be aware of the danger of punishment. In so doing, there will be no fault.

(6) Top Nine. Eradicating alternates to Taking Action (51)

The Yao Text says, "Wearing a cangue. Ears disappear." The solid line at the top is a yang element in a yin place. It is neither central nor correct. It represents one who is too stubborn and self-willed; he refuses honest advice. Because his evildoings are frequent, he deserves a heavy cangue— one so large it covers his ears. The image of ears disappearing also implies that one has stuffed one's ears and refuses to listen to honest advice. Thus Confucius's Commentary says, "Honest advice jars on the ears."

Additional Reference Information for This Gua

Image:	Fire above, Thunder below	
Recite as:	Fire above Thunder, Eradicating	
Element:	Fire	
Structure:	Three yin with three yang	
Month:	The tenth month of the lunar year, or November	
Host of the Gua:	Fifth Six	
Opposite Gua:	Replenishing	(48)
Inverse Gua:	Adorning	(22)
Mutual Gua:	Hardship	(39)

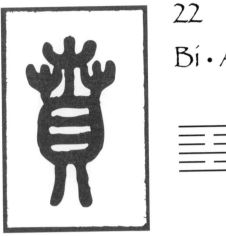

22

Bi · Adorning

$$\frac{\equiv\ \equiv}{\equiv\equiv}$$ Gen · Mountain
Li · Fire

NAME AND STRUCTURE

Bi is the inverse of the preceding gua, Shi He, or Eradicating. Eradicating is related to punishment; Adorning is connected to etiquette. The ancient Chinese thought that evil should be eradicated and goodness should be adorned. Thus, Eradicating and Adorning complement each other. Wilhelm translates Bi as Grace, Blofeld translates it as Elegance, and I use Adorning.

Sequence of the Gua: *Things cannot be exterminated and united abruptly. Thus, after Eradicating, Adorning follows.*

The ideograph consists of two parts. At the top are three sprouts of grass. This is the ideograph of hui, which means grasses. The lower part, bei, is a picture of a cowrie shell. In ancient times people used cowries with a smooth surface and brightly marked spots as ornaments and as money. When the two parts are connected, the ideograph implies that the grasses and cowrie are being used for adornment. The structure of the gua is Mountain above, Fire below—a picture of fire burning at the foot of a mountain. The flame shines upward adorning the mountain with brightness and beauty. For this reason, this book adopts Adorning as the name of the gua.

Adorning comes from Decreasing (41) ☲ or Already Fulfilled (63) ☲. When the yielding line at the third place and the solid line at the second place of Decreasing exchange places, this gua alternates to Adorning (22) ☲. And when the yielding line at the top and the solid line at the fifth place of Already Fulfilled exchange places, Already Fulfilled alternates to Adorning. In both cases the yielding lines come down to adorn the solid lines at their original place. Thus Confucius's Commentary on the Decision says, "The yielding descend and adorn the firm. . . . The firm ascend and adorn the yielding." This is another reason that I chose Adorning as the name of this gua.

When the yielding line at the third place and the solid line at the second place of Decreasing exchange positions, the inner gua alternates from Dui, Lake ☱, to Li, Fire ☲. Li represents brightness, success. When the solid line at the fifth place and the yielding line at the top of Already Fulfilled (63) ䷾ exchange places, the outer gua alternates from Kan, Water ☵, to Gen, Mountain ☶. Gen represents keeping still. Thus "a little favor" is possible.

Decision

> Adorning.
> Prosperous and smooth.
> Slightly favorable.
> There is somewhere to go.

Commentary on the Decision

> *Adorning. Prosperous and smooth.*
> *The yielding descend and adorn the firm.*
> *Therefore, there is prosperity and smoothness.*
>
> *The firm ascend and adorn the yielding.*
> *Therefore, a little favor; there is somewhere to go.*
> *This is the adornment of Heaven.*
>
> *The brightness helps people to act*
> *In accordance with the proper time and proper situation.*
> *This is the adornment of humanity.*
>
> *Watching the adornment of Heaven,*
> *One can see the changes of the four seasons.*
> *Watching the adornment of humanity,*
> *One can educate and transform all under Heaven.*

Commentary on the Symbol

Fire shines at the foot of a mountain.
An image of beautiful adorning.
In correspondence with this,
The superior person clarifies government affairs,
But dares not lightly make court decisions.

Yao Text

1. Initial Nine
   Adorning the toes,
   Leaves the carriage and walks.

   Leaves the carriage and walks,
   It is in accordance with his position that he should not ride.

2. Second Six
   Adorning the beard.

   Adorning the beard.
   He should act with the above.

3. Third Nine
   Adorning and moistening.
   Being perseveringly steadfast and upright:
   Good fortune.

   Good fortune from being perseveringly steadfast and upright.
   To the end no one will insult him.

4. Fourth Six
   Adorning plainly
   As pure white,
   Like a white horse with wings in pursuit.
   Not a robber, a suitor.

   Fourth six affords ground for doubt.
   Not a robber, a suitor.
   In the end no fault.

5. Fifth Six
Adorning hills and gardens,
Presenting a bundle of silk—little, little.
Humiliation
Ends in good fortune.

Good fortune of the fifth six.
There is joy.

6. Top Nine
Adorning with pure white.
No fault.

Adorning with pure white.
No fault.
He fulfills his will.

SIGNIFICANCE

The gua expounds the importance of etiquette. In ancient times, adorning carried the meaning of adorning one's social behavior. The ancient sages preferred to educate people to practice etiquette rather than to employ punishment to maintain social order. They set up a system of social mores so that everyone knew how to act properly according to their social status. They did not encourage punishment unless it was absolutely necessary.

The purpose of the gua is to indicate that adornment is not merely putting on external ornamentation. It is more important to bring out one's own natural beauty. Form and essence—yin and yang—should always complement each other. How can a thing exist without its basis? With reference to a human being, one must cultivate inner beauty, the beauty of the soul. Otherwise, the more ornaments are put on, the more the ugliness of one's nature is revealed.

Two lines of this gua demonstrate the truth and wisdom of how to adorn. One is the bottom line; the other is the top line. The first line advises leaving the carriage and walking. In accordance with his social position, he should not ride. The top line says to adorn with simplicity, as with pure white. He fulfills his will. One acts according to the social norm; the other acts from his heart. Comparing their attitude, the top line is more appropriate to be the host of the gua.

This gua relates that after King Wu overthrew the Tyrant of Shang, besides suppressing the rebellious he also distributed the treasures of the Shang to those who were loyal to the revolution according to their meritorious military achievements. At the same time he educated them to practice etiquette, cultivating social behavior. King Wen instructed that distributing the treasure to those who had meritorious achievement would bring progress and success, but only distributing a little was advantageous. Educating them to practice social etiquette was most significant. The Duke of Zhou encountered the result of such education. Most people responded to the mores of society and acted in accord with their social position. Education emphasized cultivating one's inner sincerity. Inner sincerity reveals one's true nature. Even one at a supreme position should still treasure one's true nature.

(1) Initial Nine. Adorning alternates to Keeping Still (52)

The Yao Text says, "Adorning the toes." This line is correct, a yang element at a yang place. It represents a person of strong character who is content to stay in a lower position. Toes symbolize walking. In ancient China common people were not allowed to ride in a carriage. For this reason, the one at the bottom prefers to leave the carriage and walk. This is a positive response to the mores of society; it exemplifies one acting in accord with one's position.

(2) Second Six. Adorning alternates to Great Accumulation (26)

The Yao Text says, "Adorning the beard." The four lines above the second line together form a mouth. Two solid lines represent the lips, and two broken lines represent the teeth. The second line, adjacent to the "mouth," symbolizes the beard. It is a yin element at a yin place, but it does not correspond to the yin element at the fifth place. However, it does connect to the firm line at the third place; they attract each other. Confucius suggests that the yielding should act together with the firm. An ancient Chinese adage says, "When the skin is gone, what can the hair adhere to?" Thus, the Commentary on the Decision says, "The yielding descend and adorn the firm. Therefore, there is prosperity and smoothness." This line suggests a model for adorning, in other words, setting a higher standard.

(3) Third Nine. Adorning alternates to Nourishing (27)

The Yao Text says, "Adorning and moistening. Being perseveringly steadfast and upright." This line is a yang element at the third place surrounded by

two yin elements. One at this place is adorned and his skin is moistened by the yin elements. But these two yin elements are not his proper mates; they are close but do not complement him. So the sage advises to remain steadfast and upright. One should not be lured by their affection. This line reminds us to maintain our own nature and not be influenced by people close by nor let adorning go to our heads.

(4) Fourth Six. Adorning alternates to Brightness (30)

The Yao Text says, "Adorning plainly as pure white." Adornment should be appropriate. Overadorning will lead to hypocrisy. If adorning is necessary, it should not cover up the true nature of what is being adorned. The Miscellaneous Notes on the Gua (the Tenth Wing) say, "Bi denotes colorless." The best way is to adorn but still retain one's true nature.

A story expounds the situation. The fourth line is a yin element at a yin place, corresponding to the yang element at the bottom. They are courting. However, a yang element at the third place lies between them, and so they cannot get together. The yang element at the third place is also interested in her, which makes her more anxious to get together with her compatible lover. Because she is a yin element at a yin place she is shy, but her love is true. Thus the Yao Text says that, while she looks adorned, she remains plain as pure white, "Like a white horse with wings in pursuit." Here the word white is used twice; it indicates sincerity. Sincerity reveals one's inner beauty, which is one's true beauty. On the other hand, the yang element at the third place is a yang element at a yang place—he is self-willed. The yin element at the fourth place tends to be overly suspicious. She suspects that the self-willed man is a robber, but he is a suitor.

(5) Fifth Six. Adorning alternates to Household (37)

The fifth line is a yin element, central to the outer gua. The outer gua is Gen (Mountain)—it represents hills and gardens. Thus, the Yao Text says, "Adorning hills and gardens." In ancient times hills and gardens were the living space of hermits, far from the luxurious city. Generally, most people adorn their outer appearance. However, one at this place stresses adorning the inner being. This line is an extension of the fourth line, emphasizing one's true nature. This location is the supreme place of a queen who adorns with only a bundle of silk. It seems too plain for a queen, but in the end there is good fortune. The message of this line is that even one at a supreme position should treasure one's true nature.

Confucius's commentary says, "Good fortune of the fifth six. There is joy." One finds joy in remaining plain at a superior position.

(6) Top Nine. Adorning alternates to Brilliance Injured (36) ☲

This is the host of the gua. The Yao Text says, "Adorning with pure white. No fault." This line has reached the uppermost place of the gua. Things that go beyond the extreme alternate to their opposites. One at this place adorns with simplicity. The upper gua is Gen (Mountain). The uppermost line here represents a person of high virtue and wisdom for whom external ornamentation is not important. Priority is given to inner beauty and simplicity. This is the key point of the gua—that while putting on adornment one must still preserve one's own beautiful nature. This attitude makes this line the host.

Additional Reference Information for This Gua

Image:	Mountain above, Fire below
Recite as:	Fire underneath Mountain, Adorning
Element:	Earth
Structure:	Three yang with three yin
Month:	The eighth month of the lunar year, or September
Host of the Gua:	Top Nine
Opposite Gua:	Exhausting (47) ䷮
Inverse Gua:	Eradicating (21) ䷔
Mutual Gua:	Relief (40) ䷧

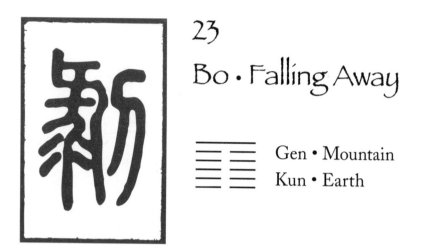

23
Bo · Falling Away

≡≡ Gen • Mountain
≡≡ Kun • Earth

NAME AND STRUCTURE

Wilhelm translates Bo as Splitting Apart, and Blofeld translates it as Peeling Off. Here I adopt Falling Away. In Chinese, when the character is pronounced bao, it means shelling or peeling—for instance, shelling peas or peeling bananas. When it is pronounced bo, it means decaying, corroding, or falling away. Applied to a mountain, it signifies a landslide. In human society, it symbolizes a process of declining, or the falling away of a social system or moral standard.

The ideograph of Bo consists of two parts. The main part, on the right, is a picture of an ancient weapon, dao, a knife. The left part was originally the character bo, providing the sound. Later this character was replaced by lü, the name of King Wen's famous sword. Lü also means a piece of carved wood. These two images represent an act of carving and engraving. During carving and engraving, pieces of wood or stone fall away.

Sequence of the Gua: *When adornment becomes excessive, beauty comes to an end. Thus, after Adorning comes Falling Away.*

The structure of the gua is Mountain ≡≡ above, Earth ≡≡ below. It symbolizes the falling away (landslide) of a mountain. The nature of a mountain is to stand high above the Earth. Here it lies on the ground, having fallen. There is only one solid line at the top of the gua; the remaining five lines are all yielding. The firm rests on the soft; obviously the foundation is not solid. All the yang elements have been nibbled away by the yin, one after the other. Now the five yin are approaching the yang at the top. They are strong enough to cause the moral degeneration of the yang.

Decision

> Falling Away.
> Unfavorable to have somewhere to go.

Commentary on the Decision

> *Falling Away is decaying.*
> *The yielding want to change the firm.*
> *Unfavorable to have somewhere to go*
> *Little fellows are growing and extending.*
>
> *Act in accordance with the situation and keep still.*
> *Contemplating the image,*
> *The superior person comprehends*
> *The alternation of increase and decrease,*
> *Also the alternation of fullness and emptiness.*
> *It is the Tao of Heaven.*

Commentary on the Symbol

> *Mountain erodes close to the Earth.*
> *An image of decaying and Falling Away.*
> *In correspondence with this,*
> *That which is above becomes benevolent to those below*
> *As if building houses on solid foundations.*

Yao Text

1. Initial Six
   Falling away at the leg of the bed.
   Erosion.
   Being steadfast: misfortune.

   > *Falling away at the leg of the bed.*
   > *Erosion.*
   > *It begins at the bottom.*

2. Second Six
   Falling away at the frame of the bed.
   Erosion.
   Being steadfast: misfortune.

   Falling away at the frame of the bed.
   Lack of associates.

3. Third Six
   Falling away.
   No fault.

   Falling away.
   No fault.
   He cuts off the relationship above and below.

4. Fourth Six
   Falling away: the skin on the bed.
   Misfortune.

   Falling away: the skin on the bed.
   Calamity is near at hand.

5. Fifth Six
   A string of fish.
   Favors them as if favoring court ladies.
   Nothing is unfavorable.

   A string of fish.
   Favors them as if favoring court ladies.
   In the end, no fault.

6. Top Nine
   A large fruit has not been eaten.
   Superior person receives a carriage.
   Inferior person's house falls.

   Superior person receives a carriage.
   He is carried along by the people.
   He ends up not being employed.

SIGNIFICANCE

This gua displays the principle of the waxing and waning of yin and yang. While the influence of the yin grows, that of the yang declines. When evil runs rampant, it is sure to affect what is good and correct. In the course of history many great empires have decayed and fallen away.

In this gua, five yin elements are covered by a yang element. Yang is substantial; yin is insubstantial. All decaying starts at the bottom. In the I Ching, Mountain also represents a bed or a house. For this reason, the image of a bed is used to explore different phases of the gua. The host of the gua is the solid line at the top. The five yielding lines are nibbling upward, trying to overthrow the solid. In a decaying situation, the solid stands firm; it is the only fruit that remains uneaten.

This gua relates that, after victory, decay in life and laxity in discipline appeared in the newly established Zhou dynasty. King Wen instructed that decaying and falling away was unfavorable for the new dynasty's development. The Duke of Zhou recounts different kinds of decay, developing from less serious to more serious cases. However, the central government represented by King Wen, King Wu, and the Duke of Zhou stood firm. Their influence produced a positive change in the situation. A new cycle began—after the falling away, a turning back followed. Falling Away is one of the twelve tidal gua, representing the ninth month of the Chinese lunar calendar. In the solar calendar, it is October.

(1) Initial Six. Falling Away alternates to Nourishing (27) ☷

Decaying starts at the bottom and damages the foundation. The first line indicates the beginning of this falling away. The floor underneath the bed has eroded. The decay reaches the leg of a bed. The evil encroaches upon the righteous. The firm and the correct are damaged. Misfortune results.

(2) Second Six. Falling Away alternates to Childhood (4) ☷

The second line suggests that the evil forces are growing gradually and steadily. If not stopped immediately, they become stronger. In the end they will cause one to fall away. In the meantime, the decay has reached the frame of the bed. The second line is a yin element at a yin place in the middle of the lower gua. The place is central and correct. Unfortunately, it does not respond to the yin element at the fifth place. One at this place lacks wise teachers and helpful friends.

(3) Third Six. Falling Away alternates to Keeping Still (52)

The third line is special. It is the only yin element responding and corresponding to the yang element. One at this place refuses to go along with evil persons and prefers to associate with the wise person at the top place. After this line moves from yin to yang, the lower gua becomes Gen, Mountain. The attribute of Mountain is standing still. At this place one is able to remain steadfast. She cuts off the relationship with the two yin elements above and the two yin elements below and maintains a close relationship with the one who is wise. In this way the evil forces can barely affect her. She loses only the evil influence from them. Therefore, there is no fault.

(4) Fourth Six. Falling Away alternates to Proceeding Forward (35)

The fourth line indicates that the situation is getting worse. The decay reaches one who is lying on the bed. This line is the beginning of the upper gua, much closer to the solid line on the top than the previous lines. If this situation does not change, no doubt, there will be misfortune.

(5) Fifth Six. Falling Away alternates to Watching (20)

The fifth line is in the central place of the upper gua. It is the top of the five yielding lines. One at this place is like a queen leading the four court ladies one after another like a school of fish, showing their submissiveness and loyalty to the king. According to ancient protocol, on the night of the full moon, the queen served the king in bed. Before the full moon, each court lady slept with the king one night, from the lowest rank to the highest rank. After the full moon, the court ladies reversed the rank order and slept with the king, one each night, until the full moon came again. This line represents a new situation. Evil forces no longer cause decay to the upright. On the contrary, they approach and show their submissiveness. After darkness comes the dawn.

(6) Top Nine. Falling Away alternates to Responding (2)

The uppermost line looks like the roof of a house; all the yin lines represent the walls. There is only one solid line, at the top. It is the only uneaten fruit, bearing the seed of new life. Because the solid line stands firm, its influence produces a change in the situation. When this solid line alternates to a yielding line, the yang element at the top will go back to the bottom of five yielding lines. A new cycle begins: Fu, Turning Back (24). Light and truth finally overcome darkness and evil and bring about a new phase of change.

Additional Reference Information for This Gua

Image:	Mountain above, Earth below	
Recite as:	Mountain falling on Earth, Falling Away	
Element:	Earth	
Structure:	Five yin with one yang	
Month:	The ninth month of the lunar year, or October	
Host of the Gua:	Top Nine	
Opposite Gua:	Eliminating	(43)
Inverse Gua:	Turning Back	(24)
Mutual Gua:	Responding	(2)

24

Fu • Turning Back

☷ Kun • Earth
☳ Zhen • Thunder

NAME AND STRUCTURE

Fu plays an important role in the I Ching. It is one of the twelve tidal gua used to explain the cosmology of the changing of the seasons—to go around and begin again. It represents the eleventh month of the Chinese lunar calendar, or December. According to the I Ching, "When yang turns back, it is Fu." This premise lies in the structure of the gua. When the solid line at the top of Falling Away ☶ alternates to a yielding line, Falling Away becomes Responding (2) ☷, the pure yin.

Responding represents the tenth month of the Chinese lunar calendar. During this period of time, the yang element seems to disappear. Actually it is brewing quietly beneath the surface. At the winter solstice, the twenty-second day of the eleventh month, the yang energy emerges. In northern China, people can actually feel the yang energy begin to surface at the turning point of that specific day. There is an ancient saying handed down over thousands of years: "At winter solstice, yang begins to surge." This idea is vividly expressed in the structure of this gua. For this reason, during the Zhou dynasty the Chinese New Year began with the winter solstice. The yang energy starts a new cycle.

This gua is the inverse of the preceding gua, Bo (Falling Away). Falling Away and Turning Back complement each other, reflecting the idea of going around and beginning again.

Wilhelm translates Bo as Splitting Apart and Fu as Return (the Turning Point). John Blofeld translates Bo as Peeling Off and Fu as Return.

The ideograph of Fu is formed of two parts. On the left side are three strokes representing three footprints going away. On the right side is the ideograph fu, which provides the sound as well as the significance of the character. At the lower right, three strokes represent three footprints returning. It was an ideograph of the remote past. At the upper right, there are two oval circles standing for two suns. In fact, the ancients employed the image of two suns to represent two yang elements. The upper sun shows that the yang is falling away, as it is at the top of Bo. The lower sun signifies that the yang is returning, as it is at the bottom of Fu. The horizontal stroke on the very top represents the number one. The whole picture of the upper right side of the ideograph explains that one yang is falling away and the other yang is turning back, going around and beginning again, in endless cyclic motion. This is the way of the Book of Changes.

Sequence of the Gua: *Things cannot go beyond the extreme. When they reach the limit, they turn back to the origin. Thus, after Falling Away comes Turning Back.*

This gua is a continuation of the previous one, Falling Away. During the time of decay, the dark forces proceed one after another until they reach the uppermost position. The situation seems hopeless. However, the Chinese believe that turning back and starting again is a universal and everlasting truth. When decaying has reached its extreme, a turning point comes. Then the light shines in the darkness, and the bright situation begins again.

Although this gua is not characterized as auspicious, it is. The inner gua is Thunder; the outer gua is Earth. The attribute of Thunder, the eldest son, is taking action; the attribute of Earth, the mother, is responding. Here, the mother responds to the action of the eldest son. The son can move forward without obstruction. Thus, King Wen's Decision on the Gua provides positive commentary.

Decision

> Turning Back.
> Prosperous and smooth.
> Going out and coming in.
> No harm.
> Friends arrive.

No fault.
The Tao of falling away and turning back,
In seven days comes the return.
Favorable to have somewhere to go.

Commentary on the Decision

Turning back is prosperous and smooth,
The firm returns.
Thus, going out and coming in, there is no harm.
Friends arrive; there is no fault.

Falling away and turning back
In accordance with the Tao of waxing and waning.
In seven days comes the return.
It is the Tao of Heaven.

Favorable to have somewhere to go.
The firm is growing and extending.
From this gua, Fu,
One can see the heart of Heaven and Earth.

Commentary on the Symbol

Thunder under Earth.
An image of Turning Back.
In correspondence with this,
The ancient king closed the gates of the passes
On the winter solstice.
Traveling merchants did not travel,
Nor did the king make inspection of his states.

Yao Text

1. Initial Nine
   Not going too far, turning back.
   No disaster, no regret.
   Supreme good fortune.

   Turning back without going too far.
   One cultivates one's virtue.

2. Second Six
   Beautifully turning back.
   Good fortune.

   The Good fortune of beautifully turning back.
   Subordinate to the kindhearted.

3. Third Six
   Repeatedly turning back.
   Adversity.
   No fault.

   The adversity of repeatedly turning back.
   Appropriate to be excused from fault.

4. Fourth Six
   Walking in the central path.
   Solitarily turning back.

   Walking in the central way,
   Solitarily turning back.
   Following the right way.

5. Fifth Six
   Sincerely turning back.
   No regret.

   Sincerely turning back.
   Being central, he is able to examine himself.

6. Top Six
   Confusedly turning back.
   Misfortune.
   There are calamity and trouble.
   Engaging in mobilizing the multitude;
   In the end: a great defeat.
   To the ruler of the state,
   Misfortune.
   Ten years:
   Unable to launch out again.

   The misfortune of confusedly turning back.
   Opposing the way of the ruler.

SIGNIFICANCE

This gua, together with the preceding one, displays the truth of changing. When things proceed to their extreme, they alternate to the opposite. Thus, after the period of falling away comes turning back. The light that has been banished returns. The change is not brought about by force—it accords with the law of Nature. The turning back arises spontaneously, like a bright spring returns after a severe winter. It is a matter of circumstance due to the appropriate time and situation. Because it is the law of Nature, no human force can alter it.

The host of the gua is the solid line at the bottom. It is the only yang element. Confucius's Commentary on the Decision says, "Turning back is prosperous and smooth, the firm returns." King Wen's Decision says, "In seven days comes the return." There are two interpretations.

The first explanation regards the seven days as a cycle. In the I Ching, each gua has six lines. For each line to move upward and return to its original place takes seven steps. If each step represents a day, the movement takes seven days. Seven days makes up a cycle. The second interpretation suggests that the seventh day might have been mistaken for the seventh month. The Chinese characters for day and month are only slightly different. The premise is that from the summer solstice in the fifth month to the winter solstice in the eleventh month there is a span of six months. The seventh month would begin a new cycle.

The Commentary on the Decision says, "From this gua, Fu, one can see the heart of Heaven and Earth." It reveals the cosmology of the Confucian school. Once Confucius said, "Heaven and Earth have a heart fond of creating and propagating." Confucian scholars advocate that one should follow the Tao of Heaven and Earth, that is, to be creative and propagate without ceasing. But the Taoists embrace a different view. Lao Tze says,

> Attain the highest void;
> Maintain the deepest stillness.
> When ten thousand beings rise and fall,
> Watch their turning back.

Taoists accept the idea of the cyclic motion of Falling Away and Turning Back and Falling Away again and Turning Back again, but they hold that existence originates from nonexistence and motion from nonmotion. Only when one reaches a state of total nonattachment is one able to see the heart of Heaven and Earth. In Chinese culture, the Confucian and Taoist schools constitute a yin-yang complement. The philosophy of the Confucian school is moving and doing. That of the Taoist school is retreating and doing nothing. Yet both philosophies originate from the I Ching.

This is an auspicious gua, because the yang energy returns. Yet the Decision does not mention its auspiciousness because the yang energy is still weak. Its achievement depends on effort. But the first line bodes supreme good fortune. In reality, no one is perfect. If one is able to turn back from not going too far toward the evil, it brings supreme good fortune. The second line presages good fortune because it is a yin element in a central place. One at this place is able to turn back happily to the good, because he is subordinate to the virtuous one beneath him.

This gua indicates that, through the influence of King Wen and King Wu, decaying was corrected in a short period of time. The social norm was reestablished. The courtesy and etiquette created by the Duke of Zhou was put back in place immediately. King Wen was happy about the situation; he claimed that turning back brought success. There was no harm for people going out and coming back. There was no harm in people of different kingdoms arriving and departing. Falling away and turning back moved in accordance with the Tao of waxing and waning. It was favorable to proceed. The Duke of Zhou records that through turning back without going too far there was no need for regret. Turning back happily to the good brings good fortune, but turning back repeatedly is dangerous. In turning back, one should walk along the central path with honesty and sincerity. Missing the proper time and direction for turning back brings about calamities.

(1) Initial Nine. Turning Back alternates to Responding (2)

This line is the host of the gua. It represents the beginning of an incident. The yang element at the bottom starts to grow and drive away the negative forces. It symbolizes the turning back of the light from the darkness. It also represents one turning back from a minor error. Because the error is at an initial stage, it is not yet serious. If one knows to amend one's mistakes at the very beginning, it is not too difficult to make a fresh start. There is nothing to regret. In the commentary on this line Confucius says, "Turning back without going too far. One cultivates one's virtue." This refers to his favorite student, Yen-hui. Once he said, "Yen-hui acts almost without fault. If there is anything not good, he never fails to recognize it. Once recognized, he never commits it a second time." This behavior, of course, is supremely auspicious.

(2) Second Six. Turning Back alternates to Approaching (19)

The second line is a yin element at a yin place, central and correct and close to the firm line at the bottom. One at this place quits the darkness and happily returns to the light. Because she attaches to and is influenced by the host, a kindhearted person, and returns to the proper path, there is good fortune.

(3) Third Six. Turning Back alternates to Brilliance Injured (36)

The third line is a yin element at a yang place, neither central nor correct. It is at the top of the inner gua, Thunder. The attribute of Thunder is unrest. One at this place tends to repeat errors, yet each time turns back. It is always possible to return to the light. Repeating errors is dangerous; however, by repeatedly turning back a person still deserves to be excused from fault.

(4) Fourth Six. Turning Back alternates to Taking Action (51)

The fourth line is in the middle of the gua surrounded by four yin elements, two above and two below. One at this place is walking with mischievous companions on a wrong path, but midway turns back to the right way. Because this line corresponds to the yang element at the bottom, it is possible not to go to the extreme. The Yao Text does not mention good fortune or misfortune because, for this gua, the yang energy has just started to turn back—it is difficult to make a prediction. On the other hand, when one acts in accord with the right way, one should ignore whether good fortune or misfortune will result. This is the proper attitude. Dong Chong-su, a great scholar of the Han dynasty, said, "A benevolent person acts in accordance with what is proper, he seeks not profit. He illuminates the Tao, counts not the merits." The true spirit of the I Ching is to do what is proper at the proper time in the proper way. Good fortune and misfortune are the consequence of one's actions.

(5) Fifth Six. Turning Back alternates to Beginning (3)

The fifth line is at a superior place, central to the upper gua, Earth. One at this place is honest and sincere. She is able to examine her own deeds and follow the ways of the Golden Mean. At the time of turning back, she endeavors to perfect herself. There is no regret.

(6) Top Six. Turning Back alternates to Nourishing (27) ☷☳

The uppermost line is a yin element at a yin place; its attribute is weakness. The place is not central, indicating that the person has lost her way and missed the opportunity to turn back from error. There will be calamities; even after a long period of time the disaster will not be repaired. In this line, the upper gua, Earth, represents the land of a country. The uppermost line represents the place of Heaven and an emperor. For this reason, the Yao Text says that the misfortune will be in the form of a natural calamity as well as calamities caused by the weakness of the emperor. The message of this line is that at the turning point—if one obstinately sticks to the wrong course and refuses to turn back—there will surely be danger.

Additional Reference Information for This Gua

Image:	Earth above, Thunder below
Recite as:	Thunder under Earth, Turning Back
Element:	Earth
Structure:	Five yin with one yang
Month:	The eleventh month of the lunar year, or December
Host of the Gua:	Initial Nine
Opposite Gua:	Encountering (44) ☰
Inverse Gua:	Falling Away (23) ☶
Mutual Gua:	Responding (2) ☷

25
Wu Wang · Without Falsehood

☰	Qian • Heaven
☳	Zhen • Thunder

NAME AND STRUCTURE

Wu Wang literally means not untruthful. Wilhelm translates Wu Wang as Innocence (the Unexpected) and Blofeld as Integrity, the Unexpected. In this book I adopt the term Without Falsehood. In Chinese, Wu means not, and Wang is untruthful, dishonest, or insincere. Thus, Wu Wang means truthful, honest, and sincere, without any fabrication. It was considered to be the natural state of the individual.

Sequence of the Gua: *When the turning point returns, there will be no untruthfulness and insincerity taking place. Thus, after Turning Back, Without Falsehood follows.*

Wu Wang is an abstract term, very difficult to express with ideographs. There are, however, two ideographs for the name of the gua. The first resembles a person bending his back carrying a heavy load. This image, suggesting having no breath, is used to express "no." The upper part consists of three strokes representing a heavy load; the lower part is the ideograph for a person, ren. The person is winded and eventually will run out of breath.

The second ideograph consists of two parts. The upper part, wang, provides the sound as well as the significance. Wang means "to walk away." The ancients drew an ideograph of a person at the top. Underneath is a vertical stroke connected to a horizontal stroke, symbolizing the act of walking away. Beneath this image is an ideograph of a woman. The

ideograph for woman is similar to the ideograph for person, except that
there is a curved line in the middle representing the breasts of a woman.
These two images together express that the woman is walking away. A
woman walking away was an ancient symbol of falseness.

In *The Biography of Prince Chun Shen*, the famous historian Si-ma
Qian of the Western Han dynasty (206 B.C. to A.D. 24) referred to Wu
Wang as "not anticipated" instead of "not false." In ancient times the
words anticipated and unfaithful shared the same sound but were written differently. This change bears a philosophical meaning: truthfulness
is the Tao of Heaven. As a human being, one does the best one can. As
for good fortune or bad fortune, blessing or calamity, events had to take
their own course. One should not live in anticipation. This is the meaning of Wu Wang.

Wu Wang comes from Retreat (33) ☰☶. When the solid line at the
top of Retreat "retreats" to the bottom, Retreat alternates to Without
Falsehood (25) ☰☳. Thus Confucius's Commentary on the Decision
says, "The firm comes from the outer [gua] and becomes the host of
the inner [gua]." When the solid line at the second place of Contention
(6) ☰☵ interchanges with the yielding line at the bottom, Contention
alternates to Without Falsehood. The yang element at the second place
and the yin element at the bottom of Contention are not correct. After
they change places, both of them are correct. This change is reasonable
and equitable—truthful.

The structure of the gua is Heaven ☰ above, Thunder ☳ below.
The inner gua is Thunder, symbolizing motion; the outer gua is Heaven,
indicating strength. The solid line at the fifth place is firm, central, and
correct and corresponds to the yielding line at the second place, which is
also central and correct. These two conditions provide a very auspicious
picture of strength with motion—a state totally free from untruthfulness, dishonesty, and insincerity. For this reason, this gua possesses the
four supreme virtues—yuan, heng, li, and zhen, the virtues of Heaven.
The ancient sages considered thunder to be the sound of Heaven. The
thunder rolling under Heaven proclaimed these virtues to myriad beings.
Those who preserved and nurtured these virtues were naturally aligned
with the will of Heaven and would be powerful and endowed with the
potential to be successful. Thus Confucius's Commentary on the Decision
says, "Movement with strength; the firm is at the central place and has a
correspondent. Great prosperity and smoothness through its correctness.
This is the will of Heaven."

Decision

> Without Falsehood.
> Sublimely prosperous and smooth.
> Favorable to be steadfast and upright.
> If one's intention is not truthful,
> There is trouble.
> Unfavorable to have somewhere to go.

Commentary on the Decision

> *Without Falsehood.*
> *The firm comes from the outer*
> *And becomes the host of the inner.*
>
> *Movement with strength;*
> *The firm is at the central place and has a correspondent.*
> *Great prosperity and smoothness through its correctness.*
> *This is the will of Heaven.*
>
> *If one's intention is not truthful,*
> *One will fall into errors.*
> *It is unfavorable for one*
> *To have somewhere to go.*
> *When truthfulness is gone,*
> *Where can one go?*
> *When the will of Heaven will not protect,*
> *How can anything be done?*

Commentary on the Symbol

> *Under Heaven, Thunder rolls.*
> *An image of all things accompanied by truthfulness.*
> *In correspondence with this,*
> *The ancient king enriches his virtue in harmony with the time*
> *And nurtures myriad beings.*

Yao Text

1. Initial Nine
   Without falsehood.

Going forward: good fortune.

Going forward with no falsehood.
His will will be fulfilled.

2. Second Six
    Not counting on the harvest while plowing,
    Nor on the results while tilling.
    Then, favorable to have somewhere to go.

    Not counting on the harvest while plowing.
    One does not aim for wealth.

3. Third Six
    A catastrophe of no falsehood,
    As if a tethered cow is carried off by a passerby.
    Passerby's gain,
    Villager's loss.

    The passerby gets the cow.
    It is a loss to the villagers.

4. Fourth Nine
    Appropriate to be steadfast and upright.
    No fault.

    Appropriate to be steadfast and upright.
    No fault.
    He is able to firmly hold fast his nature.

5. Fifth Nine
    An illness for no falsehood.
    No medicine.
    A joyful occasion.

    Medicine for no falsehood.
    One should not try.

6. Top Nine
    Without falsehood.
    Take action; there is trouble.
    Nothing is favorable.

    Action without falsehood.
    Misfortune is due to its dead end.

SIGNIFICANCE

This gua displays the wisdom of holding to the truth—that is, no matter how situations change, truthfulness never changes. The ancient Chinese did not have a personal God; they submitted to the will of Heaven and resigned themselves to their fate. They believed that to live and act in harmony with the will of Heaven was the nature and the duty of humanity. To act in accordance with the virtue of Heaven would eventually bring everlasting fortune and success. If one had this faith, then one was able to not count on the harvest while plowing. This attitude does not neglect the law of cause and effect. What is important is whether one's attitude and motivation are aligned with the virtue of Heaven. What is considered first is not the reward one will attain, but whether the work is really good for humanity. Fostering and nurturing the myriad beings is the virtue of Heaven.

The solid line at the bottom and the solid line at the fifth place are qualified to be the hosts of the gua. However, the bottom line is the starting point of a gua. In this gua, one starts with truthfulness. Truthfulness is the nature of humanity. When one approaches a task, one should start with truthfulness. For this reason, the bottom line is more suitable to be host of this gua.

This gua tells us that after King Wu overthrew the Tyrant of Shang, there was decay among the people. It was corrected before it had gone too far. The social norm returned in a short period of time. King Wen said that the principle of the new administration should be truthfulness. He accepted the lessons learned from decay and pointed out that if one's intention, especially that of a leader, was not truthful he would fall into error. It would not be favorable for him to move in any direction. The Duke of Zhou recalls that advancement with truthfulness brought good fortune. For a just cause one should count on neither the harvest nor the result while recultivating old land. Even if truthfulness encounters misfortune, one should still remain steadfast and upright. But in taking action, if the direction is lost, there would be no advantage.

(1) Initial Nine. Without Falsehood alternates to Hindrance (12) ☷

The first line is a yang element at a yang place. It is the host of the inner gua, the beginning of Without Falsehood. The yang element at the second place of Contention (6) ☰ is not in a correct place. After it descends to the initial place, swapping places with the initial six, it becomes correct, and Contention becomes Without Falsehood. Because this initial nine is firm and strong, truthful and sincere, it also becomes the host of Without Falsehood. Of course, this brings good fortune. His will will be fulfilled.

(2) Second Six. Without Falsehood alternates to Fulfillment (10)

The second line is a yin element at a yin place. Its attribute is yielding and responding, central and correct. One at this position is able to align with the will of Heaven and acts in harmony with Nature. She does not count on the harvest while plowing nor on the results while recultivating old soil. This is the true spirit of Without Falsehood. With this attitude of pursuing the truth, there will be advantage in any direction.

(3) Third Six. Without Falsehood alternates to Seeking Harmony (13)

The third line is a yin element at a yang place, which is not correct. Being truthful is virtuous, but it does not necessarily bring good fortune all the time. The case of the third line is that of a tied-up cow being carried off by a passerby. It is an unexpected misfortune. In Chinese, it is called "a misfortune of wu wang," because the one encountering this misfortune is doing nothing wrong. The truth holds that when one encounters this kind of misfortune, a truthful person still holds to being truthful. This line carries an important message. One should not have any anticipation of good fortune or misfortune, blessing or calamity. One just does the best he or she can and lets things take their natural course. This is the true meaning of Wu Wang.

(4) Fourth Nine. Without Falsehood alternates to Increasing (42)

The fourth line is a solid line at the bottom of the upper gua, Heaven. Its attribute is firmness and strength. It has no correspondent in the lower gua, which means that one at this place has no secrets. He is able to remain steadfast and upright no matter what situations may arise. This is Wu Wang. In this way, of course, there is no fault.

(5) Fifth Nine. Without Falsehood alternates to Eradicating (21)

The fifth line is a yang element at a yang place. It is central and correct and at the supreme place of the upper gua, Heaven. It corresponds to the yin element at the second place. It is one of the most auspicious lines in this gua. All these circumstances show that one at this place is firm and strong, truthful and sincere. He is not able to be hypocritical, as a healthy person is not able to be sick. If a healthy person employs medicine, it is

not truthful. An old Chinese adage says, "Truthfulness need not deal with artificiality as a healthy person need not deal with medicine."

(6) Top Nine. Without Falsehood alternates to Following (17)

The yang line at the uppermost place displays the truth of Without Falsehood. One at this place is truthful and not hypocritical. However, he has reached the extreme of Without Falsehood. Thus, the Yao Text advises that it is better not to take action. This line indicates that one should be truthful to the time and situation. Advance at the proper time to advance, and retreat in a situation favorable for retreat. To act in accordance with the proper time and the most favorable conditions is the true meaning of Without Falsehood. In this way one is able to avoid unnecessary misfortune.

Additional Reference Information for This Gua

Image:	Heaven above, Thunder below
Recite as:	Thunder rolls under Heaven, Without Falsehood
Element:	Metal
Structure:	Four yang with two yin
Month:	The ninth month of the lunar year, or October
Host of the Gua:	Initial Nine
Opposite Gua:	Growing Upward (46)
Inverse Gua:	Great Accumulation (26)
Mutual Gua:	Developing Gradually (53)

26

Da Xü • Great Accumulation

=== Gen • Mountain
=== Qian • Heaven

NAME AND STRUCTURE

In Chinese, Da means great, and Xü means accumulation. Thus, taken together Da Xü is Great Accumulation. Da Xü is the inverse of the preceding gua, Without Falsehood. Great Accumulation refers to one's virtue. If one is truthful, naturally one accumulates virtue. Wilhelm translates Da Xü as The Taming Power of the Great. Blofeld translates it as The Great Nourisher.

The name of this gua consists of two Chinese characters. The first character means great. The second character means to raise livestock or to store up something.

In Chinese, the term storing up can be applied to storing up things, nourishment, or virtue. In terms of this gua it is to store up virtue.

There are two ideographs that demonstrate the meaning of this gua. The first ideograph denotes great. The ancient Chinese, as has been mentioned earlier, believed that Heaven is great, Earth is great, and human beings are also great. Thus, the ancients employed a picture of a human to represent greatness. The picture above is of a person standing upright with arms and legs wide open, showing his greatness. The second ideograph consists of two parts. The lower part represents a field and the upper part stands for two piles of grass stored one upon the other with a cover over the top. The ideograph provides a picture of storing up or accumulating.

Sequence of the Gua: *When truthfulness is present, accumulation is possible. Thus, after Without Falsehood, Great Accumulation follows.*

When the yielding line at the uppermost place of Needing (5) ☷ is interchanged with the solid line at the fifth place, Needing alternates to Great Accumulation. It is a sign of great virtue that one at the uppermost place lets one at the fifth place take over his place and stand above him. This is the spirit of Great Accumulation.

 The structure of the gua is Mountain ☶ above, Heaven ☰ below. It presents a picture of Heaven set between the peaks of the mountains. The ancients saw the clouds in Heaven accumulating rain between the peaks. This kind of accumulation was considered great. Furthermore, the inner gua is Qian (Heaven), a symbol of pure yang. Qian is a yang gua. The outer gua is Gen (Mountain). Gen represents the youngest son and is also a yang gua. Yang represents great; thus, the ancient Chinese termed this gua great. (In the I Ching, when there are two yin lines and one yang line in a primary gua it is a yang gua and vice versa.)

Decision

 Great Accumulation.
 Favorable to be steadfast and upright.
 Eat not at home.
 Good fortune.
 Favorable to cross great rivers.

Commentary on the Decision

 Great Accumulation.
 Strong firmness,
 Substantial sincerity,
 And brilliant light.
 He renews his virtue daily.

 The firm ascends and honors the virtuous.
 He is able to keep his strength still.
 This is great and correct.

 Eat not at home. Good fortune.
 People of virtue are nourished.

Favorable to cross great rivers.
He corresponds with Heaven.

Commentary on the Symbol

Heaven between Mountains.
An image of Great Accumulation.
In correspondence with this,
The superior person has a wide learning
And memory of the words and deeds of the past,
In order to accumulate his virtue.

Yao Text

1. Initial Nine
   There is adversity.
   Favorable to stop advancing.

   There is adversity.
   Favorable to stop advancing.
   One does not expose oneself to calamity.

2. Second Nine
   A wagon's axle bracket comes off.

   A wagon's axle bracket comes off.
   It is in the central position; no wrongdoing.

3. Third Nine
   A good horse chases.
   Favorable to be steadfast and upright in hardship.
   Practice charioteering and defense daily.
   Favorable to have somewhere to go.

   Favorable to have somewhere to go.
   The will of the uppermost is in agreement with him.

4. Fourth Six
   A young bull's horns with a board attached.
   Supreme good fortune.

   The supreme good fortune of the fourth six.
   There is occasion for joy.

5. Fifth Six
   The tusks of a castrated boar.
   Good fortune.

   The good fortune of the fifth six.
   There is occasion for congratulation.

6. Top Nine
   How unobstructed Heaven's thoroughfare is!
   Prosperous and smooth.

   How unobstructed Heaven's thoroughfare is!
   The way is grandly open for advance.

SIGNIFICANCE

This gua displays the truth of great accumulation, but also the truth of holding back. When one proceeds in a situation of truthfulness, one is certain to accumulate great strength and wealth and to further his achievements vigorously. However, when things reach a climax, they will alternate to the opposite. When one possesses wealth as well as strength and knows not how to hold back, he tends to take reckless actions without care or thought. Thus, during the period of great accumulation one should remain calm and watchful, keeping still at the time when one should keep still. If it is necessary, stop taking action. During the time of advancing by leaps and bounds there is certain danger. Thus, the text gives warning instead of encouraging advancement without control.

The structure of the gua is Mountain ☶ above, Heaven ☰ below. The attribute of Heaven is creative power and that of Mountain is keeping still. The structure tells us that the creative power is kept still. It is not the appropriate time to demonstrate creative power, but to accumulate it. Accumulation of energy is preparing for release. Accumulation of knowledge is preparing for dissemination. Accumulation of wealth is preparing for benefiting society. Great accumulation is for great achievements. If the accumulation is abundant, it will be inexhaustible.

Either the yielding line at the fifth place or the solid line at the top can be the host. In his Commentary on the Decision, Confucius says, "The firm ascends and honors the virtuous." The firm denotes the top line, and the virtuous refers to the fifth line. The fifth place is the place for a king. In this gua, the sage at the top has already accumulated his

virtue and also respects people of virtue. Thus, King Wen's Decision says, "Eat not at home." A virtuous sage is advising a virtuous king to go out and search for virtuous people to serve the country. For these reasons, the top line is more suitable to be the host of the gua. However, in order to accomplish great achievements, it is wise to accumulate virtue first. The first five lines suggest that the time of great achievement has not yet come.

This gua relates that after King Wen pointed out that truthfulness should be the guideline of the new administration, he instructed his subordinates to accumulate virtue and to speak truthfully with the subordinates of the Shang dynasty. The Duke of Zhou recalled that handling conflicts between the subordinates of the Zhou and the subordinates of the Shang was difficult. It was as if the bracket of a wagon's axle had fallen off. Before virtue had been fully accumulated, the conflicts should not be dealt with lightly. Virtue should be practiced daily, like charioteering and defense. After the civil officials and the military officers of the Shang dynasty had been educated, it was as if a board had been stuck on the tips of a young bull's horns (to prevent the bull from hurting anyone) and the boars were castrated. The danger was gone. Progress and success ensued, following the way of Heaven.

(1) Initial Nine. Great Accumulation alternates to Remedying (18)

The solid line at the bottom symbolizes the initial advance. Advancement is the attribute of the inner gua, Heaven. Three solid lines of Heaven are going forward, but their advance is blocked by the outer gua, Mountain. This line corresponds to the yielding line at the fourth place, but it is blocked by that line as well. The Yao Text says, "There is adversity. Favorable to stop advancing." During the time of great accumulation, any premature move forward is dangerous.

(2) Second Nine. Great Accumulation alternates to Adorning (22)

The solid line at the second place is central. It represents one who does not tend to go to the extreme and knows how to act according to the circumstances. The Yao Text says, "A wagon's axle bracket comes off," indicating that the situation is not favorable for one to go forward. During the time of great accumulation one knows that to stop advancing is to act in accord with the central way. Therefore, there is no error.

(3) Third Nine. Great Accumulation alternates to Decreasing (41)

The third line lies at the top of the lower gua; it denotes the end of the first stage. The line responds but does not correspond to the solid line at the top of the outer gua, Mountain (Keeping Still). The situation is still not favorable to advance. One at this place is too anxious to advance, like mounting a good horse and giving chase. The Yao Text warns that one should anticipate the hardship. One should practice charioteering and defense daily before taking action; then there will be advantage in whatever direction one may advance.

(4) Fourth Six. Great Accumulation alternates to Great Harvest (14)

The Yao Text of the fourth line says, "A young bull's horns with a board attached." A board is put on the bull's horns to prevent the bull from hurting people. The upper gua, Mountain, keeps the excessive yang energy of the lower gua still. The yin element at the fourth place corresponds to the yang element at the bottom. The bottom line represents a young bull. Because the bull is still young, its strength is not yet great. A board has been put on its horns; this makes it possible to prevent the young bull's advance. It is always best to prevent trouble before it happens. In so doing, the result is supreme good fortune.

(5) Fifth Six. Great Accumulation alternates to Little Accumulation (9)

The fifth line is a yin element at a yang place, corresponding to the yang element at the second place. The yang element at the second place is much stronger than the yang element at the bottom. It is represented by the tusks of a boar, indicating trouble that is harder to deal with than the young bull in the fourth place. One at the fifth place is gentle; he walks the central path. To prevent the boar from hurting people one does not pull out its tusks, but castrates it. Castrating the boar makes it gentle. This deals with the fundamental nature of the problem, and for this reason there is occasion for congratulation.

(6) Top Nine. Great Accumulation alternates to Advance (11)

One stores up energy to release it and accumulates wealth to do something important. If accumulation and spending occur at the same time, there will be no accumulation. The uppermost line of this gua represents a situation where the accumulation of wealth has been great and the accumulation of wisdom and virtue have been abundant. It is time for releasing one's creative energy. By following the way of Heaven, the path grandly opens for one to advance.

Additional Reference Information for This Gua

Image:	Mountain above, Heaven below
Recite as:	Heaven between Mountain Peaks, Great Accumulation
Element:	Earth
Structure:	Four yang with two yin
Month:	The eighth month of the lunar year, or September
Host of the Gua:	Top Nine
Opposite Gua:	Bringing Together (45)
Inverse Gua:	Without Falsehood (25)
Mutual Gua:	Marrying Maiden (54)

27
Yi • Nourishing

Gen • Mountain
Zhen • Thunder

NAME AND STRUCTURE

Originally, Yi denoted the chin, the lower jaw. Later its meaning was extended to include nourishing for keeping fit. Wilhelm translates Yi as The Corner of the Mouth (Providing Nourishment). Blofeld translates it as Nourishment (literally Jaws).

Sequence of the Gua: *When things are accumulated in great amount, nourishing becomes available. Thus, after Great Accumulation, Nourishing follows.*

The ideograph is made up of two parts. The left looks like the side view of an oral cavity with teeth set in the upper and lower jaws. An object is placed between the teeth, symbolizing the food to be eaten for nourishing the body and spirit. The function of the right part of the ideograph is to provide the sound, yi. It is an ancient ideograph representing a head. The image at the top right looks like a head with two horizontal strokes in the middle representing a mouth. Above the head is a kerchief, and underneath two strokes represent two legs. This is, in fact, another ideograph of ren, person.

Undoubtedly King Wen derived Nourishing, the name of the gua, from insight about its shape. Only the top and bottom of the six lines are solid; they represent the jaws. All other lines are broken; they represent the teeth. The shape of the six lines gives us a picture of a mouth, symbolizing the act of eating for nourishment. The structure of the gua is Mountain ☶ above, Thunder ☳ below. The attribute of Mountain is to stand still and that of Thunder is to move. When we eat, the upper jaw holds still; only the lower jaw moves up and down. The subject of the first three lines is to nourish oneself; that of the next three lines is to nourish others.

Needing, the fifth gua, also covers the subject of nourishing. Needing follows Childhood. The orderly sequence of the gua says, "When things are in their childhood, they should not be neglected without nourishing." In Needing one nourishes the body for growth. However, the nourishing in this gua is different—it has to do less with the act of eating and drinking, and more with the wisdom of nourishing oneself as well as other people. King Wen's Decision on the Gua advises to be aware of how you nourish others and pay attention to what you eat and drink.

Decision

Nourishing.
Being steadfast and upright: good fortune.
Watch your nourishment;
Pay attention to what is in your mouth.

Commentary on the Decision

Nourishing.
Steadfast and upright: good fortune.
When nourishing is right,
Good fortune comes.

Watching how you nourish others;
It is to watch what you provide nourishment for.
Paying attention to what is in your mouth.
It is to pay attention to how you nourish yourself.

Heaven and Earth nourish all beings.
The holy sages nourish the virtuous,
And thus reach all.
Great indeed is nourishing in its time!

Commentary on the Symbol

Thunder beneath Mountain.
An image of Nourishing.
In correspondence with this,
The superior person is careful of his words
And moderate in eating and drinking.

Yao Text

1. Initial Nine
   Putting aside your spiritual tortoise,
   Staring at me with mouth drooling.
   Misfortune.

   Staring at me with drooling mouth.
   It is not a noble manner.

2. Second Six
   Turning upside down,
   Seeking nourishment.
   Contrary to normal.
   From the hill, seeking nourishment.
   Moving forward: misfortune.

   Second six, moving forward: misfortune.
   Moving forward without friends' support.

3. Third Six
   Contrary to normal,
   Seeking nourishment.
   Being steadfast: misfortune.
   Ten years, not used.
   Nothing is favorable.

   Ten years, not used.
   It is quite contrary to the proper way.

4. Fourth Six
   Turning upside down,
   Seeking nourishment.
   Good fortune.

A tiger's glare, covetous, covetous.
Its desire, chasing, chasing.
No fault.

Good fortune in turning upside down, seeking nourishment.
The one above sheds light.

5. Fifth Six
Contrary to normal.
Abide in being steadfast and upright.
Good fortune.
Not appropriate to cross great rivers.

Good fortune in abiding in being steadfast and upright,
Due to devotedly following the one above.

6. Top Nine
From this nourishing,
Adversity: good fortune.
Favorable to cross great rivers.

From this nourishing,
Adversity: good fortune.
There is great blessing.

Significance

This gua outlines the principle of nourishing. In ancient times, the Chinese concept of nourishing included nurturing, especially nurturing one's virtue. To the ancient Chinese, nourishing without nurturing was the way of animals. The revered sage Mencius says,

Filling with food,
Warming with clothes,
Living leisurely without learning,
It is little short of animals.

The ancient sages proclaimed that nourishing and nurturing were not a matter reserved for the family but concerned society as a whole. Nourishing and nurturing a family was selfish, nourishing and nurturing a society was selfless. Compared with nourishing one's virtue, nourishing one's body was secondary. Thus, the sages were cautious of words and moderate in diet and provided nourishment and nurturing to the people.

Either the yielding line at the fifth place or the solid line at the top could be the host of the gua. However, the solid line at the top is the source of nourishment. Confucius's Commentary on the Decision says, "Heaven and Earth nourish all beings. The holy sages nourish the virtuous, and thus reach all." The host of the gua refers to the person who is trying to follow in the steps of the sages. The first three lines of the gua refer to nourishing oneself. Either misfortune results or nothing will be favorable. The next three lines have to do with nourishing one's self as well as others. The results are beneficial.

The gua indicates that after King Wu overthrew the Tyrant of Shang there was a famine in the realm of the Shang dynasty. King Wen instructed the people to nourish the adherents of the Shang dynasty physically as well as spiritually. The Duke of Zhou tells how the adherents of the Shang dynasty put aside their spiritual tortoises and sought physical nourishment from the Zhou dynasty. Normally, the conquered provide sustenance to the conqueror, but here the conqueror nourishes the conquered. If the conqueror were to supply only physical nourishment to the conquered, it would lead to misfortune. Nourishing physical needs and spiritual needs brought good fortune.

(1) Initial Nine. Nourishing alternates to Falling Away (23) ☷

The solid line at the bottom represents a person of resolute character, corresponding to the yielding line at the fourth place. A tortoise is an animal able to survive without eating and drinking for a long period of time. In ancient China, the tortoise was regarded as a spiritual animal because of its longevity. The Yao Text, "Putting aside your spiritual tortoise, staring at me with mouth drooling," denotes that one at this place puts his spirituality aside and watches the person high above him eating. A drooling mouth suggests greed. There is a Chinese adage that says, "Mouth drooling with greed. It is not a noble manner." The solid line at the bottom is firm and strong. He ought to rely on himself in seeking nourishment for his physical body as well as his spiritual nature. Yet he puts aside his own resources and seeks profit from other people's toil. This behavior ends in misfortune.

(2) Second Six. Nourishing alternates to Decreasing (41) ☶

The yielding line at the second place represents a person who cannot live independently. At first she seeks nourishment from the one below, at the bottom line. They are complementary yin and yang. Yet seeking nourishment from a person below is contrary to what is normal. Then she tries to seek nourishment from the one above, at the top place. They are also complementary yin and yang. But the one at the uppermost place is too high to reach—they do not correspond with each other. It is like seeking nourishment from a hill while staying on the plain; not realistic. It is better to be independent.

(3) Third Six. Nourishing alternates to Adorning (22) ☲

The yin element at the third place corresponds to the yang element at the top. In ordinary cases, there is no danger. Here the yielding line at the third place is a yin element at a yang place, neither central nor correct. And it is at the top of the lower gua, Thunder (Taking Action), which suggests that one at this place intends to act contrary to normal. She has already reached the extreme. Acting contrary to what is appropriate goes against the principle of seeking nourishment; there is misfortune. The Yao Text warns to take no action for ten years, representing a lengthy period.

(4) Fourth Six. Nourishing alternates to Eradicating (21) ☶

This line is located at the bottom of the upper gua. At a higher position one's duty is to nourish others, but this one is unable to fulfill her duty by herself. Since she corresponds to the bottom line, she seeks nourishment from below. This is turning a relationship upside down. However, her situation is different from that of the one at the third place. This fourth six is a yin element at a yin place. The place is correct; she is not selfish. This element corresponds to the bottom line. Her motive seeking nourishment from below is not for herself but for others—thus, there is good fortune. The Yao Text explains that even glaring like a tiger, eyeing prey with insatiable craving, brings no fault. Because her motive is to nourish other people, there is good fortune instead of fault. Confucius's Commentary on the Yao Text says, "Good fortune in turning upside down, seeking nourishment. The one above sheds light." The upper gua is Mountain, which sometimes also represents fierce animals. Thus, the text uses a tiger as the analogy.

(5) Fifth Six. Nourishing alternates to Increasing (42) ☴

The yielding line at the fifth place is in the place of a ruler. It is a yin element at a yang place, central but not correct. She is not strong enough to nourish and nurture the people solely by herself; instead, she relies on the one above, the sage at the uppermost place. In this way, she acts contrary to what is appropriate. Although it is against her will, she has no choice. Her motive is pure and correct; she does it for the people. Therefore the advice is to remain steadfast and upright; good fortune will be derived from the action of devotedly following the sage. The structure of the gua is solid outside and empty inside, like a boat. After this line moves from yielding to solid, the upper gua alternates to Wind. An empty vessel encounters wind and storm—there is danger. Thus the Yao Text warns that one should not cross great rivers; in other words, do not do anything lightly.

(6) Top Nine. Nourishing alternates to Turning Back (24) ☷☳

The uppermost line is at the top of the gua. Nourishing is completed. The Tao of nourishing, in a narrow sense, is to nourish one's household. In a broad sense it is to serve the people. While a wise sage has abundance, he never forgets about the time of insufficiency. Thus the Yao Text says, "From this nourishing, adversity: good fortune." The uppermost line represents a sage. The ruler relies on him to nourish the people. The structure of the gua is solid outside and empty inside, like a boat. When this line changes from yielding to solid, the upper gua alternates to Earth, which indicates following. When an empty vessel follows the wind, it is favorable to cross great rivers. The sage is aware of the danger and overcomes all difficulties while crossing great rivers. It portends great blessing.

Additional Reference Information for This Gua

Image:	Mountain above, Thunder below
Recite as:	Thunder under Mountain, Nourishing
Element:	Earth
Structure:	Two yang with four yin
Month:	The eleventh month of the lunar year, or December
Host of the Gua:	Top Nine
Opposite Gua:	Great Exceeding (28) ䷛
Inverse Gua:	Nourishing (27) ䷚
Mutual Gua:	Responding (2) ䷁

28

Da Guo •
Great Exceeding

☱ Dui • Lake
☴ Xun • Wood

NAME AND STRUCTURE

Da is great; Guo is exceeding. Wilhelm translates Da Guo as Preponderance of the Great, and Blofeld translates it as Excess. I follow the literal Chinese meaning, Great Exceeding.

This gua is the opposite of the preceding gua. All the solid lines of the preceding gua convert to yielding lines, and the yielding lines convert to solid lines. In this way Nourishing ☶ alternates to Great Exceeding ☱. During a time of great exceeding, inevitably there is extraordinary action. Extraordinary action needs great nourishment. Therefore, Nourishing and Great Exceeding complement each other.

Sequence of the Gua: *Without nourishing it is impossible to take action. Thus, after Nourishing, Great Exceeding follows.*

Da Guo denotes greatly exceeding; taking extraordinary action. The structure of the gua is Lake ☱ above, Wood ☴ below. There are four solid lines and two yielding lines. The number of solid lines is double that of the yielding ones; the yang greatly exceeds the yin. This is one reason that King Wen named this gua Great Exceeding. The name also derives from the structure—in the layout of the lines can be seen a blueprint for the frame of a house. The six lines represent the topmost horizontal beam of a roof. The stability of a house greatly depends on the quality of this beam because all the rafters lean against this central pole. Here the ridgepole is not stable. The two ends of the pole are weak (two yielding lines), while the central part is strong (four solid lines). This picture reveals how the weight of the central portion of the ridgepole exceeds the capacity of the two ends to sustain it. This is another reason for the name Great Exceeding, which suggests that the roof is about to fall and it is time to go somewhere or to do something to remedy the situation.

There are two ideographs constituting the name of the gua. The first ideograph, da, represents "great." It is an image of a person standing upright with arms and legs wide open, showing his greatness. The second ideograph consists of two parts. Three curved strokes at the top left symbolize three footprints going forward. Underneath the footprints is the ideograph zhi, which means stop. On the right side is the ideograph guo; its function is to provide the sound of the character. It looks like a cross-section of the side view of a house. There are two pillars on each side and a beam sitting on the pillars. Underneath the beam is a tiny square representing a mouth, which was metonymical for people in ancient China, just as we say "many mouths to feed" in English. Placing the person underneath the beam and between the pillars suggests that the structure is a house. Above the beam is an extra structure which gives the beam an extra load, symbolizing excess.

In this gua, the solid line at the second place and the solid line at the fifth place are central. The inner gua is Wind. Here, Wind represents "smooth," for example, sailing with a smooth wind. The outer gua is Lake (Happy). Sailing with a favorable wind makes people happy. It is possible to obtain support and help and to advance smoothly without obstruction. Thus the Decision says that it is favorable to advance; there will be success.

Decision

Great Exceeding.
The ridgepole sags.
Favorable to have somewhere to go.
Prosperous and smooth.

Commentary on the Decision

Great Exceeding.
It indicates that the exceeding is great.

The ridgepole sags;
Two ends are weak.

The firm exceeds the yielding
At the central place.

Smooth and joyous in action.
Favorable to have somewhere to go.
There is success.
Truly great is the time of Great Exceeding!

Commentary on the Symbol

The lake rises over the tree.
An image of Great Exceeding.
In correspondence with this,
The superior person stands alone without fear
And withdraws from the world with no depression.

Yao Text

1. Initial Six
   For a mat
   Use white cogon grasses.
   No fault.

   For a mat, use white cogon grasses.
   It is to put soft materials underneath.

2. Second Nine
   Withered willow produces sprouts;
   Old man takes a young wife.
   Nothing is unfavorable.

   Old man takes a young wife.
   The excess and the insufficiency can be adjusted.

3. Third Nine
   Ridgepole sags.
   Misfortune.

   The misfortune of the sagging ridgepole,
   Being unable to get support.

4. Fourth Nine
   Ridgepole curves upward.

Good fortune.
If responding with others,
Humiliation.

The good fortune of the ridgepole curving upward.
Rely not on support from below.

5. Fifth Nine
Withered willow produces flowers.
Old woman takes a young husband.
No fault. No praise.

A withered willow produces flowers.
How could this last long?
Old woman takes a young husband.
Could it be disgraceful?

6. Top Six
Passing through a river,
Water over head.
Misfortune.
No fault.

Misfortune of passing through a river;
There is no ground for blame.

SIGNIFICANCE

Great Exceeding suggests a situation that is out of balance. It denotes an extraordinary situation requiring extraordinary action. Confucius's Commentary on the Symbol says, "The superior person stands alone without fear and withdraws from the world with no depression." This is the proper attitude for taking extraordinary action in an extraordinary situation. Because the situation is unusual, not everyone is able to take such action; one should stand alone without fear. If one fails, one is able to withdraw from the world without suffering. In so doing, one acts in accordance with the spirit of taking extraordinary action in an extraordinary situation.

Things that are too big are difficult to control, and things that are too firm are easy to break: this is the defect of Great Exceeding. This gua expounds the truth of adjustment between the strong and the weak, the excessive and the deficient. If one masters the principle of adjustment, no matter how difficult the situation, any problem can be solved. For instance, if something is likely to break easily, one can put soft materials, like cogon grasses, underneath it to protect it. Amending the firmness and balancing the deficiency rely on adjustment.

This gua also expounds the principle of taking extraordinary actions. In the process of taking action, during the time of Great Accumulation and Nourishing, one is able to develop strength, store up knowledge, accumulate experience, and bring up followers and successors to realize one's aspiration and ambition. Up to the point of Great Exceeding, one is able to take extraordinary action. Taking extraordinary action is not an easy task. One should be extremely cautious, employing the theory of balancing the yin and the yang. That is to moderate the yang with the yin and to elevate the yin with the yang. In this way, people will be happy to follow and support.

The host of the gua is unusual—it is the solid line at the fourth place. Normally the solid line at the second place or the fifth place is the host. They are firm and strong, central and correct. However, in this gua, both of them are not qualified. The solid line at the second place is firm and central, yet it has not gone beyond the lower gua. The solid line at the fifth place is firm, central, and correct, yet it is too close to the yin element at the top. That is where the ridgepole could break. Only the fourth line—firm and strong—is located in the middle of the ridgepole and curves upward. It is appropriate to be the host of the gua. Among the six lines, only the solid line at the third place is in an unfortunate situation. The rest are able to adjust from yin to yang or yang to yin without problem.

This gua tells us that after the Zhou dynasty was established, its territory was greatly expanded, and administrative work was extensive. Adjustment was demanded. King Wen instructed that Great Exceeding was like a ridgepole sagging. Although it was favorable to advance, it required extraordinary actions to make adjustments. The Duke of Zhou records that the adjustment was carried on with reverence and caution, as if offering a sacrifice to Heaven and the ancestors. At first the result was good, like a withered willow producing sprouts. However, there were too many surviving adherents of the Shang dynasty waiting for adequate arrangements and dispositions. King Wu worked hard, as if passing through a river. The water was over his head, but there was no fault.

(1) Initial Six. Great Exceeding alternates to Eliminating (43) ☱

The Yao Text says, "For a mat use white cogon grasses." In ancient times there were no tables and chairs. People sat on the floor. When offering

sacrifices to Heaven or their ancestors, white cogon grasses were spread on the ground, and all vessels were put on the grasses, showing the offerer's reverent mood. The bottom line is yielding, symbolizing that one at this place is humble and cautious. The line is at the bottom of the lower gua, Wind, which represents a gentle character. During the time of taking extraordinary action, such a person is cautious and reverent, as when spreading white cogon grasses on the ground while offering a sacrifice. If there should be an accident, it would not damage the vessels. There is nothing at fault.

(2) Second Nine. Great Exceeding alternates to Mutual Influence (31) ☲

Willows grow close to water. The lower gua is Wind or Wood. The four yang lines in the middle of this gua can be seen as a single yang element, which gives this gua the appearance of the primary gua Water ☵. Thus willow was employed as a symbol. The solid line at the second place is the lowest among the four yang lines. It symbolizes the beginning of Great Exceeding. This yang element does not respond to the yang element at the fifth place; they are both yang. However, it is close to the yin element on the bottom. These yin and yang attract each other, like an old man taking a young wife. The old man gets nourishment from the young wife and has children, like a withered willow producing new sprouts. The old man and young wife symbolize excess and insufficiency. When they are balanced, nothing is unfavorable. This line reveals the truth that excess and insufficiency can be adjusted and balanced.

(3) Third Nine. Great Exceeding alternates to Exhausting (47) ☵

The third line and the fourth lines are in the middle of the gua. The text uses a ridgepole, the topmost horizontal beam of a roof, as an analogy. The third line is a yang element at a yang place—too firm, too rigid, and too easy to break. It suggests that a rigid, self-willed person is facing a dangerous situation, like a sagging ridgepole about to break. One at this place corresponds to the yin element at the uppermost place. One at the uppermost place wants to help, but nobody can help an extremely self-willed person. This situation is dangerous.

(4) Fourth Nine. Great Exceeding alternates to Replenishing (48) ☵

The fourth line is a yang element at a yin place; it possesses the attributes of both yin and yang. It is more balanced than the element at the third place. One at this place is able to carry a heavy burden. Thus, the Yao

Text says that there is good fortune. However, this line corresponds to the yin element at the bottom; there is temptation for one at this place to rely on the yin in taking action. The bottom line is a yin element at a yang place, which is too much yin. When one who is at a balanced yin and yang situation relies on someone who has an excessive amount of yin, there will be humiliation. This is why the Yao Text says, "If responding with others, humiliation."

(5) Fifth Nine. Great Exceeding alternates to Long Lasting (32)

The yang element at the fifth place is at the top of the four yang elements. It reaches the end of Great Exceeding. It does not correspond to the yang element at the second place. Thus, one at this place tends to seek union with the uppermost yin element. The fifth line is a yang element at a yang place, symbolizing a young man. The top line is a yin element at a yin place, symbolizing an old woman. This union is as unusual as a withered willow producing a flower. There is no fault, yet no praise.

(6) Top Six. Great Exceeding alternates to Encountering (44)

The yin element at the uppermost place is at the end of the gua. It is too weak to cross a river. Owing to a lack of self-understanding, her over-reacting gets her in water over her head. Of course, there is danger. She is a yin element at a yin location; she might not be too self-willed. If this overreacting is necessary and can be handled with caution, there will be no ground for blame.

Additional Reference Information for This Gua

Image:	Lake above, Wind or Wood below
Recite as:	Lake over Wood, Great Exceeding
Element:	Metal
Structure:	Four yang with two yin
Month:	The tenth month of the lunar year, or November
Host of the Gua:	Fourth Nine
Opposite Gua:	Nourishing (27)
Inverse Gua:	Great Exceeding (28)
Mutual Gua:	Initiating (1)

29
Kan • Darkness

$$\begin{array}{c}\rule{2em}{0.4pt}\ \ \rule{2em}{0.4pt}\\ \rule{5em}{0.4pt}\\ \rule{2em}{0.4pt}\ \ \rule{2em}{0.4pt}\end{array}$$ Kan • Water

Kan • Water

NAME AND STRUCTURE

Kan is a pit. It can also be interpreted as falling. Wilhelm translates Kan as Abysmal and Blofeld as Abyss. In this book the word Darkness is used. The ancient ideograph selected for this gua is a very old and beautiful form. The left half of the ideograph is a symbol for Earth. The right half is made up of two parts. The upper portion depicts a person standing on one foot with the other foot off the ground, which indicates that the person is falling. Directly underneath one foot, there is a vertical line symbolizing a falling movement. The lower portion of the ideograph looks like a pit. We have here the image of someone falling into a pit. The meaning of Kan is twofold, either a pit or falling. In the later version of the ideograph, it should be noted, the picture of the pit was left out.

The central theme of this gua is: falling but not drowned; in danger but not lost. Maintain your confidence: soothe your mind. With assurance and faith, caution and trust, you can pass through any difficult situation. Both Abysmal and Abyss carry the sense of being bottomless. Kan is a pit, but it is not bottomless. There is hope.

Kan is made up of two primary gua, Water ☵ above and Water ☵ below. In ancient times, the Chinese lived inland; they were not a sea-faring people. For this reason, Water was associated with difficulty or danger. According to the system of the five elements, the color of Water is blue-black. There is no light in a pit. Thus, the meaning of Kan can also be interpreted as falling into darkness. In the I Ching, yin lines of a gua alternating to yang lines, or vice versa, are called inverse. The inverted form of this gua is Li, meaning "attaching to brightness."

According to Fu Xi's arrangement of the eight primary gua, Qian stands for Heaven, Kun for Earth, Li for sun, and Kan for moon. Besides Heaven and Earth, sun and moon were the two most important symbols to the ancient Chinese. The sun and moon up in the sky were the first two natural objects they noticed to display the principle of yin and yang. The ancients recognized that the sun was the source of heat and light. They named the sun tai yang, which means the most yang or the hottest, the brightest. They also perceived that the moon itself had neither heat nor light; its light was merely the reflection of the sun. They named the moon tai yin, which means the most yin or the coldest, the darkest. From the waxing and waning of the moon derived the principle of change and also that of the continuity of change—the two principles that are the basis of the I Ching. Heaven and Earth, sun and moon were the four deities that the ancient Chinese revered the most. Heaven and Earth, respectively, represent the pure yang and the pure yin. Sun and moon represent yin within yang and yang within yin, respectively. The ancients named these four gua as the symbols of the four cardinal directions—Qian for south, Kun for north, Li for east, and Kan for west. Qian, Kun, Li, and Kan were the most significant gua in the I Ching; therefore, Qian and Kun were placed at the beginning of the Upper Canon and Kan and Li at the end.

The whole I Ching expounds the principle of yin and yang. Yin and yang exist in everything. They are opposite but mutually interdependent; without yin, there would be no yang and vice versa. Sun and moon, fire and water, brightness and darkness are the most obvious examples of yin and yang. The symbol of the sun is Li, meaning the Fire or the Brightness; the symbol of moon is Kan, signifying the Water or the Darkness. For these reasons, I feel comfortable employing Darkness as the name of this gua and referring to its inverted form, Li, as Brightness.

Darkness represents not only a pit but also a situation of difficulty or danger. The structure of this gua is a doubling of the primary gua, Water. The image of Water is a yang line plunging between two yin lines, like running water flowing along and between the banks of a river. In ancient times, crossing a river represented a great danger. Thus, the attribute of Water was designated a situation of difficulty or danger. Here, Water is doubled, suggesting that one is plunging into a situation fraught with difficulties or danger. However, the ancient Chinese believed that no matter how dangerous or dark a situation was, if one was able to follow the way of Heaven, one could pass through it as safely as water passes through a ravine.

Sequence of the Gua: *Things cannot forever be in an excessive state. Thus, after Great Exceeding, Darkness follows.*

Decision

> Doubled darkness.
> Be sincere and truthful.
> Rely on heart and mind.
> Prosperous and smooth;
> Deeds will be honored.

Commentary on the Decision

> *Darkness is doubled.*
> *Dangers succeed one after another.*
>
> *Water flows and fills,*
> *Not accumulating but running.*
> *Pass through dangerous places;*
> *Never lose self-confidence.*
>
> *Rely on heart and mind.*
> *The firm are in the central places.*
> *Deeds will be honored.*
> *Going forward, there is success.*
>
> *The danger in Heaven,*
> *No one can ascend.*
> *The danger on Earth,*
> *There are mountains and rivers.*
>
> *Kings and princes*
> *Took advantage of these dangerous situations*
> *To protect their realms.*
>
> *It is great indeed, at the proper time,*
> *To take advantage of these dangerous situations.*

Commentary on the Symbol

Water flows on twice over,
Darkness is doubled.
In correspondence with this,
The superior person cultivates and practices virtue constantly
And responds through teaching.

Yao Text

1. Initial Six
   Doubled darkness.
   Falling into a pit within a pit.
   Misfortune.

   Darkness doubled.
   Falling into a pit under a pit.
   One has lost the way;
   There will be misfortune.

2. Second Nine
   Darkness; there is danger.
   Strive for little things.
   Obtain.

   Strive for little things,
   Still along the middle way.

3. Third Six
   Coming or going, darkness, darkness.
   Danger, just wait.
   Already fallen into a pit within a pit;
   Do not act.

   Coming or going, darkness, darkness.
   Any effort ends without success.

4. Fourth Six
   A jug of wine, two baskets of food.
   Plain earthen vessels.
   Simple offerings through a window
   End in no fault.

A jug of wine, two baskets of food.
Firm and yielding meet.

5. Fifth Nine
   Water in the pit, not overflowing,
   Fills only to the rim.
   No fault.

   Water in the pit, not yet overflowing.
   The central line is not yet great enough.

6. Top Six
   Bound with black cords,
   Confined in a thicket of thorns.
   Three years, no remission.
   Misfortune.

   Top six has missed the proper way.
   Misfortune for three years.

SIGNIFICANCE

This gua is one of the eight that are made by doubling one of the primary gua—in this case, Water ☵.

The image of the gua is darkness following darkness, difficulty after difficulty, and danger after danger. The main theme is how to deal with difficult situations or danger. The ancient sages always taught people to be cautious. There is an old saying that "where there is precaution, there is no danger." However, in the course of life, sometimes one cannot avoid difficult situations or danger. How should one deal with them? First, it is important to remain calm and establish a positive attitude. Be cautious and trusting. When passing through darkness, one should stay as calm as if walking on level ground. Consider how to prevent the situation from worsening, then find a way to solve the problem. One can always transform bad situations into something positive. This is the core spirit of the I Ching.

There are two solid lines in this gua, one at the second place and the other at the fifth place. The host of the gua is the solid line at the fifth place. Water here symbolizes a pit. The nature of water is to flow. But first the water must fill up the pit; only then can it move forward. The solid line at the second place is capable of being the host, but it is not as

suitable as the one at the fifth place, which is a yang element at a yang place.

After King Wu overthrew the Tyrant of Shang, he still needed to conquer 99 minor kingdoms and subdue 652 lords. Returning in victory, King Wu selected Gao-jing as the capital. Here the Zhou dynasty was established. This gua tells us how in this period of time the situation bred darkness following darkness, difficulty upon difficulty, and danger after danger. King Wu maintained his confidence and calmed his heart and mind. The Duke of Zhou narrates several difficulties and dangers overcome by King Wu.

(1) Initial Six. Darkness alternates to Restricting (60) ≣≣

Six at the beginning is a yin element at the bottom of the gua. It indicates a very bad situation; the circumstances have reached the extreme of darkness and difficulty. This yao gives warning that one should not fall into the depth of darkness from which it would be difficult to extricate oneself. The message is that even when one's difficulty is doubled, one should not lose one's way or one's self-confidence.

(2) Second Nine. Darkness alternates to Union (8) ≣≣

Nine at the second place is a yang element at a yin place. It is still a difficult situation. In the darkness there is danger. Fortunately, this line is a central yang element. One at this place is not able to overcome the difficulty or danger totally; but, by being cautious and self-confident and understanding the situation, one can strive to make little changes.

(3) Third Six. Darkness alternates to Replenishing (48) ≣≣

Six at the third place is a yin element at a yang place, neither central nor correct but yielding and gentle. One in this place has difficulty going forward or backward. It is like falling into a dark well. This line suggests that when one has fallen into such a situation, one should cease struggling and wait for a favorable time and set of circumstances.

(4) Fourth Six. Darkness alternates to Exhausting (47) ≣≣

This line is in a better situation. The fourth place is for a minister, close to the king at the fifth place. Here there is a yin element at a yin place, gentle and submissive. But the king is firm and strong. In ordinary circumstances, there are numerous requirements concerning etiquette between a king and a minister. During a time of difficulty and darkness, they treat each

other with respect. A jug of wine and baskets of food are enough for their entertainment. They do not rely on material things, but only on a spirit of faithfulness and reverence. This is the attitude to adopt in dealing with a difficult situation: one should be as sincere as the king and minister and as faithful and reverent as when offering a sacrifice.

(5) Fifth Nine. Darkness alternates to Multitude (7) ☷☵

Nine at the fifth place is in the center of the upper gua, but it is close to the end, the top place. The text employs the analogy of water filling a pit. When running water falls into a pit, the pit fills up before the water can run out. In this place, the water has come close to the rim—sooner or later it will flow out and move forward again. This line shows that no matter how dark and difficult a situation is, if one does not lose one's self-confidence, there is always a way out.

(6) Top Six. Darkness alternates to Dispersing (59) ☴☵

This line is a warning. One cannot deal with difficulty and danger by leaving things to chance. That is a negative attitude. The one at the upper-most place is a yin element whose character is weak. One who keeps this negative attitude is likened to a prisoner bound by cords and confined in a thicket of thorns. In ancient times, this was actually done to prisoners. If one could not get remission within three years, one would be confined forever. In other words, if one holds on to a negative attitude, there is no way to extricate oneself from difficulty and danger. One should cultivate an attitude of self-understanding and self-preservation.

Additional Reference Information for This Gua

Image:	Water above, Water below	
Recite as:	Water is doubled, Darkness	
Element:	Water	
Structure:	Two yang with four yin	
Month:	Winter Solstice	
Host of the Gua:	Fifth Nine	
Opposite Gua:	Brightness	(30) ☲☲
Inverse Gua:	Darkness	(29) ☵☵
Mutual Gua:	Nourishing	(27) ☶☳

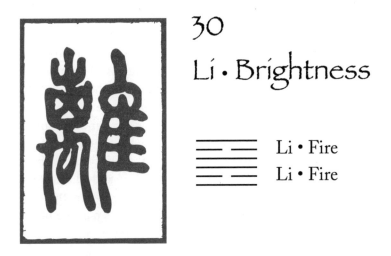

30
Li · Brightness

☲ Li · Fire
☲ Li · Fire

NAME AND STRUCTURE

Li is the opposite of the preceding gua, Kan. It represents Fire or Brightness. When the lines of a gua alternate from yin to yang or yang to yin, a new gua—the opposite of the original gua—comes forth. Wilhelm translates Li as The Clinging, Fire; Blofeld translates Li as Flaming Beauty. Here I use Brightness. Li means to leave, to part from, to be away from, but in ancient times it also meant to attach. This is why the orderly sequence of the gua refers to attaching.

The left half of this ideograph is an ancient animal named li; the right half is an ancient bird with bright yellow feathers called zhui. A Chinese character, in most cases, is made up of two parts: one part provides the sound, the other part provides the meaning. In this ideograph, the left side gives the sound of the character Li, while the right provides the meaning. The ancients picked the bright color of the bird to signify the character Li; thus, Li symbolizes brightness, though that is not its literal meaning. It is associated with Fire, the sun, and the most yang energy. On this basis, I use Brightness for the name of this gua. Complications such as this, and the need to know the history and changing meanings of each word and character, is why it can be so difficult to properly translate the I Ching.

It is of great significance that King Wen placed this gua, Li, together with the previous gua, Kan, as the last two chapters of the Upper Canon. The I Ching expounds the truth of yin and yang; they oppose each other and yet also complement each other. The Upper Canon demonstrates the yin-yang principle in natural phenomena, starting with Qian and Kun and ending with Kan and Li. These four gua have special significance in the I Ching. King Wen regarded Qian and Kun as the symbols of Heaven and Earth and Kan and Li as the symbols of the sun and the moon. Heaven and Earth represent the pure yang and the pure yin. The sun and moon tell us that within the yang there is yin, and within the yin there is yang. According to Fu Xi's arrangement of the eight primary gua, Qian, Kun, Kan, and Li were designated as the four cardinal directions of the universe. King Wen placed Qian and Kun at the head of the Upper Canon and Kan and Li at the end. These four gua were the most distinguished symbols of the natural phenomena. The purpose of the Upper Canon is to trace the Tao of Heaven and apply it to human life. The ancients believed that the truth expounded in the Upper Canon was as perpetual as Heaven and Earth, as correct as the four cardinal directions, and as bright as the sun and moon. Actually the Chinese put the ideographs of the sun and the moon together to form a new character, ming, which means brightness.

Sequence of the Gua: *When falling into darkness, one is certain to attach to something. Thus, after Darkness comes attaching to each other and to Brightness.*

The structure of the gua is Fire ☲ above, Fire ☲ below. The attribute of Fire is attachment as well as brightness. When two Fire gua are combined, the Brightness is doubled. During times of darkness and danger people should cling to one another. When they do, things get brighter.

Decision

Brightness.
Favorable to be steadfast and upright.
Prosperous and smooth.
Raise a cow:
Good fortune.

Commentary on the Decision

Brightness.
It means being attached.

The sun and moon attach to Heaven.
Grains and plants attach to Earth.

Doubled brightness attaches to what is correct.
Thus, all under Heaven are transformed.

The yielding attaches to the central and correct places.
For this reason, there is prosperity and smoothness.
It is like raising a cow;
It brings good fortune.

Commentary on the Symbol

Brightness is doubled,
An image of the brightness of the sun.
In correspondence with this,
A great person continuously radiates
Brilliant virtue and deeds all over the world.

Yao Text

1. Initial Nine
   Steps confused.
   Tread with reverence.
   No fault.

   Reverence for confused steps.
   Avoid faults.

2. Second Six
   Yellow brightness.
   Supreme good fortune.

   The supreme good fortune of yellow brightness.
   He is stepping in the central way.

3. Third Nine
   Sunset brightness.
   Not beating an earthen pot and singing,
   Sighing in sorrow for old age.
   Misfortune.

Sunset brightness.
How can it last long?

4. Fourth Nine
   Comes all of a sudden.
   Flaring up,
   Dying down,
   Discarded away.

   Comes all of a sudden.
   There is no place for it.

5. Fifth Six
   Tears in floods,
   Sighing with sorrow.
   Good fortune.

   The good fortune of the fifth six;
   It is attached to the king's place.

6. Top Nine
   The king engages in launching an expedition.
   There is a decree:
   Kill the leader,
   Capture the followers.
   No fault.

   The king engages in launching an expedition.
   Bring rectification to the country.

SIGNIFICANCE

This gua is one of the eight gua made up by doubling one of the eight primary gua. The name of the gua symbolizes heat and light. The source of heat and light is the sun. The attribute of Li is brightness, which symbolizes intelligence and wisdom. Being embarrassed by unresolved problems feels like falling into darkness. Finding a solution is compared to a light that casts out the darkness. The preceding gua, Darkness, displays the way to deal with a difficult or dangerous condition. It teaches caution together with sincerity, trustfulness, and wholeheartedness. This gua, Brightness, sheds light upon the distinction between right and wrong. If one's attitude is not sincere and wholehearted, one is not able to distinguish between what is appropriate and what is inappropriate.

There are two yielding lines in this gua, one at the second place and the other at the fifth place. The host of the gua is at the second line. The flame of a fire begins at the lower level, where it shines brighter. Although the yielding line at the fifth place is at a supreme place—central but not correct—it is not suitable to be the host.

This gua is a continuation of the preceding gua, which tells us that during the time that King Wu was conquering minor kingdoms and subduing lords, he remembered that as people came to join the brightness there would be prosperity. It was favorable to be steadfast and upright. The submission of those who were as docile as a cow would bring good fortune. The Duke of Zhou tells how different kinds of people were dealt with in different ways. The policy was to kill the leader and not his followers. In this there was no fault.

(1) Initial Nine. Brightness alternates to Traveling (56) ☶

Nine at the beginning is a yang element at a yang place. It is the beginning of Brightness and symbolizes an intelligent person who is firm and active but too eager to advance. Unfortunately, at the very beginning of a new situation, it is difficult for one to see the end. In this way, one's steps are confused. Treading with caution, there will be no fault.

(2) Second Six. Brightness alternates to Great Harvest (14) ☰

Six at the second place is in a supremely auspicious situation. The Yao Text mentions yellow brightness. This is similar to the fifth six in the second gua, Kun—"A yellow lower garment. Supreme good fortune." Yellow is the color of the Earth. In the system of the five elements, Earth occupies the central place. For this reason, the Duke of Zhou employed yellow to indicate the center. The yielding line at the second place is central and correct and therefore auspicious. The message of this gua is that when one attaches to someone or something, one should follow the principle of being central and correct.

(3) Third Nine. Brightness alternates to Eradicating (21) ☳

Nine at the third place is a yang element at a yang place, in the midst of two primary gua, Fire and Fire. In this situation, the lower gua represents the sun setting in the west, and the upper gua represents the sun rising in the east. The ancient Chinese used sunset as a metaphor to indicate old age. The sun declines quickly, like the end of one's life. In this gua, we are told that life and death are natural phenomena, just like sunrise and sunset. When one ages, one should beat the earthen pot, sing, and fully enjoy the blessings of life. If one sighs in sorrow for old age, it is a great misfortune.

(4) Fourth Nine. Brightness alternates to Adorning (22) ☲

Nine at the fourth place is also in the middle of two primary gua, Fire and Fire. Six at the fourth place is firm and strong. Its situation is likened to the rising of the sun. The Yao Text says, "Comes all of a sudden" because the lower mutual gua is Wind ☴. When fire catches wind it blazes up instantly; the result is "Flaring up, dying down, discarded away." A story used to explain this gua says that once there was an old king who suddenly passed away and a young king was crowned. Power struggles followed. The dark forces would flare up, die down, and be discarded. This line shows that in the course of life brightness may arise suddenly and then die out as quickly. One should be intelligent and wise enough to deal with the varying course of life.

(5) Fifth Six. Brightness alternates to Seeking Harmony (13) ☰

Six at the fifth place is a yin element at a yang place. It is central but incorrect. Although this line is in a supreme place, it is too weak. One at this place feels pressure coming from the two yang elements above and below, leading to tears in floods and sorrowful sighs. Fortunately he is gentle and walks in the central path, so there is still good fortune. Confucius's commentary says, "The good fortune of the fifth six; it is attached to the king's place." This yao shows that one at this place is not as confused as one at the bottom, yet he does not have a positive attitude. He sheds tears and sighs. How can he enjoy life?

(6) Top Nine. Brightness alternates to Abundance (55) ☳

Nine at the top is at the uppermost place of the gua. It reaches the peak of Brightness. Eventually, one at this place becomes mature. A parable is used to explain the meaning of this gua, which says that one at this place should be able to see clearly the whole situation of one's realm, like a king. He is firm and strong but kind and gentle, able to undertake an expedition to bring light to the country. The one in this place should also cultivate the virtue and wisdom of a superior person. "Kill the leader, capture the followers" is the key line of this gua. This is to say that one should deal with the root of a problem, not the minor problems. This principle is useful in cultivating one's own virtue and practicing in daily life. Then there will be no fault.

Additional Reference Information for This Gua

Image:	Fire above, Fire below
Recite as:	Fire is doubled, Brightness
Element:	Fire
Structure:	Two yin with four yang
Month:	Summer Solstice
Host of the Gua:	Second Six
Opposite Gua:	Darkness (29)
Inverse Gua:	Brightness (30)
Mutual Gua:	Great Exceeding (28)

THE
LOWER
CANON

The Lower Canon contains thirty-four gua, from Xian and Heng to Ji Ji and Wei Ji. Xian and Heng represent the Mutual Influence and Long Lasting union of a man and a woman. Ji Ji and Wei Ji represent the endless cycle of human affairs from Already Fulfilled to Not Yet Fulfilled. This canon sheds light upon the yin aspect of natural phenomena, the Tao of Humanity.

31

Xian • Mutual Influence

☱ Dui • Lake
☶ Gen • Mountain

Name and Structure

Sequence of the Gua: *After Heaven and Earth have come into existence, there are myriad beings. After myriad beings have come into existence, there are male and female. After male and female are distinguished, there comes the relationship of husband and wife. After husband and wife have united together, there arrive father and son. After there are father and son, there come ruler and minister. After there are ruler and minister, there come high and low. After high and low exist, then etiquette can be appropriately practiced.*

Xian originally meant all, together, or mutual. Wilhelm translates Xian as Influence (Wooing); Blofeld translates Xian as Attraction, Sensation. In this book, it is called Mutual Influence. Pictured here are two ancient ideographs with a close relationship. The upper one is xian, and the one in the left margin is gan. When the ideograph for heart, xin, appears underneath xian, then xian becomes gan. According to Confucius's Commentary on the Decision, xian should be gan. Gan means influence. It has the connotation of moving one's heart. If we consider the whole context of this gua, gan makes more sense. It has been suggested that the ideograph for heart might have been left out in the ancient text. In ancient Chinese writings, a radical or root of a complicated character was frequently left out.

The structure of the gua is Lake ☱ over Mountain ☶. Because a lake contains water, Lake is bestowed with the attribute of sinking downward. It is obvious that the nature of a mountain is to tower aloft. Lake over

Mountain presents the picture that one is sinking downward and the other is towering upward. The mountain underneath affords the foundation for the lake, and the lake above supplies moisture to nourish the mountain. They mutually influence each other, like a man and woman courting. Mutual Influence is the main theme of this gua.

In the system of the I Ching, Lake represents the youngest daughter, and Mountain represents the youngest son. Lake above, Mountain below symbolizes an attractive young man wooing a beautiful maiden. Since, as they are young and energetic, their mutual influence is powerful and sincere. This gua symbolizes newlyweds. The lower gua, Mountain, keeps still; the upper gua, Lake, is pleasant. Mutual love cannot be obtained with half-heartedness. It should be as stable as the mountain and as pure as the water in the lake. To the Chinese, mutual love between man and woman is the will of Heaven and Earth. Mutual love should not be actuated by selfish motives, otherwise the union will not be successful and long lasting. For this reason, King Wen arranged Mutual Influence and Long Lasting at the start of the Lower Canon, matching the arrangement of Qian and Kun, the creative force of Heaven and the responsive force of Earth, at the beginning of the Upper Canon. One can see that King Wen's sequence of the sixty-four gua is very well organized.

The purpose of the I Ching is to explore the Tao of Heaven and the Tao of Humanity. Heaven is the Chinese term for Nature or God. Following the Tao of Nature or the Tao of God to establish the Tao of Humanity is the ancient Chinese way to guide one's personal life and to manage one's social affairs. The Upper Canon was designed to explore the law of Heaven, and therefore it begins with the interplay of Heaven and Earth and ends with the interaction of Water and Fire. Heaven and Earth are the yin and yang aspects of natural phenomena. Water and Fire are the yin and yang aspects of human affairs. The Chinese believed that the male nature was akin to Fire and the female nature was like Water. Fire and Water stand for male and female. When they interact, these opposites become complementary.

When King Wen rearranged the sixty-four gua, he was able to follow Fu Xi's system of the eight primary gua. According to Fu Xi's system, the eight primary gua represent the eight directions. Heaven, Earth, Fire, and Water symbolize the four cardinal directions, namely, south, north, east, and west. King Wen appointed Heaven and Earth to initiate and Water and Fire to end the Upper Canon. The Lower Canon was designed to explore human affairs and begins with the union of a husband and wife.

Following the pattern of the Upper Canon, King Wen employed the four diagonal directions of Fu Xi's Earlier Heaven Sequence to begin and end the Lower Canon. This gua, Xian, is composed of Mountain and Lake. In Fu Xi's system of the eight primary gua, Mountain is northwest, and Lake is southeast, opposite in direction. King Wen put them together and gave them the quality of mutual influence. When Lake and Mountain interact, these opposites become complementary.

Decision

Mutual Influence.
Prosperous and smooth.
Favorable to be steadfast and upright.
Take a maiden as a wife.
Good fortune.

Commentary on the Decision

Xian, Mutual Influence.
The gentle is above, the firm below.
The love of the two induces and corresponds;
A union is formed.
Keeping still and joyful,

The man subordinates himself to the woman.
For this reason, there is prosperity and smoothness
In being steadfast and upright.
Taking a maiden as a wife brings good fortune.
Heaven and Earth influence each other;
Then all things take shape and come into being.
The holy sage influences the hearts of people;
Then the world attains peace and harmony.
Contemplating their mutual influence,
We can see the nature of Heaven and Earth and all beings.

Commentary on the Symbol

Lake on Mountain.
An image of Mutual Influence.
In correspondence with this,

The superior person opens his heart and mind
To accept people without prejudice.

Yao Text

1. Initial Six
Mutual influence on one's big toes.

   Mutual influence on one's big toes.
   His will is directed outward.

2. Second Six
Mutual influence on one's calves.
Misfortune.
Tarrying: good fortune.

   Even as misfortune threatens,
   Tarrying brings good fortune.
   Be yielding and reasonable.
   There will be no harm.

3. Third Nine
Mutual influence on one's thighs.
Insist on his following.
Going forward: humiliation.

   Mutual influence on one's thighs.
   Hard to get along with one another.
   Insisting on following others,
   One holds a low standard.

4. Fourth Nine
Being steadfast and upright: good fortune.
Regret vanishes.
Hesitating, hesitating,
Coming or going?
Friends follow your thought.

   Steadfast and upright: good fortune.
   Regret vanishes.
   Hesitating, hesitating; coming or going?
   One has not yet become brilliant and great.

5. Fifth Nine
   Mutual influence on one's upper back.
   No regret.

   Mutual influence on one's upper back.
   His will is skin deep.

6. Top Six
   Mutual influence
   On one's jaw, cheek, and tongue.

   Mutual influence on one's jaws, cheeks, and tongue.
   The open mouth makes empty promises.

SIGNIFICANCE

Hui-yuan, an eminent monk of the Eastern Jin Dynasty (317–420), says the root of the I Ching is mutual influence. The theme of the gua is to cultivate mutual influence between people. In the Chinese concept, mutual influence between husband and wife is most powerful and long lasting. The ancient sages employed the image of husband and wife to expound the truth of Mutual Influence. In order to influence each other, no matter what kind of relationship, both parties should be sincere and free from judgment. Their hearts and minds should be as pure as the clear sky and as open as the vast ocean. Thus, acting in harmony, the superior person opens his heart and mind fully to accept people without prejudice.

In Chinese, influence (gan) is made up of two characters—mutual (xian) plus heart (xin). When the "heart" is taken away from gan, gan becomes xian. In the text of the I Ching, it is possible that the author removed the "heart." To the ancient Chinese, the heart had a mental function. It is understandable that in order to obtain mutual influence one has to overcome or get rid of one's selfish heart to become unselfish, or selfless. Thus, the name of the gua is Xian, Mutual Influence without selfishness. The Duke of Zhou's Yao Text uses different parts of the human body to expound different situations of Mutual Influence. All the lines in the lower gua respond to their corresponding lines in the upper gua, balancing the yin with the yang. In other words, every line pursues its corresponding mate. The problem is that in seeking mutual influence, it is difficult to act without selfishness.

The theme of the Lower Canon is human affairs. It begins with the relationship of a husband and wife. The mutual influence of a male and female is a natural as well as a social phenomenon. Nevertheless, for this kind of relationship to endure, both parties must be selfless, truthful, and humble. Otherwise they won't be able to communicate with or enjoy each other and be accepted. This principle and process can be applied to all kinds of human relationships. Such relationships begin with mutual influence without selfishness. In this way, mutual influence arises spontaneously.

The host of the gua is the solid line at the fourth place. The fourth place is in the middle of the gua, equivalent to the location of the heart within the body. Mutual influence should radiate from the heart. The solid fifth line is at a supreme place—firm, central, and correct—but it is not at the heart position and therefore is not as suitable to be the host of this gua.

After the Zhou dynasty was established, King Wen encouraged the people to set up homes and start careers to stabilize his kingdom as well as people's lives. The Duke of Zhou formulated etiquette and composed music to change prevalent social customs. In this gua the Duke of Zhou narrates different ways and stages of seeking mutual influence and their consequences.

(1) Initial Six. Mutual Influence alternates to Abolishing the Old (49) ☰

The big toes are at the lowest part of the body, as the bottom line is at the lowest part of a gua. The yin element at the bottom corresponds to the yang element at the fourth position. The one at this place intends to pursue the one at the fourth place—there is mutual influence. However, this element is too weak to move forward because the bottom line symbolizes an initial stage. At this stage mutual influence has just begun, and good fortune or misfortune is still uncertain. They depend on one's sincerity and steadfastness.

(2) Second Six. Mutual Influence alternates to Great Exceeding (28) ☰

"Mutual influence on one's calves" signifies that one at this position is taking action. The yin element at the second place corresponds to the yang element at the fifth place. One at this place intends to pursue. This line is in the middle of the lower gua, Mountain, or Keeping Still. This situation suggests that in seeking mutual influence it is better to wait until the other party is prepared. Any premature action is not favorable. The secret of proper timing is hidden in one's physical and mental balance

with nature. For this reason, living in peace and being content will bring good fortune.

(3) Third Nine. Mutual Influence alternates to Bringing Together (45) ☷☳

The yang element at the third place corresponds to the uppermost yin element. One at this place is anxious to pursue the one at the uppermost place since the Yao Text says that Mutual Influence has reached the thighs, which indicates that one is ready to move. On the other hand, because one at this place is at the top of the inner gua, Mountain (Keeping Still), one needs patience to wait until the other party is ready. For mutual influence, the worst thing is to take reckless action. If one at this place lacks patience and follows the one at either the second place or the bottom through any ill-considered action, there will be regret.

(4) Fourth Nine. Mutual Influence alternates to Hardship (39) ☵☶

In the Yao Text, every line relates to a part of the human body, except this line. There are three yang lines in this gua. The fourth line is the middle of the three yang lines—underneath the neck and above the thigh. It is believed that the word heart was intentionally left out of the ideograph, because a human heart (Chinese consider the heart to be equivalent to the mind) is unpredictable. One at this place needs to work on the heart, feeling. Mutual influence greatly depends on the feeling of one's heart. Only by being steadfast and upright will one's regret disappear. This is a yang element at a yin place, an unsettled mind. If one continues to hesitate, only a few friends will follow one's lead, but at the same time one should be aware of being influenced by other people. This is the host of the gua. The message is that one should eliminate selfish intentions and become open and honest; then hesitation will disappear.

(5) Fifth Nine. Mutual Influence alternates to Little Exceeding (62) ☳☶

There are three solid lines in this gua: the third, fourth, and fifth lines. The fourth line in the middle represents the heart. The fifth line is above the heart, representing the upper back. Here, another analogy is used. The upper gua is Lake, which symbolizes the mouth. The broken line at the top of two solid lines looks like two lips. Therefore the top line symbolizes someone who is adept with sweet words and honeyed phrases and at making up stories. One at this place should disregard these sweet words and honeyed phrases as the back ignores the mouth; then there will be no regret.

The fifth line is a yang element at a yang place, central and correct. It corresponds to the yin element at the second place. However, another two solid lines lie between them. One at this place tends to give up the one at the second place and approaches the one at the top. This is to seek what lies close at hand and turn one's back on what is far away. The message is that when one makes a decision, one should not be nearsighted.

(6) Top Six. Mutual Influence alternates to Retreat (33)

The yielding line at the top is a yin element at a yin place at the end of the gua. At the same time, it is at the top of the upper gua, Lake, representing a mouth. Inside the mouth is the tongue. This line denotes that one at this place is fond of using sweet words and honeyed phrases. If one merely opens one's mouth and makes empty promises, there is no way to achieve mutual influence.

Additional Reference Information for This Gua

Image:	Lake above, Mountain below
Recite as:	Lake on Mountain, Mutual Influence
Element:	Metal
Structure:	Three yang with three yin
Month:	The fifth month of the lunar calendar, or June
Host of the Gua:	Fourth Nine
Opposite Gua:	Decreasing (41)
Inverse Gua:	Long Lasting (32)
Mutual Gua:	Encountering (44)

32

Heng •
Long Lasting

Zhen • Thunder
Xun • Wind

NAME AND STRUCTURE

Heng means persistence, perseverance, long lasting.

Sequence of the Gua: *The union of husband and wife should not be short-lived. Thus, after Mutual Influence, Long Lasting follows.*

Heng is translated by Wilhelm as Duration; by Blofeld as The Long Enduring. In this book, it is translated as Long Lasting. The structure of the gua is Thunder ☳ above, Wind ☴ below. It is the inverse of the preceding gua, Xian ䷞, or Mutual Influence. The preceding gua symbolizes a new marriage. In the I Ching, Thunder represents an eldest son, and Wind an eldest daughter. Thus, this gua symbolizes the long-term union of an old married couple.

In the preceding gua the youngest son, Mountain, constitutes the lower gua, which is a subordinate position. In courtship, usually the young man tends to subordinate himself to the young woman. Here the lower gua is replaced by Wind, which symbolizes an older woman at a subordinate place. The attribute of Wind is gentleness. The lower gua also represents an inner situation. It suggests that the woman takes more responsibility at home. The attribute of the man, Thunder, is strength and activity. The upper gua is also known as the outer gua, which represents an outer situation. Here it indicates that the man takes more responsibility in the outside world.

There are two horizontal lines in the ideograph of this gua, one at the top and the other at the bottom. These two lines represent the two shores of a river. Between the shores there are two images—a boat on the right, and a heart on the left. Three people are sailing across the river in the boat. In ancient China, crossing a river was not an easy task. An old Chinese saying describes the situation: "People in the same boat share weal and woe." Sharing weal and woe means working together in full cooperation with a united purpose—with one heart. For this reason, the ancient sage placed a heart beside the boat. Originally, the boat between two shores indicated the distance from this shore to that shore. Later on, the meaning was extended to suggest simply from here to there and, finally, from beginning to end. When the ancient sage drew a heart beside the boat, the meaning was further extended to include everlasting.

The main theme of Zhou I is twofold: Follow the Tao of Heaven to establish the Tao of Humanity. To follow the Tao of Heaven, the ancient sage employed Qian and Kun, characterizing the function of Heaven and Earth, to open the Upper Canon. To establish the Tao of Humanity, the ancient sage selected Xian and Heng, the prerequisite of a husband and wife, to commence the Lower Canon. The relationship of Heaven and Earth is interactive and everlasting. In the same way, the relationship of a husband and wife should have the quality of long-lasting mutual influence.

The union of a man and woman, to the Chinese, is a sacred event. In the ancient ceremony of a wedding, the man and woman made a sacred vow before Heaven and Earth and to the person in charge of the marriage. Qian represented the bridegroom's side, and Kun stood for the bride's side. In this way, the union of a man and woman was akin to the union of Heaven and Earth. The message of this gua is that sincerity, purity, and unselfishness are the essential elements of a long-lasting relationship.

Decision

> Long Lasting.
> Prosperous and smooth.
> No fault.
> Favorable to be steadfast and upright.
> Favorable to have somewhere to go.

Commentary on the Decision

> *Heng is Long Lasting.*
> *The firm is above, the gentle below.*

Thunder and wind are in mutual support.

Be gentle and in motion,
The firm and the gentle respond.
This signifies Long Lasting.

Long Lasting brings success; there is no fault.
It is favorable to be steadfast and upright.
This indicates that Long Lasting accords with the Tao.
The Tao of Heaven and Earth is long lasting; it never ends.

It is favorable to go somewhere.
An end is always followed by a new beginning.

Sun and moon rely on the Tao of Heaven;
Thus can their shining be long lasting.

The four seasons change and transform;
Thus can their production of beings long endure.
The holy sage remains long lasting in his way of life;
Then all things under Heaven are transformed to completion.
Contemplate the Tao of Long Lasting,
To see the nature of Heaven and Earth and of all beings.

Commentary on the Symbol

The union of Thunder and Wind.
An image of Long Lasting.
In correspondence with this,
The superior person stands firm without changing his aim.

Yao Text

1. Initial Six
    Deeply long lasting.
    Being steadfast: misfortune.
    Nothing is favorable.

    The misfortune of deeply long lasting
    Because of seeking deepness and profundity at the very beginning.

2. Second Nine
   Regret vanishes.

   Regret vanishes for the second nine,
   It holds to the central place.

3. Third Nine
   Not long lasting, one's virtue.
   Probably meets with disgrace.
   Being steadfast: humiliation.

   Not long lasting, one's virtue.
   No one tolerates him.

4. Fourth Nine
   Field.
   No birds.

   Staying away from one's proper place for long,
   How can one catch game?

5. Fifth Six
   Long lasting, one's virtue.
   Being steadfast and upright.
   Wives: good fortune.
   Husbands: misfortune.

   Docility brings good fortune for a wife;
   She follows one to the end.
   A man must make resolute decisions.
   Following a woman obediently: bad end.

6. Top Six
   Long lasting agitation.
   Misfortune.

   Long-lasting agitation at the uppermost position.
   Greatly without merit.

SIGNIFICANCE

This gua takes the image of the union of Thunder and Wind to display a long-lasting relationship. Thunder and wind correspond to each other

as natural phenomena. Thus, the superior person stands firm and does not change his aim. The Chinese believe that the way of Nature is always correct. Because it is always correct, it is long lasting. The Chinese concept of correctness is that it is free from deviation. Any excess or insufficiency represents deviation and is not right. The secret of success is to walk along the central path, that is, never overreact. Whatever is exactly right can be long lasting.

According to the structure, the upper gua, Thunder, is yang, the elder son. The lower gua, Wind, is yin, the eldest daughter. In the Commentary on the Decision, Confucius says, "The firm is above, the gentle below. Thunder and Wind are in mutual support." This is the typical ancient Chinese concept of marriage—that a husband should take the initiative, and the wife should be subordinate. This is the way of a harmonious marriage. It is also a natural phenomenon that wind and thunder work together in making a thunderstorm. The lower gua, Wind, supports the actions of the upper gua, Thunder. According to the ancient sages, one should follow the natural law. This is the Tao of Heaven and Earth, which is long lasting, never ending. The main theme of this gua is stated by Confucius:

> *Sun and moon rely on the Tao of Heaven;*
> *Thus can their shining be long lasting.*
> *The four seasons change and transform;*
> *Thus can their production of beings long endure.*
> *The holy sage remains long lasting in his way of life;*
> *Then all things under Heaven are transformed to completion.*
> *Contemplate the Tao of Long Lasting,*
> *To see the nature of Heaven and Earth and of all beings.*

In this gua, the first and the fourth lines are complementary yin and yang, as are the fifth and second lines and the sixth and third lines. All six lines are in harmony with their counterparts. This is necessary if something is to endure. If one does something that has long-lasting effects, it is certain to result in achievement. However, there is one essential prerequisite: to be steadfast and upright. Then there will be no fault, and it will be favorable to go anywhere.

The host of the gua is the solid line at the second place. According to the I Ching, only walking in the central path can have enduring effects. There are two central lines in this gua, the solid line at the second place and the yielding line at the fifth place. In most gua the fifth line is the superior position. But here, the line at the fifth place is weak. Although it is central, it is not as firm and strong as the solid line at the second place. Therefore, the solid line at the second place is more suitable to be the host of this gua. For stabilizing the social order and to affect the prevalent social customs, King Wen encouraged people to cultivate the virtue of perseverance and constancy of purpose. In this gua the Duke of Zhou narrates different ways of seeking long-lasting relationships and their results.

(1) Initial Six. Long Lasting alternates to Great Strength (34) ☳

This is a yin element at a yang place—neither central nor correct. It corresponds to the yang element at the fourth place. The lower gua is Wind ☴ (Penetrating), which gives a hint that one on the bottom place would be eager to establish a relationship with one at the fourth place. However, there are two solid lines between them. The situation is not favorable. One cannot expect a deep and profound relationship at a beginning stage. Mutual love and everlasting relationships take time to cultivate.

(2) Second Nine. Long Lasting alternates to Little Exceeding (62) ☳

The solid line at the second place is a yang element at a yin place. The position is not correct. This line is in the central place of the lower gua and corresponds to the yin element at the fifth place. Unfortunately, two yang lines lie between them. One at this place cannot move forward smoothly. Knowing the situation, one here keeps to the central path and acts reasonably. In this way regret disappears. This line indicates that those who walk in the central way are able to stand firm and obtain their final goal. There is no ground for regret.

(3) Third Nine. Long Lasting alternates to Relief (40) ☳

The solid line at the third place is a yang element at a yang place, but it has gone beyond the central path. Although one at this place is firm and strong and corresponds to the topmost yin element, there is, unfortunately, a lack of contentment with the present situation. One at this place intends to move forward but there are two yang lines around it, both below and above. If one in this position insists on moving forward, it probably will result in disgrace. Even remaining steadfast and upright, there is still ground for regret. In this situation, it is favorable to keep still and not move forward, because no one would tolerate him. In the Confucian Analects, Confucius says, "Long Lasting without virtue, one will be visited with disgrace." Obviously, Confucius adopted the idea from this yao.

(4) Fourth Nine. Long Lasting alternates to Growing Upward (46)

The solid line at the fourth place is at the bottom of the upper gua, Thunder. The attribute of Thunder is action. The text uses hunting in the field as an analogy. One at this place intends to move forward. The fourth line corresponds to the bottom line of the lower gua, Wind. Wind, in the I Ching, also represents a rooster. Thus the Yao Text mentions birds. The solid line at the fourth place is a yang element at a yin place. Its place is not proper, and so it catches no birds. Thus Confucius says, "Staying away from one's proper place for long, how can one catch game?" In other words, nothing can be accomplished.

(5) Fifth Six. Long Lasting alternates to Great Exceeding (28)

The yielding line at the fifth place is a yin element, indicative of a gentle character. This line is in the central place of the upper gua, Thunder. One at this place is not merely gentle but also truthful. This line corresponds to the solid line at the second place, suggesting that the element at this place maintains gentleness and truthfulness firmly with the one attached to it. In ancient China, gentleness is one of the highest virtues of a woman, but not of a man. A man needs to make worldly decisions. The core message of this line is that by acting properly one will be free from unnecessary action later. Even while maintaining the virtue of gentleness, a man or a woman still needs to consider each situation. In the course of history, different times have had different social mores and constraints. Different cultures recognize different standards. Different roles carry different responsibilities. One has to adjust one's deeds and perspective in accordance with the situation. Any excess or insufficiency of action is not correct. Walking the central path is the way to succeed.

(6) Top Six. Long Lasting alternates to Establishing the New (50)

The attribute of Thunder is motion. The topmost line is at the end of a movement—it is time to stop. If one persists in moving, misfortune will result. "Sun and moon rely on the Tao of Heaven; thus can their shining be long lasting. The four seasons change and transform; thus can their production of beings long endure." The way of Long Lasting is to let the situation determine one's changes and transformations.

Additional Reference Information for This Gua

Image:	Thunder above, Wind below
Recite as:	Thunder over Wind, Long Lasting
Element:	Wood
Structure:	Three yang with three yin
Month:	The seventh month of the lunar calendar, or August
Host of the Gua:	Second Nine
Opposite Gua:	Increasing (42)
Inverse Gua:	Mutual Influence (31)
Mutual Gua:	Eliminating (43)

33

Dun • Retreat

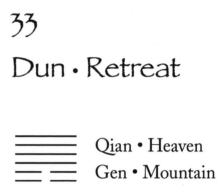

Qian • Heaven
Gen • Mountain

NAME AND STRUCTURE

Dun is to hide, to withdraw, to retreat. Wilhelm translates Dun as Retreat and Blofeld as Yielding, Withdrawal. In this book, the term Retreat is used. The ideograph of Dun consists of two parts. On the left is an ideograph from the remote past. Three curved strokes represent three footprints moving forward. Underneath the three strokes is a tiny ideograph, zhi, meaning "stop." These two ideographs create a picture of going forward and stopping abruptly. The ideograph on the right is complicated, consisting of three pictures: a little pig, a piece of meat, and a hand. A piece of pork is offered as a sacrifice at a memorial ceremony. The little pig is cut into two portions—shown at the top and the bottom of the ideograph. In the middle, there is a piece of meat at the left and a hand at the right. Taken together, this is a picture of someone performing a sacrificial ceremony during a retreat.

Sequence of the Gua: *Things cannot abide long in the same place. Thus, after Long Lasting, withdrawal and retreat follow.*

The structure of the gua is Heaven ☰ above, Mountain ☶ below. The attribute of Heaven is creative power. In this gua it represents a sage who lives in accordance with the will of Heaven. The attribute of Mountain is keeping still. The structure shows that a sage confronts stillness and retreats.

There are four solid lines and two yielding lines in this gua. The two yielding lines stand at the bottom. They are moving forward. This is a situation where inferior persons were multiplying and increasing in power. It is time for the wise to retreat. Retreat is not flight. To flee, to escape danger in any circumstance, is cowardly. But retreating can also be aimed at preserving one's strength, waiting for the right time for future advance. A wise person uses strength properly. When the time is not right, retreat. King Wen's Decision says that for the little it is favorable to be steadfast and upright. The word little denotes inferior people. In the time favoring the inferior, it is better for the wise to retreat, keeping steadfast and upright for future advancement.

This gua, Dun, is one of the twelve tidal gua. It represents the sixth month of the Chinese lunar calendar.

Decision

> Retreat.
> Prosperous and smooth.
> The little: favorable to be steadfast and upright.

Commentary on the Decision

> *Retreat, prosperous and smooth.*
> *Prosperity and smoothness lies in retreat.*
>
> *The firm is at the right place*
> *And properly corresponds.*
> *It accords with the time.*
>
> *The little:*
> *Favorable to be steadfast and upright.*
> *It is advancing and growing.*
>
> *Great indeed is the significance of retreat*
> *At the proper time.*

Commentary on the Symbol

> *Mountain under Heaven,*
> *An image of Retreat.*
> *In correspondence with this,*

The superior person keeps inferior persons at a distance,
With dignity but without ill will.

Yao Text

1. Initial Six
   Retreat at the tail.
   Adversity.
   Do not use anything.
   There is somewhere to go.

   Adversity of retreating at the tail.
   If no action be made,
   What misfortune could there be?

2. Second Six
   Holding fast
   With hide of yellow ox.
   No one is able to loosen.

   Holding fast with hide of yellow ox.
   It denotes a firm will.

3. Third Nine
   Attached, retreats.
   There is illness.
   Adversity.
   Feed manservants and handmaidens:
   Good fortune.

   Attached, retreats: adversity.
   He is distressed and exhausted.
   Feed manservants and handmaidens: good fortune.
   He cannot do big things.

4. Fourth Nine
   Being fond of retreat:
   Superior person—good fortune;
   Little fellow—nay!

   Superior person, being fond of retreat.
   Little fellow cannot do that.

5. Fifth Nine
   Appropriate retreat.
   Being steadfast and upright:
   Good fortune.

   Appropriate retreat.
   Being steadfast and upright: good fortune.
   He rectifies his will.

6. Top Nine
   Elegant retreat.
   Nothing is unfavorable.

   Elegant retreat.
   Nothing is unfavorable,
   No doubt at all.

SIGNIFICANCE

This gua employs the image of a high mountain and faraway Heaven to expound the constructive meaning of retreat. When the dark forces spread and the brightness is too high to reach, one should retreat rather than compromise with the darkness. Thus, Retreat has a positive meaning. Because Retreat is constructive, most of the lines are auspicious, except the bottom line and the third line. One is too late to retreat, and the other has already retreated but still attaches to the darkness. The topmost line represents the highest level of retreat.

Three lines in this gua are qualified to be the host—the two yielding lines at the bottom and the solid line at the fifth place. Confucius's Commentary on the Decision says, "The firm is at the right place and properly corresponds. It accords with the time." This is said with reference to the solid line at the fifth place. However, the name of the gua is Retreat. The cause of the retreat is the two yielding lines at the bottom. They are proceeding forward and thus forcing the solid lines to retreat. One of the yielding lines is thus the most appropriate host of Retreat. The yielding line at the second place is central and correct and makes the best host. The two yielding lines of this gua represent the dark forces multiplying and increasing in strength. The four solid lines symbolize the bright forces. They are retreating, but their retreat is constructive. Since the time is not favorable for the light, their retreat comes at the right moment and with the proper attitude. Their goal is to preserve their strength for future advancement and success.

During the period of establishing feudal lords and stabilizing people's lives, conditions were not always smooth. King Wen shouldered heavy responsibilities. When inferior persons around the Tyrant of Shang were multiplying and gaining power, King Wen retreated. To retreat was a strategy of concession in order to determine the hostile intentions of such inferior persons. The Duke of Zhou mentions different ways to retreat. He indicates that during the time favorable for retreat, one hides his capacities and bides his time. Retreat is constructive—to preserve one's strength, waiting for the right time for future advance.

(1) Initial Six. Retreat alternates to Seeking Harmony (13) ☷

The Yao Text says, "Retreat at the tail." The tail is the rear part of an animal. It represents the last one to take action to retreat. When the dark force begins to close in, it is difficult to distinguish. If one cannot take action to prevent its growing, there lies the potential of adversity. According to the experience of the ancient sages, "If no action be made, what misfortune could there be?" The lower gua is Mountain, whose attribute is keeping still. Keeping still is one aspect of Retreat.

(2) Second Six. Retreat alternates to Encountering (44) ☰

The second line, in the middle of the lower gua, represents one who is following the principle of the Golden Mean, that is, walking in the central path. During the time favorable for one to retreat, he hides his capacities and bides his time. His retreat is constructive. The Duke of Zhou employed an analogy to describe his steadfastness: "Holding fast with hide of yellow ox. No one is able to loosen." That no one can loosen it means that nobody is able to interrupt him. Yellow is the color of Earth, and its attribute is being central and obedient. One at this place should bow to the time and situation and walk in the middle path. A constructive retreat is made for future advance.

(3) Third Nine. Retreat alternates to Hindrance (12) ☶

The third line is a yang element at a yang place. It is firm and correct but encumbered with the two yin elements underneath it. One at this place has already retreated from the dark forces but still attaches to the darkness. If he cannot completely keep the darkness at a distance, there is distress, such as illness. The text advises that it is better to stay at home and care for little things. In ancient times, there were many servants at a feudal noble's house. "Feed manservants and handmaidens" means staying at home.

(4) Fourth Nine. Retreat alternates to Developing Gradually (53)

The solid line at the fourth place is at the bottom of the upper gua, Heaven. It possesses a strong and firm character and responds to the yin element at the bottom of the lower gua, which represents the dark force. At the time of retreat, it is favorable for one to cut the bond with the dark forces abruptly. The Yao Text says that the superior person can succeed by retreating, but not the little fellow. Severing oneself from the dark forces is not an easy task. Only a sage can preserve his purity by retreating; a little fellow cannot.

(5) Fifth Nine. Retreat alternates to Traveling (56)

The fifth line is a yang element at a yang place, central and correct. It corresponds to the yin element at the second place. The yin element at the second place is also central and correct—it would not constitute a hindrance for one at the fifth place to retreat. Retreat without attachment to the darkness is an admirable retreat. There is good fortune. In comparison with the one at the topmost position, here one is still not able to totally abandon the affairs of human society. Therefore, remaining steadfast and upright is still necessary.

(6) Top Nine. Retreat alternates to Mutual Influence (31)

The topmost line represents the end of a situation. There is no more space to advance and progress. It is beyond the position of a king; it represents a sage. Here one is free from bonds. He embraces the spirit of nonattachment, which is favorable in every respect. Even where there is advance, there is still no bond.

Additional Reference Information for This Gua

Image:	Heaven above, Mountain below
Recite as:	Heaven above Mountain, Retreat
Element:	Metal
Structure:	Four yang with two yin
Month:	The sixth month of the lunar calendar, or July
Host of the Gua:	Second Six
Opposite Gua:	Approaching (19)
Inverse Gua:	Great Strength (34)
Mutual Gua:	Encountering (44)

34
Da Zhuang ·
Great Strength

Zhen • Thunder
Qian • Heaven

NAME AND STRUCTURE

Da is great. Zhuang means strength. Both Wilhelm and Blofeld translate Da Zhuang as The Power of the Great. This book adopts its literal meaning, Great Strength. The name consists of two ideographs. The first one, da, looks like a person standing upright with arms and legs wide open. The attribute of greatness was associated with Heaven, Earth, and human beings.

The second ideograph, zhuang, consists of two parts. On the left is an ideograph from antiquity. It looks like a weapon. In ancient times a weapon was made of bamboo or wood. On the right is another ideograph, shi. In ancient times shi was the lowest class of feudal subordinate. Later on, it came to represent an intellectual. At the very beginning, people of robust strength were selected as guards to protect the royalty. They were as stout and strong as the trunks of trees. The ideograph employs a picture of a strong man with arms stretching out like a cross standing on the ground. When these two pictures are put together, zhuang has the meaning of strength.

Sequence of the Gua: *Things cannot retreat forever. Thus, after Retreat, Great Strength follows.*

This gua is the inverse of the preceding one, Retreat. Retreat is a negative means to a positive end. Great Strength represents a positive advance for further achievement. The structure of the gua is Thunder ☳ above, Heaven ☰ below. The ancient Chinese believed thunder to be yang energy. When yang energy permeates Heaven, its strength is incredibly great. In Retreat, two yielding lines lie at the bottom of four solid lines. In Great Strength, the two yielding lines withdraw to the top of the gua. Four firm lines at the bottom ascend higher and higher and grow stronger and stronger. This is where the name Great Strength comes from. The attribute of Thunder is motion, and that of Heaven is strength. This gua is a union of motion with strength, resulting in Great Strength. Great Strength is one of the twelve tidal gua. It represents the second month of the Chinese lunar calendar.

Decision

> Great Strength.
> Favorable to be steadfast and upright.

Commentary on the Decision

> *Great Strength.*
> *Strength becomes great.*
>
> *Firm in motion.*
> *The strength is great.*
>
> *Great strength.*
> *Favorable to be steadfast and upright;*
>
> *What is great should be righteous.*
> *When righteousness is great,*
> *The truth of Heaven and Earth can be seen.*

Commentary on the Symbol

> *Thunder above Heaven.*
> *An image of Great Strength.*
> *In correspondence with this,*
> *The superior person does not act contrary to courtesy.*

Yao Text

1. Initial Nine
   Strengthening the forward toes.

Moving forward: misfortune.
Be sincere and truthful.

Great strength at the toes.
It certainly leads to failure.

2. Second Nine
   Being steadfast and upright:
   Good fortune.

   Good fortune of the second nine.
   It is at the central place.

3. Third Nine
   Little fellow uses strength;
   Superior person uses nothing.
   Being steadfast: adversity.
   A ram butting against a hedge
   Entangles its horns.

   Little fellow uses strength.
   Superior person never runs wild like that.

4. Fourth Nine
   Being steadfast and upright: good fortune.
   Regret vanishes.
   The hedge falls apart,
   No more entanglement.
   Strength at the spokes of a big cart.

   The hedge falls apart, no more entanglement.
   He can go forward.

5. Fifth Six
   Lose a ram in the field.
   No regret.

   Lose a ram in the field.
   The place is not appropriate.

6. Top Six
   A ram butts against a hedge,
   Unable to go backward,
   Unable to go forward.

Nothing is favorable.
Difficulty, then good fortune.

Unable to go backward or forward,
It is not auspicious.
If one realizes the difficulty,
There is good fortune.
In this way, one's fault will not last long.

SIGNIFICANCE

This gua expounds the principle of how to use one's great strength. The main theme is that one should not become too self-willed and opinionated. To the ancient Chinese, great strength should not merely appear as physical strength. Moral strength was more important and powerful than physical strength. Relying on physical strength, one's achievement could not endure. Only moral strength could radiate its brilliance and be everlasting. For this reason, the first, third, and topmost lines show that for those who rely too much on strength and lose their equanimity, nothing is favorable and there is danger. The host of this gua is unusual. There are four solid lines; the one at the second place is central, in a good location to be the host. Yet the fourth line is the leader of four yang elements—it deserves the host position.

King Wen's strategy in dealing with inferior persons around the Tyrant of Shang was successful. After retreating, King Wen accumulated great strength. He instructed his people that it was necessary to be steadfast and upright. The Duke of Zhou warns that during a time of gaining strength, people tend to become opinionated and run wild. Conquering the inferior merely by using strength would not assure success. One should employ righteousness and act according to the principle of the Golden Mean. When situations are not conducive to moving forward, one should not overdo.

(1) Initial Nine. Great Strength alternates to Long Lasting (32)

Toes are the lowest part of a human body, as the bottom line is the lowest part of a gua. The bottom line of this gua is a yang element at a yang place. One at this place has a strong desire to move forward. Since the bottom line is just the beginning of Great Strength, it is not yet strong enough to carry the whole body. And it does not correspond to the yang element at the fourth place. Thus, proceeding brings misfortune. The Yao Text says, "Moving forward: misfortune. Be sincere and truthful." This yang element at a yang place, at the bottom of the inner gua, Heaven, bears too much yang. Parading one's strength and striving to outshine others brings about misfortune.

(2) Second Nine. Great Strength alternates to Abundance (55)

The second line is a yang element at a yin place. Although the place is not correct, it is central to the lower gua. One at this place is able to act according to the principle of the Golden Mean. In a position of great strength, one tends to overdo. If he is able to restrain himself and persist in doing right, there will be good fortune.

(3) Third Nine. Great Strength alternates to Marrying Maiden (54)

The third line is a yang element at a yang place. There are three yang elements in the lower gua. The third line has already proceeded beyond the middle; one at this place bears too much yang. He might become opinionated and run wild. In a position of great strength, inferior persons may bully and humiliate others. The Duke of Zhou gives warning that this is like a ram butting against a fence and getting its horns entangled. A superior person would never run wild.

(4) Fourth Nine. Great Strength alternates to Advance (11)

The fourth line is the host of the gua. It is the head of the four yang elements and the principal factor overcoming the inferior. Conquering the inferior merely by using strength cannot asssure success. One should employ righteousness. This is the theme of this line and the gua as a whole. As the head of the yang elements, this line has already reached the upper gua. It is extremely strong. In this situation, relying on one's great strength will bring danger and regret. Thus the Yao Text says, "Being steadfast and upright: good fortune. Regret vanishes." Fortunately, this is a yang element at a yin place; he does not blindly proceed further with force and strength. Thus, regret disappears.

The upper gua is Thunder. When this line alternates from solid to yielding, the upper gua becomes Kun. Here, Thunder is seen as bamboo, a hedge, and Kun represents a big cart. Because this person is able to restrain himself, the Yao Text says, "The hedge falls apart, no more entanglement. Strength at the spokes of a big cart." In this way, he can go forward.

(5) Fifth Six. Great Strength alternates to Eliminating (43) ☱

If one combines every two lines of the gua into one, Great Strength ☱ becomes Dui ☱. Dui symbolizes a ram, and the lines resemble the face of a ram. The Yao Text originally said, "Lose a ram in I." Here, I, in Chinese, is exactly the same character as the I of the I Ching. I means easy, lightly, or change. For this reason, other translations give this text as "Lose the goat with ease," "He sacrifices a goat too lightly," or "Losing the sheep due to changes." However, in ancient times I also meant field. This translation retains the ancient meaning "Lose a ram in the field."

This line is a yin element at a yang place—it is a gentle ram. Since it is in a central location, the ram will not act wildly. He knows the situation of great strength will decline. When the four yang elements approach menacingly, he yields. The mood is as calm as if the ram is lost in the field without regret. Because he understands that his position is not conducive to moving forward, he has no regret.

(6) Top Six. Great Strength alternates to Great Harvest (14) ☲

The topmost line represents the waning of great strength. The ancient sage employs the analogy of a ram butting against a hedge to explain the situation. Because the line is at the top, there is no way to go forward. Moreover, it is weak; it has no strength to turn back. Nothing is favorable. Fortunately, this line is a yin element. Its yielding character frees it from overdoing. The spirit of the I Ching is to remind people to act without error. If one in this position can realize the difficulty and yield, there will be good fortune. Confucius says in his commentary on the Yao Text: "If one realizes the difficulty . . . one's fault will not last long."

Additional Reference Information for This Gua

Image:	Thunder above, Heaven below
Recite as:	Thunder above Heaven, Great Strength
Element:	Wood
Structure:	Four yang with two yin
Month:	The second month of the lunar calendar, or March
Host of the Gua:	Fourth Nine
Opposite Gua:	Watching (20) ☶
Inverse Gua:	Retreat (33) ☶
Mutual Gua:	Eliminating (43) ☱

35

Jing · Proceeding Forward

☲ Li • Fire
☷ Kun • Earth

NAME AND STRUCTURE

Jing is to advance, to promote, or to proceed. Both Wilhelm and Blofeld translate Jing as Progress. I adopt the term Proceeding Forward.

Sequence of the Gua: *Things cannot remain forever in great strength. Thus, after Great Strength, Proceeding Forward follows.*

The structure of the gua is Fire ☲ above, Earth ☷ below. Fire is a symbol of Li, which represents the sun. The structure of this gua shows that the sun is rising over the Earth, an image of progress or a process.

The ideograph of Jing is a beautiful picture of the sun rising over the Earth. The circle at the bottom is a symbol of the sun. The horizontal stroke in the middle of the sun is believed to represent a dark spot on its surface. Above the sun, there are two straight lines that symbolize the horizon of the Earth. Upon the earth, two plants are flourishing and blooming upward with the yang energy from the sun, glowing like the flame of a fire. The ideograph shows not only an act of proceeding but also the radiance of the energy.

Decision

> Proceeding Forward.
> Lord Kang is honored with numerous horses.
> In a single day, thrice received at interview.

Commentary on the Decision

Proceeding Forward.
It denotes advancing.

The bright is appearing over the earth.
The submissive is clinging to the brilliant.
The gentle is proceeding and moving upward.

It symbolizes that the lord who maintains the country in order
Is honored with numerous horses
And received at interviews three times a day.

Commentary on the Symbol

The Light comes forth over the Earth.
An image of Proceeding Forward.
In correspondence with this,
The superior person cultivates his virtues
And brightens them by himself.

Yao Text

1. Initial Six
   Proceeding forward, being held back.
   Being steadfast and upright: good fortune.
   No confidence.
   Being calm and unhurried:
   No fault.

   Proceeding forward, being held back.
   All alone, he walks in the right path.
   Being calm and unhurried.
   He has not received an appointment.

2. Second Six
   Proceeding forward with worry.
   Being steadfast and upright: good fortune.
   Receiving this great blessing
   From his grandmother.

Receive this great blessing
Owing to central and correct position.

3. Third Six
   From the multitude obtain trust.
   Regret vanishes.

   From the multitude obtain trust.
   The will is to move upward.

4. Fourth Nine
   Proceeding forward like a rat.
   Being steadfast: adversity.

   A rat faces adversity
   Even remaining steadfast.
   The position is not appropriate.

5. Fifth Six
   Regret vanishes.
   Lose or gain,
   Stop worrying.
   Going forward: good fortune.
   Nothing is unfavorable.

   Win or lose, stop worrying.
   To proceed will afford ground for congratulation.

6. Top Nine
   Proceeding forward into his horn.
   Appropriate to conquer one's own domain.
   Adversity: good fortune.
   No fault.
   Being steadfast: humiliation.

   Appropriate to conquer one's own domain.
   His way is not yet brilliant.

SIGNIFICANCE

This gua expounds the principle of proceeding. If one's strength is great, one is able to progress and contribute one's talent to society. It is like the rising sun shining upon all beings on the Earth. In the

process of proceeding, one's motivation should be pure. If the situation is not smooth, one should remain steadfast and upright and hold to the principle of the Golden Mean. Then people around will lend support. This gua also displays the truth of the complementary nature of yin and yang. Yin is yielding; yang is firm. The ancients thought that being too firm in one's character would lead to difficulty in dealing with people. If one was not firm enough, one would find it difficult to deal with the course of life. Proceeding should be stable, gradual, and steady.

The host of this gua is the yielding line at the fifth place, in the middle of the upper gua, Li (Fire). When yin takes over the middle place of Heaven, Heaven ☰ becomes Fire ☲. The image of the gua is a rising sun over the Earth. After gaining great strength, King Wen had the opportunity to proceed. Helping the Shang maintain the country in order, he was honored with numerous horses. In a single day he was received at interview three times. The Duke of Zhou mentions that to proceed was auspicious, but being too close to the tyrant was like being a rat in the court. There was humiliation and adversity. By gaining trust from the people and allaying concern over whether plans would fail or succeed, nothing was unfavorable. Continuing to proceed without restraint would have led to regret.

(1) Initial Six. Proceeding Forward alternates to Eradicating (21) ☷

All lines in this gua intend to proceed. However, the bottom line symbolizes that one has just entered society. Without experience, she wants to proceed but holds back. This line is a yin element at a yang place. The place is not correct. Although it responds to the yang element at the fourth place, there are two yin elements between them. It is difficult to respond. Thus the Yao Text says, "No confidence." Nevertheless, the bottom line and the fourth line are correspondent yin and yang. When the bottom line accumulates experience, they will support each other. The Yao Text advises one to be calm and unhurried. The key is keeping steadfast and upright; then there will be good fortune.

(2) Second Six. Proceeding Forward alternates to Not Yet Fulfilled (64) ☷

The second line is a yin element at a yin place, central and correct. It does not respond to the yin element at the fifth place, which is a place for a king. One at this place cannot gain support from above. She proceeds with worry. However, she is central and correct; if she is able to keep steadfast and upright, she will receive great blessing, as from a grandmother. There will be good fortune. Grandmother, in Chinese, is wang mu. Literally, wang means king, and mu means mother. For this reason, Wilhelm translates wang mu as ancestors, and Blofeld translates it as Queen Mother. According to the oldest Chinese dictionary of characters, *Er Ya*, wang mu means father's mother. In this gua, all yin elements symbolize females. The yielding line at the third place is the mother, and the fifth line is the grandmother. Don't worry; it is certain that the central and correct will bring good fortune—this is the message of the gua.

(3) Third Six. Proceeding Forward alternates to Traveling (56) ☷

The Yao Text says, "Obtain trust from the multitude. Regret vanishes." The lower gua is Kun, which represents a multitude. The third line is the topmost of three yin lines; thus she gains their trust. This line is a yin element at a yang place, neither central nor correct—there is regret. Fortunately, the two yielding lines underneath intend to proceed with her. The three together are of the same mind. Thus regret disappears. Because the multitude trust, one in this place is able to move upward (forward) and carry out her will.

(4) Fourth Nine. Proceeding Forward alternates to Falling Away (23) ☶

The fourth line is a yang element at a yin place, neither central nor correct. He is at a minister's place, close to the king. However, he is not qualified for this position, being a yang element at a yin place. When this line changes from a yang to a yin element, the upper gua alternates from Li ☲ to Gen ☶. Gen also represents a rat. Yang has the attribute of large size. Thus, the Yao Text says, "Proceeding forward like a rat." The nature of a rat is to act without a goal and to be greedy. One in this place needs self-knowledge. If he is not virtuous and as greedy as a big rat, even being steadfast will bring evil. The message of this gua is that one should not act without a goal, or be greedy, especially in a high position.

(5) Fifth Six. Proceeding Forward alternates to Hindrance (12) ☶

This is the host of the gua. Being a yin element at a yang place, there is regret. However, it has the dominant position of the upper gua, Fire, which represents the light. The lower gua is Earth which is submissive. If one in this place possesses a humble attitude and is open and straightforward, she will receive the support of the solid line at the fourth place. If she is able to humble herself to accept advice from a wise man (the solid line at the top), stop being concerned over whether plans will fail or succeed, and proceed gradually and steadily like the rising sun, her light will illuminate every corner of the land as does the sun. People will follow. Nothing is unfavorable.

(6) Top Nine. Proceeding Forward alternates to Delight (16) ☷☳

The topmost line is a yang element at a yin place, neither central nor correct. One at this place has reached an extreme, like proceeding into the point of a horn. There is no way out. Owing to his firmness, he still has the strength to conquer his own domain. To conquer one's own domain refers to having self-control. Be aware of the danger, and there will be good fortune. Continuing to proceed will bring regret.

Additional Reference Information for This Gua

Image:	Fire above, Earth below
Recite as:	Sun arises on Earth, Proceeding Forward
Element:	Fire
Structure:	Two yang with four yin
Month:	The second month of the lunar calendar, or March
Host of the Gua:	Fifth Six
Opposite Gua:	Needing (5) ☵☰
Inverse Gua:	Brilliance Injured (36) ☷☲
Mutual Gua:	Hardship (39) ☵☶

36

Ming Yi •
Brilliance Injured

☷	Kun • Earth
☲	Li • Fire

NAME AND STRUCTURE

Ming signifies brightness, brilliance. Yi has more than ten meanings in the Chinese language. As a verb, it means to raze, to exterminate, to injure. Literally, Ming Yi means that one's brilliance is injured. Wilhelm translates Ming Yi as Darkening of the Light; in Blofeld it is Darkening of the Light, Injury. However, in Chinese guang is the word that refers to the brightness of a light. Ming indicates the brilliance of one's mind, intelligence, and virtue.

Sequence of the Gua: *Proceeding Forward without restraint, surely someone will be hurt. Thus, after Proceeding Forward, Brilliance Injured follows.*

This gua is the inverse of the preceding one, Proceeding Forward ☷☲. There is a well-known Chinese maxim: tao guang yang hui, which means hide one's light and bide one's time. This is the connotation of Brilliance Injured. By proceeding one is taking a risk, even risking injury. When one's brilliance is injured, it forces one to hold back, nurse one's wounds. It is then favorable to proceed further.

The name of the gua consists of two ideographs. The first one, ming, is composed of the symbols for a sun, on the left, and a moon, on the right. The Chinese saying "Sun and moon, brightness" indicates the character of ming. The second ideograph, yi, is composed of two symbols, a big man and a bow. If one is familiar with the gua Great Harvest (14), Great Accumulation (26), Great Exceeding (28), and Great Strength (34), one can recognize that the ideograph of "great," da, forms the background of yi. Here, yi represents a great man or a big man. In the middle there is a bow. The text employs the image of a large man with a bow to express the act of injury.

The structure of the gua is Earth ☷ above, Fire ☲ below—a picture of the setting sun. The brightness of the sun is hidden by the Earth. Darkness envelopes more and more, representing a situation of hardship. Such a situation was encountered by King Wen when he was imprisoned by the Tyrant of Shang. King Wen was bright within and gentle without. He adopted the art of tao guang yang hui—hiding his brilliance and biding his time—in dealing with an extremely difficult situation. To be bright within and gentle without was one of the highest virtues in ancient China. To the ancient sages, only the bright and the gentle could overcome the dark and the unyielding. Only the wisest and, at the same time, the strongest could appreciate this virtue and cultivate it.

Decision

> Brilliance Injured.
> Favorable to be steadfast and upright in hardship.

Commentary on the Decision

> *Brightness has sunk under the Earth.*
> *It is Brilliance Injured.*
>
> *Inside is grace and brightness.*
> *Outside is gentle and yielding.*
> *Confronted by great hardship.*
> *This was what King Wen experienced.*
>
> *Favorable to be steadfast and upright in hardship.*
> *This is to cover one's brilliance.*
>
> *In the midst of hardship,*
> *Nonetheless keeping his mind still and his will righteous.*
> *This was what Ji Zi encountered.*

Commentary on the Symbol

Brightness has sunk under the Earth.
An image of Brilliance Injured.
In correspondence with this,
The superior person remains in harmony with the multitude.
Covering his brilliance, yet his light is still shining.

Yao Text

1. Initial Nine
    Brilliance injured is flying,
    Drooping its wings.
    The sage evades,
    Three days, ignores eating.
    There is somewhere to go.
    The host gossips.

    The sage evades;
    It is righteous not to eat.

2. Second Six
    Brilliance injured,
    Injured in the left thigh.
    Needs aid, a strong horse.
    Good fortune.

    The good fortune of the second six.
    He acts in accordance with the principle and the situation.

3. Third Nine
    Brilliance injured
    Hunting in the south.
    Captured the great chief.
    Act not with undue haste;
    Be steadfast and upright.

    Hunting in the south.
    A great achievement has been accomplished.

4. Fourth Six
Entering the left belly,
Knowing the heart of the injured brilliance.
Quit the dwelling place.

Entering the left belly,
Learn the intention of his mind.

5. Fifth Six
Ji Zi's brilliance injured.
Favorable to be steadfast and upright.

The steadfastness and uprightness of Ji Zi;
His brilliance could not be extinguished.

6. Top Six
No brightness,
Only darkness.
At first, ascend to Heaven.
Afterward, fall to Earth.

At first, ascend to Heaven.
He illuminated the four quarters of the Earth.
Afterward, fall to Earth.
He lost the code of conduct.

SIGNIFICANCE

This gua expounds the truth of hiding one's brilliance and biding one's time during an extremely difficult situation. There are two lines qualified to be the host of this gua, the yielding at the second place and the yielding at the fifth place. Both of them are central but not correct. This gua represents a time of darkness and a situation of hardship, as experienced by both King Wen and Ji Zi. Thus, the two principal lines represent these two sages who were injured the most. The main theme of the gua expresses the wisdom of realizing the difficulty and hardship and remaining steadfast and upright during a time of darkness, as did King Wen and Ji Zi.

(1) Initial Nine. Brilliance Injured alternates to Humbleness (15) ☷☶

The bottom line represents the situation of one injured during a time of darkness, as a bird is injured while flying. The line represents the initial injury. The injury of the bird is not serious—the bird can still fly with its wings drooping. The Duke of Zhou associated this line with an incident in the life of the sage Bai Yi. It is well known in Chinese history that Bai Yi refused to eat the millet of the Zhou dynasty.

Bai Yi and his brother, Shu Qi, lived in the kingdom of Zhou. When King Wu launched the revolution against the Tyrant of Shang, they did not agree with it, because they believed to overthrow any king was wrong. When the tyrant was overthrown, they retreated to the mountain of Shou Yang, refused to eat the millet of the Zhou dynasty, and died. This is what Confucius refers to in his commentary when he says, "It is righteous not to eat." Bai Yi and Shu Qi were honored as the most righteous figures in Chinese history. Mencius said,

> Bai Yi would not serve a lord of whom he did not approve.
> He would not associate with a friend whom he did not esteem.
> He would not stand in an evil lord's court nor speak with an evil man.

They held fast to what they believed and even refused to eat the food they thought unrighteous.

(2) Second Six. Brilliance Injured alternates to Advance (11)

The injury of the second line is more serious than that of the bottom line. At the bottom line the bird is still able to fly, while at the second line it has become difficult to walk. This is a yin element at a yin place, central and correct. One in this place is gentle and acts in accordance with the situation, obtaining support, and matters end in good fortune. When this line changes from yielding to solid, the lower gua alternates from Li to Qian. Qian also represents a stallion. The Yao Text says to get aid from a strong horse. The strong horse is King Wen, who rescued the people of the Shang dynasty from the Tyrant of Shang.

(3) Third Nine. Brilliance Injured alternates to Turning Back (24)

The third line is a yang element at a yang place—extremely firm. It is at the top of the lower gua, Li, a most brilliant position. However, it is surrounded by yin elements. Moreover, it responds to the topmost yin element, signifying darkness. The situation is not good. One must hide one's brilliance and be patient. Because one in this position is firm and brilliant, during a hunt in the south the great chief will eventually be captured. In ancient times, south was placed at the top of a map. Thus in this gua south indicates the host yin element at the fifth place—the host

of darkness. This hunt in the south will bring light to the darkness. It is an immense action, a revolution; as such, it will take time; hasty correction should not be expected. This line tells us that after King Wen, who had been imprisoned by the Tyrant of Shang for seven years, was released, he instructed his son, King Wu, to launch a revolution against the tyrant.

(4) Fourth Six. Brilliance Injured alternates to Abundance (55)

The text of this line is difficult to understand. The fourth line is at the bottom line of the upper gua, Earth. In the I Ching, Earth represents a belly as well as darkness. The fourth line is also in the middle (the heart) of this gua, Brilliance Injured; thus, the Yao Text says, "Entering the left belly, knowing the heart of the injured brilliance." A Chinese adage says, "Without entering the tiger's lair, how can one catch tiger cubs?" In other words, having experienced the danger of a situation, one is able to use that information to avoid being a helpless victim.

This line is associated with a historical event. When Wei Zi, an elder brother of the Tyrant of Shang, saw his brother tyrannize the country, he remonstrated several times and was rejected. He realized that the tyrant's mind would not change. He left the palace and took refuge in King Wen's domain. After the Tyrant of Shang was overthrown, Wei Zi returned and became a virtuous ruler of his own.

(5) Fifth Six. Brilliance Injured alternates to Already Fulfilled (63)

The fifth line is the host of the gua. It is in the center of the upper gua, Darkness, and also adjacent to the topmost line, representing the most darkness. One at this place has fallen into a very difficult situation. Because of the central place, one is able to be steadfast and upright, like Ji Zi. The light cannot be extinguished. To the ancient Chinese, remaining steadfast and upright was the highest virtue when dealing with darkness and hardship. This line represents Ji Zi. Ji Zi was the virtuous uncle of the Tyrant of Shang. He remonstrated with the tyrant for his misbehavior and was rebuffed. His close friends advised Ji Zi to go into exile; otherwise he would be put to death. Ji Zi responded, "As a subordinate of a king, after being rejected from dissuading His Majesty from cruelty, to leave would expose the king's evil and gain favor from people. I cannot bear to do that." Although Ji Zi knew that the king was wrong, he also knew that as a loyal servant it would be wrong for him to betray the king. With his hair disheveled, he pretended to be insane. He was driven out of the palace and became a slave. This is how Ji Zi intentionally hid his brilliance to avert an impossible situation. The message of this line and of the gua is, as Confucius says, "The steadfastness and uprightness of Ji Zi; his brilliance could not be extinguished."

(6) Top Six. Brilliance Injured alternates to Adorning (22) ☶

The Yao Text says, "No Brightness, only darkness," representing the worst situation. The darkness reaches an extreme. In this situation one must remain faithful. If one realizes that the darkness has already ascended to Heaven, it will soon fall into the depths of the Earth. With this faithfulness, steadfastness, and uprightness, King Wen and the sage Ji Zi survived. What they could do, we can do also. On the other hand, the Tyrant of Shang never acted in accord with the will of Heaven and the wishes of people; he insisted upon tyranny to the end. As Confucius says, he fell because "he lost the code of conduct."

Additional Reference Information for This Gua

Image:	Earth above, Fire below
Recite as:	Fire under Earth, Brilliance Injured
Element:	Earth
Structure:	Two yang with four yin
Month:	The ninth month of the lunar calendar, or October
Host of the Gua:	Fifth Six
Opposite Gua:	Contention (6) ☰
Inverse Gua:	Proceeding Forward (35) ☷
Mutual Gua:	Relief (40) ☵

37
Jia Ren •
Household

$$\overline{}\ \underline{}\ \overline{}$$ Xun • Wind
Li • Fire

NAME AND STRUCTURE

Jia is family, and ren means person. Jia Ren denotes all the members of a family. This gua named Jia Ren instead of Jia, because Jia Ren includes all the members of a family and also domestic relationships and affairs. Jia Ren expounds the relationships among the family members and the ethics of a family. Both Wilhelm and Blofeld translate Jia Ren as The Family. I adopt the term Household.

Someone asked Confucius, "Master, why are you not engaged in the government?" Confucius said, "What does the *Shu Ching* [the oldest of the Chinese classics] say about piety? 'Oh, filial piety. Nothing but filial piety!' If one is filial, one is able to show brotherly love. If these qualities can be maintained in a family, they will also be exercised in governing. Why must one be engaged in the government?" Confucius also tells us that the government of a state depends on the regulation of the family. When a ruler acts as a father, a son, and a brother, he becomes a model; then the people will follow his example.

Sequence of the Gua: *One who is injured abroad is sure to return home. Thus, after Brilliance Injured, Household follows.*

The name of the gua consists of two ideographs. A house and a pig were employed to represent family, jia, because moral principles should be practiced in a family. Family members should be educated just as animals should be tamed. The frame of the ideograph represents a house with walls and roof. On the roof there is a chimney and under the roof, a pig. In ancient times households commonly raised pigs. The second ideograph is the image of a person, ren. The person is bending down with hands and feet touching the ground. We see the beautiful contour of a lifted head, a curved spine, and a plump buttock. When these two images are are put together, the composite represents Household.

The structure of the gua is Wind ☴ above, Fire ☲ below. According to the positioning of the lines, this gua represents a harmonious family. The four solid lines stand for four men. The top line is the father; the other three lines are the sons. The bottom line is the youngest son, and the third and fifth lines are the two elder sons, both of whom are married—the two yielding lines at the second and fourth places are their wives. The image of the gua is Wind coming forth from Fire, indicating warmth and harmony.

Decision

> Household.
> Favorable for a woman
> To be steadfast and upright.

Commentary on the Decision

> *Household.*
> *The women obtain the proper place within;*
> *The men obtain the proper place without.*
> *When men and women obtain their proper places,*
> *They fulfill the great norm of Heaven and Earth.*
>
> *In a household there are authoritative rulers,*
> *They are the parents.*
>
> *When a father is in truth a father and the son a son,*
> *When the elder brother is in truth an elder brother*
> *And the younger brother a younger brother,*
> *And the husband a husband and a wife a wife,*
> *Then the way of that family is in proper state.*
>
> *When every family is in proper state,*
> *Then all under Heaven is in a stable condition.*

Commentary on the Symbol

The wind comes forth from the fire.
An image of Household.
In correspondence with this,
The superior person is substantial in his words
And consistent in his deeds.

Yao Text

1. Initial Nine
   Take precautions within a household.
   Regret vanishes.

   Take precautions within a household,
   Before any change of will has happened.

2. Second Six
   Making no arbitrary decision,
   Taking no irresolute action.
   In charge of feeding the household,
   Being steadfast and upright: good fortune.

   The good fortune of the second six,
   Due to her docility and gentleness.

3. Third Nine
   The household, grumbling, grumbling.
   Regret for adversity: good fortune.
   Women and children, joking, joking.
   Ends in humiliation.

   The household, grumbling, grumbling.
   No indulgence occurs.
   Women and children, joking, joking.
   The control of the household might be lost.

4. Fourth Six
   Enrich the household.
   Great good fortune.

   Enrich the household—
   Great good fortune,

Due to her docility and correct place.

5. Fifth Nine
   The king influences his household.
   Do not worry.
   Good fortune.

   The king influences his household.
   They associate with one another with mutual love.

6. Top Nine
   Being sincere and upright,
   With dignity,
   Ends in good fortune.

   Good fortune of dignity.
   He relies on self-examination.

SIGNIFICANCE

This gua expounds the principle of managing a household. In ancient China, filial piety toward one's parents and respect of one's elder brother were considered the root of all morality. The atmosphere of a household should be harmonious and smooth. To be either too stern or too indulgent is not right. The main theme of the gua lies in the fifth line. It indicates mutual love.

The image of the gua is Wind ☴ above, Fire ☲ below. The wind springs forth from the fire. This gua symbolizes that the wind of harmony is fed by the flames of love. The harmonious atmosphere of a household starts at the very beginning, the bottom line, and extends from within (the inner gua) outward, to the outer gua. This gua has two hosts, because a man and a woman compose a household. The Commentary on the Decision says, "The women obtain the proper place within; the men obtain the proper place without." "Within" refers to the inner gua; "without" indicates the outer gua. The solid line at the fifth place represents the husband. The yielding line at the second place is his wife.

The ancient sages always applied the principle of managing a household to governing a country. In their view, a country was simply a big household. With the spirit of sincerity and mutual love, one is able to create a harmonious situation anywhere, in any circumstance. In his Analects, Confucius says,

From the loving example of one household,
A whole state becomes loving.
From the courteous manner of one household,
A whole state becomes courteous.

This gua relates that after King Wen was released from prison he returned home. Realizing that the stability of the country depended upon the stability of the families, he encouraged people to establish families and careers. He said that it was most favorable in a household for the women to be steadfast and upright. The Duke of Zhou narrates different ways to regulate a household. In a spirit of sincerity and dignity the influence of a household can extend to the whole community.

(1) Initial Nine. Household alternates to Developing Gradually (53) ☶

The bottom line is the beginning of the gua. It is a yang element at a yang place, firm and correct. One in this place is able to take precautions in the household to prevent any regret. In this way, regret will disappear. Yan zhi-tui (531–590), a famous Confucian scholar of the Northern Qi dynasty (550–577), says in his *Instructions for the Household* that influencing a daughter-in-law should begin at the time when she first comes into the family. Educating sons and daughters should start in their infancy. The idea is to make provisions before troubles occur.

(2) Second Six. Household alternates to Little Accumulation (9) ☴

The second line represents a housewife. It is a yin element at a yin place, but she seems too gentle. However, she is in the central position of the inner gua. This is an ideal place for a housewife. Being gentle and steadfast is an essential virtue for a wife. The Yao Text says, "Making no arbitrary decision, taking no irresolute action," she is in charge of feeding the household, and being steadfast and upright brings good fortune. It is good fortune for a household that a woman be the hostess. In The Book of Poetry, Confucius's collection of ancient folk songs, it says,

How delicate and elegant that peach tree is;
How luxuriant is its foliage.
The maiden is going to her husband's house,
She will appropriately manage her household.

Let the household be appropriately managed;
Then the people of the state may be taught.

(3) Third Nine. Household alternates to Increasing (42) ☰☰

The third line is at the top of the inner gua. It represents the authoritative ruler of the household. It is a yang element at a yang place—too firm. He treats the household with a stern attitude and this leads to regret. But still there is good fortune. The idea that women and children laughing and joking ends in humiliation was a typical Chinese viewpoint in ancient times. This line indicates that being neither too stern nor too indulgent is best for cultivating a harmonious family life. Moderation is the Golden Mean.

(4) Fourth Six. Household alternates to Seeking Harmony (13) ☰☰

The fourth line is a yin element at a yin place; it lies at the beginning of the outer gua—Xun, Modesty. The one at this place is gentle and modest; she is able to walk in the central path and thus enrich the household. There is great good fortune.

(5) Fifth Nine. Household alternates to Adorning (22) ☰☰

This line is the host of the gua. It is a yang element at a yang place, firm, correct, and central and at the supreme place. It corresponds to the yin element at the second place. The second place is the hostess of the household; thus this line symbolizes that the king has reached his household. The firm and the yielding associate with each other on terms of mutual love. A harmonious family life will bring good fortune.

(6) Top Nine. Household alternates to Already Fulfilled (63) ☰☰

The top line represents the head of a household. He is full of love but not without dignity. Relying on his sincerity and self-discipline, he is able to set an example for the whole family. His influence not only affects his own family but also extends beyond the family, bringing good fortune. Mencius says, "If a man himself does not follow the Tao, he will not be able to expect his wife and children to follow the Tao. If he does not deal with people according to the Tao, he will not be able to expect his wife and children to deal with people according to the Tao. . . . There is no greater delight than to be conscious of sincerity and of self-examination."

Additional Reference Information for This Gua

Image:	Wind above, Fire below
Recite as:	Wind comes forth from Fire, Household
Element:	Wood
Structure:	Four yang with two yin
Month:	The fifth month of the lunar calendar, or June
Host of the Gua:	Fifth Nine
Opposite Gua:	Relief (40)
Inverse Gua:	Diversity (38)
Mutual Gua:	Not Yet Fulfilled (64)

38
Kui • Diversity

Li • Fire
Dui • Lake

NAME AND STRUCTURE

Kui means to go against, to be incompatible with; diversity.

Sequence of the Gua: *When the proper way of a household comes to an end, there is surely diversity. Thus, after Household, Diversity follows.*

Wilhelm translates Kui as Opposition. Blofeld translates it as the Estranged, Opposites. In this book the term Diversity is adopted.

The original meaning of kui was "eyes do not look at each other," indicating that people's lines of vision are different. There is diversity among them. The ideograph of Kui demonstrates this sense of diversity. In this ideograph, an eye is drawn on the left side in a vertical position. There are two tiny strokes at the middle of the eye. Early on these two strokes were represented by a tiny circle, the pupil. At the top of the right side, there are two hands, showing the fingers and palms. The palms of the hands are not facing each other; instead, they are back to back. This placement suggests diversity. A bow and arrow are drawn underneath the hands. Two feathers are fastened to the end of the arrow to show that the arrow is moving as the feathers fly. The route of the arrow is between the two hands, making the space of their diversity bigger.

This gua is the inverse of the preceding gua, Household, which characterized the centripetal force holding the family together. Diversity, on the other hand, shows a centrifugal force diversifying the family. An old Chinese adage says, "In a harmonious family, everything is prosperous. In a disharmonious family, everything is obstructed."

The structure of the gua is Fire ☲ above, Lake ☱ below. The flame of a fire flares upward, while the water in a lake sinks downward. These movements, upward and downward, diverge. Lake, symbolizing joy, joyfully clings to Fire, Brightness. In the course of diversifying, there is still similarity—this is the unique wisdom of the I Ching. Fire represents the middle daughter and Lake the youngest daughter. They originated from the same parents. However, when they grow up they will go to different families through marriage. Their interests will naturally take them in different directions. Thus, diversity is unavoidable. The key is in seeking harmony out of diversity.

When the second line and the third line of Brightness interchange, Brightness alternates to Diversity. Likewise, when the fourth and fifth lines of Innermost Sincerity (61) exchange places, and when the second and third lines and fourth and fifth lines of Household (37) interchange, they become this gua. With all these changes, the yielding lines proceed upward. As a result, the yielding line in the fifth place is central and corresponds to the solid line at the second place. In this way, although great things may not be accomplished, there will be good fortune in little ways. Thus the Commentary on the Decision says, "The joyous clings to the brilliant. The yielding advances and moves upward. It attains the central place and corresponds to the firm. This is why there is good fortune in little things."

Decision

> Diversity.
> Little things:
> Good fortune.

Commentary on the Decision

> *Diversity.*
> *Fire moves upward; Lake moves downward.*
> *Two daughters live together;*
> *Their minds do not move in the same direction.*
>
> *The joyous clings to the brilliant.*
> *The yielding advances and moves upward.*

It attains the central place and corresponds to the firm.
This is why there is good fortune in little things.

Heaven and Earth diversify,
But their achievements are concerted.
Man and woman diversify,
But their passion is in unison.
All beings diversify,
But their functions are the same.

Great indeed is the time and significance of diversity.

Commentary on the Symbol

Fire above, Lake below.
An image of Diversity.
In correspondence with this,
The superior person seeks common ground on major issues
While reserving differences on minor ones.

Yao Text

1. Initial Nine
   Regret vanishes.
   Lose a horse, do not chase.
   Of its own accord, returns.
   Meet with evil people.
   No fault.

   Meet with evil people;
   Guard against mistakes.

2. Second Nine
   Meet lord in a narrow lane.
   No fault.

   Meet lord in a narrow lane.
   He has not deviated from the proper way.

3. Third Six
   Seeing a wagon dragged,
   One's ox pulled,

As if one's forehead were tattooed and nose cut off.
Without a beginning,
There is an end.

Seeing a wagon dragged,
The place is not correct.
Without a beginning, there is an end;
He meets someone who is firm.

4. Fourth Nine
   Diversity isolated.
   Meets the initiator.
   Fused sincerity and truthfulness.
   Adversity.
   No fault.

   Fuse sincerity and truthfulness: no fault.
   Their minds can be communicated and fulfilled.

5. Fifth Six
   Regret vanishes.
   Clansmen respond
   As if biting soft meat.
   Going forward, what mistake?

   Clansmen respond
   As if biting soft meat.
   There is ground for congratulation.

6. Top Nine
   Diversity isolated.
   See a pig covered with dirt,
   A wagon carrying devils.
   First draw the bow,
   Then lay it aside.
   Not an invader, but a suitor.
   Going forward, encounter the rain,
   Then good fortune.

   The good fortune of encountering rain.
   All doubts wash away.

SIGNIFICANCE

Diversity is natural and unavoidable. The key is in seeking harmony. To the Chinese, all diversity can be harmonized, no matter whether it is between members of a household, or members of a society, or between nations of the world. The clue lies in one's attitude. If both sides are willing to come together in sincerity and truthfulness, no problem cannot be solved. The symbol of the gua is Fire ☲ above, Lake ☱ below. The ascending flame of the fire and the downward flowing of the water of the lake move in opposite directions. In correspondence, the superior person seeks common ground while reserving differences. This is the correct attitude with which to neutralize diversity. Based on this attitude, there will be no misfortune. However, integrating diversity also requires proper timing and an appropriate situation. Either the yielding line at the fifth place or the solid line at the second place could be the host. The Commentary on the Decision says, "The yielding advances and moves upward. It attains the central place and corresponds to the firm." This commentary tells us that the yielding line at the fifth place is the host.

This gua relates that the people of the Shang dynasty responded to King Wen's policy of welcoming persons of talent and virtue to his country. Those who opposed the tyranny of the Shang dynasty went to Zhou for shelter one after another. King Wen instructed them that being aware of diversity and beginning with little things would bring good fortune. The Duke of Zhou narrates the different experiences of those who diverged from the Tyrant of Shang.

(1) Initial Nine. Diversity alternates to Not Yet Fulfilled (64) ☲

The bottom line is a yang element at a yang place; it responds to but does not correspond to the yang element at the fourth place. Since they do not work together, how could there be regret? But during the time of diversity, those who should correspond to each other diversify, and those who should diversify, respond—the diversity between one at the bottom and one at the fourth position vanishes. It is as if one who has lost his horse does not chase it, and it comes back. In the time of diversity, one should be generous and magnanimous. In dealing with bad people, it is not necessary to keep a good distance from them. Even encountering them face to face, there would be no fault. This line suggests that to smooth out a misunderstanding takes time; the lost horse will come back of its own accord. With the

proper attitude, even in meeting a person with different ideas there will be no problem.

(2) Second Nine. Diversity alternates to Eradicating (21)

The second line is a yang element at a yin place. This line corresponds to the yin element at the fifth place. This is the lord. They are complementary yin and yang—they should meet. But during the time of diversity, they cannot. One at the second place looks for his lord elsewhere. Eventually he finds the lord in a narrow lane, which is unusual. The narrow lane in question is a lane outside the palace wall. The subordinate and his lord are able to meet humbly in this informal place. In this there is no fault. This line indicates that in a time of diversity one should maintain a spirit of conciliation and compromise to best serve the general interest.

(3) Third Six. Diversity alternates to Great Harvest (14)

The third line is a yin element at a yang place, corresponding to the topmost yang element. One in this place should go to meet the one at the topmost place. Nevertheless, her personality is too weak. She is hindered by the surrounding yang elements. It is as if a wagon is being dragged by the solid line at the second place and an ox is being pulled by the solid line at the fourth place. The situation is bad—as when a man's forehead is tattooed and his nose cut off. These were two forms of ancient punishment. Nevertheless, since they are corresponding elements and the one at the top is firm and strong, in the end they meet.

(4) Fourth Nine. Diversity alternates to Decreasing (41)

The fourth line is a yang element at a yin place; it does not correspond to the yang element at the bottom. Furthermore, it is surrounded and isolated by yin elements above and below. But the yang element at the bottom is strong and firm, truthful and upright. They are both yang. Thus the Yao Text says, "Diversity isolated. Meets the initiator. Fused sincerity and truthfulness. Adversity. No fault." The initiator is the bottom line.

(5) Fifth Six. Diversity alternates to Fulfillment (10)

The fifth line is a yin element at a yang place. Although it is in a supreme place, its attribute is weakness and its place is incorrect. There is regret. On the other hand, it is central and corresponds to the yang element at the second place, which supports it like a clansman. Regret vanishes. What mistake can there be?

(6) Top Nine. Diversity alternates to Marrying Maiden (54)

The Yao Text of this line is very imaginative. One at the topmost place represents a person who acts contrary to reason and is isolated. This line corresponds to the yin element at the third place, but he has a doubtful attitude. He wants to meet this corresponding yin element, but she is surrounded by two solid lines, above and below. He suspects that she is like a pig covered with dirt or a wagon loaded with devils—something useful covered by something unpleasant. At first, he draws a bow; then he lays it aside. At last he recognizes that she is not an enemy but is someone who is wooing. Eventually his doubts are dispelled as the rain washes away the dirt, and in the end they meet. There is good fortune. This line tells us that resolving diversity should be as natural as the clouds accumulating and bringing down rain. It takes time.

Additional Reference Information for This Gua

Image:	Fire above, Lake below
Recite as:	Fire above Lake, Diversity
Element:	Fire
Structure:	Four yang with two yin
Month:	The twelfth month of the lunar calendar, or January
Host of the Gua:	Fifth Six
Opposite Gua:	Hardship (39)
Inverse Gua:	Household (37)
Mutual Gua:	Already Fulfilled (63)

39
Jian · Hardship

Kan • Water
Gen • Mountain

NAME AND STRUCTURE

Originally, Jian meant lame or a lame person. From lame, its meaning extends to encompass difficulty in walking or hardship. Wilhelm translates Jian as Obstruction; Blofeld translates it as Trouble. In this book I use Hardship.

Sequence of the Gua: *If there is misunderstanding and diversity in a household, surely hardship will result. Thus, after Diversity, Hardship follows.*

The ideograph of the gua shows its original meaning—a lame person having difficulty walking. At the top of the ideograph is the roof of a house with a chimney. Below it there is an ideograph of a person, ren. Between the roof and the person, there are two bundles of grass, representing bedding. These images form the upper part of the ideograph: a picture of a person under the roof of a house covered with two pieces of thick bedding to resist the cold. At the bottom, there is an ideograph of a foot. On each side of the foot and underneath the person a pair of crutches is drawn. One can visualize the crutches under the armpits of the person with a lame leg. The blood circulation of a lame leg is poor, thus the image of a cold foot was used to demonstrate a lame person's difficulty with walking.

The structure of the gua is Water ☵ above, Mountain ☶ below. It represents a situation of hardship following hardship. Climbing a mountain and crossing a river are arduous undertakings. The attribute of

Water is darkness and of Mountain is keeping still. If it is not the right time to overcome hardship, one should keep still. Keeping still does not mean giving up. It is just yielding to the situation and waiting for a more auspicious time. If the proper time comes, it is favorable to seek union or to consult a noble person for constructive advice. Any premature advance will entail risk. Overcoming hardship depends on the correct time, situation, and companions—in Chinese terms Heaven, Earth, and human beings, the three primary elements.

When the solid line at the fourth place and the yielding line at the fifth place of Little Exceeding (62) ䷽ interchange, Little Exceeding becomes Hardship ䷦. As a result, the solid line at the fourth place of Little Exceeding moves forward to the center of the upper gua. Thus, the Commentary on the Decision says, "Going forward obtains the central place." If the solid line at the fourth place of Little Exceeding moves backward, it confronts the lower gua, Mountain (Keeping Still). The commentary tells us, "There is no way out." In the I Ching, Earth represents the southwest. The upper gua is Water, which is derived from Earth; for this reason it also represents southwest. The commentary says there is advantage in the southwest. The lower gua, Mountain, represents northeast, and the commentary correspondingly says, "It is unfavorable in the northeast."

In the I Ching, there are two gua that betoken hardship: the third one, Beginning, and this one. In Beginning, the Commentary on the Decision says, "The firm and the yielding united at the very beginning; difficulties come into being." Hardship in that case is attendant upon the creation of all beings. In this gua, the hardship occurs during the course of one's life journey. One has already grown and matured. Confucius instructs us that the superior person should be introspective to cultivate virtue. Resonating with Confucius, Mencius says,

> If one loves others, and they do not respond in the same way, one should turn inward and examine one's own love. If one treats others politely, and they do not return politeness, one should turn inward and examine one's own politeness. When one does not realize what one desires, one must turn inward and examine oneself in every point.

This passage reveals the true spirit of what the ancient sages learned from this gua.

Decision

> Hardship.
> Favorable to the southwest.
> Unfavorable to the northeast.
> Favorable to see a great person.
> Being steadfast and upright: good fortune.

Commentary on the Decision

> *Jian is Hardship.*
> *Danger in front.*
> *Seeing the danger and knowing to stand still,*
> *Being conscious and wise.*
>
> *Hardship.*
> *Favorable in the southwest.*
> *Going forward obtains the central place.*
> *Unfavorable in the northeast.*
> *There is no way out.*
>
> *Favorable to see a great person;*
> *Going forward, there is achievement.*
>
> *Proper position,*
> *Being steadfast and upright,*
> *Good fortune,*
> *Rectifying the country.*
> *Great indeed is the function and time of hardship!*

Commentary on the Symbol

> *Water on the Mountain.*
> *An image of Hardship.*
> *In correspondence with this,*
> *The superior person is introspective to cultivate his virtue.*

Yao Text

1. Initial Six
   Going forward: hardship.
   Coming back: praise.

Going forward, hardship.
Coming back, praise.
Waiting for the proper time.

2. Second Six
   King and minister, hardship, hardship.
   Not for one's own affairs.

   King and minister
   Hardship upon hardship,
   Ending with no resentment.

3. Third Nine
   Going forward: hardship.
   Come back instead.

   Going forward, hardship.
   Coming back instead.
   Those inside rejoice with him.

4. Fourth Six
   Going forward: hardship.
   Coming back: union.

   Going forward, hardship.
   Coming back, union.
   The proper place possesses solidity.

5. Fifth Nine
   Great hardship.
   Friends come.

   Great hardship.
   Friends come.
   Rely on the virtue of the central.

6. Top Six
   Going forward: hardship.
   Coming back: a great achievement.
   Good fortune.
   Favorable to see a great person.

   Going forward: hardship.
   Coming back: a great achievement.

Wishes placed on the internal.
Favorable to see a great person.
Follow the one of noble rank.

Significance

Water above Mountain is an image of hardship following hardship. There is no way to totally avoid hardship in one's life. Hardship should be overcome; calamity can be prevented. One should not always let things take their own course and resign oneself to one's fate. This gua tells us how to deal with hardship. The ancient sages experienced the hardship of climbing a mountain as well as crossing a river. They also experienced all kinds of hardship in their life journey. Some hardships were avoidable, but others were unavoidable. If one has the right attitude, no matter what kind of hardships there are, they can be overcome. In times of hardship a country needs a great leader, associated with loyal officials and supported by the people with one heart and one mind. This is what the Commentary on the Decision means when it advises to see a great person; and that proper position brings good fortune. When the time is not auspicious, one should keep still. Any premature advance will lead to possible danger.

The host of the gua is the solid line at the fifth place. The Commentary on the Decision says, "Going forward obtains the central place." This is the position for a great person. During the time of hardship, moving forward is not favorable. The Yao Text mentions hindrance and advises returning.

The gua relates how King Wen noticed that the people of the Shang who came to Zhou to seek shelter suffered hardship. He told them that it would be better for them to stay in the realm of Zhou (southwest), but unfavorable to return to the Shang realm (northwest). It was favorable for them to see the great person (probably King Wen) and remain steadfast and upright. Good fortune would prevail. The Duke of Zhou tells us how these people dealt with various hardships in different situations.

(1) Initial Six. Hardship alternates to Already Fulfilled (63) ☰

The bottom line is a yin element at a yang place. Its attribute is weakness, and its place is not correct. It does not correspond to the yin element at the fourth place. All these conditions indicate that it is not favorable to go forward. The bottom line is at the beginning of the hardship—it is better to seek an understanding of the situation before acting. If one at this place acts blindly, she will fall into the darkness of the upper gua, Water. If she understands the situation and returns, staying in the lower gua, Keeping Still, she will be praised.

(2) Second Six. Hardship alternates to Replenishing (48)

The second line is a yin element at a yin place, central and correct. It corresponds to the yang element at the fifth place. Normally this line can move forward smoothly without hindrance. However, the fifth line is in the midst of the upper gua, Water, or Darkness. In the I Ching, the second line represents a general in the service of a king. When a king at the fifth place is facing hardship, it is the duty of the general to dash forward to help, regardless of his own safety; otherwise he will feel guilt and regret his whole life. In Chinese history, the Yao Text of this line has been quoted to refer to the loyal subordinate of a king.

(3) Third Nine. Hardship alternates to Union (8)

The third line is at the top of the inner gua. It is the only yang element of the inner gua and thus acts to support the yin elements. It corresponds to the topmost yin element. However, the topmost element is weak. In this situation, it is difficult to proceed. If one in this position comprehends the circumstances and returns, staying within the inner gua, the yin elements will rejoice and he himself will be safe.

(4) Fourth Six. Hardship alternates to Mutual Influence (31)

The fourth line has reached the bottom line of the upper gua, Water, representing the Darkness. It is a yin element at a yin place, but it does not respond to the yin element at the bottom. One at this place is weak and surrounded by two yang elements above and below. She has the opportunity to seek union with the yang element below, but the yang element at the fifth place is lost in the midst of darkness (water). Thus the commentary says, "Going forward, hardship. Coming back, union. The proper place possesses solidity."

(5) Fifth Nine. Hardship alternates to Humbleness (15)

This line is the host. It represents a leader. He is in the midst of the upper gua. But he is solid and firm and associates with the one at the second place. They are complementary and supportive yin and yang. Their positions are proper, their attitudes right. Both of them are working hard, not simply for their own advantage. In his Analects Confucius says, "If one is virtuous, one will not be left to stand alone. It is certain that associates of like mind will come and join with one."

One at this place will reap good fortune, but the text does not mention good fortune because the situation of hardship prevails.

(6) Top Six. Hardship alternates to Developing Gradually (53)

By the topmost line, further advance will lead to further hardship. If one understands the situation and returns, she has two choices. She can rely on the one at the fifth place, who is firm and strong, central and correct. Or she can associate with the one at the third position, since they are complementary yin and yang. She is extremely wise; he associates with the one at the third place and goes along with him to see the great person at the fifth place. Thus Confucius's Commentary on the Yao Text says, "Going forward: hardship. Coming back: a great achievement. Wishes placed on the internal. Favorable to see a great person. Follow the one of noble rank." The internal refers to the inner gua, where the third line is located. Noble rank indicates the fifth line, a king's place.

Additional Reference Information for This Gua

Image:	Water above, Mountain below
Recite as:	Water above Mountain, Hardship
Element:	Water
Structure:	Two yang with four yin
Month:	The eleventh month of the lunar calendar, or December
Host of the Gua:	Fifth Nine
Opposite Gua:	Diversity (38)
Inverse Gua:	Relief (40)
Mutual Gua:	Not Yet Fulfilled (64)

40
Jie • Relief

$$\begin{array}{c}\equiv\ \equiv\end{array}$$ Zhen • Thunder
Kan • Rain

NAME AND STRUCTURE

Jie has many meanings. Originally it meant to separate or to remove and, later, to release or to relieve—especially to relieve pain or distress. In this gua, it signifies relief of the cause of hardship. Wilhelm translates Jie as Deliverance, and Blofeld translates it as Release. Deliverance and release both denote an act of allowing to go, setting free, or unfastening. Relief is closer in meaning to alleviation—lessening or ending pain, distress, or anxiety. Given the content of this gua, I adopt the name Relief.

Sequence of the Gua: *Things cannot remain in hardship without end. Thus, after Hardship, Relief follows.*

The ideograph of Jie pictures its original meaning, to separate or to remove. It consists of three parts. On the left, there is a horn, and at the bottom right, there is an ox. The image looks like the face of an ox with horns curved upward. Resting on the top of the ox is a knife. Taken as a whole, the ideograph shows that a horn is separated and removed from the head of an ox by a knife. This gua is the inverse of the preceding gua, Hardship—after one's hardship is relieved, one tends to indulge in pleasure again and creates new hardship. Thus, Hardship and Relief complement each other.

The structure of the gua is Thunder ☳ above, Water ☵ below, signifying a thunderstorm with heavy rain. Thunder represents motion, and Water stands for darkness. One can imagine that the thunderstorm is wild and

violent. When the tremendous strength of the storm has passed through the dark, the danger is relieved. There is an old Chinese saying, "After a thunderstorm, the sky becomes clearer." Rain and storms wash away dirt, but they cannot last long. After the hot and suffocating atmosphere is relieved, people can breathe freely again. Tension is relieved. A new cycle begins.

When the solid line at the third place and the yielding line at the fourth place of Growing Upward (46) ☷ interchange, Growing Upward alternates to Relief ☵☷. The upper gua of Growing Upward is Earth, representing the southwest. The solid third line of Growing Upward ascends to the upper gua, Earth, and Growing Upward becomes Relief. Thus the Decision says, "Relief. Favorable in the southwest." It drops the hint that, to relieve a difficult situation, one should follow the way of yin like the Earth, gently and amiably. After relieving the hardship, one should rest and recuperate like the Earth, nourishing and nurturing myriad beings.

Decision

> Relief.
> Favorable in the southwest.
> Nowhere to go—
> Come back, return to normal.
> Good fortune.
> Somewhere to go—
> No delay: good fortune.

Commentary on the Decision

> *Relief.*
> *Danger produces motion.*
> *Through motion, danger is removed.*
> *This is what relief means.*
>
> *Relief.*
> *Favorable in the southwest.*
> *Going forward, win the multitude.*
> *Returning back brings good fortune.*
> *He obtains the central position.*
>
> *If there is somewhere to go,*
> *Acting without delay brings good fortune.*

He will receive merit by going forward.

Heaven and Earth obtain relief;
Thunderstorm and rain come together.
When thunderstorm and rain come together,
The buds of plants and fruit trees begin to burst.

Great indeed is the time of relieving!

Commentary on the Symbol

Rolling Thunder with heavy Rain.
An image of Relief.
In correspondence with this,
The superior person pardons mistakes
And deals gently with misdeeds.

Yao Text

1. Initial Six
   No fault.

   Junction between yin and yang.
   There should be no fault.

2. Second Nine
   In the field
   Three foxes are caught.
   Obtain a golden arrow.
   Being steadfast and upright: good fortune.

   Good fortune for the second nine,
   Due to the middle path.

3. Third Six
   Carrying a burden,
   Riding in a carriage,
   Tempting robbers to come.
   Being steadfast: humiliation.

   Carrying a burden, riding in a carriage,
   It is a shame.

When I myself tempt the robbers to draw near,
On whom shall I lay the blame?

4. Fourth Nine
Removing your big toe,
Friends come.
Be sincere and truthful.

Removing your big toe.
The place is not appropriate.

5. Fifth Six
Superior person
Relieves hardship:
Good fortune.
Be sincere and truthful to the little fellow.

The superior person relieves the hardship;
Little fellows have to retreat.

6. Top Six
The prince is engaged in shooting a falcon
On top of a high city wall.
Hits it.
Nothing is unfavorable.

The prince is engaged in shooting a falcon;
He relieves the rebellious.

SIGNIFICANCE

This gua is the inverse of Hardship, the preceding one. Now, hardship is relieved. To relieve hardship, timing is important; if the time is not favorable, one must remain still. The Decision indicates that if there is nowhere to go, returning will be propitious. On the other hand, if there is somewhere to go, acting immediately will bring good fortune. Beside timing, harmony between people is absolutely important.

The gua has two hosts: the yielding line at the fifth place and the solid line at the second place. The yielding line at the fifth place represents a king who is humble and gentle. The solid line at the second place represents an official who is strong and firm. These two elements are complementary yin and yang. They mutually support each other. A wise leader is working with an able subordinate—they relieve hardship together. The yielding lines at the second, third, and sixth places use the fox, the robber, and the falcon, respectively, as images of potential dangers, suggesting that during a time when hardship is relieved, one should still be cautious.

The gua tells us that the hardship of those who came to the Kingdom of Zhou for shelter from the Tyrant of Shang was relieved. It was best for those who came to stay in the realm of Zhou (southwest). For those who moved on, if there was nowhere else to go, returning still brought good fortune if they acted without delay. The Duke of Zhou tells us how the hardship of these people was relieved only through the retreating of the little fellows.

(1) Initial Six. Relief alternates to Marrying Maiden (54)

The bottom line denotes the transition between Hardship and Relief. It is a turning point. Thus the Commentary on the Yao Text says that there should be no fault. This line is a yin element at a yang place. The element is weak, and the position is low; therefore it is safe. It corresponds to the yang element at the fourth place. When hardship begins to find relief, although there is not yet good fortune, at least there is no fault.

(2) Second Nine. Relief alternates to Delight (16)

The second line is a yang element at a yin place. The position is not correct, but it is central. It corresponds to the yin element at the fifth place, and is able to obtain support from this element at the king's place. Three foxes represent the other yin elements. Foxes are considered crafty and tricky. One at this place is firm and strong, able to banish those who try to trick the king. The Yao Text says, "In the field three foxes are caught." The firmness of this line is represented by the golden arrow. With its resolve, the three foxes are caught. The color of gold, yellow, in the system of the five elements is the color of Earth, which is in the central place. This brings good fortune.

(3) Third Six. Relief alternates to Long Lasting (32)

The yielding line at the third position symbolizes a little fellow. It is a yin element at a yang place. Its placement is not correct, but it occupies the top position of the lower gua. Its status is not compatible with its position. In ancient times, only those with rank were allowed to ride in a carriage. This is a little fellow who is carrying a burden. While carrying a burden, one rides in a carriage, tempting robbers to draw near.

However steadfast and upright, there will be regret. The Chinese sages emphasized that appearances should match reality. Otherwise people will not trust and follow.

(4) Fourth Nine. Relief alternates to Multitude (7)

The Yao Text says, "Removing your big toe, friends come." The big toe denotes the bottom line. The fourth line is a yang element at a yin place, while the bottom line is a yin element at a yang place. These two lines are complementary yin and yang, but both are in incorrect places. The one at the fourth place represents a gentle man, and the one at the bottom symbolizes a petty fellow. They cannot support each other. In order to relieve hardship, the one at the fourth place should cut off relationships with petty persons. After he has done so, he is able to move forward. The yin element at the fifth place can be a good friend. She is in a central place, indicating that she is sincere and trustworthy. An ancient Chinese maxim says, "Things of the same kind come together." If one has a petty person as a companion, how can upright friends come forward?

(5) Fifth Six. Relief alternates to Exhausting (47)

There are four yin elements in this gua. Only this yin element is brilliant and wise, because it is at a supreme place. The other three yin elements are petty fellows who cause hardships. The ancient sages thought that a brilliant and wise person should keep a distance from petty fellows. Thus the Yao Text says that contemplating relieving hardship brings good fortune.

(6) Top Six. Relief alternates to Not Yet Fulfilled (64)

The topmost line of a gua is generally the place for a sage or a hermit. In this gua, it is the place of a lord. This line, at the end of the gua, symbolizes a situation where all hardships are relieved. The predatory falcon is an inauspicious bird, representing the yin element at the third place who is striving for a high position. The high wall mentioned here is the top line of the gua. Confucius's commentary says, "The prince is engaged in shooting a falcon; he relieves the rebellious." The "rebellious" element is the yin line at the third place.

Additional Reference Information for This Gua

Image: Thunder above, Water below
Recite as: Thunder above Rain, Relief
Element: Wood
Structure: Two yang with four yin
Month: The second month of the lunar calendar, or March
Host of the Gua: Fifth Six
Opposite Gua: Household   (37)
Inverse Gua: Hardship   (39)
Mutual Gua: Already Fulfilled   (63)

41

Sun • Decreasing

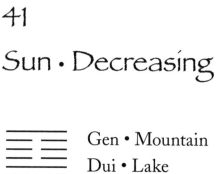

Gen • Mountain
Dui • Lake

NAME AND STRUCTURE

Sun means decreasing, losing, or damaging. Wilhelm translates Sun as Decrease while Blofeld chooses Loss, Reduction. I use the term Decreasing.

Sequence of the Gua: *Relieving continues to excess; surely something is to be lost. Thus, after Relief, Decreasing follows.*

The ideograph consists of three parts. On the left is the image of a hand, shou, holding something in a fist. At the bottom right is an ancient sacrificial vessel, usually used to hold liquors. At the top of the sacrificial vessel is the ideograph of an open mouth, kou. The union of these three ideographs tells us that a hand holds a sacrificial vessel pouring the liquor out from its open mouth. As it pours out, the quantity of the liquor decreases. When the vessel is empty, the liquor is gone. Thus, Sun signifies either decreasing or losing.

The structure of the gua is Mountain ☶ above, Lake ☱ below. At the foot of the mountain there is a lake. This symbol shows how it was imagined that an increase of the mountain was at the same time a decrease of the lake. For example, the evaporation of water from the lake precipitates on the mountain. This gua has an inner connection with Tai, or Advance (11) ䷊. Confucius's Commentary on the Decision says, "To decrease what is lower is to increase what is above." In Advance, there are three solid lines in the lower gua. When the solid line at the bottom moves to the top, Advance alternates to this gua, Decreasing.

The structure of the Upper Canon and the Lower Canon of the I Ching is well knit. The Upper Canon begins with the Initiating (1) and the Responding (2). After ten changes, we have moved to Advance (11) and Hindrance (12). The Lower Canon begins with Mutual Influence (31) and Long Lasting (32). After ten changes, we have Decreasing (41) and Increasing (42). Thus, Decreasing and Increasing have inner connections with Advance and Hindrance. From this inner connection, we can see that the sequence of the sixty-four gua is an integrated whole.

Decision

Decreasing.
Being sincere and truthful:
Supreme good fortune, no fault.
Appropriate to be steadfast and upright.
Favorable to have somewhere to go.
How is it to be used?
Two bamboo trays can be used for offering.

Commentary on the Decision

Decreasing.
To decrease what is lower
Is to increase what is above.
The way is to benefit the above.

Decreasing and being sincere and truthful
There will be supreme good fortune
Without fault.
One can be steadfast and upright.
It is favorable to go somewhere.

How can the principle of decreasing be used?
With truthfulness and sincerity
Two bamboo trays can be used for sacrifice.
But employing two bamboo trays should be decided
In accord with the time.

There is a time for decreasing the firm
And increasing the yielding.

Decreasing and increasing,
Being full and being empty,
These take place in accord with the conditions of time.

Commentary on the Symbol

At the foot of the Mountain,
There is a Lake.
It is an image of Decreasing.
In correspondence with this,
The superior person controls his anger
And restrains his desire.

Yao Text

1. Initial Nine
   Suspend one's own affairs.
   Hurry forward, no fault.
   Weigh how much one can decrease.

   Suspend one's own affairs and hurry forward.
   Uphold working in full cooperation with one mind.

2. Second Nine
   Favorable to be steadfast and upright.
   Moving forward: misfortune.
   Without decreasing,
   Increase.

   The favor and steadfastness of the second nine,
   The central position makes him uphold his will.

3. Third Six
   Three people walk together;
   Then decrease by one.
   One walks alone,
   Then finds a friend.

   One should walk alone.
   Three people together, doubts arise.

4. Fourth Six
   Decrease one's ailment,
   Hasten to help.
   There is rejoicing, no fault.

   Decrease one's ailment.
   It is indeed worthy of joy.

5. Fifth Six
   Probably being increased.
   A tortoise worth ten pairs of shells
   Cannot be refused.
   Supreme good fortune.

   The supreme good fortune of the fifth six,
   Due to the blessing from above.

6. Top Nine
   Without decreasing, increase.
   No fault.
   Being steadfast and upright: good fortune.
   Favorable to have somewhere to go.
   Obtain subordinates
   Without consideration of their own households.

   Without decreasing, increase.
   He attains what he wants in great measure.

SIGNIFICANCE

The theme of the gua is the law of balance between decreasing and increasing, giving and receiving. What is excessive should be decreased. Likewise, what is insufficient should be increased. This is the way of the universe. The gua is based on the idea that to decrease what is lower is to increase what is above. When the solid line at the third place of Advance alternates to a yielding line, and the yielding line at the top alternates to a solid line, then Advance changes to Decreasing. In this gua what is lower indicates the people; what is above refers to the king. Therefore, the yielding line at the fifth place is the host. Among the six lines, the three in the lower gua are the givers and the three in the upper gua are the receivers.

After making adequate arrangements for those seeking shelter in the realm of Zhou, King Wen tried to promote prosperity. On one hand, he began to levy taxes from the people, and, on the other, he instructed people how to profit and practice economy. To set an example, he performed a grand ceremony, but used just two bamboo trays instead of the traditional eight, offering a very simple sacrifice with truthfulness and sincerity. The Duke of Zhou describes the way to restrain oneself to allow others to prosper.

(1) Initial Nine. Decreasing alternates to Childhood (4)

The bottom line indicates that it is time to decrease what is lower in order to increase what is above. The yang element at the bottom is firm and strong and has the potential to help others. He corresponds to the yin element at the fourth place, who needs help. He suspends his own affairs, hurrying away to help. There is no fault. However, he must consider how much he can diminish himself to benefit others.

(2) Second Nine. Decreasing alternates to Nourishing (27)

The yang element at the second place is firm and strong, in the central position of the lower gua. He is able to follow the principle of the Golden Mean and would not take rash actions. It is favorable to remain steadfast and upright. Premature advance always leads to misfortune. Bringing increase to others without diminishing oneself is the best way to deal with the matter of giving and receiving.

(3) Third Six. Decreasing alternates to Great Accumulation (26)

The Yao Text explains that this gua, Decreasing, comes from Advance. When the lower gua of Advance loses a yang element and this yang element moves to the top of the upper gua, then Advance becomes Decreasing. In the first case the Yao Text says, "Three people walk together, then decrease by one." In the second case, when the yang element moves to the top of the upper gua and meets the yin elements, the Yao Text says, "One walks alone, then finds a friend." This line delves into human relationships. When one walks alone, one can meet a harmonious companion. When two people come together, it is easy to build a close relationship. But when three people are in a relationship, doubts arise.

(4) Fourth Six. Decreasing alternates to Diversity (38)

The Yao Text says, "Decrease one's ailment," recommending a mitigation of one's shortcomings. The fourth line is a yin element at a yin place, surrounded by two yin elements above and below. There is too much yin and thus there is a shortcoming. One at this place corresponds to the yang element on the bottom. She relies on the help of the one at the bottom, who is strong and firm. When she obtains help and support, her ailment is alleviated. This line tells us that a true friend is beneficial and important in helping diminish one's shortcomings.

(5) Fifth Six. Decreasing alternates to Innermost Sincerity (61) ☲

The fifth line, in the middle of the upper gua, is a yin element at a yang place. One in this place is gentle and modest, able to accept benefits with grace. Because she is at a supreme place and is virtuous, during the time of diminishing what is lower to increase what is above, people are willing to sacrifice to augment her. This line shows the importance of the quality of modesty. An ancient saying goes, "Modesty helps one to go forward, whereas conceit makes one lag behind." Modesty brings supreme good fortune.

(6) Top Nine. Decreasing alternates to Approaching (19) ☷

All three lines in the upper gua are receivers. The topmost line is a yang element—one at this place has more than enough. He does not need to diminish others to benefit himself. To increase one's benefits without diminishing others is not only without fault, it is the best way to obtain constant increase. Moreover, in this situation, it is right to scale down one's excess to alleviate other people's deficiency. In this way one obtains support from his subordinates and attains what he wants in great measure.

Additional Reference Information for This Gua

Image:	Mountain above, Lake below
Recite as:	Lake under Mountain, Decreasing
Element:	Earth
Structure:	Three yin with three yang
Month:	The seventh month of the lunar calendar, or August
Host of the Gua:	Fifth Six
Opposite Gua:	Mutual Influence (31) ☱
Inverse Gua:	Increasing (42) ☳
Mutual Gua:	Turning Back (24) ☳

42
Yi · Increasing

☴ Xun • Wind
☳ Zhen • Thunder

NAME AND STRUCTURE

Yi means profit, benefit, increase. Wilhelm translates Yi as Increase; Blofeld translates it as Gain. In this book the translation Increasing is used. This gua is the inverse of the preceding one. Decreasing and Increasing are opposite but complementary. Thus the forms of these two gua are reversed.

Sequence of the Gua: *When decreasing reaches its end, surely increasing is certain to come. Thus, after Decreasing, Increasing follows.*

The ideograph of Yi is simple and clear. The lower part is the image of a household container. Above the container is an ancient ideograph for water, shui. It looks exactly like the symbol of the original gua Kan, Water ☵. Water above a container symbolizes that water is pouring into the container, an act of increasing. The structure of the gua is Wind ☴ above, Thunder ☳ below. When wind and thunder support each other, their energy is doubled. It is also an image of increase. The inner gua, Thunder, indicates that there is firm resolution within. The outer gua, Wind, indicates that there is penetrating outward action. Confucius's Commentary on the Symbol says, "The superior person follows the good when he sees it, and corrects his fault when he finds it." This tells us that a superior person follows the good as quickly as the wind and corrects his faults as firmly as thunder.

The theme of the previous gua is to decrease what is lower in order to increase what is higher. This gua discusses how to decrease what is above in order to increase what is below. When Heaven ☰ loses a yang element, it becomes Wind. And when Earth ☷ gains a yang element, it becomes Thunder. This is precisely an image of diminishing the lower to increase the upper. Increasing comes from Pi, Hindrance (12)☶☰. In Hindrance, there are three solid lines in the upper gua and three yielding lines in the lower gua. When the topmost solid line of Hindrance moves to the bottom, Hindrance alternates to Increasing. The Commentary on the Decision says, "To decrease what is above is to increase what is lower." The upper gua is Wood as well as Wind. Here it symbolizes that a wooden boat is moving forward, driven by the wind. The lower gua is Thunder, symbolizing action. Thus King Wen's Decision says, "Favorable to have somewhere to go. Favorable to cross great rivers."

Decision

Increasing.
Favorable to have somewhere to go.
Favorable to cross great rivers.

Commentary on the Decision

Increasing.
To decrease what is above
Is to increase what is lower.
The joy of the people is boundless.
Increase of what is lower comes from what is above.
Its way is greatly brightened.

Favorable to have somewhere to go
Because it is central and correct
And, therefore, is blessed.
Favorable to cross great rivers
Because the wood is floating on the water
And sent forward by the wind.

Increase moves with gentleness and mildness.
It proceeds daily without limit.
Heaven bestows and Earth accepts.
Thereby things increase without restriction.
The Tao of increasing always proceeds in harmony with the time.

Commentary on the Symbol

Wind and Thunder support each other.
An image of Increasing.
In correspondence with this,
The superior person follows the good when he sees it,
And corrects his fault when he finds it.

Yao Text

1. Initial Nine
    Favorable to engage in conducting great accomplishments.
    Supreme good fortune, no fault.

    Supreme good fortune. No fault.
    Though the lower is not suitable to engage in great affairs.

2. Second Six
    Probably being increased.
    A tortoise worth ten pairs of shells;
    Cannot be refused.
    Being perseveringly steadfast and upright:
    Good fortune.
    The king is engaged in presenting to the Lord of Heaven.
    Good fortune.

    Accept benefits with an open mind.
    It comes from without.

3. Third Six
    Being increased.
    Engaging in unfortunate events.
    No fault.
    Being sincere and truthful,
    Walking the central path,
    Reporting to the lord with jade gui.*

    Being increased, engaging in unfavorable events.
    It is just as it should be.

---

*An elongated pointed tablet of jade held in the hands by ancient rulers on ceremonial occasions.

4. Fourth Six
   Walking the central path,
   Reporting to the lord.
   The lord follows.
   Favorable to use this as the basis to move a capital.

   Reporting to the lord, the lord follows.
   His purpose is to increase the benefit of the public.

5. Fifth Nine
   With sincerity and truthfulness,
   Benefiting their hearts.
   No need to ask.
   Supreme good fortune.
   Being sincere and truthful,
   My virtue will be favored.

   With sincerity and truthfulness,
   Benefiting their hearts.
   No need to ask the reaction.
   My virtue will be favored.
   This is what he really wants.

6. Top Nine
   No increase, but a strike.
   Not keeping the heart steady: misfortune.

   No increase.
   He has an erroneous tendency.
   But a strike—
   It comes from without.

SIGNIFICANCE

The message of the gua is that those above provide benefit to those below. The three lines of the upper gua represent the persons who give, and the three lines of the lower gua represent those who receive. The way to gain relies on doing something substantial. This is why the Decision says, "Favorable to have somewhere to go. Favorable to cross great rivers." The host of the gua is the solid line at the bottom. It is the principal line of the lower gua, and thus the most appropriate line to be the host.

After King Wen levied taxes from the people and instructed them in increasing production and practicing economy, both the government and the people accumulated wealth. King Wen believed that it was favorable for the government to overcome hindrance for the public welfare. The Duke of Zhou narrates that work for the welfare of the people always brought good fortune. The administration helped people live through natural disasters and moved the capital from Cheng to Feng, which is both a place name and the Chinese word for abundance.

(1) Initial Nine. Increasing alternates to Watching (20) ☴☷

The upper gua, Xun, comes from Qian. When Qian loses a yang element, it becomes Xun. The lower gua is Zhen, which derives from Kun. When Kun gains a yang element, it becomes Zhen. In the I Ching, decreases and increases are counted from the bottom. Here, the bottom line is the first to be increased. Normally, the bottom line is not able to accomplish much. During a time of gain, however, what is above amplifies what is below. Because the one above provides benefits, the one below accumulates assets. A favorable situation can bring one supreme good fortune, even when the position is not suitable for great affairs.

(2) Second Six. Increasing alternates to Innermost Sincerity (61) ☴

The Yao Text of this line matches that of the fifth line of the preceding gua, Decreasing, because this gua is the inverse form of the preceding gua. The second line of this gua is equivalent to the fifth line of the preceding one, but now one who increases is at the lower position. The yin element here is gentle, modest, and central. It corresponds to the yang element at the fifth place. One in this position is able to obtain benefits. Because it is weak, remaining steadfast and upright is necessary. In ancient times, before the king presented offerings to Heaven he divined. If he obtained this line, it boded well. To the ancient Chinese, accepting benefits from an offering should be as truthful and sincere as presenting offerings to Heaven.

(3) Third Six. Increasing alternates to Household (37) ☴

The Yao Text of the third line is related to an ancient tradition. In ancient times when unfortunate events happened, such as the death of a nobleman, famine, flood, or war, the lord reported them to the king and informed the neighboring states, seeking help. Thus the Yao Text says, "Being increased. Engaging in unfortunate events. No fault." When the envoy went to other states reporting the misfortune, he carried presents, like jade gui and chime stones, symbolizing truthfulness and sincerity. This sincerity is further indicated by the fact that the envoy walks the central path, which is the key to relieving hardship. Normally one at the third place is not in a favorable situation, but owing to her truthfulness and sincerity and pursuit of the middle path, her gain is just as it should be. The ancients thought that an extremely hard situation could temper and steel one's ability and capacity for endurance. Mencius said:

> When Heaven is about to confer a great mission upon a person, it first exercises his mind with suffering and his body with toil. It subjects him to hunger and poverty and perplexes his undertakings. By all these means it stimulates his mind, hardens his nature, and relieves his incompetence.

In this spirit, the situation described here is unfavorable but without fault.

(4) Fourth Six. Increasing alternates to Without Falsehood (25) ☰☰

The Yao Text of the fourth line is related to the third line. The fourth line is a minister; the third line represents the envoy who comes to report. The fourth line is not central, but it is in the middle of the six lines. One in this place is walking in the central path, and for this reason one's advice is accepted by the envoy. The minister is close to the king at the fifth place. Their trusting relationship means that they can accomplish everything successfully, even such a big undertaking as moving a capital. In ancient times, when moving the capital, a state usually obtained support from neighboring states. "Walking the central path" also denotes being just and fair-minded. When the fourth line of Hindrance (12) ☰☰ moves to the bottom, it becomes this gua. This is what is meant by moving a capital for the benefit of the people.

(5) Fifth Nine. Increasing alternates to Nourishing (27) ☰☰

The yang element at the fifth place is firm and strong. It is central, at a king's place, and corresponds to the yin element at the second place, an official, who is also central. The fifth line is the key to this gua. Sincerity and truthfulness benefits their hearts. There is no question that one will reap supreme good fortune.

(6) Top Nine. Increasing alternates to Beginning (3) ☰☰

The theme of this gua is to decrease what is above in order to increase what is below. The topmost line has reached the extreme, and when things reach an extreme they alternate to their opposite. One at this place is selfish and unreliable. Because he is greedy, nobody wants to aid him. Somebody might even attack him. If he does not keep his heart constantly steady, misfortune will befall him.

Additional Reference Information for This Gua

Image:	Wind above, Thunder below
Recite as:	Wind above Thunder, Increasing
Element:	Wood
Structure:	Three yang with three yin
Month:	The first month of the lunar calendar, or February
Host of the Gua:	Initial Nine
Opposite Gua:	Long Lasting (32)
Inverse Gua:	Decreasing (41)
Mutual Gua:	Falling Away (23)

43

Guai •
Eliminating

≡≡ Dui • Lake
≡≡ Qian • Heaven

NAME AND STRUCTURE

Guai is a Chinese character from the remote past. At present, it is used exclusively in the I Ching; some modern Chinese dictionaries do not include it at all. Originally, Guai meant to set apart. Later, its meaning was extended to include dredging a channel to eliminate the overflow of a river. A radical of three dots was later placed at the left and it was pronounced jue. Still later, its meaning was further extended to encompass making a resolution. In Chinese, making a resolution is equivalent to casting aside hesitation. The Sequence of the Gua explains the name guai in terms of jue. Translated into English, it means to eliminate hesitation. Wilhelm translates Guai as Breakthrough (Resoluteness). Blofeld uses the term Resolution. I follow the Sequence of the Gua, adopting the word Eliminating.

Sequence of the Gua: *When increase continues to excess, surely it will burst. Thus, after Increasing, eliminating hesitation follows.*

The ideograph illustrates the original meaning, to set apart. At the top of the ideograph there are two horizontal lines crossed by two vertical lines. The two horizontal lines and the vertical line on the right represent an object. The vertical line in the middle represents an act of separation. Underneath the central vertical line is the ideograph of a hand, shou, with three fingers and an arm. The hand is holding something—exactly what we no longer know—to set it apart. It can be interpreted as either to set apart good from evil or to set apart resolution from hesitation. In this gua, a yin element is set apart (eliminated) by five yang elements.

The structure of the gua is Lake ☱ above, Heaven ☰ below. When water on the ground has risen up to Heaven and accumulated as a lake of cloud in the sky, surely there will be a cloudburst. This gua signifies the rupture of an accumulation of tension in human society, like a river bursting over its banks. It is time for the righteous to eliminate the inferior forces and their influences through an act of resolution. There are five solid lines, representing the just, under a yielding line. Their influences are blending together and growing stronger. As a result, they take resolute actions to eliminate negative forces. Guai, Eliminating, is one of the twelve tidal gua, representing the third month of the Chinese lunar calendar.

Decision

> Eliminating.
> Declaring at the king's court;
> Sincerely howling:
> There is adversity.
> Notify one's own city:
> Unfavorable to use arms,
> Favorable to have somewhere to go.

Commentary on the Decision

> *Eliminating.*
> *It is a resolution to eliminate something.*
> *The firms eliminate the yielding.*
>
> *Strong and joyous.*
> *Eliminate with harmony.*
> *Declaring at the king's court.*
> *A yielding mounts on five firms.*
>
> *Sincerely howling.*
> *There is adversity.*
> *Exposing the danger is to make the elimination brilliant.*
>
> *Notifying one's own city,*
> *Unfavorable to use arms.*
> *Relying on arms,*

There is no way out.

Favorable to have somewhere to go.
After the firms grow, the elimination will be ended.

Commentary on the Symbol

Water of the lake accumulates in Heaven.
An image of Eliminating.
In correspondence with this,
The superior person bestows his wealth upon those below him
And considers not his own merits.

Yao Text

1. Initial Nine
   Strengthening the forward toes.
   Going forward, unable to compete.
   Instead becomes a fault.

   Unable to compete, still going forward.
   This is a fault.

2. Second Nine
   Being on the alert, howling
   Late at night.
   There are men with arms.
   Fear not.

   There are men with arms; fear not.
   He obtains the central path.

3. Third Nine
   Strengthening the cheek,
   There is misfortune.
   Superior person, eliminating, eliminating.
   Walking alone, encountering the rain.
   Dripping, getting mad.
   No fault.

   Superior person, eliminating, eliminating.
   In the end, no fault.

4. Fourth Nine
   On the buttocks, no skin.
   Going forward, difficult to proceed.
   Tie up a ram;
   Regret vanishes.
   Hearing the words,
   Not believing.

   Going forward; difficult to proceed.
   The position is not appropriate.
   Hearing the words, not believing.
   He is unable to comprehend.

5. Fifth Nine
   Weeds, eliminating, eliminating.
   Walking the central path, no fault.

   Walking the central path, no fault.
   The center is not bright enough.

6. Top Six
   Howling, no response.
   In the end there is misfortune.

   The misfortune of howling with no response.
   One cannot remain any longer.

SIGNIFICANCE

This gua expounds the principle of eliminating evil. There are five solid lines and one yielding line. The five solid lines represent the just; they combine their influence and strength to eliminate the dark forces. Thus, the solid line at the fifth place stands for the leader of the just (the host of the gua), and the yielding line at the top represents the dark force. Five solid lines unite as one to eliminate the evil, but the text still warns that evil forces are sinister and treacherous and their schemes and intrigues should not be overlooked. To eliminate the evil, their evil nature should be exposed in order to gain support from the public. It is better to rely on both courage and resourcefulness.

After the court of Zhou recruited many surviving adherents of the Shang, there were still some hostile elements at large. King Wen decided to eliminate those evil forces. He advised that the matter should be revealed at the king's court and notified the people. It was advisable to do something other than use arms. The Duke of Zhou describes how eliminating the evil forces was not an easy task. There should be no outward animosity, but it should be done without tolerance.

(1) Initial Nine. Eliminating alternates to Great Exceeding (28)

The Yao Text for the bottom line of this gua is the same as for the bottom line of Great Strength (34). In Great Strength there are four yang elements and two yin elements at the top. Here, there are five yang elements and only one yin element at the top. The yang element of this gua has proceeded one step farther than that of Great Strength. The lower gua is Qian, the root of all strength. Thus, the Yao Text for the bottom line says, "Strengthening the forward toes." One at this place intends to move forward to eliminate the evil. Nevertheless, he is too weak owing to his being at a beginning stage. His spirit is willing, but his flesh is weak. His will is unable to give him strength to do what he wants to do. The time and situation are not appropriate.

(2) Second Nine. Eliminating alternates to Abolishing the Old (49)

The lower gua, Qian, symbolizes raising an alarm and calling out. The solid line here corresponds to the solid line in the center of the upper gua, Dui, which also represents night and attacking. The Yao Text says, "Being on the alert, howling late at night. There are men with arms. Fear not." The second line and the fifth line do not correspond to each other, thus there is no reason to fear. The second line is a yang element at a yin place, but central. One at this place is able to mold his firmness with gentleness and temper his strength with wisdom. When eliminating the evil, he is able to be on guard against his opponent's attack and does not take any reckless action. He pursues the middle course.

(3) Third Nine. Eliminating alternates to Joyful (58)

This line is a yang element at a yang place, at the top of the three yang lines in the lower gua. He is firm enough to make a strong decision to eliminate the evil regardless of danger, but his decision shows on his face (cheek), bringing about the enmity of the evil forces. On the other hand, the third line is a yang element that corresponds with the yin element at the topmost place, representing the evil; thus this yang element is doubted by the other yang elements around him. He is isolated and upset, like one walking alone and encountering the rain, but because he is firm and strong, there is no fault.

(4) Fourth Nine. Eliminating alternates to Needing (5) ☵

The fourth line is a yang element at a yin place. It has gone beyond the center, and its position is not correct. One at this place is unstable and suspicious. The upper gua, Dui, also represents a ram. The proper way to lead a ram is to tie a rope to it but let it move on its own. If one forces the ram forward, it will resist. When eliminating evil, one should not be alone in taking the initial step. Wait until all the rams are ready to take part, then one will have no cause for regret.

(5) Fifth Nine. Eliminating alternates to Great Strength (34) ☳

The fifth line is a yang element at a yang place—firm and strong, central and correct. It is in the supreme place of a king and at the top of the five solid lines. It acts as a leader in the course of eliminating evil. Because it is too close to the yin element at the top, firm resolution is necessary. Walking in the central path will create no cause for blame.

(6) Top Six. Eliminating alternates to Initiating (1) ☰

The topmost line is a yin element representing evil. With a long record of misdeeds, it can call no helpers to its aid. There is misfortune. The ancient sages believed that if one plants melons, one reaps melons, and when one sows beans, one gets beans.

Additional Reference Information for This Gua

Image:	Lake above, Heaven below
Recite as:	Lake above Heaven, Eliminating
Element:	Metal
Structure:	Five yang with one yin
Month:	The third month of the lunar calendar, or April
Host of the Gua:	Fifth Nine
Opposite Gua:	Falling Away (23) ☶
Inverse Gua:	Encountering (44) ☴
Mutual Gua:	Initiating (1) ☰

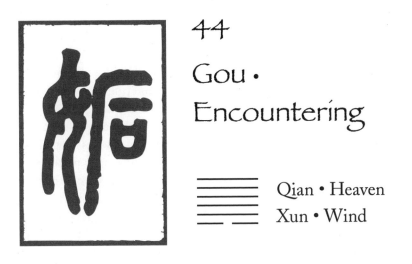

44

Gou •
Encountering

Qian • Heaven
Xun • Wind

NAME AND STRUCTURE

Gou is a character from remote antiquity, which appears at present only in the I Ching. According to the ancient dictionary of characters, Gou denotes a couple, especially a married couple. Later, it meant to pair or to copulate; it also meant good. The Great Treatise, one of the most important commentaries of the Ten Wings, says that Gou is to meet or to encounter. Traditionally it is understood as a meeting, an encounter between a male and a female.

Sequence of the Gua: *After eliminating, surely there will be something to encounter. Thus, after Eliminating, Encountering follows.*

This gua is the inverse of the preceding gua, Eliminating. Eliminating means to separate; Encountering is to meet. After separation people meet again; after meeting again, people separate. That is human life. Eliminating and Encountering mutually complement each other. Wilhelm translates Gou as Coming to Meet. Blofeld translates it as Contact (or Sexual Intercourse, Meeting). Here, following the suggestion of the commentary, the term Encountering is used.

The ideograph of Gou is simple. It is composed of a woman and a queen. On the left is a buxom maiden. On the right side is the ideograph hou, a queen. Because a queen always follows the king, hou also means behind. The queen is standing upright and bowing. Underneath her bending body is an open mouth, kou, and above the mouth a horizontal stroke indicating the number one. This one person that the queen is encountering is the king. They meet and come together. The queen greets the king with respect and her best wishes.

The structure of the gua is Heaven ☰ above, Wind ☴ below. The wind blows everywhere under Heaven, encountering every being. It should be an auspicious gua. However, there is only one yielding line beneath five solid lines, symbolizing that the yin element is advancing and approaching the yang elements. When King Wen saw this happening, he heightened his vigilance. He realized that an unworthy person was worming his way into favor at the court. The growing negative influences would displace good people one after another. Darkness and difficulties had been eliminated, but their negative influences had not totally faded. These influences were permeating different areas. One must beware of this tendency and take prompt precautions against possible misfortune. Thus King Wen's Decision and the Duke of Zhou's Yao Text are full of warnings. But Confucius's commentaries still shed light on the positive side. This gua is one of the twelve tidal gua. It represents the fifth month of the Chinese lunar calendar.

Decision

> Encountering.
> The maiden is strong.
> Do not engage in marrying such a woman.

Commentary on the Decision

> *Encountering.*
> *Meet someone unexpectedly.*
> *The yielding encounters the firms.*
>
> *Do not engage in marrying such a woman.*
> *The union cannot last very long.*
>
> *When Heaven and Earth meet*
> *All creatures are fully displayed.*
> *When the firm meets the central and the correct*
> *His aspiration will be fulfilled under Heaven.*
>
> *Great indeed is the time and significance of Encountering!*

Commentary on the Symbol

Under Heaven, there is Wind.
An image of Encountering.
In correspondence with this,
The prince delivers his commands
And makes them known to the four quarters of his kingdom.

Yao Text

1. Initial Six
   Fasten with a metal brake.
   Being steadfast and upright: good fortune.
   There is somewhere to go.
   Misfortune appears—
   Impetuous lean pig,
   Pacing up and down.

   Fasten with a metal brake.
   It is tied down—the way of the yin.

2. Second Nine
   Grass sack,
   There are fish.
   No fault.
   Not favorable for the guests.

   Grass sack, there are fish.
   It is not appropriate to let it approach the guests.

3. Third Nine
   On the buttocks, no skin.
   Going forward, difficult to proceed.
   Adversity.
   No great harm.

   Going forward, difficult to proceed.
   His steps have not been tied down.

4. Fourth Nine
   Grass sack, no fish.
   Misfortune arises.

Misfortune of no fish.
He keeps himself far away from the people.

5. Fifth Nine
   Willow twigs wrap the melon,
   Concealing brilliance.
   There are meteorites descending from Heaven.

   Fifth nine conceals his brilliance,
   Owing to his middle position and correct place.
   There are meteorites descending from Heaven;
   He does not abandon the ordinance of Heaven.

6. Top Nine
   Encountering in a horn.
   Humiliation.
   No fault.

   Encountering in a horn.
   Reaching the topmost; there is ground for regret.

SIGNIFICANCE

This gua discusses the principle of encountering. In Chinese, meeting a person (or anything) unexpectedly is defined as encountering. When people encounter each other, either they are attracted, making adjustment for a harmonious relationship, or they reject each other, creating conflict between them. In human life sometimes one cannot refrain from misunderstanding and conflict. But one should not indulge in it and think that conflict is unavoidable and cannot be resolved. The ancient sages advocated adopting a conciliatory attitude. Here one yin element approaches five yang elements. She dares to come forward because her strength grows stronger. In this situation, one should not overlook taking preventive measures.

King Wen's strategy of eliminating evil forces was to show no animosity but to act without tolerance. His administration constrained evil elements like tying up rams. But evil elements still wormed themselves into the favor of the court. King Wen realized that the evil forces had been eliminated, yet their influence had not totally faded. His analogy was that the maiden was too strong; it was not good to marry such a woman.

The Duke of Zhou describes the evil forces as waiting to move forward like a lean pig. They should be stopped as if fastened with a metal brake. It is wise to restrain their influence by not letting them influence other people, but it was wiser to influence people with positive virtue.

(1) Initial Six. Encountering alternates to Initiating (1) ☰

The bottom line is a yin element starting to grow under five yang elements. It is better to stop its growth at the beginning so its evil influence will not extend any further. The Yao Text says, "Fasten with a metal brake. Being steadfast and upright: good fortune. There is somewhere to go. Misfortune appears." But the yin element is unwilling to lag behind. It is like a lean pig waiting to move forward. One should be alert and take precautions, as in using a metal brake to stop a moving carriage.

(2) Second Nine. Encountering alternates to Retreat (33) ☶

This is a yang element at a yin place, central but not correct. It does not correspond to the yang element at the fifth place, but it is close to the yin element at the bottom. In this gua, more emphasis is laid on encountering than corresponding because people are more easily influenced in person than at a distance. As a matter of fact, the bottom yin element tries to move forward. It is held back by this yang element, like a fish packed in a grass sack. It is wise to restrain a negative force and not let it influence other people. Thus Confucius says, "It is not appropriate to let it approach the guests." The guests referred to are the other four yang elements.

(3) Third Nine. Encountering alternates to Contention (6) ☰

The Yao Text of this line begins exactly the same as the fourth line of Eliminating (43), which is the inverse form of Encountering. This line is a yang element at a yang place—it has moved beyond the center. The character of one at this place is too strong. He is too anxious to look for a mate. Looking for a mate is human nature, yet here it is an unfavorable situation.

There is one yin element at the bottom, the only yin element in this gua. The yang element is going to chase her. However, the bottom yin element has already encountered the yang element at the second position. So this yang turns his eyes to the one at the topmost position. The topmost element does respond but not correspond, because they are both yang. This yang is in a bind and is able to neither proceed nor draw back. He feels uneasy whether sitting or walking, like one with no skin on his buttocks. The Yao Text says, "Going forward, difficult to proceed." This is an adverse situation, but the difficulty in proceeding means that he is unlikely to encounter any evil, thus there is no great harm.

(4) Fourth Nine. Encountering alternates to Proceeding Humbly (57)

This is a yang element at a yin place, neither central nor correct. It corresponds to the yin element at the bottom place. The element at the bottom is obstructed by the yang element at the second place. He cannot move forward. "Grass sack, no fish" means that there are no friends gathered round. The misfortune of one at this place is that he keeps himself away from people. In Chinese, "sack" also means accepting others. If one is able to be magnanimous and tolerant toward others, then he is able to obtain support from them.

(5) Fifth Nine. Encountering alternates to Establishing the New (50)

This line is the host of the gua. It is a yang element at a yang place—central, correct, and in the supreme position. This line represents a person of high virtue who is righteous and powerful. The Yao Text says, "Willow twigs wrap the melon, concealing brilliance." One at this place has the brilliant quality of tolerating others' opinions and behaviors, but still restrains the evil influence from spreading. Melon represents the yin element at the bottom. It is sweet, but it rots easily and creeps along the ground, denoting the insidious influence of evil.

Confucius's Commentary on the Yao Text says, "He does not abandon the ordinance of Heaven." One should live in accordance with the ordinance of heaven, natural law. The rising of evil is as natural as the rotting of a melon, and its influence extends much more easily and faster than that of the righteous, but by understanding natural law one endowed with brilliance can radiate it as easily as meteorites drop from Heaven. In other words, live with virtue.

(6) Top Nine. Encountering alternates to Greet Exceeding (28)

The topmost line is a yang element at a yin place. According to the I Ching, one at the top has no position. It is at the end of the gua, so it falls into an isolated situation. The only yin element in this gua is at the bottom. She is too far away for him to meet. He is proud and does not want to descend. Pride drives him to a dead end, like finding himself at the tip of a horn. There is no way for him to encounter the yin element at the bottom. Although there is no reason for blame, there is regret.

Additional Reference Information for This Gua

Image:	Heaven above, Wind below
Recite as:	Wind under Heaven, Encountering
Element:	Metal
Structure:	Five yang with one yin
Month:	The fifth month of the lunar calendar, or June
Host of the Gua:	Fifth Nine
Opposite Gua:	Turning Back (24)
Inverse Gua:	Eliminating (43)
Mutual Gua:	Initiating (1)

45
Cui · Bringing Together

≡≡≡ Dui • Lake
≡ ≡ Kun • Earth

NAME AND STRUCTURE

Originally Cui designated bundles of thickly grown grasses. From this meaning, it grew to signify collecting things together.

Sequence of the Gua: *After encountering, things begin to gather together. Thus, after Encountering, Bringing Together follows.*

Wilhelm translates Cui as Gathering Together (Massing). Blofeld translates it as Gathering Together, Assembling. I use the term Bringing Together. Bringing Together means bringing *people* together. Bringing bears a sense of causing to come and implies a purposeful togetherness. Gathering expresses only a general idea, usually with no implication of an arrangement. Bringing Together is more active and productive and has a purpose.

The ideograph consists of two parts. At the top, there are two bundles of grasses. The lower part is the ideograph zu, providing the sound. Zu carries several meanings. At present, it generally indicates a soldier. In ancient times it meant a servant. And in very early days it denoted a servant exclusively retained to make clothes for his or her master. The ideograph zu looks like an upper garment on a hanger with two pieces of girdle. In making clothes, pieces of cloth are purposefully sewn together. Taken together these images portray the character's original meaning: either collecting bundles of thickly grown grasses or bringing a multitude of people together.

·The structure of the gua is Lake ☱ above, Earth ☷ below. In its form and content, this gua has a close connection to Union (8) ䷇. The structure of Union is Water ☵ above, Earth ☷ below. A lake is a place where a great amount of water accumulates. The ancient Chinese realized that this sort of bringing together is more powerful than that of Union. Union symbolizes a small community, such as a neighborhood, while Cui symbolizes a large community, such as a nation.

In Union, there is only one solid line, at the fifth place. This gua has two solid lines, at the fourth and the fifth places. These two solid lines, a king and a minister, are powerful in their leadership. They work in tandem to bring people together in a larger community with a strong mutual bond.

Decision

> Bringing Together,
> Prosperous and smooth.
> The king arrives at the ancestral temple.
> Favorable to see a great person.
> Prosperous and smooth,
> Favorable to be steadfast and upright.
> Use big animals: good fortune.
> Favorable to have somewhere to go.

Commentary on the Decision

> *Bringing Together.*
> *It is bringing people together.*
> *Devoted and joyous.*
> *The firm is central and has correspondence.*
> *Therefore people come and assemble together.*
>
> *The king arrives at the ancestral temple.*
> *With filial piety, he presents his offerings.*
>
> *Favorable to see a great person.*
> *This will bring prosperity and smoothness,*
> *Bringing people together in a proper way.*
>
> *Use big animals:*
> *Good fortune.*

He is following the will of Heaven.

By observing how all beings are brought together,
One can see the truth of Heaven and Earth and all beings.

Commentary on the Symbol

Lake over Earth.
An image of Bringing Together.
In correspondence with this,
The superior person repairs his weapons
To guard against unexpected happenings.

Yao Text

1. Initial Six
   Being sincere and truthful,
   Not to the end.
   Confused,
   Still bringing together.
   If crying out,
   Once grasping hands: laughing.
   Do not worry.
   Going forward: no fault.

   Confused,
   Still bringing together,
   One's mind is in confusion.

2. Second Six
   Being drawn together: good fortune.
   No fault.
   Be sincere and truthful;
   Favorable, even using a small offering.

   Being drawn together: good fortune.
   No fault.
   The central principle remains unchanged.

3. Third Six
   Bringing together: sighs.
   Nothing is favorable.

Going forward: no fault.
Slight humiliation.

Going forward, no fault.
Gentle breeze is above.

4. Fourth Nine
   Great good fortune. No fault.

   Great good fortune. No fault.
   Even the place is not appropriate.

5. Fifth Nine
   Bringing together.
   There is a position. No fault.
   No confidence.
   Sublimely persevering, steadfast and upright.
   Regret vanishes.

   Bringing together, there is a position.
   His will has not yet become brilliant.

6. Top Six
   Lamenting and sighing.
   Bitter tears; no fault.

   Lamenting and sighing,
   Bitter tears.
   He does not feel safe at the top.

SIGNIFICANCE

This gua displays a state of strong union between a sovereign and his minister. In bringing people together, a great leader is critically important. Besides the leader, there should be a common belief. For this reason, the ancient king arrived at his ancestral temple and offered large animals to Heaven. In ancient China, Heaven and the ancestors were the two most powerful bonds of union. When people have faith in Heaven and trust in their leader, they are happy to work together with one heart and one mind, especially in difficult times.

The gua has two solid lines—at the fourth and the fifth places. One is the king and the other a minister; they are working together harmoniously to draw all people together. Bringing Together means gathering people together to protect the country. The king and minister are equally important, but the king is the leader, the commander in chief. It is appropriate that he be the host of the gua.

After eliminating the evil and encountering the good, King Wen brought together a multitude of people at his ancestral temple. He offered an ox, a ram, and a pig to Heaven and to the ancestors of the Zhou and the Shang as well for unification and celebration. The Duke of Zhou kept a memorandum about the ceremony. Many people gathered. The gathering was successful and ended with great good fortune. There was no fault.

(1) Initial Six. Bringing Together alternates to Following (17)

The bottom line is a yin element incorrectly positioned at a yang place. It corresponds to the yang element at the fourth place. They want to get together. However, there are two yin elements obstructing them. Although she is sincere, she is unable to reach the end. If she were to call out sincerely, one at the fourth place would hear and come. Then she would burst out laughing and grasp the other's hand. The Yao Text says, "Do not worry. Going forward, no fault." This line tells us that sincerity is one of the basic factors of a strong union.

(2) Second Six. Bringing Together alternates to Exhausting (47)

The yin element at this place corresponds to the yang element at the fifth place. They long to get together. This yin element is surrounded by two other yin elements above and below. This is a yin element at a yin place; she is gentle, modest, and central. She needs help from the one at the fifth place, which is a yang element at a yang place. He is firm, strong, and also central. They are a perfect match. The Yao Text says, "Being drawn together: good fortune. No fault. Being sincere and truthful; favorable, even using a small offering."

The small offerings mentioned were part of a Chinese ceremony known as *you*. The spring ceremony of the Shang dynasty and the summer ceremony of the Zhou dynasty were called *you*. Spring and summer are not seasons of harvest; thus the offering was simple. Blessing is based on sincerity and truthfulness, not on material wealth. Confucius says that the blessing of this line derives from the central path it maintains.

(3) Third Six. Bringing Together alternates to Mutual Influence (31)

At the third place is a yin element at a yang place, neither central nor correct. It does not correspond to the topmost line since they are both

yin. There is no way to bring them together. She tries to bring the neighborhood together. However, the lower neighbor, the yin element at the second place, corresponds to the yang element at the fifth place. The upper neighbor, the yang element at the fourth place, corresponds to the yin element at the bottom. Thus, the Yao Text says, "Bringing together: sighs. Nothing is favorable." The text still encourages him to go forward because the topmost yin is devoted and gentle. Although the union might not be perfect, there is no fault, only slight regret. Confucius's commentary says, "Going forward, no fault. Gentle breeze is above." This gentle breeze above refers to the topmost yin element.

(4) Fourth Nine. Bringing Together alternates to Union (8) ☵☰

This is a yang element at a yin place, neither central nor correct. However, he is at a minister's place and close to the king. He can bring together those people in the lower gua. Owing to these excellent conditions, his words and deeds have great influence, but he should act with extreme caution, for the suspicions of the king as well as the people might be aroused by one wielding such influence from an improper place. Generally, one who is at a place neither central nor correct is not in a favorable situation. However, this element carries the yang element at the fifth place and corresponds to the yin element at the bottom. He is sincere in bringing people together for the king and the country. Although his place is neither central nor correct, other conditions are excellent. Thus, his plans will reap great good fortune and are without fault.

(5) Fifth Nine. Bringing Together alternates to Delight (16) ☳☷

The fifth line has the quality of a brilliant leader; he is a yang element at a yang place. He is firm and strong, central and correct, and obtains the supreme place of a king. He has dignity—there is no ground for blame. However, one in this situation tends to be proud and willful. The text warns that there is no confidence in him. He must persevere. Confucius indicates that his will has not yet become brilliant and he should not be insincere. Only if he is able to keep to the central path consistently and be steadfast and upright will regret disappear.

(6) Top Six. Bringing Together alternates to Hindrance (12) ☴☷

The topmost line represents the last stage of bringing people together. Here is a yin element at a yin place. She is weak and unable to unite people. She feels isolated and helpless, and so she laments, sighs, and sheds tears.

She needs instead to examine her motivation and conduct. Setting the blame on fate and destiny is not the right attitude to adopt.

Additional Reference Information for This Gua

Image:	Lake above, Earth below
Recite as:	Lake on Earth, Bringing Together
Element:	Metal
Structure:	Two yang with four yin
Month:	The eighth month of the lunar calendar, or September
Host of the Gua:	Fifth Nine
Opposite Gua:	Great Accumulation (26)
Inverse Gua:	Growing Upward (46)
Mutual Gua:	Developing Gradually (53)

46
Sheng · Growing Upward

$$\begin{array}{cc}\equiv\!\equiv & \text{Kun} \cdot \text{Earth} \\ \overline{} & \text{Xun} \cdot \text{Wood}\end{array}$$

NAME AND STRUCTURE

Sheng signifies growing upward.

Sequence of the Gua: *Bringing together in an upward motion is called growing upward. Thus, after Bringing Together, Growing Upward follows.*

Originally, Sheng meant to rise, to ascend, to promote. In terms of this gua, it is to promote in an upward direction. Wilhelm translates Sheng as Pushing Upward and Blofeld as Ascending, Promotion. The symbol of this gua is wood growing upward from the earth; thus Growing Upward is the term adopted here.

The ideograph consists of two parts. The upper part is a rising sun. The Chinese say, "The brilliant sun is growing upward in the eastern sky." The lower image is the ideograph sheng, which provides the sound. Traditionally, only this lower part is used for the name of this gua. Sheng was an ancient unit of measure for grain or cloth. Today, one sheng is approximately one liter.

This gua is the inverse of the preceding gua, Bringing Together. Bringing Together indicates bringing *people* together. Growing Upward takes a further step, upgrading the action to doing something more productive. Some I Ching scholars suggest that while Bringing Together means unifying people to protect the country, Growing Upward signifies opening up the border regions of the country. The structure of the gua is Earth ☷ above, Wood ☴ below. Wood underneath Earth is an image of upward growth.

In the I Ching, there are three gua related to the movement of advancing: Proceeding Forward (35) ☶☷; Growing Upward; and Developing Gradually (53) ☴☶. The structure of Developing Gradually is Fire ☲ above Earth ☷ (the image of a rising sun) and the movement is simply forward advance, Fire representing the south and south symbolizing advance. The image of Growing Upward is wood breaking through the ground and growing out of the earth. It is a movement of promotion from a lower level to a higher level and is associated with an effort of growth. The image of Developing Gradually is Wood ☴ above Mountain ☶. It suggests a tree growing gradually to its height on a mountain, stressing the slowness. Growing gradually keeps the tree strong, firm, and stable. This is the wisdom of nature. Weeds grow quickly—they are neither strong nor stable. Growing Upward means advancing smoothly. The lower gua of Growing Upward is Wood ☴; the upper gua is Earth ☷. Both of their attributes suggest moving smoothly without hindrance. During the time of upward growth, there is no obstruction.

Decision

> Growing Upward.
> Sublimely prosperous and smooth.
> Appropriate to see a great person.
> Do not worry;
> Moving forward toward the south:
> Good fortune.

Commentary on the Decision

> *The yielding ascends in accord with the time.*
> *Gentle and submissive.*
> *The firm is central and obtains a correspondense.*
> *There is great prosperity and smoothness.*
>
> *Appropriate to see a great person.*
> *Do not worry;*
> *There is blessing.*
> *Moving forward toward the south: good fortune.*
> *His will will be fulfilled.*

Commentary on the Symbol

Within the earth, wood grows.
An image of Growing Upward.
In correspondence with this,
The superior person cultivates his virtue in proper order.
He accumulates the small achievements
And develops them higher and greater.

Yao Text

1. Initial Six
   With confidence, growing upward.
   Great good fortune.

   With confidence, growing upward: great good fortune.
   Those above agree with his will.

2. Second Nine
   Being sincere and truthful.
   Then, favorable, even using a small offering.
   No fault.

   The sincerity and the truthfulness of the second nine.
   It brings joy.

3. Third Nine
   Growing upward
   Into an empty village.

   Growing upward into an empty village.
   There is no reason to hesitate.

4. Fourth Six
   The king is engaged in
   Presenting offerings to Mount Ji.
   Good fortune.
   No fault.

   The king is engaged in presenting offerings to Mount Ji.
   He follows the way of the royalty.

5. Fifth Six
   Being steadfast and upright: good fortune.
   Ascending step by step.

   Being steadfast and upright: good fortune.
   He greatly achieves what he wills.

6. Top Six
   Darkness, growing upward.
   Favorable to be ceaselessly steadfast and upright.

   Darkness, growing upward, reaching the highest place.
   It is going to decrease his wealth.

SIGNIFICANCE

This gua expounds the principle of growing upward. Upward growth needs support from people. People are a source of strength for achieving goals. Such growth also needs to follow in the steps of precedent—experience provides a precious reference. One who wishes to ascend needs an attitude of truthfulness and sincerity; otherwise people will not lend support. The gua uses the image of wood growing up from within the earth. It takes effort for a tree's roots and trunk to break up the soil. Applied to human society, this tells us the way to approach advancement. When one's fame and position grows, it is not accidental. It is based on the law of cause and effect. One should cultivate virtue, build up character, accumulate knowledge and experience, and work hard to establish credibility. This is the proper way to approach personal growth and promotion.

King Wen's Decision says, "Growing Upward. Supremely prosperous and smooth. Appropriate to see a great person. Do not worry; moving forward toward the south: good fortune." This passage refers to the promotion of the yang element at the second place, which is central to the lower gua—an auspicious location. It is a place for a general, which corresponds to the yin element at the fifth place, representing the king. Because the second element is firm and resolute and walks in the central path, he is able to see a great person, in other words, to gain an opportunity for promotion. It is believed that the great man refers to King Wen. "Moving forward toward the south" indicates King Wen's punitive expedition toward the place called Shu, which was the ancient name for Sichuan.

The hosts of the gua are the yielding fifth line and the yielding line at the bottom. The Commentary on the Decision says, "The yielding ascends in accord with the time." The "yielding" designates the yin element at the fifth place, which grows upward to the supreme position. She is gentle and humble, and her upward growth is in accord with her virtue without her needing to curry favor. However, the bottom line is the root of the lower gua, Xun, Wood, and is also appropriate to be the host.

After he brought the multitude of people together with great success, King Wen took a further step and opened up the border regions of the kingdom. He decided to advance toward the south, a place known as Shu. The Duke of Zhou narrates that the punitive expedition toward the south was carried out with sincerity and confidence. Before launching the expedition, King Wen held a ceremony and presented offerings to Mount Ji, the native place of the Zhou. The expedition brought supreme prosperity and smoothness, and great good fortune, as King Wen had predicted.

(1) Initial Six. Growing Upward alternates to Advance (11) ☷

The bottom line is a yin element at a yang place at the bottom of the lower gua, Wood. This bottom line suggests that the root of a tree penetrates deep underneath the ground. The second and the third lines represent the trunk. The root consumes nutrition from the soil while the trunk with its leaves assimilates light from the sun. The roots cannot grow alone—they should grow in accord with the trunk. The commentary on the Yao Text says, "Those above agree with his will." The root and the trunk grow steadily with sincerity and confidence. There is great good fortune.

(2) Second Nine. Growing Upward alternates to Humbleness (15) ☷

The second line is a yang element at a yin place. The Yao Text of this line is the same as for the yielding line at the second place of the preceding gua, Bringing Together. In the preceding gua, the yin element at the second place corresponds to the yang element at the fifth place. In this gua, it is just reverse—the yang element at the second place corresponds to the yin element at the fifth place. Although the positions are different, the principle is the same. If one is sincere and truthful in his or her heart, a small offering is enough to obtain blessing. The commentary says that his sincerity and truthfulness brings joy. The bottom line and the second line thus tell us that an attitude of sincerity and truthfulness is proper for attaining upward growth.

(3) Third Nine. Growing Upward alternates to Multitude (7) ☷

The third line is a yang element at a yin place at the top of the lower gua. If it grows upward, it will enter into the upper gua, Earth, which is made up of three broken lines. The broken lines leave an empty space in the middle of the gua, symbolizing an empty village. The element at the third place is firm. He intends to grow upward. The place ahead of him is empty. It is human nature to fear the empty place, the unknown. For this reason, there is no comment about good fortune or misfortune. The commentary advises only, "There is no reason to hesitate."

(4) Fourth Six. Growing Upward alternates to Long Lasting (32) ☳

The fourth line is a yin element at a yin place, central and correct. It is in a minister's position. In ancient times, only the king presented offerings to Heaven and Earth. Lords and princes presented offerings to mountains and rivers. Here one is appointed by the Lord of Heaven to take charge of the ceremony to present offerings to the mountain. It shows how his utmost faithfulness and sincerity wins the trust of the Lord of Heaven. There is good fortune and no fault. Mount Ji was also known as the West Mountain. It was the place of origin of the Zhou dynasty.

(5) Fifth Six. Growing Upward alternates to Replenishing (48) ☵

The fifth line is a yin element at a yang place. Its attribute is weakness, and its place is not correct. One at this place corresponds to the yang element at the second place, which is strong and firm. She obtains his support and ascends to the supreme place. The Yao Text says, "Being steadfast and upright: good fortune. Ascending step by step." Moving upward step by step is the best way to gain promotion. Thus, "he greatly achieves what he wills," bringing good fortune.

(6) Top Six. Growing Upward alternates to Remedying (18) ☶

The topmost line is a yin element at a yin place. Its attribute is weakness. Its upward growth has already reached the limit. There is darkness. One at this place should not become dizzy with success. If one cannot remain steadfast and upright, one will become exhausted. There is the possibility of losing one's wealth.

Additional Reference Information for This Gua

Image:	Earth above, Wood below
Recite as:	Wood under Earth, Growing Upward
Element:	Earth
Structure:	Two yang with four yin
Month:	The twelfth month of the lunar calendar, or January
Host of the Gua:	Initial Six and Fifth Six
Opposite Gua:	Without Falsehood (25)
Inverse Gua:	Bringing Together (45)
Mutual Gua:	Marrying Maiden (54)

47
Kun • Exhausting

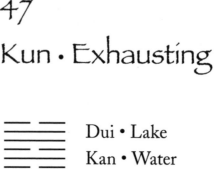

Dui • Lake
Kan • Water

NAME AND STRUCTURE

Kun means difficulty and hardship. It suggests a difficult position or situation. In ancient times it meant being surrounded by enemies, poverty-stricken, extremely tired, or exhausted.

Sequence of the Gua: *When growing upward goes on without stopping, surely one will become exhausted. Thus, after Growing Upward, Exhausting follows.*

Wilhelm translates Kun as Oppression (Exhaustion). Blofeld translates it as Adversity, Weariness. I use the translation Exhausting. The ideograph of Kun is a tree placed within a big mouth, kou. Here "mouth" signifies an enclosure. The symbol of the preceding gua is wood growing upward from the earth. The ideograph of this gua is wood confined in an enclosure. It can no longer grow. In the end it will become exhausted and die. Before the Zhou dynasty, the ideograph of Kun was represented by wood and the sign for stop, indicating that the wood stops growing; it becomes exhausted. The structure of the gua is Lake ☱ above, Water ☵ below. Water below Lake is a picture of an empty lake. The water here has been used up completely.

Exhausting defines a situation where the water is drained away, one's energy is used up. This is one of the most difficult situations described by the sixty-four gua in the I Ching, fraught with restriction, obstruction, oppression, and exhaustion. All six lines are unfavorable. The situation seems extremely gloomy and hopeless. But this is the best time for one to hide one's capacities and bide one's time. In an exhausting situation, one must still seek prosperity and smoothness and remain steadfast and upright. Only the great person possesses these traits, which will bring about good fortune. In the spirit of the I Ching, an extremely exhausting situation bears the seeds of great regeneration. The sage accepts every situation with faith and ease. Not many people understand and believe this truth.

Decision

> Exhausting.
> Prosperous and smooth.
> Being steadfast and upright.
> Great person: good fortune.
> No fault.
> There are words
> Not believed.

Commentary on the Decision

> *Exhausting.*
> *The firm is covered.*
>
> *Facing danger, still be joyous.*
> *In an exhausting situation*
> *One does not lose his prosperity and smoothness;*
> *Only the superior person is able to do it.*
>
> *Being steadfast and upright.*
> *Only the great person possesses these traits.*
> *It will bring about good fortune*
> *Because he is firm and central.*
>
> *There are words*
> *Not believed.*
> *He who considers the words important*
> *Falls into exhaustion.*

Commentary on the Symbol

> *Lake without water.*
> *An image of Exhausting.*

In correspondence with this,
The superior person spares no effort
In fulfilling his inspiration.

Yao Text

1. Initial Six
    Buttocks, exhausted, on the stump of a tree.
    Entering into a gloomy valley.
    Three years, one does not appear.

    Entering into a gloomy valley.
    One is dark and not clear.

2. Second Nine
    Exhausted with wine and food.
    A pair of scarlet kneecaps has just arrived.
    Favorable to use them for ceremonial offerings.
    Moving forward: misfortune.
    No fault.

    Exhausted with wine and food.
    He is in a central position;
    There is ground for congratulation.

3. Third Six
    Exhausted with rocks.
    Resting on thorns and thistles.
    Entering his house,
    Seeing not his wife: misfortune.

    Resting on thorns and thistles.
    He lies on a hard line.
    Entering his house, not seeing his wife.
    Not a good omen.

4. Fourth Nine
    Coming, slowly, slowly.
    Exhausted in a golden carriage.
    Humiliation.
    There is an end.

    Coming slowly, slowly.

His will is directed to the lower.
Though the place is not appropriate,
There is response.

5. Fifth Nine
   Nose and feet are cut off.
   Exhausted with scarlet kneecaps.
   Gradually and slowly, there is joy.
   Favorable to use them for ceremonial offerings.

   Nose and feet are cut off;
   He does not fulfill his aspiration.
   Gradually and slowly, there is joy.
   The line is straight and central.
   Favorable to use it for ceremonial offerings.
   He will receive blessing.

6. Top Six
   Exhausted with creeping vines,
   And also danger and perplexity.
   Saying, "Moving: regret."
   Probably repenting,
   Then moving forward: good fortune.

   Exhausted with creeping vines.
   One does not handle it properly.
   "Regret for taking action. There is regret."
   Good fortune comes from moving forward.

SIGNIFICANCE

This gua discusses the way to deal with an extremely difficult time or situation. The text is enigmatic. The image of the gua suggests that the yin forces overwhelm the yang, but the yang will not be overcome. The virtuous and the wise might fall into a destitute situation, but it is only a temporary condition. Because they know how to practice self-examination, and to regret and repent, they always learn something from their former errors. The little fellows might be successful and prosperous for a time, but they will surely end up destitute. They refuse to understand the law of cause and effect—one who damages others will eventually damage oneself.

A lake without water dries out. A man without money breaks down.

Financial pressure is one of the most stressful situations in human lives. The ancient Chinese remind us, "A man with no money is like a fish with no water." In such a situation, it is difficult to survive. This truth pertains to a person and to a government. There are different ways to understand exhausting. One can become exhausted by not having enough, or by having too much. When one is stuck in an exhausting situation, it is wise to discover the cause and seek the solution. This is what the wise do. Merely complaining and being resentful will only make the situation worse. The virtuous exhaust themselves with the Tao. They worry not for material things, only for spirituality. Their exhaustion is in being completely absorbed, even forgetting food and sleep.

The hosts of the gua are the solid lines at the second and fifth places. The solid second place is exhausted with wine and food. The solid element at the fifth place is exhausted with "scarlet kneecaps," symbolizing an imperial robe. Imperial robe, in Chinese, is zhu fu. Zhu means bright red. Fu has two meanings. One denotes the silk ribbon for fastening an official seal. The other is an imperial robe worn for attending ceremonial offerings; it was a robe for covering the knees when bending and kowtowing. Only officials of high rank could wear the zhu fu. In this gua it represents a high position.

The expedition to the south encountered difficulties which cast a pall over the proceedings. King Wen remained steadfast and upright, still seeking prosperity and smoothness. The Duke of Zhou narrates the tale of hardship. There was occasion for regret, but King Wen believed it would end in good fortune. The people would not believe the truth. So, to inspire the multitude's enthusiasm, King Wen twice performed a sacrificial ceremony to Heaven and the ancestors. He was able to reach the end.

(1) Initial Six. Exhausting alternates to Joyful (58) ☷

The bottom line is a yin element at a yang place, at the bottom of the lower gua, Water, or Darkness. It represents one who is exhausted and in a difficult situation. Generally, the bottom line is represented by the toes. In this gua, it is represented by the buttocks, which are on the bottom when one is sitting. This line is described in terms of a person who is sitting on the stump of a tree. He cannot walk; he is like a stump stuck in the ground. It is as if he has entered into a gloomy valley, and for a long period of time (not necessarily three years) he sees nothing. The line tells us that when one is in a gloomy situation, one needs to gain enlightenment and wisdom.

(2) Second Nine. Exhausting alternates to Bringing Together (45) ☷

The second line is a yang element at a yin place, central but not correct. It represents a person with noble character and high prestige. His exhaustion derives from excess. Good wine and expensive food as well as imperial robes (scarlet kneecaps) are appropriate for offering sacrifice, but not in daily life. One in this place knows that overindulging will bring misfortune. Therefore he avoids this temptation and no fault is involved.

There is an unusual feature to this gua. In the I Ching, usually, if the second line and the fifth line are complementary yin and yang, they correspond to each other and there is good fortune. Only in this gua and Little Accumulation (9) ☴ do the second and the fifth lines not correspond, and yet there is still good fortune. The reason is that, because the yang is suppressed by the yin, it needs the support of another yang.

(3) Third Six. Exhausting alternates to Great Exceeding (28) ☱

The third line is a yin element at a yang place, neither central nor correct. It bears two yang elements at the fourth and fifth places, as if carrying two rocks on its shoulders. It mounts another yang element at the second place, as if resting on thorns and thistles. This is a situation where it is difficult to advance or to retreat. The only choice is to return home. However, it does not see its partner, who should be at the top place, to which the third place responds. Unfortunately, the topmost line is another yin element, and so it does not correspond. Thus the Yao text says, "Seeing not his wife: misfortune." In his Great Treatise, Confucius comments on this line:

> *Exhausted in a situation where one should not be exhausted,*
> *It is sure that his reputation is humiliated.*
> *Occupying what one should not occupy,*
> *It is certain that he is falling into danger.*
> *Being humiliated and falling into danger,*
> *The time to perish is near at hand.*
> *How can he see his wife?*

(4) Fourth Nine. Exhausting alternates to Darkness (29) ☵

This line is exhausted in a golden carriage. In ancient times, the prince rode in a golden carriage to greet the bride at his wedding. The fourth line mounts on the lower gua, Kan. Kan represents water, but also wheels and a carriage. The Water is below and the Lake above. Lake represents a youngest daughter; Water represents a middle son. They are going to marry. This is the most joyful time in one's life, yet he still feels exhausted. In ancient times, a superior person worried not about poverty but about the Tao of Humanity. One who could not carry out one's aspiration, even in a superior position and at a significant time, still remembered those who were in an arduous situation.

The fourth line is a yang element at a yin place, neither central nor correct, corresponding to the yin element at the bottom. The bottom line is stuck in a gloomy valley. This yang line should go forward to help, but he is in a golden carriage. In the I Ching, a line moving upward is said to "go," one moving downward is said to "come." This line wants to move downward toward the bottom line. The lower gua is Water; he cannot move quickly through it. Thus the Yao Text says, "Coming, slowly, slowly. Exhausted in a golden carriage. Humiliation. There is an end."

(5) Fifth Nine. Exhausting alternates to Relief (40) ☷☲

There are two primary types of exhaustion—from insufficiency or from excess. This element is exhausted from neither of these, but instead because his aspirations cannot be fulfilled. This place is a yang element at a yang place, central and correct. Being in a supreme position, he wants to give rein to his noble will. However, he is surrounded by the yin elements at the top and at the third place. These yin elements are high-ranking officials whose knees appear scarlet because they are cloaked in imperial robes. He is restricted by them, as if his nose and feet were to be cut off. Nevertheless, he is central and correct and in the middle of the upper gua, Joy. The Yao Text says, "Gradually and slowly, there is joy."

Under normal conditions, it is inauspicious when the fifth line does not correspond to the second line. But at an exhausting time, the situation changes. If both yang are sincere and truthful, as one is in making ceremonial offerings, they are able to support each other. In the end they will receive blessings. The fifth and second lines show that the wise handle a trying situation with calm and ease, as in offering a sacrifice with devotion. They proceed slowly with self-confidence. They understand that joy will come gradually if they remain hopeful and have faith.

(6) Top Six. Exhausting alternates to Contention (6) ☰☷

The Yao Text of this line is clear. The topmost line is a yin element at a yin place, both weak conditions. The line is at the end of the gua. Mounting on two yang elements is similar to becoming exhausted creeping through vines. One in this place is capable of self-examination and understands that taking action will bring misfortune. But this is the end of the road—the turning point is at hand. If she truly regrets former faults, her sincerity is auspicious. If she moves forward, good fortune will follow.

Additional Reference Information for This Gua

Image:	Lake above, Water below
Recite as:	Water under Lake, Exhausting
Element:	Metal
Structure:	Three yang with three yin
Month:	The ninth month of the lunar calendar, or October
Host of the Gua:	Second Nine and Fifth Nine
Opposite Gua:	Adorning (22) ☶
Inverse Gua:	Replenishing (48) ☵
Mutual Gua:	Household (37) ☲

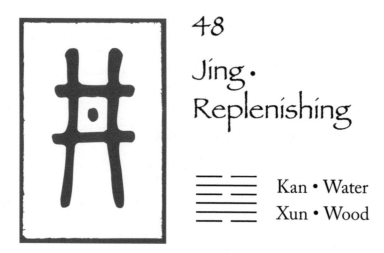

48
Jing ·
Replenishing

Kan • Water
Xun • Wood

NAME AND STRUCTURE

Jing is a well, a place of replenishment. This gua is the inverse of the preceding one, Exhausting. The ideograph of the preceding gua shows wood (a tree) held in confinement and becoming exhausted trying to grow. The image of this gua is the watering of the wood, replenishing. After becoming exhausted, one needs replenishing. Exhausting and Replenishing are opposite but complementary. Wilhelm and Blofeld as well as most of the other translators give Jing as The Well. I adopt Replenishing, because the well is a symbol of being replenished.

Sequence of the Gua: *Those who are exhausted from above are sure to return back to the lower. Thus, after Exhausting, Replenishing follows.*

The ideograph of Jing shows the image not of a well, but of the ancient Jing land system, adopted in the time of the early Zhou dynasty. Two horizontal lines and two vertical lines intersect each other with a dot in the middle of the square, representing a well or bucket. The ideograph jing is a picture of a piece of land divided into nine equal portions. Each portion occupied 100 mu, equaling 16.47 acres. All the lands belonged to the government or the lord. The central portion was planted exclusively to benefit the government or the lord and contained the well. It was cultivated by the joint labor of the eight families who used the other eight portions of land. When a male reached a certain age he received a portion of land from the government or the lord. When he grew old, he returned the land. Every day, the eight families worked on the central portion first. In their spare time, they worked on their own piece of land.

The well nourished all the people who lived on the lord's land. Later on, four plots of Jing land made up a village. Because people in the village took water from the well, the well became a marketplace and gained importance in the daily life of the people. For this reason, the true spirit of Jing is to replenish people. The serfs worked on the lands all day long, becoming exhausted; they went to the well to get replenished. The Commentary on the Decision says, "The well supplies replenishment but is never exhausted."

The structure of the gua is Water ☵ above, Wood ☴ below. This image gave the ancient sage the picture of a well. The water in a well was practically an inexhaustible resource. It was in constant use yet continually refilled. It was the source of life. The image also suggests that the roots of a plant draw water from the soil to nourish the stalk and leaves.

Decision

> Replenishing.
> The site of a village may be moved,
> Not the well.
> Neither loses nor gains.
> Coming and going, drawing, drawing.
> Nearly out of the well,
> Break one's bucket—misfortune.

Commentary on the Decision

> *Penetrating into the water and bringing the water up.*
> *It indicates a well.*
> *The well supplies replenishment*
> *But is never exhausted.*
>
> *The site of a village may be moved,*
> *Not the well,*
> *Because the solids are in the central positions.*
>
> *Nearly out of the well,*
> *The achievement has not yet been fulfilled.*
> *Break one's bucket;*
> *There is misfortune.*

Commentary on the Symbol

Water over Wood.
An image of Replenishing.
In correspondence with this,
The superior person encourages the people at their work
And urges them to help one another.

Yao Text

1. Initial Six
   Mud in the well.
   No drinking.
   Old well, no birds.

   Mud in the well; no drinking.
   The position is too low.
   Old well, no birds.
   As time passes, it has been deserted.

2. Second Nine
   Bottom of the well—
   Tiny carp.
   Bucket leaks.

   Bottom of the well—
   Tiny carp.
   Nobody responds to him.

3. Third Nine
   Well is dredged.
   No drinking.
   Sorrow in my heart.
   It could be used and drawn.
   King is enlightened
   And receives his blessing.

   Well is dredged, no drinking.
   This is the sorrow of the passersby.
   May the king be enlightened and bright;
   Then blessing will be received.

4. Fourth Six
   Well is tiled.
   No fault.

   Well is tiled. No fault.
   It is renovated.

5. Fifth Nine
   Well is pure.
   Icy spring is drunk.

   Drinking from the pure and icy spring.
   The position is central and correct.

6. Top Six
   Well is fully drawn.
   Do not cover.
   Being sincere and truthful:
   Supreme good fortune.

   Supreme good fortune at the top place.
   Great accomplishment.

SIGNIFICANCE

The gua shows the wisdom of replenishing the people. In order to replenish people, the head of a household or the leader of a community must first have a source that is inexhaustible. According to the wisdom of the ancient sages, the only way to assure that the supply is inexhaustible is to make the best possible use of the people and resources, and let the commodities flow abundantly into the market. This gua also explores the wisdom of employing virtuous people. Water in a stream is a gift of nature. Water in a well results from the accomplishment of human beings. All the underground streams are there, but without digging the water is wasted. So it is with able and virtuous people. In ancient times, selecting the virtuous and the able was always an important task of a great king.

The host of the gua is unusual—it is the yin element at the topmost place. The yang element at the fifth place is the king—firm and strong, central and correct. Confucius's Commentary on the Decision says, "The site of a village may be moved, not the well, because the solids are in the central positions." The firm is the king at the fifth place. He is the well, the source of replenishment. Things may change, but his desire to replenish the people never changes. This line has the correct attributes to be the host, but it is not the host.

There is another yang element that is firm and strong, central and correct—the yang element at the second place. This yang element could also act as the host, but it doesn't. Since this gua is about drawing water from the well, or selecting the virtuous and the able from the multitude, which can only be accomplished by the person at the top. The topmost yin element symbolizes a well without a cover, indicating that the resource of the well is fully used. This line represents the ideal society—a society of great harmony in which the leader and the people work in full cooperation and with unity of purpose.

After the success of King Wen's southern expedition, the Zhou population increased and the territory expanded. In order to replenish the people's latent productive capacity, King Wen abolished the old slavery system, setting the slaves free. Likewise, the old personnel system was accordingly changed, and new talent and able officials were recruited. King Wen stated that the system could be changed, but not the principle. The old system could not function well, like an old bucket already broken. If the old system were to remain in place, there would be misfortune. The Duke of Zhou records the problems of the old system. The new social system and the new personnel system functioned better, as if the well had been tiled. The water was pure and cold and could be used again. Supreme good fortune ensued.

(1) Initial Six. Replenishing alternates to Needing (5) ☷

The bottom line is a yin element at a yang place. It is at the bottom of the well where there is mud and no water. Nobody drinks, not even a bird. The lower gua is Xun, Wood, which represents a cock. Thus the Yao Text takes a bird as the symbol. The well is too old and not well maintained. The situation is bad. If one in this place is not able to live in accord with the time and make adjustments, one will be deserted.

(2) Second Nine. Replenishing alternates to Hardship (39) ☵

The second line is a yang element at a yin place, symbolizing water in the well. It does not correspond to the yang element at the fifth place. The water cannot flow from the bottom up to the top, so it flows away. The situation of this line is similar to that of the bottom line.

(3) Third Nine. Replenishing alternates to Darkness (29)

The third line is a yang element at a yang place, at the top of the lower gua. It is water, not mud, but nobody drinks it. This line indicates that a person of wisdom and virtue is not appreciated. His time has not come. The line explains how an enlightened and bright leader should recognize the potential of virtuous and intelligent people.

(4) Fourth Six. Replenishing alternates to Great Exceeding (28)

The fourth line is a yin element at a yin place. Its place is correct, but its attribute is being too weak. This symbolizes that the well is tiled but still not able to supply large amounts of water. It is time for one to prepare for the future. An auspicious time is coming. After the renovation is finished, there will be an opportunity to advance and progress.

(5) Fifth Nine. Replenishing alternates to Growing Upward (46)

The fifth line is a yang element at a yang place, central and correct. Now the well is pure, and the water is cold. It can be used. With his firm and steadfast character, together with his proper position, one at this place is able to benefit the multitude.

(6) Top Six. Replenishing alternates to Proceeding Humbly (57)

The topmost line is a yin element at a yin place. Its position at the top of the gua symbolizes that the well is used without a covering. It shows that the resource of the well is being fully used. Usually, in the I Ching the topmost line has no position. The supreme place is the fifth place. In this gua, however, the topmost line is the host. Interpretation of the I Ching is not dogmatic and rigid—it depends on the situation. This line also represents an ideal society of great harmony in which the leader and the people work in full cooperation and with unity of purpose.

Additional Reference Information for This Gua

Image:	Water above, Wood below
Recite as:	Water watering Wood, Replenishing
Element:	Water
Structure:	Three yang with three yin
Month:	The fifth month of the lunar calendar, or June
Host of the Gua:	Top Six
Opposite Gua:	Eradicating (21) ☷
Inverse Gua:	Exhausting (47) ☱
Mutual Gua:	Diversity (38) ☲

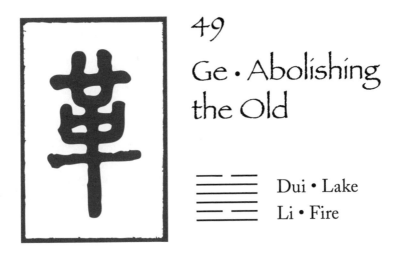

49

Ge · Abolishing
the Old

Dui • Lake
Li • Fire

NAME AND STRUCTURE

Ge originally meant the hide of an animal. After an animal's skin is tanned, it becomes hide. On this basis, Ge also meant to alternate, to change, to innovate. Later on, the meaning extended to encompass revolution, in the sense of abolishing the old and making way for the new. These are integral parts of one action.

Sequence of the Gua: *The silt at the bottom of the well needs to be removed. Thus, after Replenishing, Abolishing the Old follows.*

Wilhelm translates Ge as Revolution (Molting) and Blofeld translates it as Revolution, Leather, or Skin. I use the phrase Abolishing the Old.

The ideograph of Ge is a picture of a raw animal skin, with a head, body, and tail stretched out over three horizontal lines representing three twigs. The skin is exposed to the sun for drying. The structure of the gua is Lake ☱ above, Fire ☲ below. Lake contains water, which can extinguish fire. Fire, in turn, is able to dry up water. Water and fire overcome each other. This phenomenon suggests a picture of revolution—abolishing the old. Confucius's Commentary on the Decision says, "Heaven and Earth abolish the old and bring about the new, then the four seasons complete their changes. Tang and Wu . . . brought about the new. They obeyed the will of Heaven in accord with the wishes of people. The time and meaning of abolishing the old is truly great!"

This gua has an inner connection with Diversity (38) ☲. Both gua

are made up of Lake and Fire. According to the system of the eight primary gua, Lake represents a youngest daughter, and Fire represents a middle daughter. In Diversity, the middle daughter is above the youngest daughter (Fire above Lake). This symbolizes two daughters living in the same house who will separate, marrying into different families. Their interests will naturally diversify in different directions. In this gua, the youngest daughter is above the middle daughter (Lake above Fire). They are incompatible with each other, like fire and water. Each of them tries to change the other, and each of them does not allow the other to change herself. Conflict arises. Confucius's Commentary on the Decision says, "Water and Fire destroy each other. Two daughters live together, but their minds are not in chorus. This is called revolution."

Decision

Proper day.
Upon it obtain confidence from people.
Supremely prosperous and smooth.
Favorable to be steadfast and upright.
Regret vanishes.

Commentary on the Decision

Abolishing the Old.
Water and Fire destroy each other.
Two daughters live together,
But their minds are not in chorus.
This is called revolution.

Proper day.
Upon it obtain confidence from people.
When the revolutionary tempest breaks out,
Faith will accord with it.

Enlightened intelligence makes people joyful.
Great success comes through justice.
Since the revolution is proper,
All regret disappears.

Heaven and Earth abolish the old and bring about the new,
Then the four seasons complete their changes.

Tang and Wu abolished the old and brought about the new.
They obeyed the will of Heaven
In accord with the wishes of people.

The time and meaning of abolishing the old is truly great!

Commentary on the Symbol

Fire in the midst of the Lake.
An image of Abolishing the Old.
In correspondence with this,
The superior person watches the changes of the planets
And sets the calendar in order,
Making the time of the seasons clear.

Yao Text

1. Initial Nine
   Bound with the hide of a yellow ox.

   Bound with the hide of a yellow ox.
   One should not take action in such circumstances.

2. Second Six
   Proper day.
   Upon it abolish the old.
   Moving forward: good fortune.
   No fault.

   Proper day;
   Abolish the old.
   Taking action brings praiseworthy success.

3. Third Nine
   Moving forward: misfortune.
   Being steadfast: adversity.
   Declaring to abolish the old three times,
   Being sincere and truthful.

   Declaring to abolish the old three times.
   Besides revolution, what else can he do?

4. Fourth Nine
Regret vanishes.
Be sincere and truthful;
Change the old.
Good fortune.

The good fortune in changing the old.
His conviction meets with his belief.

5. Fifth Nine
Great person
Changes like a tiger.
No need to divine;
There is sincerity and truthfulness.

Great person changes like a tiger.
He is brilliant and distinct.

6. Top Six
Superior person
Changes like a panther.
Petty fellows
Change faces.
Moving forward: misfortune.
Abide in being steadfast and upright:
Good fortune.

Superior person changes like a panther,
Brilliant and elegant.
Little fellows change faces.
They are devoted to obeying the superior.

SIGNIFICANCE

This gua takes the image of the conflict between Fire and Water. It describes the truth of revolution. Revolution takes place not merely to overthrow the old. Its purpose is to establish the new. The new should be better than the old. It is progress, an improvement. Revolution does not happen by accident. There is always a reason. One can never create a revolution. On the other hand, if a revolution is on the road, no one can stop it. Only by following the will of Heaven and acting in accord with the wishes of people, can revolution be made unnecessary. Following the will of Heaven and acting in accord with the wishes of people, first of all, is to care for and nourish the people.

In the course of ancient Chinese history there were two most important revolutions. One was the rebellion led by King Tang who overthrew the tyrant Jie of the Xia dynasty and established the Shang dynasty. The other was the revolution led by King Wu, son of King Wen, who overthrew the Tyrant of Shang and established the Zhou dynasty. The Chinese believed that both revolutions carried out the will of Heaven and realized the wishes of the people. Mencius says,

> The son of Heaven receives instruction from Heaven and becomes King. Whether there is instruction from Heaven depends on the wishes of people. Those who oppose the wishes of people oppose the will of Heaven. It is certain that they will be abolished by the new one authorized by Heaven.

According to the tradition of the Zhou dynasty, before any important event, ceremonial ritual and divination should take place in order to gain the confidence of people. To the ancient Chinese, the emperor was the Son of Heaven. Whatever the emperor commanded was as true as whatever the divination instructed. In terms of this gua, King Wu was preparing to take action for a revolution against the tyrant of the Shang dynasty. Before he took action, he reformed the old social system by abolishing slavery. In this way he replenished his people and strengthened his territory. Before he abolished the old system he performed ceremonial rituals and divination. In the thirty-four gua of the Lower Canon, only this gua is bestowed with the most auspicious blessing of "Supremely prosperous and smooth. Favorable to be steadfast and upright." People had confidence in the change of the old system; thus all regret disappeared.

The host of the gua is the solid line at the fifth place. It is firm and strong, central and correct, and in a supreme place. One at this place is capable of being the leader of the great change. Traditionally it is believed that this gua has a historical background associated with the revolution led by King Wu to overthrow the tyrant of the Shang dynasty in the year 1066 B.C. However, according to history, the revolution led by King Wu took place four years after King Wen passed away. If that is true, then the author of the I Ching would not be King Wen or King Wen alone. Adhering to the traditional opinion that the author of the I Ching was

King Wen, I suggest that this gua is associated with King Wen's abolishing of the old social system and establishing of the new.

(1) Initial Nine. Abolishing the Old alternates to Mutual Influence (31)

The bottom line represents the dawn of a revolution. The time is not mature—one should not act lightly. He should consolidate his forces, as if binding them with the hide of a yellow ox. The ox is represented by the yielding line at the second place in the middle of the lower gua. The color of the middle place is yellow. A yielding line belongs to the family of Earth, which is represented by a cow. Thus a hide of yellow ox is used as an image. The bottom line is a yang element at a yang place. It does not correspond with the yang element at the fourth place. Although it is firm, it is at the bottom of the gua and has no correspondent. In this situation, one is not able to act productively. One should not take action in such circumstances.

(2) Second Six. Abolishing the Old alternates to Eliminating (43)

The second line is a yin element at a yin place, central and correct. It is the principal line of the lower gua, Li, or Brilliance. One at this place is gentle and bright and corresponds to the yang element at the fifth place, who is firm and strong. They have the same goal and can support each other. The time is right and the situation excellent. As the proper day approaches, one may expedite revolution. Taking action brings good fortune and success. But one still needs to walk with firm steps. This line indicates that after the ceremonial ritual and divination had been conducted, the revolution against the old system was launched. There was no resistance. Good fortune prevailed, and there was no fault.

(3) Third Nine. Abolishing the Old alternates to Following (17)

The third line is a yang element at a yang place. It has already gone beyond the center place. It is time to take action, but one at this place tends to act with undue haste. So the Yao Text says, "Moving forward: misfortune." In this position, one should be steadfast and upright and explain the purpose of change over and over again. If the purpose of change has been fully discussed, confidence and trust can be restored. In taking action for sudden change, communication with people is important. This line relates to a historic event. After King Wu successfully led the revolution against the Tyrant of Shang, he did not bring about radical reform. He declared the purpose of the revolution three times. Furthermore, he pardoned the tyrant's family members, such as sage Ji Zi, his uncle. Afterward, he consoled the people and helped them settle down in their native places. He gained the love and esteem of the people of the Shang dynasty.

(4) Fourth Nine. Abolishing the Old alternates to Already Fulfilled (63) ☵☲

The fourth line is a yang element at a yin place, neither central nor correct. There is regret. When this line alternates to a yin element, this gua becomes Already Fulfilled (63) ☵☲, which indicates the time is ripe. Regret vanishes. The line says that when the time of revolution strikes, correctness of purpose, sincerity, and truthfulness of the leadership still play important roles. This line is a continuation of the third line. After King Wu declared the purpose of the revolution three times, regret on the part of the people disappeared. King Wu began to revamp the system and make personnel changes. Good fortune accrued to the new order.

(5) Fifth Nine. Abolishing the Old alternates to Abundance (55) ☳☲

The fifth line is a yang element at a yang place, central and correct, firm and strong and in a supreme place. He is the leader of the great change. Before he effects reformation a great man changes himself first. In this way he is able to win the faith and confidence of the people. People trust him because of his virtue, even before the oracle is consulted. The Yao text says the great person changes like a tiger, which means his merit is as brilliant and distinct as a tiger's fur. The great person of this line denotes King Wen. King Wen totally supported the revolution and the changes in the personnel system. Based upon his prestige, people had confidence even before the oracle was consulted.

(6) Top Six. Abolishing the Old alternates to Seeking Harmony (13) ☰☲

The top line tells us that the revolution is over. Success has been obtained. Now it is time for public order to return to normal. Any further advance of revolution will lead to misfortune. Remaining steadfast and upright is crucial. One has to learn when to lead a revolution and also when to stop. On the other hand, the one who led the revolution should at this time renew himself to make constructive advancements. The ancient Chinese believed that the color and specks of a panther change according to the seasons. This image symbolizes how a sage makes a fresh start in accord with the change of time. This line is a warning. Even after the great success of a change, not everyone sincerely changes his opinion. Little fellows change only their faces; some day they will stage a comeback.

Additional Reference Information for This Gua

Image:	Lake above, Fire below.
Recite as:	Lake above Fire, Abolishing the Old
Element:	Metal
Structure:	Four yang with two yin
Month:	The third month of the lunar calendar, or April
Host of the Gua:	Fifth Nine
Opposite Gua:	Childhood (4)
Inverse Gua:	Establishing the New (50)
Mutual Gua:	Encountering (44)

50

Ding ·
Establishing
the New

<table>
<tr><td>≡≡≡</td><td>Li • Fire</td></tr>
<tr><td>≡ ≡</td><td>Xun • Wind</td></tr>
</table>

NAME AND STRUCTURE

Ding originally denoted an ancient Chinese sacrificial vessel with two loop handles and three or four legs. Later on, its meaning was extended to include establishing the new. A ding was cast with bronze and decorated with sacred inscriptions and auspicious pictures of birds and animals. It was popular during the period of the Xia, the Shang, and the Zhou dynasties. The three-legged ding is round, and the four-legged ding is square.

It is said that Xia Yu, the originator of the Xia dynasty, cast nine ding, symbolizing nine continents. They were treasured as heirlooms. Where the nine ding were, the capital was located. King Tang moved them to Shang, the capital of the Shang dynasty; King Wu moved them to Lo, the capital of the Zhou dynasty. When a new dynasty began or a new emperor was enthroned, the first thing done was to cast a new ding and inscribe the new constitution on it, symbolizing that a new era had begun. The emperor employed the ding to prepare sacrificial offerings for the Lord of Heaven and to nourish persons of wisdom and virtue. For this reason, the Chinese scholars call the change of a dynasty *ding ge*, a phrase derived from the I Ching. Ding is to establish the new; ge is to abolish the old.

Later on, ding was also used in the temple of ancestors at a family memorial ceremony. For this sort of occasion the ding was much smaller. The food in the ding was first served to the ancestors. Then the head of

the household distributed the food into the bowls of each member according to his position in the family. The ceremony symbolized the union of the family and the care of its members.

Sequence of the Gua: *For changing things absolutely, there is nothing better than a ding. Thus, after Abolishing the Old, Establishing the New follows.*

Wilhelm translates Ding as The Caldron while Blofeld translates it as A Sacrificial Vessel. I adopt the symbolic meaning of Ding—Establishing the New. This gua is the inverse of the preceding one, Abolishing the Old. Abolishing the Old and Establishing the New are opposite, but complementary. The ideograph of Ding looks exactly like a front view of the ancient sacrificial vessel: a round bowl on top with two loop handles and two legs. The structure of the gua is Fire ☲ above, Wood ☴ below. The wood nourishes the fire. It is an image of cooking. The six lines of the gua also construct a picture of a ding. The yielding line on the bottom represents the legs. The three solid lines at the second, third, and fourth positions are the body. The fifth, a broken line, represents the opening of the ding. The solid line at the top serves as the cover, or carrying handle.

Decision

Establishing the New.
Supreme good fortune.
Prosperous and smooth.

Commentary on the Decision

Ding.
An image of a sacrificial vessel.
When wood is put into fire,
It is cooking.

When the holy person cooked,
He was preparing offerings to the Lord of Heaven.
When he made a great feast,
He was nourishing holy persons and those with worthy virtues.

Through gentleness,
His ears become clear and eyes sharp.
The yielding advances and goes upward.

It obtains the central position
And finds respondence with the firm.
There is supreme prosperity and smoothness.

Commentary on the Symbol

Fire over Wood.
An image of Establishing the New.
In correspondence with this,
The superior person rectifies his position
And fulfills the will of Heaven.

Yao Text

1. Initial Six
   Sacrificial vessel, toes upside down.
   Favorable to get out the stale stuff.
   Take a concubine to obtain a son.
   No fault.

   Sacrificial vessel, toes upside down.
   This is not contrary to the truth.
   Favorable to get out the stale stuff.
   It is to follow the noble.

2. Second Nine
   Sacrificial vessel: full.
   My mate has illness,
   Cannot approach me.
   Good fortune.

   Sacrificial vessel: full.
   Be cautious about where he goes.
   My mate has illness.
   No fault in the end.

3. Third Nine
   Sacrificial vessel, ears removed.
   Activities are obstructed.
   Pheasant gravy, not eaten.
   When rain falls,

Regret vanishes.
Ends in good fortune.

Sacrificial vessel, ears removed.
It loses what it should be.

4. Fourth Nine
Sacrificial vessel, broken legs,
Spilled prince's soup.
He gets dripping wet.
Misfortune.

Spilled prince's soup.
How about his popular trust?

5. Fifth Six
Sacrificial vessel,
Yellow ears, golden handle.
Favorable to be steadfast and upright.

Sacrificial vessel, yellow ears.
There is firm substance in the central.

6. Top Nine
Sacrificial vessel, jade ring.
Great good fortune.
Nothing is unfavorable.

The jade handle is in the highest place.
The firm and the yielding complement each other properly.

SIGNIFICANCE

This gua takes the image of a sacrificial vessel to expound upon the importance of honoring and nourishing wise and virtuous persons for the growth of a new country or a new situation. The image of the gua is an inverse form of the preceding one. The preceding one is an act of revolution to abolish the old system or condition. The purpose of revolution is not merely to overthrow the old but, more important, to establish a new situation and a better order. Abolishing the old is difficult; establishing the new is even more so. Both abolishing the old and establishing the new need qualified personnel of extraordinary ability. This gua offers a proper way to reorganize the old order. The key point is to respect wise and virtuous persons and rely on them to establish the new order. On the other hand, eliminating those who are mean and unqualified for their position is equally important.

The image of this gua is Fire ☲ above, Wood ☴ below. It is the wood that nourishes the fire. This is a picture of preparing food. In the I Ching, there are four gua dealing with nourishment: Needing (5), Nourishing (27), Replenishing (48), and Establishing the New (50). The first three deal with nourishing an individual, a household, or a small group. This gua deals with a large group of people and with solemn ceremony. During the ceremony, food is offered first to the most honorable—Heaven and Earth, the ancestors, or honorable and virtuous persons. The fifth line represents the person who is in charge of the ceremony, and the topmost line represents the person who is honored. The Commentary on the Decision says, "When the holy person cooked, he was preparing offerings to the Lord of Heaven. When he made a great feast, he was nourishing holy persons and those with worthy virtues." The host of the gua is the yielding line at the fifth place, the one who takes charge of the ceremony. He honors and nourishes the person of great virtue and ability at the topmost place.

After King Wen abolished slavery and established a new feudal system, the methods of production changed, latent productive capacity was released, and productivity greatly increased. King Wen felt happy about those changes. He claimed that abolishing the old and establishing the new brought supreme good fortune as well as great prosperity and smoothness. The Duke of Zhou describes the defective old systems as a sacrificial vessel turned upside down, saying that it was favorable to get rid of the "stale stuff." Encountering his enemies' envy, King Wen obtained the support of people with wisdom and virtue and reaped great good fortune; nothing was unfavorable.

(1) Initial Six. Establishing the New alternates to Great Harvest (14) ☰

The bottom line represents the beginning of the new order. The first thing to do is to abolish the old system. An upside-down sacrificial vessel with its toes upturned indicates that a firm decision has been made to purge the old order thoroughly. Generally, overturning a sacrificial vessel is not auspicious. However, the bottom line represents the beginning—the food is not yet cooked. Overturning the vessel helps eliminate the stale stuff. A bad thing is turned to a good end.

The lower gua is Xun ☴, which represents an eldest daughter. After the bottom line alternates from yin to yang, the lower gua becomes Qian, a male. A marriage is employed as an image. Because the sacrificial vessel is not upright, a concubine, instead of a wife, is used as a symbol. In ancient times, taking concubines was allowed, though it was considered a cause of family trouble. Only for the purpose of trying to have a son was the practice considered acceptable. The yin element at the bottom corresponds to the solid line at the fourth place, which represents a noble person. Thus, Confucius's Commentary on the Yao Text says, "It is to follow the noble."

In terms of the historical background, this gua is a continuation of the preceding gua. The preceding gua relates to the abolishing of the old system led by King Wen. This gua discusses establishing a new system after the victory. The first step is to overturn the old system and then employ a new staff. Concubines represent personnel of the higher ranks of the Shang dynasty. The sons represent their followers. The policy of the Zhou dynasty was to use those who worked for the Shang dynasty in the new order. In this way, stability and unity could be obtained.

(2) Second Nine. Establishing the New alternates to Traveling (56) ☶☴

The yang element at the second place symbolizes a sense of fulfillment. It is in the middle of the lower gua, suggesting that there is plenty of food in the sacrificial vessel. "My mate has illness" refers to the bottom line. This line is a yin element who is wrong in some way. Because she cannot approach the one at this second place there is good fortune. Otherwise it would be a different story. The message of this line is that, although one might be able and firm, one still needs to be cautious about where one goes and whom one associates with. After the revolution led by King Wen, the task of establishing a new order had been fulfilled. Those who were eliminated were envious but could not approach the new order.

(3) Third Nine. Establishing the New alternates to Not Yet Fulfilled (64) ☲☵

The yang element at the third place represents the body of the sacrificial vessel. There is plenty of food. The third line is a yang element at a yang place, but it goes beyond the center. There is too much yang. The third place is the intersection between the upper gua and the lower gua, which means that it is time for one at this place to change. This line does not respond to the fifth line, which represents the handle of the sacrificial vessel. Thus the Yao Text says, "ears removed." When the earlike handles of a sacrificial vessel are removed, one's activities are obstructed. The pheasant gravy not being eaten indicates that one at this place does not get nourishment from the noble one at the fifth place. But they are complimentary yin and yang. Once they find harmony, it is as if the rain has fallen. All regret is washed away, and in the end there is good fortune. This line tells us that there was some obstruction affecting the personnel reform after the revolution. The benefits of the reformation had not been fully obtained. Further attempt should be made to flush out the obstruction, as with rainfall; then regret would disappear and good fortune would arrive.

(4) Fourth Nine. Establishing the New alternates to Remedying (18)

The fourth line is a yang element at a yin place. It corresponds to the yin element at the bottom. The yin element at the bottom is a sacrificial vessel, upside down with toes upturned. This line represents the broken leg of the sacrificial vessel. The situation is more serious. The fourth line is at the top of the body of the vessel and next to the fifth line, representing a prince. The text says the leg was broken, the vessel fell, and the food spilled over the prince's robe and the floor. This line refers to the fact that during reformation, important work should not be given to people who are not qualified. Otherwise it will spoil the whole situation, as when the prince's soup is spilled and he gets dripping wet as a result. There will be misfortune.

(5) Fifth Six. Establishing the New alternates to Encountering (44)

The broken line at the fifth place represents two ears of the sacrificial vessel. There is a handle attached to the ears for carrying the vessel. The fifth line is in the middle of the upper gua, Li. Li is yellow brightness. When the fifth line moves from yin to yang, the upper gua alternates from Li to Qian. Qian is gold. Thus, the Yao Text says, "yellow ears, golden handle." The fifth line is the host of the gua. He takes charge of the ceremony and also honors and nourishes the person of great virtue and ability. He "rectifies his position and fulfills the will of Heaven," as Confucius's Commentary on the Symbol says. Nevertheless he is a yin element at a yang place. He needs support. Fortunately, he corresponds to the yang element at the second place. Thus Confucius's Commentary on the Yao Text says, "There is firm substance in the central." This line is a continuation of the previous line. The previous line indicates that the prince's soup was spilled. This line tells us that King Wen obtained the

support of persons with wisdom and virtue. The situation got better, but it was still wise to be steadfast and upright.

(6) Top Nine. Establishing the New alternates to Long Lasting (32) ☳

The topmost line represents the ring for carrying the sacrificial vessel. Without the ring the sacrificial vessel cannot be moved from place to place. This line represents a person of high wisdom and distinguished virtue. It is believed that it refers to King Wen. It is a yang element at a yin place, indicating that his attribute is a perfect integration of yin and yang in harmonious proportion. He is both firm and gentle, as a jade is hard, yet softly lustrous. Here one has the honor of being chosen as the advisor of the leader at the fifth place. It is great good fortune. Nothing is unfavorable. Thus Confucius's Commentary on the Yao Text says, "The firm and the yielding complement each other properly."

Additional Reference Information for This Gua

Image:	Fire above, Wind below	
Recite as:	Wind under Fire, Establishing the New	
Element:	Fire	
Structure:	Four yang with two yin	
Month:	The six month of the lunar calendar, or July	
Host of the Gua:	Fifth Six	
Opposite Gua:	Beginning	(3)
Inverse Gua:	Abolishing the Old	(49)
Mutual Gua:	Eliminating	(43)

51
Zhen ·
Taking Action

$$\equiv\equiv$$ Zhen • Thunder
$$\equiv\equiv$$ Zhen • Thunder

NAME AND STRUCTURE

Zhen means shake, shock, or quake. In the I Ching, it is the symbol of Thunder. Wilhelm translates Zhen as The Arousing (Shock, Thunder), and Blofeld translates it as Thunder. Here I consider the significance of Thunder and employ the term Taking Action.

Sequence of the Gua: *For taking charge of a sacrificial vessel, no one is more suitable than the eldest son. Thus, after Establishing the New, Taking Action follows.*

The ideograph of Zhen comes from the form inscribed on bronze objects in the Zhou dynasty. The original form was very complicated, including pictures of rain and lightning. This image has been simplified. The upper part of the ideograph is the rain—water falling from clouds. The horizontal stroke at the top represents Heaven, and the *n*-shaped curved stroke illustrates the clouds. A vertical stroke in the middle symbolizes an act of falling. The four dots are the raindrops.

The lower part of the ideograph is the character chen. At present, it means time, but in ancient times it meant shock. According to the Chinese lunar calendar, there are twenty-four solar terms in the year. Zhen was related to the third solar term, called the Waking of Insects, which takes place on the sixth day of the third month of the Chinese lunar calendar. During this period, thunder roars. The thunder proclaims that spring is arriving. All hibernating insects and animals awaken and tiny sprouts emerge. Peasants and farmers prepare to plant crops.

The structure of the gua is Thunder ☳ above, Thunder ☳ below. The action is dual and the power doubled. The image of the primary gua is a solid line buried underneath two yielding lines. The solid line intends to burst upward forcefully against the yin pressure. It is an explosion of yang energy. One can feel that the quake is tremendous and has extraordinary power. It is also an image of the interaction of yin and yang energy creating the thunder and lightning. In addition, it is Earth, pure yin, uniting with pure yang, Heaven, for the first time—an eldest son is conceived.

A quake is a way to make an advance smooth without obstruction. When there is an earthquake, everyone is fearful. Afterward, they forget the fearfulness and begin talking and laughing as usual. They learn no lessons from the quake, so it is not beneficial. Only the sage is on the alert. When the thunder shocks a hundred li (a Chinese unit of length about one half of a kilometer), he is still able to remain calm and at ease.

Decision

> Taking Action.
> Prosperous and smooth.
> Thunder comes—alarm! alarm!
> Laughing and talking—ha, ha!
> Thunder shocks a hundred li.
> The sacrificial spoon and chalice do not fall.

Commentary on the Decision

> *Thunder—Taking Action.*
> *Prosperous and smooth.*
>
> *Thunder comes—alarm! alarm!*
> *Being fearful brings good fortune.*
> *Laughing and talking—ha, ha!*
> *After that, there is a principle to follow.*
>
> *Thunder shocks a hundred li.*
> *It startles the distant and frightens the near.*
> *Coming forth, he is able to protect the temple of ancestors,*
> *And the state as well,*
> *And take charge of all sacrifices.*

Commentary on the Symbol

Thunder is dual.
Action is doubled.
In correspondence with this,
The superior person with fearful mind
Is cultivating his virtue and examining his fault.

Yao Text

1. Initial Nine
   Thunder comes—alarm! alarm!
   Afterward, laughing and talking—ha, ha!
   Good fortune.

   Thunder comes, alarm, alarm;
   Being alert brings good fortune.
   Laughing and talking—ha, ha!
   After that, there is a principle to follow.

2. Second Six
   Thunder comes.
   Adversity.
   Greatly losing treasures.
   Climbing over nine hills,
   Do not pursue.
   Seven days: regained.

   Thunder comes: adversity.
   It rests on a solid line.

3. Third Six
   Thunder comes, dispiriting, dispiriting.
   Going forward like thunder:
   No trouble.

   Thunder comes, dispiriting, dispiriting.
   The position is not appropriate.

4. Fourth Nine
   Thunder comes.
   Stuck in the mud.

Thunder comes, stuck in the mud.
Its radiance is not able to shine.

5. Fifth Six
Thunder comes, back and forth.
Adversity.
No great loss.
Something will happen.

Thunder comes, back and forth. Adversity.
One takes risk in doing.
Important matters are central.
Nothing at all is a great loss.

6. Top Six
Thunder comes, trembling, trembling.
Gazes flustered, flustered.
Moving forward, misfortune:
Thunder affects not oneself,
But one's neighbors.
No fault.
The in-laws gossip.

Thunder comes, trembling, trembling.
One does not obtain the central position.
Misfortune but no fault.
One is aware of what is warned by neighbors.

SIGNIFICANCE

This gua is one of the eight among the sixty-four accomplished gua that is made by doubling one of the eight primary gua. Here, the accomplished gua is Zhen ☳, Taking Action, and the primary gua is Thunder ☳. The structure of the gua is Thunder ☳ above, Thunder ☳ below. When Thunder is doubled, the potential energy is tremendous. In the I Ching, Thunder represents the eldest son of Heaven and Earth. It symbolizes the beginning of a created being. After the eldest son is born, a new cycle starts, and a new generation sets out. Thunder is a gua of the spring season. An ancient Chinese adage says, "Once the spring thunder bursts, myriad beings on Earth are awakened." After that, the Earth will be green again and farmers can begin work in the field. This is a picture of prosperity.

Taking Action advises people to adopt a cautious heart and a cautious mind in dealing with a new situation before expecting success. Taking action brings success, and it is tempting to try to enhance success. But the wise man keeps himself calm and remains at ease. He does not let the excitement lead to failure in important matters. With a cautious mind, he cultivates his virtues and examines his errors. This is the key to success. The host of the gua is unusual—it is the solid line at the bottom. It hints that the positive energy is taking action and moving upward from below.

After King Wen's new system was established, people were shocked, feeling as if a thunderstorm was striking. Some felt alarm. When the benefits became known, they talked to each other and laughed together. However, King Wen, from beginning to end, was as calm in carrying out the reformation as a priest holding a sacrificial spoon and chalice without letting them fall. The Duke of Zhou records how the people were happy, but not the slave owners. Dangerous counterattacks were anticipated, for some in-laws of the tyrant stood against the reformation.

(1) Initial Nine. Taking Action alternates to Delight (16) ☷

The bottom line is the principal line of the lower gua; it is the beginning of the thunder and shock. When the thunder and shock arrives, if one can be alert about past lessons, good fortune will follow. The gua says that if preventive measures or action against possible trouble are taken, one will be free from mistake. This line suggests that the reformation brought about by King Wen put fear into the people of the Shang dynasty. After people understood and experienced the benefits, they laughed and talked. Thus, there was good fortune.

(2) Second Six. Taking Action alternates to Marrying Maiden (54) ☳

Because the bottom line represents the source of the shock, the second line becomes the first one to be affected. The situation is most dangerous. Losing treasures is anticipated, and it is necessary to climb over nine hills to escape. But the second line is a yin element at a yin place. One at this place is able to take action in accordance with the principle of the Golden Mean. He does not need to pursue what he has lost; after seven days what he has lost will come back. This gua indicates that if one takes action correctly, with sincerity, one can turn the situation from bad to good. Seven days represents a cycle. Once a line moving upward has occupied each of the six places, on the seventh change it returns to its original place. This is what is meant when the Yao Text says that after

seven days what he has lost will come back. This line relates that King Wen's reformation struck relentless blows at the rebellious group. Danger was everywhere. Members of the rebellious group escaped to the hills. After they understood the situation, they came back.

(3) Third Six. Taking Action alternates to Abundance (55)

The third line is a yin element at a yang place. It has gone beyond the center. The place is not right—the shock startles the one who is here. If the shock can urge her to correct her errors and take action to make a fresh start, she will be free of mistakes. This line tells us that King Wen's reformation made people feel nervous and uneasy and it turned him to introspection. No blunder affected his seeing the situation clearly.

(4) Fourth Nine. Taking Action alternates to Turning Back (24)

The fourth line is a yang element at a yin place, neither central nor correct. There are two yin elements above and another two below. They restrict his motion. Thus the Yao Text says, "Stuck in the mud." One at this place is lost in the darkness. If one lowers one's guard and becomes careless, even if success ensues, one will not know how to deal with it. One of the main aspects of the Tao of I is that events move forward in waves. After King Wen's reformation went smoothly for a while, it became stuck in the mud again.

(5) Fifth Six. Taking Action alternates to Following (17)

"Thunder comes, back and forth" suggests moving forward and backward. The line is a yin element at a yang place, central but not correct. If it moves forward, it reaches the top line—at the end of the action. There is no way to go forward. If it comes back, its responding line at the second position is also a yin element, and there will be no correspondense. It is an unfavorable situation.

This line describes the time during the reformation when King Wen surveyed the whole situation. He remained calm and at ease. Although the shock of reformation affected everyone in a radius of a hundred li, he would not let the sacrificial spoon and chalice (political power) fall. There was no great loss at the moment, but he sensed that matters of importance could be affected.

(6) Top Six. Taking Action alternates to Eradicating (21)

The topmost line is a yin element at a yin place, correct but not central. It encounters the thunder and shock from beginning to end and becomes exhausted. Taking any action will bring misfortune. If the shock has not affected one, but only one's neighbors, one is able to be alert and take preventive measures. There will be no fault. Otherwise one's in-laws will speak against one. In the I Ching, marriage often symbolizes a political alliance. This line, a continuation of the preceding line, indicates that the reformation did not affect political alliances but did affect the in-laws of the tyrant. At that moment, there was no great loss, but King Wen sensed that some serious problems could arise. The main theme of the gua is to prepare people for the shock of a new situation. One should always be cautious, even when success seems inevitable.

Additional Reference Information for This Gua

Image:	Thunder above, Thunder below
Recite as:	Thunder is dual, Taking Action
Element:	Wood
Structure:	Four yin with two yang
Month:	Spring Equinox
Host of the Gua:	Initial Nine
Opposite Gua:	Proceeding Humbly (57)
Inverse Gua:	Keeping Still (52)
Mutual Gua:	Hardship (39)

52

Gen ·
Keeping Still

$$\begin{array}{c} \equiv\!\equiv \\ \equiv\!\equiv \end{array}$$ Gen · Mountain
Gen · Mountain

NAME AND STRUCTURE

In the northern Chinese dialect, gen means straightforward, forthright, and blunt. In written language, it is used only in the I Ching, to represent one of the eight primary gua, Mountain, which symbolizes keeping still. Wilhelm translates Gen as Keeping Still, Mountain, and Blofeld translates it as Desisting, Stillness. In this book, it is termed Keeping Still.

Sequence of the Gua: *Events cannot continue in motion without stopping; they must take a rest. Thus, after Taking Action, Keeping Still follows.*

The ideograph of Gen consists of two parts. The upper portion is a picture of an eye, mu. The lower part is a remote form of bi, which meant "close by." An eye close by indicated somebody staring, which came to be the symbol for keeping still. This gua is the inverse of the preceding one, Taking Action. They are opposite but complementary. The structure of the gua is Mountain ☶ above, Mountain ☶ below. The attribute of Mountain is stillness. When Mountain is doubled, it is extremely still. The structure of Mountain is one solid line above two yielding lines, which indicates that the yang has ascended to the top. There is no room for the yang to ascend further; it is time for the yang to keep at rest. Then a new cycle will start again.

From the very beginning of Chinese culture, ancient sages emphasized keeping still. Keeping still is not keeping merely the body still but the mind and spirit as well, and is called "sitting in stillness" or "nourishing the spirit." While sitting still in a lotus posture, one is shaped like a mountain. Sitting in stillness, or in meditation as Westerners call it, is a self-disciplinary training. While doing this, one is able to control the mind and the breath, to be introspective about one's shortcomings and to cultivate inner strength and virtue. Mencius says, "I am skillful in nourishing my imperishable noble spirit." When one is in a state of stillness, one is oblivious to one's surroundings. This is the highest stage of nonattachment. In such a state there is no fault in one's being. It is believed that when Heaven is about to confer a great mission on a person, it first exercises his or her mind and spirit with discipline. Keeping still is meant to prepare one's mind and spirit to progress when the time comes.

Decision

> Keeping still, at his back.
> Feels not his body.
> Walking in his courtyard,
> Sees not his people.
> No fault.

Commentary on the Decision

> *Mountain.*
> *It is keeping still.*
>
> *Keep still when it is time to keep still.*
> *Remain active when it is time to remain active.*
> *When action and resting do not miss their time,*
> *Their way becomes promising and brilliant.*
>
> *Keeping still in stillness*
> *Is keeping still in the place where one should be still.*
>
> *The corresponding lines above and below are repelling.*
> *They do not respond to each other.*
> *Thus he is no longer feeling his body.*
> *Even walking in the courtyard*
> *He is no longer seeing his people.*
> *There is no fault.*

Commentary on the Symbol

Mountains, one over the other.
An image of Keeping Still.
In correspondence with this,
Whatever the superior person thinks
Does not go beyond his duties in his position.

Yao Text

1. Initial Six
   Keeping still at his toes.
   No fault.
   Favorable to be perseveringly steadfast and upright.

   Keeping still at his toes.
   What is correct is not yet lost.

2. Second Six
   Keeping still at his calves.
   Cannot rescue his leader.
   His heart unhappy.

   Cannot rescue his leader,
   Because this one does not retreat to listen to him.

3. Third Nine
   Keeping still at his waist.
   Strains his spinal muscles.
   Adversity
   Heats up the heart.

   Keeping still at his waist.
   The danger inflames the heart.

4. Fourth Six
   Keeping still at his trunk.
   No fault.

   Keeping still at his trunk.
   He keeps free from reckless action.

5. Fifth Six
   Keeping still at his jaws.

Words have order.
Regret vanishes.

Keeping still at the jaws.
He is in harmony with its central position.

6. Top Nine
Honestly and sincerely keeping still.
Good fortune.

The good fortune of honesty and sincerity.
He keeps these virtues to the end.

SIGNIFICANCE

This is one of the eight among the sixty-four accomplished gua that is made by doubling one of the eight primary gua. Here, the accomplished gua is Gen ☶, Keeping Still, and the primary gua is Mountain ☶. Keeping Still expounds the truth of knowing when and where to stop before one's action goes too far. According to the structure of the gua, when a solid line appears at the bottom of Earth ☷, it becomes Thunder ☳. Its attribute is taking action. The action builds. When the solid line advances to the central position, it becomes Water ☵. Its attribute is flowing. The action continues; it flows onward. When the solid line advances to the top, it beomes Mountain ☶. Its attribute is keeping still. In this situation, one must stop flowing forward and remain at rest. The key to success is to advance when it is time to advance and to stop when it is time to stop. Every action should accord with the time and situation. Never act subjectively and blindly. Keeping still means to be tranquil and stable. It is a phase of advancement. Advance and stillness complement each other. Keeping still is preparing oneself for a new advance. All the lines of this gua take images of different parts of the body to indicate paticular times and situations.

When King Wen abolished slavery and reestablished the Jing land system, people were shocked, as if a thunderstorm had struck. Those who were liberated were happy, but not the slave owners—especially those who were close to the tyrant. Dangerous counterattacks were anticipated. King Wen retreated, sitting in stillness to contemplate the situation and foresee the future. The Duke of Zhou describes King Wen's different stages and moods of stillness. Eventually his honesty and sincerity brought

good fortune. He remained virtuous to the end. In this gua, King Wen employed the word "his" four times in the Decision, and the Duke of Zhou used it eight times in the Yao Text. For this reason, it is believed that a specific person is being referred to, and this person is thought to be King Wen himself.

(1) Initial Six. Keeping Still alternates to Adorning (22) ☷☷

The toes are at the bottom of a body, as the beginning line is at the bottom of the gua. Keeping still at the toes maintains the whole body in stillness. Before one takes any action, if one knows where to stop before going too far, there is no impropriety, and therefore there is no fault. The bottom line is a yin element at a yin place. It is gentle and weak and might not be able to remain steadfast and upright. For this reason, the Yao Text indicates that keeping steadfast and upright is favorable.

(2) Second Six. Keeping Still alternates to Remedying (18) ☷☶

The second line is represented by the calves. It is a yin element at a yin place, central and correct. One at this place knows when to take action and when to keep still. On the other hand, he is in a subordinate position, following the one at the third place. The third place is a yang element at a yang place—self-willed, refusing to accept any advice, and tending to go to extremes. The yin element is not able to help him remain still in such a situation. He must follow his superior, and it makes him sad.

(3) Third Nine. Keeping Still alternates to Falling Away (23) ☷☷

The third line is between the upper gua and the lower gua. It symbolizes the waist. The line is a yang element at a yang place and has gone beyond the center. It represents a person who is too self-willed and intransigent. He keeps still in the extreme. There are four yin elements around him with whom he cannot deal harmoniously. The situation gives him trouble, as if he has injured his spinal muscles, and this brings anger to his heart. How can he have peace?

(4) Fourth Six. Keeping Still alternates to Traveling (56) ☲☶

The fourth line represents the trunk of the body, where the heart lies. It is a yin element at a correct yin place. One in this place is able to keep free from taking reckless action. He knows how to remain still in his heart. There is no fault.

(5) Fifth Six. Keeping Still alternates to Developing Gradually (53) ☶

The broken line at the fifth place represents the jaws. When one speaks, the jaws open and close. Because this line is in the center, this person is walking the central path. "Keeping still at his jaws" does not mean to stop talking, but instead refers to knowing when and where to talk and when and where to stop talking. The place of the fifth line is not correct since it is a yin element at a yang place. Normally there is regret. But he is able to choose his words correctly; therefore, regret vanishes. This line gives warning that one should be responsible for what he says.

(6) Top Nine. Keeping Still alternates to Humbleness (15) ☷

The topmost line represents the final stage of keeping still, and is thus the host. In his treatise The Great Learning, Confucius says,

> *The way of the Great Learning is to illustrate brilliant virtue,*
> *to love people, and to rest in conduct that is perfectly good.*
> *By knowing how to keep still,*
> *one is able to determine what objects he should pursue.*
> *By knowing what objects he should pursue,*
> *one is able to attain calmness of mind.*
> *By knowing how to attain calmness of mind,*
> *one is able to succeed in tranquil repose.*
> *By knowing how to succeed in tranquil repose,*
> *one is able to obtain careful deliberation.*
> *By knowing how to obtain careful deliberation,*
> *one is able to harvest what he really wants to pursue.*

In the final stage of one's life, if one can manifest one's brilliant virtue, love people, and maintain one's goodness till the end, it is a true blessing, and there will be good fortune.

Additional Reference Information for This Gua

Image:	Mountain above, Mountain below
Recite as:	Mountain is doubled, Keeping Still
Element:	Earth
Structure:	Four yin with two yang
Month:	The tenth month of the lunar calendar, or November
Host of the Gua:	Top Nine
Opposite Gua:	Joyful (58)
Inverse Gua:	Taking Action (51)
Mutual Gua:	Relief (40)

53
Jian ·
Developing
Gradually

Xun · Wood
Gen · Mountain

Name and Structure

Jian means gradual, developing gradually, or progressing step by step. Wilhelm translates Jian as Development (Gradual Progress). Blofeld also translates it as Gradual Progress. Here I adopt the term Developing Gradually. The ideograph of Jian consists of three parts. Jian was the name of a river whose fountainhead lay in the mountains in central China at a place called Dan-yang in the kingdom of Zhou. The Jian river crossed the vast area of central China and gradually became vast itself as it flowed east to the ocean. The ancients chose this river as a symbol of gradual development. The left part of the ideograph is the sign for water, which looks like the primary gua Water ☵ turned vertically. The central and the right images put together provide the sound of the character Jian.

Sequence of the Gua: *Events cannot continue in stillness without moving. Thus, after Keeping Still, Developing Gradually follows.*

The structure of the gua is Wood ☴ above, Mountain ☶ below. It denotes a tree that is growing gradually to its height on a mountain. When the trunk of a tree grows upward above the ground, its roots develop deep underneath the earth. The progress of upward and downward growth are in positive proportion. In this way, the tree remains strong, firm, and stable. This is the wisdom of nature. Weeds grow fast; they are neither strong nor stable.

In the text of the gua the analogy of a marrying maiden describes a gradual process of development. In ancient China, before the wedding of a couple there was a process of several ceremonies. First, there should be a proposal. After an agreement was reached, both presented betrothal gifts to each other, and then a ceremony of engagement was performed. These ceremonies proceeded gradually. In this gua, from the second line to the fifth line, every line is correct in its placement. It symbolizes the pureness and correctness of the maiden's virtue. There is good fortune. In the Yao Text, the landing of a swan at different places is used to demonstrate the process of gradual development.

Decision

Developing Gradually.
The maiden is given in marriage.
Good fortune.
Favorable to be steadfast and upright.

Commentary on the Decision

Developing Gradually,
Good fortune to the maiden given in marriage.

Progressing will make the place proper;
Going forward, there is merit.
Advancing in what is correct,
One is able to rectify his country.

About his place,
It is firm and central.
Keeping still with gentleness,
This makes the forward movement without ending.

Commentary on the Symbol

On the mountain, there are trees.
It is an image of Developing Gradually.
In correspondence with this,
The superior person lives a life of virtue
And improves the morals and mores of his people.

Yao Text

1. Initial Six
   Developing gradually.
   The swan approaches the shore.
   Little fellow: adversity.
   There is gossip; no fault.

   The adversity of the little fellow.
   He should not be at fault.

2. Second Six
   Developing gradually.
   The swan approaches the cliff.
   Eat and drink, joyfully, joyfully.
   Good fortune.

   Eat and drink, joyfully, joyfully.
   He does not reap without sowing.

3. Third Nine
   Developing gradually.
   The swan approaches the plateau.
   The husband goes on an expedition;
   Does not return.
   The wife conceives;
   Does not give birth.
   Misfortune.
   Favorable to fight off invaders.

   The husband goes on an expedition;
   Does not return.
   He keeps himself away from his group.
   The wife conceives,
   Does not give birth.
   She has lost her proper way.
   Favorable to fight off invaders.
   Yielding to their own nature, they can protect one another.

4. Fourth Six
   Developing gradually.
   The swan approaches the tree;

Probably finds a flat rafter.
No fault.

Probably finds a flat rafter.
One is docile and gentle.

5. Fifth Nine
Developing gradually.
The swan approaches the hill.
Woman, three years, does not conceive.
In the end, no one conquers her.
Good fortune.

In the end, nothing can defeat.
One obtains one's wish.

6. Top Nine
Developing gradually.
The swan approaches the avenue high in the sky.
Its feathers can be used in ceremony.
Good fortune.

Its feathers can be used in ceremony.
The sequence of the progress cannot be disturbed.

SIGNIFICANCE

This gua indicates that after a period of keeping still there is opportunity to advance. In advancing, one should move gradually. Here the image of the growth of a tree is used to expound the truth of development. Any kind of development should proceed in an orderly way and advance step by step. The ancient sages took the idea of the marriage of a young maiden as an example. She is going to marry, but she has to wait until the appropriate time arrives. True love, mutual understanding, and a harmonious relationship take time to cultivate. They develop gradually and steadily step by step. So the Decision says, "Good fortune. Favorable to be steadfast and upright." There are two hosts in the gua—the yielding line at the second place, the maiden, and the solid line at the fifth place, the prospective husband.

During King Wen's sitting in stillness he considered the rise of his kingdom. It grew up and developed gradually. He realized that he was

appointed to a mission to manifest the will of Heaven, as a maiden is given to a husband. It was the will of Heaven asking him to remain faithful. The Duke of Zhou uses the image of a swan to show the orderly progress of the Kingdom of Zhou. When swans fly, they follow one another in order. They come and go according to the seasons. Likewise, the Kingdom of Zhou would move forward in proper sequence, as a swan from the water approaching the shore, the cliff, the plateau, the tree, the hill. Eventually it flies high in the sky, and its feathers that fall can bring a touch of the sacred to others.

(1) Initial Six. Developing Gradually alternates to Household (37) ☲☲

The bottom line is the beginning of Developing Gradually. It is a yin element at a yang place, symbolizing a young person who is not mature enough to take his place in society. There is gossip and trouble. An immature person needs someone's support. Nevertheless, she does not correspond to the yin element at the fourth place. This yin element is not able to support her. Relying on her own strength, there should not be any reproach in her gradual progress.

(2) Second Six. Developing Gradually alternates to Proceeding Humbly (57) ☴☴

The second line is a yin element at a yin place, central and correct. Thus, the Yao Text says, "The swan approaches the cliff." A cliff is a safe haven for birds. This yin element corresponds to the yang element at the fifth place. The fifth position is the supreme place for a king. One at the fifth place is willing to support her and supply her with a good living. The one at the second line is an honest person who would not reap without sowing. Her work deserves his earnings. There is good fortune.

(3) Third Nine. Developing Gradually alternates to Watching (20) ☶☶

The third line is a yang element at the top of the lower gua. The Yao Text says, "The swan approaches the plateau." For swans, it is best to fly high in the sky or stay close to the water. It is dangerous to live on dry land. There will be misfortune. This line does not correspond to the topmost yang element since they are both yang. One at this place, acting against his will, becomes involved with the nearby yin element at the fourth place. Unfortunately, they are not compatible. A bad relationship is formed. Thus, "the wife conceives; does not give birth." On the other hand, both of them are at their correct places. If they can overcome their prejudices and yield to their own attributes, they can complement each other and protect each other in difficult times. In this way it is "favorable to fight off invaders."

(4) Fourth Six. Developing Gradually alternates to Retreat (33)

The fourth line is a yin element at a yin place; it is not central, but it is correct. This time the swan approaches a tree. The tree is not a suitable place—she needs a flat perch, represented by the solid line at the third place. The fourth line is a yin element at the bottom of the upper gua; because she is docile and gentle and close to the yang element at the third place, there is no doubt that the swan will find the flat rafter.

(5) Fifth Nine. Developing Gradually alternates to Keeping Still (52)

The fifth line is in a supreme position. The swan has approached the hill. This yang element corresponds to the yin element at the second place; they are a perfect match. However, two lines lie between them—the yang element at the third place and the yin element at the fourth place. They cannot see each other. For this reason, the Yao Text tells us, for three years the woman does not conceive. Both of them are in central and correct places, however, and they are also compatible and would not take unreasonably reckless action. Nothing can conquer their love, and ultimately there is good fortune.

(6) Top Nine. Developing Gradually alternates to Hardship (39)

The topmost line symbolizes the swan flying in the sky. The Yao Text of this line is similar to that of the topmost line of Great Accumulation (26), which says, "How unobstructed Heaven's thoroughfare is!" It indicates that one has become like the clouds flowing back and forth in the sky without hindrance. In classical Chinese literature, especially in poems, swans represent hermits. The hermit is totally free from social bonds, and his dropped feathers (virtuous words and deeds) are sacred.

Additional Reference Information for This Gua

Image:	Wood above, Mountain below
Recite as:	Wood on Mountain, Developing Gradually
Element:	Wood
Structure:	Three yin with three yang
Month:	The first month of the lunar calendar, or February
Host of the Gua:	Second Six and Fifth Nine
Opposite Gua:	Marrying Maiden (54)
Inverse Gua:	Marrying Maiden (54)
Mutual Gua:	Not Yet Fulfilled (64)

54

Gui Mei •
Marrying Maiden

☰☰ Zhen • Thunder
☰☰ Dui • Lake

NAME AND STRUCTURE

Gui originally meant marrying a maiden to her husband's house. Later on,
its meaning was extended to include return. Mei means a young maiden
or a younger sister. Thus, Gui Mei denotes a marrying maiden.

Sequence of the Gua: *Through advancing and developing, surely one needs
a home to return to. Thus, after Developing Gradually, Marrying Maiden
follows.*

Wilhelm translates Gui Mei as The Marrying Maiden and Blofeld translates
it as The Marriageable Maiden. I also use the name Marrying Maiden.
   The name of the gua is made up of two characters. The ideograph of
the first character, gui, consists of two parts. The upper left looks like
two pennants with a tassel at the top of a pole, held in the procession of
a marrying maiden. The lower part is the ideograph zhi, representing
"stop." At the upper right is an image of a hand with three fingers and an
arm. The lower right is a picture of a hand-held broom. Taken together,
these images describe the procession of a marrying maiden. It stops at
the groom's house, where the maiden will take charge of the household,
as symbolized by the holding of a broom. The ideograph of the second
character of the name is Mei, consisting of two parts. The left side of the
ideograph is an image of a maiden with a well-shaped bust. The ideograph
on the right provides the sound of the character.
   This gua is the inverse of the preceding one, Developing Gradually.

Developing and returning are opposite, but they complement each other. The structure of the gua is Thunder ☳ above, Lake ☱ below. In the I Ching, Thunder represents an eldest son, and Lake represents a youngest daughter. This picture brought to mind a young maiden going to the groom's house to be his wife. King Wen's Decision on the Gua says, "Marrying Maiden. Moving forward: misfortune. Nothing is favorable." Marriage should be one of the most auspicious events in one's life. Why does it bring misfortune in this gua?

It is said that the marriage system originated with the Yellow Emperor, Huang-di (twenty-seventh century B.C.), who had nine wives. Eight of them were chosen by his first wife. At the time of the Zhou dynasty this system was still practiced. When the elder sister got married, frequently, a younger sister would be assigned as the second wife. Sometimes more than one younger sister would be brought into the marriage. This gua speaks of the marriage of a younger sister as a junior wife. The role of a second wife was to be a concubine; she had no primary power in the household. The second wife had to be totally submissive to the first wife, or else there would be a power struggle in the household. The situation was not always happy. In Chinese literature, a concubine often symbolizes an official of secondary importance or the state of being out of favor. It is one who must obey what his superior says even when it opposes his own will.

Decision

> Marrying Maiden.
> Moving forward: misfortune.
> Nothing is favorable.

Commentary on the Decision

> *Marrying Maiden*
> *Exposes the relation between Heaven and Earth.*
>
> *If Heaven and Earth do not unite,*
> *All beings fail to flourish.*
> *Marrying Maiden*
> *Represents the end and beginning of human relations.*
>
> *Joy with movement,*

Marrying off a young maiden.
Moving forward: misfortune;
Places are not correct.
Nothing is favorable;
Yieldings are mounted on the firms.

Commentary on the Symbol

Thunder over Lake.
An image of Marrying Maiden.
In correspondence with this,
The superior person persists in the everlasting relationship
And avoids anything that would hurt the harmony.

Yao Text

1. Initial Nine
   Marrying maiden as a junior wife.
   Lame on one leg,
   Still able to walk.
   Moving forward: good fortune.

   Marrying maiden as a junior wife.
   Two sisters marry one husband.
   It is a common practice.
   Lame on one leg.
   Good fortune for still being able to walk,
   Because they help each other.

2. Second Nine
   Blind in one eye,
   Still able to see.
   Favorable to be steadfast and upright.
   A solitary person.

   Favorable for a solitary person to be steadfast and upright;
   The everlasting principle does not change.

3. Third Six
   Marrying maiden is waiting.
   Returns back as a junior wife.

Marrying maiden is waiting.
She is not in an appropriate place.

4. Fourth Nine
Marrying maiden stays unmarried,
Marrying late—the proper time.

The decision of staying unmarried
Is to wait for the proper person.

5. Fifth Six
King Yi married off his sister.
Her garment was not as gorgeous as that of the junior wife.
The moon was nearly full.
Good fortune.

King Yi married off his younger sister.
Her garment did not look as gorgeous as that of the junior wife.
She is in the central place.
She values noble character more than ornaments.

6. Top Six
The woman holds a basket:
No fruits.
The man sacrifices a goat:
No blood.
Nothing is favorable.

The yielding line at the top has no fruits.
She holds an empty basket.

SIGNIFICANCE

This gua takes the image of a marriage to show the human relationship between a couple. The foundation of all marriage is love. Caring, concern, and mutual understanding are the essential elements of a harmonious and happy marriage. If married life is not harmonious, how can it be happy? In ancient times, for two sisters to marry one husband was common. In such a case, the elder sister became the wife, and the younger sister naturally stayed in a secondary position. She helped the elder sister manage the household. They loved each other and supported each other. In such an atmosphere, the family life could be harmonious. While the system

is out of date, the principle of cultivating and maintaining a harmonious relationship is still useful.

In ancient Chinese literature the relationship between a husband and a wife was used as an analogy to describe the relationship between a king and an official. In the preceding gua, King Wen used the image of a marrying maiden to describe the relationship between himself and the Lord of Heaven. He was assigned a mission to overthrow the tyrant and rescue the people from the tyrant's cruel rule. In this gua King Wen employed the image of marriage to describe his relationship with the tyrant.

During King Wen's sitting in stillness he recalled the situation when he was working in the tyrant's court. It was exactly like that of a marrying maiden. He had no initial power in the court. Any advance would bring misfortune; nothing was favorable. The Duke of Zhou tells about King Wen's problems with the court. King Wen maintained his gentleness and docility. He acted with humility—even his garment did not look as gorgeous as that of the attendants.

(1) Initial Nine. Marrying Maiden alternates to Relief (40) ☷☳

The bottom line is a yang element at the lowest place. It does not correspond to the yang element at the fourth place since they are both yang. This symbolizes a younger sister following the elder sister into marriage as a junior wife, a common practice in ancient times. As a junior wife she is likened to a lame person who is still able to walk. This system of marriage is, of course, not suitable to the present day, but the message is that one should act in accord with one's position. Mutual help brings harmony and good fortune.

(2) Second Nine. Marrying Maiden alternates to Taking Action (51) ☳☳

The second line is still in a lower place. The bottom line is a lame person who is still able to walk. This one is blind in one eye but still able to see. They are in a similar situation. But this line is a yang element in the center, symbolizing a firm and strong character. Although he is in a gloomy situation, he remains steadfast. It is advisable to keep one's self-confidence and to look forward positively.

(3) Third Six. Marrying Maiden alternates to Great Strength (34) ☳

The third line is a yin element at a yang place, neither central nor correct. It does not correspond to the topmost yin element. Under these conditions, one at this place can do nothing but wait. It is better to return home; she can be married as a junior wife. This line shows that those who are in subordinate positions are still able to make contributions.

(4) Fourth Nine. Marrying Maiden alternates to Approaching (19)

The fourth line is a yang element at a yin place. It does not correspond to the yang element at the bottom. The Yao Text says, "Marrying maiden stays unmarried, marrying late—the proper time." In other words, she waits for the right person. The message of this line is that when one plans an important undertaking, one should carefully consider all the possibilities and take no hasty action.

(5) Fifth Six. Marrying Maiden alternates to Joyful (58)

The Yao Text says, "King Yi married off his sister." This topic also appears at the fifth line of Advance (11). King Yi was a king of the Shang dynasty. This line is a yin element at the fifth place, the place for a king. Here it represents a king's sister. It corresponds to the yang element at the second place and symbolizes that the king has married his sister to his subordinate. This yin element is in a central place, indicating one who is gentle and docile. Her virtue is as brilliant as the full moon. It is not necessary for her to put on gorgeous clothes to show her prestige. For this reason her garment does not look as gorgeous as that of her maid attendant, who accompanies her to marry her husband as a junior wife. This line, the host of the gua, tells us that one should value spirituality more than materialism.

(6) Top Six. Marrying Maiden alternates to Diversity (38)

The Yao Text says, "The woman holds a basket: no fruits. The man sacrifices a goat: no blood. Nothing is favorable." In ancient wedding ceremonies, the bride carried a basket of fruits as a gift for her father-in-law and mother-in-law. The groom killed a goat to offer its blood in sacrifice to the ancestors, and the meat was used for the feast. This line is a yin element at a yin place. It represents a maiden with a weak character in a bad situation. It does not correspond to the yin element at the third place. Either she cannot find the right person or she is engaged but cannot marry or she can be married but the marriage is not good. There are no fruits in the basket and no blood from the sacrificed goat. These are bad omens. Partners, whether in marriage or in business, should be truthful and sincere. Otherwise, trouble awaits.

Additional Reference Information for This Gua

Image:	Thunder above, Lake below
Recite as:	Thunder above Lake, Marrying Maiden
Element:	Wood
Structure:	Three yang with three yin
Month:	The ninth month of the lunar calendar, or October
Host of the Gua:	Fifth Six
Opposite Gua:	Developing Gradually (53)
Inverse Gua:	Developing Gradually (53)
Mutual Gua:	Already Fulfilled (63)

55
Feng·
Abundance

☰☰ Zhen • Thunder
☰☰ Li • Fire

Name and Structure

Feng means full, plentiful, abundant.

Sequence of the Gua: *Those who find a home surely will reap abundance. Thus, after Marrying Maiden, Abundance follows.*

Wilhelm translates Feng as Abundance (Fullness), as does Blofeld. I also use the name Abundance. The ideograph of Feng takes the image of beans flourishing to express abundance. The ideograph consists of two parts. The lower part is a cooking vessel. The upper part shows the stems and leaves of beans. The overall picture is one of flourishing and abundance.

   The structure of the gua is Thunder ☰☰ above, Fire ☰☰ below. The attribute of Thunder is taking action. Fire represents flame and electricity. When a thunderstorm and lightning come together, the energy is tremendously abundant. It denotes a time of outstanding greatness and abundance, like the sun blazing at noon. Unfortunately, this tremendous abundance cannot last very long. There is no room for the excessive abundance to grow, to expand. Such a time of abundance should be treasured and well used.

Decision

   Abundance.
   Prosperous and smooth.

The king reaches this point.
Be like the sun at noon.

Commentary on the Decision

Abundance.
It denotes greatness.
Brilliance with motion,
Hence abundance.

The king reaches this point.
He values abundance and greatness.

Do not worry.
Be like the sun at noon.
One should radiate his light on Earth.

When the sun reaches its height,
Declining begins.
When the moon attains its fullest,
Waning starts.
The waxing and waning of Heaven and Earth
Accord with the course of time.
How much more true is this of humans?
How much more true is this of spirits and gods?

Commentary on the Symbol

Thunder and lightning come together.
An image of Abundance.
In correspondence with this,
The superior person decides lawsuits with clarity
And carries out punishment with exactness.

Yao Text

1. Initial Nine
   Meets his corresponding lord.
   Although alike, no fault.
   Going forward,
   There is esteem.

Although alike, no fault.
Exceeding alikeness, there is calamity.

2. Second Six
   Abundant, his screen.
   The sun is at noon;
   Polestar can be seen.
   Going forward brings a suspicious illness.
   There is sincerity and truthfulness to inspire
   Good fortune.

   There is sincerity and truthfulness to inspire.
   Truthfulness and sincerity sprout from his will.

3. Third Nine
   Abundant, his curtain.
   The sun is at noon;
   Tiny stars can be seen.
   Breaks his right arm; no fault.

   Abundance, his curtain.
   One should not attempt to do great things.
   Breaks his right arm.
   In the end, he would not be employed.

4. Fourth Nine
   Abundant, his screen.
   The sun is at noon;
   Polestar can be seen.
   Meets his lord of like nature.
   Good fortune.

   Abundance, his screen.
   The place is not appropriate.
   The sun is at noon; polestar can be seen.
   There is dimness and no light.
   Meets his lord of like nature.
   Good fortune for taking action.

5. Fifth Six
   Brilliant persons come around.
   There is congratulation and praise.
   Good fortune.

Good fortune of the fifth six.
There is congratulation and blessing.

6. Top Six
Abundant, his house.
Sheltering his household,
Peers through his gate.
So quiet, no people.
Three years, he does not appear.
Misfortune.

Abundance, his household.
It is like floating in Heaven.
Peers through his gate.
So quiet, no people.
He keeps himself away from others.

SIGNIFICANCE

The name of the gua is Abundance, yet a gloomy atmosphere overwhelms the lines. This gua reminds us that after abundance there is a decline. One should treasure and enjoy a time of abundance. When thunder and lightning act together, there is tremendous energy and explosive sound. Afterward, ominous quiet descends. The sound and the light do not last long. Based on this natural phenomenon, the ancient Chinese considered how to slow down the process of decline after extreme abundance.

A decline after extreme abundance is the law of Nature, like the waxing and waning of the moon. However, in human affairs we can delay the coming of decline by careful management. When a relationship or a business is in a period of abundance and prosperity, great caution should be taken to prevent disharmony and overdoing. People become used to the easy situation, but they may neglect the law of cause and effect.

The text of this gua is difficult to translate into modern language. The ancient text was inscribed on bamboo slips, and the ancient sage simplified it as much as he could to express its full meaning. Every character is equivalent to the content of a whole sentence. There are eight instances where the word "his" is used in the Yao Text and four times that it is said that the sun is at noon, one in the Decision and three in the Yao Text. They echo each other. What is being spoken of here? The host of the gua is the yielding line at the fifth place. This is what King Wen's

Decision refers to: "The king has reached this point. Do not worry. Be like the sun at noon."

During King Wen's sitting in stillness, he meditated upon abundance. He realized that after abundance there would be a decline. When a king has abundance, he should not worry about decline. To the contrary, he should share his abundance with his people without delay because the sun at noon does not last very long. The Duke of Zhou describes how the abundance of the Shang dynasty was masked by its tyranny as the sun's light is blocked by a screen and curtains. Because King Wen was magnanimous and humble, brilliant persons were willing to gather around him. Thus he enjoyed good fortune. The Tyrant of Shang, on the other hand, confined his abundance to his own palace; he cared not for his people. Peering through his gate, he saw nothing of people's suffering and hardship. Misfortune was in store for the tyrant.

(1) Initial Nine. Abundance alternates to Little Exceeding (62)

The bottom line is a yang element at a yang place—positive and productive. It corresponds to the yang element at the fourth place, who is its lord.

(2) Second Six. Abundance alternates to Great Strength (34)

The second line is in the middle of the lower gua, Li, or Fire, representing the sun. It does not respond to the yin element at the fifth place, which represents a screen. The Yao Text says, "Abundant, his screen. The sun is at noon; polestar can be seen." This indicates that one's abundance is covered by a screen as in a solar eclipse: the polestar can be seen although the sun is at noon. This is a bad situation. One's intelligence is overshadowed by another's ignorance. The one at the fifth place is not as bright as the one at the second place. Following him, the latter will be suspected and envied. Since the second line is a broken line, there is an opening in the middle, symbolizing an open heart and humility. When the line alternates to a solid line, it symbolizes truthfulness. Thus the Yao Text recommends truthfulness and sincerity.

(3) Third Nine. Abundance alternates to Taking Action (51)

The third line is a yang element at a yang place, extremely bright. He is at the top of the lower gua, denoting that brightness has reached its climax, like the sun at noon. He responds to the topmost yin element, his curtain. This yin covers the brightness of the third line more than that of

the second line. For the second line, the brightness is eclipsed; here it is covered by a curtain. The situation of this line is darker than that of the second line; even tiny stars can be seen at noon. The broken right arm is a metaphor for losing a capable assistant. However, the place of this line is correct, so there is no fault.

(4) Fourth Nine. Abundance alternates to Brilliance Injured (36)

The first part of this line of the Yao Text is the same as that of the second line. The second line is in the middle of the lower gua, while the third and fourth lines are in the middle of the accomplished gua; thus, the situation of the fourth line is similar to that of the second line. The fourth line does not correspond with the bottom line. They are both yang lines, and their situations are the same. The bottom line thinks of the fourth line as "his corresponding lord." The fourth place considers the yang element at the bottom as "his lord of like nature." During the time of darkness, seeking a positive companion and taking productive action will bring good fortune.

(5) Fifth Six. Abundance alternates to Abolishing the Old (49)

The fifth line is the host of the gua. It is the supreme place of a king. This is the king whom King Wen mentions in his Decision. This line is a yin element at a yang place, suggesting that it is magnanimous, gentle, and humble. For that reason, brilliant persons are willing to gather around. Thus "congratulation and praise" are in order. In seeking abundance, a leader should be magnanimous, gentle, and humble and respect those who are brilliant and able.

(6) Top Six. Abundance alternates to Brightness (30)

The topmost line is in a bad situation, at the end of the action. It is the topmost line of the accomplished gua, Abundance, and the topmost line of the upper gua, Thunder. There is no room for further advance. Its abundance is confined in a house in the dark. As a yin element he is reserved, peering through doors. For "three years" he sees nothing. Three years represents a period of time, the number "three" deriving from the fact that the topmost line is the third line of the upper gua. The misfortune of the topmost line is that he keeps himself apart from others either through arrogance and imperiousness or by wallowing in luxury and pleasure.

Additional Reference Information for This Gua

Image:	Thunder above, Fire below		
Recite as:	Thunder above Fire, Abundance		
Element:	Wood		
Structure:	Three yang with three yin		
Month:	The sixth month of the lunar calendar, or July		
Host of the Gua:	Fifth Six		
Opposite Gua:	Dispersing	(59)	䷺
Inverse Gua:	Traveling	(56)	䷷
Mutual Gua:	Great Exceeding	(28)	䷛

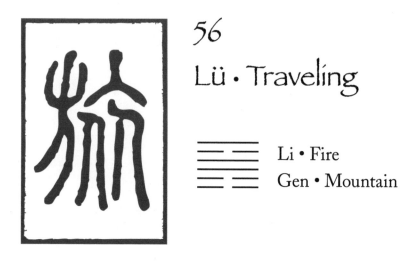

56
Lü · Traveling

$$\overline{}\ \overline{}$$ Li · Fire
Gen · Mountain

NAME AND STRUCTURE

Lü means to travel, to move from place to place. In ancient times, an army of five hundred soldiers was called Lü.

Sequence of the Gua: *If abundance proceeds to the utmost and becomes poor, surely one would lose his home. Thus, after Abundance, Traveling follows.*

Wilhelm translates Lü as The Wanderer, and Blofeld translates it as The Traveler. In this book I adopt Traveling.

It was challenging to create an ideograph to express an act of moving. The ideograph of this gua employed the image of an army chasing its enemy to express traveling. The left half of the ideograph is an ancient character, fang. During the Shang dynasty and the beginning of the Zhou dynasty, the minorities on the northern border were called fang. The ideograph of fang looks like a dancing warrior with his two arms swinging in the air. The minority groups usually performed a dance ceremony before fighting. On the right side are three soldiers. The leader at the top moves forward with two soldiers following him. The heads of the soldiers face the minority warrior, and their feet move toward him, suggesting that they are giving chase.

This gua is the inverse of the preceding one, Abundance. Abundance denotes a time of outstanding greatness and plenitude. However, this period cannot last very long. Abundance advises people to treasure and use well the plenitude and to sustain the state of abundance as long as possible. The gua

Traveling suggests that after the declining of Abundance, one should move forward, exploring the new world and starting a new cycle. Staying at the old place and moving with the old pace is only to stagnate. Thus, Abundance and Traveling are opposite in content but still complementary.

The structure of the gua is Fire ☲ above, Mountain ☶ below. The image of fires burning on the mountain, their flames blown by the wind from place to place, is where the name Traveling came from. When one is traveling, life is not stable, and everyone is a stranger. Moving from place to place makes one physically and emotionally tired. Under every circumstance, a traveler should remain steadfast and upright. In this way there will be good fortune.

Decision

> Traveling.
> Little prosperity and smoothness.
> Traveler,
> Being steadfast and upright: good fortune.

Commentary on the Decision

> *Traveling.*
> *Little prosperity or smoothness.*
>
> *The yielding is central in the outer;*
> *It follows the solids.*
> *Keeping still and clinging to the brilliance,*
> *There is chance for a little prosperity and smoothness.*
>
> *Traveler,*
> *Being steadfast and upright: good fortune.*
>
> *The time and significance of Traveling are truly great!*

Commentary on the Symbol

> *Fire on Mountain.*
> *An image of Traveling.*
> *In correspondence with this,*
> *The superior person is prudent and precise in punishment*
> *And does not lengthen the period of imprisonment.*

Yao Text

1. Initial Six
   Traveling,
   Dwelling upon trivial things, trivial things.
   This is how one finds calamities.

   Traveling,
   Dwelling upon trivial things, trivial things.
   One's intention is low,
   Which causes the misfortune.

2. Second Six
   Traveling,
   Staying at a lodge
   With one's belongings.
   Obtains a boy attendant,
   Being steadfast and upright.

   Obtains a boy attendant;
   In the end, no discontentment.

3. Third Nine
   Traveling,
   His lodge burns.
   Loses his boy attendant.
   Being steadfast: adversity.

   Traveling,
   His lodge burns.
   It is too sad.
   He treats his boy attendant with pride;
   It is certain he should lose him.

4. Fourth Nine
   Traveling.
   Resting in a shelter.
   Gets his traveling expenses.
   "My heart is not glad."

   Traveling, rest in a shelter.
   He has not yet got a proper position.
   Gets his traveling expenses.

He is not glad in his heart.

5. Fifth Six
   Shooting a pheasant.
   One arrow: dead.
   In the end,
   Obtains fame and nobility.

   In the end, obtains fame and nobility.
   It comes from above.

6. Top Nine
   The bird burns the nest.
   The traveler first laughs,
   Then laments and weeps.
   Loses a cow in the field.
   Misfortune.

   As traveler at the top place,
   That is just as it should be burned.
   Loses a cow in the field.
   No news will ever be heard.

SIGNIFICANCE

This gua expounds the principle of stability and unity. When abundance reaches the extreme, an unstable situation arises. Further progress and advance is not as easy and smooth as before. The gua takes the image of traveling to display the truth of change and development in human life. Life is a journey, and we are all travelers. Every event in our daily lives is part of a continuum of change and development. Time and space are a process. Every individual event enhances change and development. We must respond to the changes and discover the most suitable way to deal with them. Responding to isolated changes merely leads to a little success. Only by responding to the changes within the whole process can great success be achieved. This is the key to success. In this gua, all the yielding lines bring good fortune because they are docile and tend to be central and harmonious with others. On the other hand, all the solid lines are not that auspicious because they tend to be willful and opinionated and difficult for others to deal with.

During King Wen's sitting in stillness he recalled the changes and

development of the Shang dynasty as well as that of the Zhou. He realized that the life of a country, and of a person, is a journey. Before one settles down, chances for progress and success are few. Only being steadfast and upright can bring good fortune. The Duke of Zhou describes the different situations in one's life journey. Dwelling upon trivial things, one cannot create good fortune. With a place to stay, enough money, and a companion, one's life is better.

(1) Initial Six. Traveling alternates to Brightness (30) ☲

The bottom line describes a person who cares only for trivial things. She has neither a goal nor a career. In her life journey she is just a traveler and her sights are set low. She creates her own misfortune.

(2) Second Six. Traveling alternates to Establishing the New (50) ☴

The second line represents the best situation for traveling. Staying in an inn is safe and comfortable. One also has enough money; there is no worry about any shortage. One has a loyal boy attendant who is a faithful servant and companion, thus there is no discontentment.

(3) Third Nine. Traveling alternates to Proceeding Forward (35) ☷

The third line is a yang element at a yang place at the end of the lower gua, Mountain, or Keeping Still. There is no way to advance. It is also close to the upper gua, Fire—thus, the inn burns down. He is too willful and treats his boy attendant unkindly and so he loses a loyal servant and companion. On a journey one should be gentle and humble and treat people with trust and sincerity.

(4) Fourth Nine. Traveling alternates to Keeping Still (52) ☶

The fourth line is a yang element at a yin place, not as firm as the third line nor as gentle as the second line. One at the second place is able to stay in a comfortable inn. At this place one can only rest in a shelter. He is unhappy.

(5) Fifth Six. Traveling alternates to Retreat (33) ☰

The fifth line is a yin element at a yang place, central but not correct. One at this place is gentle and follows the principle of the Golden Mean, thus this line is the host of the gua. When shooting the pheasant, a single arrow makes the bird die. As a result, one obtains fame and nobility. In ancient times, when one was ordained as an official, one presented pheasants to the king as a gift.

(6) Top Nine. Traveling alternates to Little Exceeding (62)

The topmost line is at the highest place of the gua, symbolized by the image of a bird. It is a yang element, which indicates a person possessing a stubborn and proud character. While traveling, this kind of person is not at all welcome. The image of a bird's nest on fire suggests that he cannot find a place to stay. He might be successful for a while, but he laments and weeps at last. He loses a cow in the field, indicating that he loses an important assistant; in this way he creates his own misfortune.

Additional Reference Information for This Gua

Image:	Fire above, Mountain below
Recite as:	Fire on Mountain, Traveling
Element:	Fire
Structure:	Three yang with three yin
Month:	The fourth month of the lunar calendar, or May
Host of the Gua:	Fifth Six
Opposite Gua:	Restricting (60)
Inverse Gua:	Abundance (55)
Mutual Gua:	Great Exceeding (28)

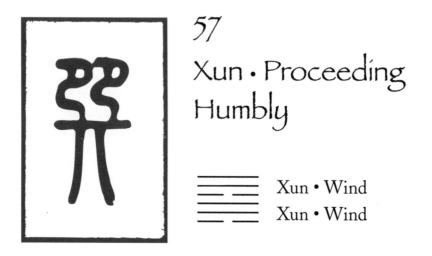

57
Xun · Proceeding Humbly

☰
☰ Xun · Wind
Xun · Wind

Name and Structure

Xun ☴ is one of the eight primary gua; doubled, it forms this accomplished gua. As a primary gua it represents Wind or Wood. The Commentary on the Symbol says, "Following the wind; an image of Proceeding Humbly." "Following the wind" suggests proceeding, but the proceeding should be gentle, flowing easily into wherever the wind goes. Applied to human affairs, it means to proceed humbly, or to resign sovereign authority.

Sequence of the Gua: *When the traveler has no place to take shelter, Proceeding Humbly follows.*

Wilhelm translates Xun as The Gentle (The Penetrating, Wind). Blofeld calls it Willing Submission, Gentleness, Penetration. Xun is an action, a proceeding. The ideograph employs the image of two snakes to represent the act of continuing. The upper part of the ideograph depicts two snakes, si. The lower part is an ideograph of gong, which means "together." Two snakes proceed together—the power of proceeding is doubled.

The structure of the gua is Wind ☴ above, Wind ☴ below, or Wood above, Wood below. According to the structure, a yielding line lying underneath two solid lines shows the submissive, humble, and obedient personality of the yielding element. The attribute of the wind is to proceed gently. The Chinese consider a gentle breeze with bright sun or a gentle breeze with mild rain to be the best weather. When the wind blows softly, it goes everywhere. When the wood proceeds gently, it penetrates the soil deeply. Gently proceeding is the most effective way to influence events. It never violates and is therefore easily accepted.

Decision

> Proceeding Humbly.
> Little prosperity and smoothness.
> Favorable to have somewhere to go.
> Favorable to see a great person.

Commentary on the Decision

> *The symbol of Wind is doubled.*
> *It is to repeat one's order once more.*
>
> *The firm proceeds humbly to the central and to the correct position.*
> *Its will is able to be fulfilled.*
>
> *The yieldings submit to the firm.*
> *Only little prosperity and smoothness are available.*
> *It is favorable to have somewhere to go.*
> *It is favorable to see a great person.*

Commentary on the Symbol

> *Following the wind;*
> *An image of Proceeding Humbly.*
> *In correspondence with this,*
> *The superior person repeats his order*
> *And carries out his command.*

Yao Text

1. Initial Six
   Going forward or coming back?
   Favorable to have a warrior's firmness and steadfastness.

   > *Going forward, or retreating?*
   > *His mind is perplexed.*
   > *Favorable to have a warrior's firmness and steadfastness.*
   > *His will is controlled.*

2. Second Nine
Proceeding humbly underneath the bed.
Priests and exorcists are used in profusion.
Good fortune.
No fault.

The good fortune of employing in profusion.
He attains the central place.

3. Third Nine
Repeatedly proceeding humbly.
Humiliation.

The regret of repeatedly proceeding humbly.
He loses his sincerity and truthfulness.

4. Fourth Six
Regret vanishes.
In the field, caught three grades of game.

In the field, caught three grades of game.
He achieves merit.

5. Fifth Nine
Being steadfast and upright: good fortune.
Regret vanishes.
Nothing is unfavorable.
No beginning, there is an end.
Before changing, three days.
After changing, three days.
Good fortune.

The good fortune of fifth nine.
Its place is correct and central.

6. Top Nine
Proceeding humbly underneath the bed.
Loses his means of substance.
Being steadfast: misfortune.

Proceeding humbly underneath the bed.
At the top, the end has come.
Loses his means of substance.
This is what misfortune is!

Significance

This gua is one of the eight gua among the sixty-four accomplished gua that is made by doubling the primary gua, here, Wind ☴. Proceeding Humbly explains the reason to be humble and gentle. In an unstable situation, if one is humble and gentle one is able to make friends with people, gaining their trust and obtaining their support. The ancients believed that humility and gentleness were the basic moral qualities which one should possess, but that these did not equate with inferiority and weakness.

This gua takes the image of a yielding line humbly lying underneath two solid lines. It symbolizes that one is waiting with patience for the right time to accomplish an aim. On the other hand, the winds following one upon the other symbolize the driving force continuously pushing one forward to achievement. In his Analects, Confucius says:

> Before one's mood of pleasure or anger, sorrow or joy, is released, one's mind is in a state of equilibrium. When those feelings have been released and are at an appropriate degree, they are in a state of harmony. This equilibrium is the great basis of all human activities, and this harmony is the universal path for all to pursue. We must devote ourselves to achieving this state of equilibrium and harmony and to establishing the proper order between Heaven and Earth. Then all things will be nourished and will flourish.

Thus, equilibrium is the potential before it has been released, and harmony is the result of the proper way of releasing the potential. When we intend to do something, both before and afterward every step should be taken in the proper way. The host of the gua is the solid line at the fifth place. The Commentary on the Decision says, "The firm proceeds humbly to the central and to the correct position. Its will is able to be fulfilled."

During King Wen's sitting in stillness he meditated upon traveling, being humble, and proceeding. He realized that one should proceed with humility on a life journey. When only a little success can be achieved, there is still room for more. Great success is the result of the building up of little successes. The Duke of Zhou records the results of different attitudes of proceeding humbly. Progressing in this way, one still needs a warrior's firmness and steadfastness. Being too humble and meek makes one lose self-confidence. Proceeding humbly with sincerity and trust brings good fortune. When one intends to make a change, one should consider matters carefully before taking action and reconsider after the action is completed.

(1) Initial Six. Proceeding Humbly alternates to Little Accumulation (9) ☴

The bottom line is the principal line of the lower gua. It represents a gentle and humble person. Its position indicates that it is too humble and lacks self-confidence. Thus it is torn between advancing and retreating, perplexed. What it needs is steadfastness. Thus the Yao Text says, "Favorable to have a warrior's firmness and steadfastness."

(2) Second Nine. Proceeding Humbly alternates to Developing Gradually (53) ☶

The second line is a yang element at a yin place, representing a person of truthfulness and sincerity. He is as humble and devoted as a priest or an exorcist praying before an altar. There is good fortune and no fault.

(3) Third Nine. Proceeding Humbly alternates to Dispersing (59) ☵

The third line is a yang element at a yang place, the top of the lower gua. One at this place is not really gentle and humble, but repeatedly acts like a gentle and humble person. This hypocritical conduct will bring humiliation. One can fool others for a while, but cannot dissemble forever.

(4) Fourth Six. Proceeding Humbly alternates to Encountering (44) ☰

This line uses the analogy of hunting. In ancient times animals caught in a hunt were divided into three grades. Those hit in the heart were of the first grade. They could be used as sacrifices in ceremonies. Those hit in the leg were of the second grade. They could be used for banquets. Those hit in the intestine were of the third grade. They could be eaten only by the one who caught them. The fourth line is a yin element at a yin place. It has no correspondent—there are two solid lines above it and below it. In this situation there is regret. But its place is correct, a yin element at the bottom of the upper gua, gentle and humble. For this reason, regret vanishes. It will achieve merit, as when three grades of game are caught in the field.

(5) Fifth Nine. Proceeding Humbly alternates to Remedying (18) ☶

The fifth line is a yang element at a yang place. One at this place is firm and strong, but too much firmness and strength is not appropriate in this situation of proceeding humbly, and would cause problems. However, one at this place is central and correct, and will not show excess firmness and strength. Thus regret vanishes, and nothing is unfavorable. "No beginning; there is an end" means that although there is no good at first, there will be eventually. The Commentary on the Symbol says, "The superior person repeats his order and carries out his command." This yang element is the superior person in question. The Duke of Zhou suggests that before one intends to make any change, one should consider it for three days, and after the change is made reconsider it for another three days. Then regret will vanish, and good fortune will result.

(6) Top Nine. Proceeding Humbly alternates to Replenishing (48)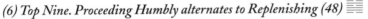

The topmost line is at the extremity of gentleness and humility. One at this place is too humble and meek, as if lying underneath a bed. To be overly humble and meek makes one lose self-confidence. It is the same as when a traveler loses all his money. Even if he remains steadfast and upright, there will be misfortune.

Additional Reference Information for This Gua

Image:	Wind above, Wind below
Recite as:	Wind is doubled, Proceeding Humbly
Element:	Wood
Structure:	Four yang with two yin
Month:	The eight month of the lunar calendar, or September
Host of the Gua:	Fifth Nine
Opposite Gua:	Taking Action (51)
Inverse Gua:	Joyful (58)
Mutual Gua:	Diversity (38)

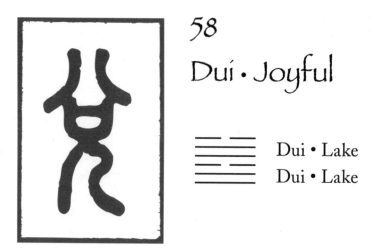

58
Dui · Joyful

☱ Dui · Lake
☱ Dui · Lake

NAME AND STRUCTURE

Dui is the root of the Chinese character "speaking." There is an open mouth in the middle of the character, talking and smiling. Dui has a variety of meanings. Originally it signified speaking with joy, but it also means exchange in the sense of giving and taking. Giving and receiving makes people joyful. Dui is the inverse of the preceding gua, Proceeding Humbly, which makes people joyful.

Sequence of the Gua: *Proceeding humbly makes people feel joyous. Thus, after Proceeding Humbly, Joyful follows.*

Wilhelm translates Dui as The Joyous, Lake, and Blofeld translates it as Joy. I adopt the name Joyful.

The ideograph uses the image of a person singing and dancing to express the mood of joy. It consists of three parts. In the middle is an open mouth singing. The lower part is made up of two legs, which seem to be moving and dancing. The upper part depicts two arms swinging in the air, expressing joy. The structure of the gua is Lake ☱ above, Lake ☱ below. Lake's attribute is joy. When Lake is doubled, the joyfulness is also doubled. According to Western tradition, Dui has been translated as Lake, and people are accustomed to it. In fact, it should be marsh or swamp. Rice is the staple of life for the Chinese people, and rice paddies are marshes. An abundance of Dui, marshes, leads to an abundance of food—a situation that makes everyone joyful.

In the I Ching, the uppermost line represents the outer reality and the lowest line represents the inner reality. A yielding line mounting upon two solid lines makes Lake ☱. Thus, the yielding line at the top represents one's gentle and joyful personality. The two solid lines on the bottom symbolize one's inner principle and strength. When one is gentle and joyful and has inner strength, one is easily accepted in any situation.

Decision

Joyful.
Prosperous and smooth.
Favorable to be steadfast and upright.

Commentary on the Decision

Joyful.
It is a symbol of joy.

The solids are in the center,
And the yieldings outer.
Joy is favorable to being steadfast and upright.
It is acting in accordance with the will of Heaven
And in correspondence with the wishes of people.

When one's priority is to give people joyfulness,
They forget their toils.
When people are willing to encounter danger,
They forget their fear of death.

How great is the power of giving people joyfulness.
It stimulates them to do everything possible!

Commentary on the Symbol

Lakes clinging one to the other.
An image of Joyful.
In correspondence with this,
The superior person makes friends with people,
Discussing and practicing the Tao of Truth.

Yao Text

1. Initial Nine
   With inner harmony, joyful.
   Good fortune.

   Good fortune of joyfulness with inward harmony.
   There is no doubt about his conduct.

2. Second Nine
   With inner sincerity, joyful.
   Good fortune.
   Regret vanishes.

   Good fortune of joyfulness with inner sincerity.
   He has faith in his will.

3. Third Six
   With flattery, coming for joyfulness.
   Misfortune.

   The misfortune of coming for joyfulness with flattery.
   He is not in a proper place.

4. Fourth Nine
   Deliberating over joyfulness.
   Not at ease.
   Keep away from illness;
   Then there is happiness.

   The joyfulness of the fourth nine.
   There is ground for congratulation.

5. Fifth Nine
   Sincerity toward decadence.
   There is adversity.

   Sincerity toward decadence
   Because his position is appropriate and correct.

6. Top Six
   Induced joyfulness.

   The yielding line at the top induces.
   His virtue is not brilliant.

SIGNIFICANCE

This is one of the eight gua made by doubling the primary gua. Here, the accomplished gua is Dui ☱, Joyful, and the primary gua is Lake ☱. Joyful expounds the principle of joyfulness and happiness. If one is joyful and happy, one makes people feel joyful and happy. If one is able to make people joyful and happy, one feels joyful and happy, too. Joyfulness and happiness can promote harmonious relationships.

This gua takes the image of a person who is outwardly gentle and joyful but firm and truthful inside. It discusses the way to deal with human affairs. Before one takes action, one should make a decision. This is using inner strength. But one still should accept others' ideas and not stubbornly adhere to one's own opinion. This is the way to cultivate outward harmony. Dealing with people, one should be gentle and joyful but not flattering and fawning. Dealing with events, one should be firm and stable but not stubborn and opinionated. In this way, there will be progress and success, and nothing will be unfavorable.

The Commentary on the Decision says, "The solids are in the center, and the yieldings outer." The solid line at the second place or the fifth place could be the host. However, because the fifth line is at the supreme position, it is more suitable to be the host of the gua.

During King Wen's sitting in stillness, he realized that one should know the purpose and goal of one's life journey and should proceed humbly and joyfully toward that goal. The Duke of Zhou elucidates the proper attitude to make people joyful. Good fortune derives from inward harmony and sincerity and a peaceful heart. This attitude makes oneself as well as others joyful. Inducing joyfulness in a disingenuous way invites misfortune.

(1) Initial Nine. Joyful alternates to Exhausting (47) ☱

The bottom is a yang element at a yang place. Of the four solid lines in this gua, only the bottom one has no connection to a yielding line. Firm and strong, it makes people joyful with inward harmony, not flattery. This is the one Confucius refers to when he says, "The superior person is in harmony with people, but does not go along with them in evil deeds." There is good fortune.

(2) Second Nine. Joyful alternates to Following (17) ☱

The second line is a yang element in the center of the lower gua. One at this place is trustworthy and sincere. Making people joyful with trustfulness and sincerity, of course, brings good fortune. On the other hand, the position of this line is not correct. There might be regret. Owing to his faith in one's trust and sincerity, regret will disappear.

(3) Third Six. Joyful alternates to Eliminating (43) ≣

The yin element at the third place is the principal line of the inner gua. It is neither central nor correct and does not correspond to the topmost line; they are both yin. One at this place has no alternative but to descend to please the yang elements at the second and bottom places. According to Chinese cosmology, yang energy rises and yin energy descends. In this gua, the yin element at the third place comes down to please the two yang elements with flattery. However, those two elements are firm and strong—they do not respond. There is misfortune.

(4) Fourth Nine. Joyful alternates to Restricting (60) ≣

The yang element at the fourth place is close to the yin element at the third place. The yin element is neither central nor correct, leading to deliberation over whom to be joyful with. There is no peace in his heart. Eventually, he makes a decision and refuses to be seduced by the one at the third place. Forsaking the dark for the light, he avoids illness. It is a joyful and happy event. There is ground for congratulation.

(5) Fifth Nine. Joyful alternates to Marrying Maiden (54) ≣

The fifth line is a yang element at a yang place, firm and strong and in a supreme place. It is close to the topmost line—a yin element at a yin place, representing a sycophant. The text warns that when one is in a supreme position, one should be aware of the danger of trusting such people, who tend to please others to gain benefit from them or mislead them. There is danger.

(6) Top Six. Joyful alternates to Fulfillment (10) ≣

This topmost line uses all kinds of methods to lure people in a wrong direction or allows itself to be lured. The Yao Text does not mention good fortune or misfortune, but it does warn that joyfulness is induced in a wrong direction. It is the worst situation found in this gua. Beware of the consequences.

Additional Reference Information for This Gua

Image:	Lake above, Lake below
Recite as:	Lake is doubled, Joyful
Element:	Metal
Structure:	Four yang with two yin
Month:	Autumn Equinox
Host of the Gua:	Fifth Nine
Opposite Gua:	Keeping Still (52)
Inverse Gua:	Proceeding Humbly (57)
Mutual Gua:	Household (37)

59
Huan · Dispersing

Xun • Wind
Kan • Water

NAME AND STRUCTURE

Originally Huan meant ice breaks, melts, and vanishes. Later on, it came to mean to separate and scatter.

Sequence of the Gua: *After happiness and joyfulness, there comes dispersing. Thus, after Joyful, Dispersing follows.*

Wilhelm translates Huan as Dispersion (Dissolution). Blofeld translates it as Scattering, Disintegration, Dispersal. I adopt the term Dispersing.

The ideograph of Huan expresses its original meaning. The image on the left represents water. It resembles the primary gua for Water ☵, turned vertically. On the top right is a knife, and on the bottom are two hands with fingers and arms. In the middle are two pieces of ice. Taken as a whole, this ideograph pictures a knife used to break up the ice, with two hands separating the pieces of ice. The ice melts and becomes water, at last dispersing and vanishing. The structure of the gua is Wind ☴ above, Water ☵ below. The wind blows over the water and disperses the waves. The inner gua is Water; its attribute is danger. It symbolizes one's vital energy blocked within. The outer gua is Wind; its attribute is penetration. Penetrating and breaking the blockage leads to dispersion.

This gua derives from Developing Gradually (53) ䷴. When the solid line at the third place of Developing Gradually descends to the second place, Developing Gradually alternates to Dispersing. The Commentary on the Decision says, "The firm comes [descends] without hindrance." When the yielding line at the second place of Developing Gradually ascends to the third place, Developing Gradually alternates to this gua. The yielding third line is similar to the yielding fourth line. The Commentary on the Decision says, "The yielding is at the proper place. It goes out [ascends] to meet its similarity above."

In this gua, the yang element at the fifth place is central and correct. It represents the king. The elements at the third and fourth places are both yin. They serve the king in full cooperation and with unity of purpose. Thus there is success. During a time of dispersion, the king should arrive at the temple to pray and ask the blessing of Heaven. When people see the sincerity and truthfulness of the king, they will be influenced and gather together to uphold and support the king. The upper gua, Xun, can symbolize either Wind or Wood. Wood above Water is a favorable omen to cross great rivers, thus Confucius's Commentary on the Decision says, "The merit comes from mounting on the wood."

Decision

> Dispersing.
> Prosperous and smooth.
> The king arrives at the temple.
> Favorable to cross great rivers.
> Favorable to be steadfast and upright.

Commentary on the Decision

> *Dispersing.*
> *Prosperous and smooth.*
>
> *The firm comes without hindrance.*
> *The yielding is at the proper place.*
> *It goes out to meet its similarity above.*
>
> *The king arrives at the temple.*
> *He is in the central place.*
> *Favorable to cross great rivers.*
> *The merit comes from mounting on the wood.*

Commentary on the Symbol

The wind moves over the water.
An image of Dispersing.
In correspondence with this,
The ancient king offers sacrifice to the Lord of Heaven
And establishes temples.

Yao Text

1. Initial Six
   Engaged in rescuing; a strong horse.
   Good fortune.

   Good fortune of the initial six.
   It follows its submissive nature.

2. Second Nine
   Dispersing.
   Hurrying to an opportune moment.
   Regret vanishes.

   Dispersing.
   Hurrying to an opportune moment.
   His will is fulfilled.

3. Third Six
   Dispersing one's selfishness.
   No regret.

   Dispersing one's selfishness.
   One's will is for others.

4. Fourth Six
   Dispersing one's group.
   Supreme good fortune.
   Dispersing brings a mound.
   Beyond common people's imagination.

   Dispersing one's group.
   Supreme good fortune.
   It is brilliant and great.

5. Fifth Nine
    Dispersing
    Like perspiration, speaking out loudly.
    Dispersing king's belongings.
    No fault.

    No fault for dispersing king's belongings.
    He is in a proper place.

6. Top Nine
    Dispersing one's worry.
    Get out,
    Keep a distance,
    Go away.
    No fault.

    Dispersing one's worry.
    Keep the calamity at a distance.

SIGNIFICANCE

The gua takes the image of the wind moving over the water to demonstrate the act of dispersing people's resentment. During the time of dispersing, having a leader with wisdom and foresight is crucial. The king approaching his temple gives us an image of his connection with the spiritual world. Crossing great rivers signifies the hardship and difficulty of the work. Steadfastness and uprightness should be the virtue of a great leader. He has self-confidence, so he is able to live and work in peace. The host of the gua is the solid line at the fifth place. This line represents the king who approaches his temple to connect himself with the Lord of Heaven. During the time of dispersing he is the only one who, in the honored place, is able to establish order throughout his nation. The fourth line represents the king's minister, while the second line is his officer. They faithfully assist the king to unite the people in the time of dispersing.

During King Wen's sitting in stillness he meditated upon joyfulness and dispersion. After people had been joyful, their energy dispersed, and their focus was scattered. At such a time, a leader with wisdom and foresight was needed. He arrived at his temple and communicated with the deity. His sincerity and trustworthiness encouraged people to work in full

cooperation and with unity of purpose. The Duke of Zhou narrates that to be of help at such a time, one should have the speed of a strong horse. Dispersing self-serving groups led to a union as solid as a mound.

(1) Initial Six. Dispersing alternates to Innermost Sincerity (61)

The bottom line is the beginning of Dispersing. The situation is not serious. Using the speed of a strong horse, it is possible to rescue the situation. Therefore, there is good fortune. The bottom line is a weak yin element at a yin place. It relies on the strength of a speedy horse, which is represented by the solid line at the second place. Thus, the Commentary on the Yao Text says, "Good fortune of the initial six. It follows its submissive nature." Its submissive nature makes it follow the solid line in the second place.

(2) Second Nine. Dispersing alternates to Watching (20)

The second line is a yang element at a yin place, central but not correct. A yang element in a central place represents a person who has his own definite view. The lower gua, Water, also symbolizes a horse. One at the second place is able to take his own view. He grasps the opportune moment, hurrying to rescue the situation of dispersing. All regrets disappear. This line shows that to act in accord with the time is important.

(3) Third Six. Dispersing alternates to Proceeding Humbly (57)

The third line is a yin element at a yang place, neither central nor correct. It represents a selfish and shortsighted person, but because she is at a yang place, she is able to overcome her shortsightedness and rid herself of selfishness. In this way she can do good for others. There is no regret.

(4) Fourth Six. Dispersing alternates to Contention (6)

The fourth line is a minister's place. It is a yin element at a yin place, not central but correct. Although it responds to the one at the bottom, they are both yin; the fourth line refuses to form what would be a selfish union. She prefers to serve the king at the fifth place loyally and faithfully. Her act of refusing a selfish bond leads to a union as strong as a mound. There is supreme good fortune.

(5) Fifth Nine. Dispersing alternates to Childhood (4)

The fifth line is at the supreme place representing a brilliant leader. He is a yang element at a yang place, central and correct. As a leader he makes a great pronouncement, likened to perspiration dispersing, which serves to relieve the body. This image symbolizes that a pronouncement made by a brilliant king will never be without virtue or benefit. Thus the Yao Text says, "Dispersing like perspiration, speaking out loudly." He also gives away his own accumulated property. There is no fault. This line is a continuation of the previous line, which discussed avoiding a selfish bond in order to promote the unity of people. This line focuses on dispersing one's own wealth to induce a flourishing prosperity of the whole community.

(6) Top Nine. Dispersing alternates to Darkness (29) ☵

The topmost line has arrived at the end of Dispersing. It is far away from the lower gua, Water, representing the danger; thus, one at this place is able to avoid calamity. The Yao Text gives warning: Get out, keep a distance, and go away. There will be no fault.

Additional Reference Information for This Gua

Image:	Wind above, Water below
Recite as:	Wind above Water, Dispersing
Element:	Wood
Structure:	Three yang with three yin
Month:	The sixth month of the lunar calendar, or July
Host of the Gua:	Fifth Nine
Opposite Gua:	Abundance (55) ☳
Inverse Gua:	Restricting (60) ☵
Mutual Gua:	Nourishing (27) ☶

60

Jie • Restricting

Kan • Water
Dui • Lake

NAME AND STRUCTURE

Jie has a variety of meanings. Originally it indicated a joint, or node, of a stalk of bamboo. Because these nodes delimit sections of stalk, its meaning extended to "set the bounds." Setting boundaries means to restrict, and from restricting came the meanings to limit, to restrain, to economize, or to save. This connotation loosened the definition to encompass moral principle. To save is to restrict one's expenses, and moral principle restrains one's behavior. All these meanings have the sense of keeping or containing something within a specified area. Wilhelm translates Jie as Limitation. Blofeld translates it as Restraint. For this book, the term Restricting is adopted, to keep the focus on keeping persons, things, or activities within a prescribed area.

Sequence of the Gua: *Things cannot disperse forever. Thus, after Dispersing, Restricting follows.*

The ideograph attempts to express the original meaning of Jie, to set bounds. At the top there are two sets of lance-shaped bamboo leaves. Below the leaves is the character ji, providing the sound. Ji means immediately or instantly; it sets a time restriction. The left side of ji depicts a seed of grain with a tiny sprout at the top and two tiny roots at the bottom. On the right is a sickle. These two images suggest a picture of cutting grain and eating it immediately. Originally the righthand image represented an ancient verifying token made of bamboo. When a piece of bamboo has been

464

split in two, each half becomes a verifying token. If the two pieces match each other, then each person who has one holds a trustworthy credential. Tokens made of bamboo slips were commonly used by ancient governments to verify the identity of an individual on a mission.

This gua is the inverse of the preceding one, Dispersing, a movement of scattering. Restricting is to set a boundary for the movement. They are opposite, but complementary. The structure of the gua is Water ☵ above, Lake ☱ below. Water flows into a lake. Too much water pouring into a lake results in flooding unless there is restraint. The space of a lake is restricted by its boundary. Only a certain amount of water can be held within this boundary, otherwise calamity would result. This is where the name Restricting comes from. In ancient China, to set limits on one's expenses and bounds for conduct was regarded as a sign of moral excellence. But to be overly restrictive causes pain. Thus King Wen did not encourage painful restriction.

Decision

Restricting.
Prosperous and smooth.
Not appropriate to be steadfast
In bitter restriction.

Commentary on the Decision

Restricting.
Prosperity and smoothness.

The firm and the yielding are equally divided,
And the firms obtain the central places.
Not appropriate to be steadfast in bitter restriction.
Its way leads to the end.

Passing the danger with joy,
Carry out restriction in the proper position.
From the central and correct place,
His advance is without limitation.

When Heaven and Earth regulate their restriction,
Then the four seasons complete their functions.
When restriction is put into regulation,

Then resources will not be exhausted
And people will not be hurt.

Commentary on the Symbol

Water over Lake.
An image of Restricting.
In correspondence with this,
The superior person creates numbers and measures for restriction
And discusses a moral code for social conduct.

Yao Text

1. Initial Nine
   Not going out of the inner courtyard.
   No fault.

   Not going out of the inner courtyard.
   One knows when his time is smooth
   And when it is obstructed.

2. Second Nine
   Not going out of the outer courtyard.
   Misfortune.

   Not going out of the outer courtyard.
   Misfortune.
   He misses the crucial moment.

3. Third Six
   No restriction,
   Then laments and sighs.
   No one else is at fault.

   Laments and sighs over no restriction.
   Who should be blamed?

4. Fourth Six
   With ease, restriction.
   Prosperous and smooth.

   The prosperity and smoothness of restriction with ease.
   He accepts the way of the one above.

5. Fifth Nine
   Sweet restriction.
   Good fortune.
   Going forward: esteem.

   The good fortune of sweet restriction.
   He abides in the central place.

6. Top Six
   Bitter restriction.
   Being steadfast: misfortune.
   Regret vanishes.

   Bitter restriction.
   Being steadfast: misfortune.
   Its way comes to an end.

SIGNIFICANCE

The gua takes the image of water in a lake to illustrate that there is a need to regulate the excessiveness and insufficiency of water and applies the principle to adjusting right and wrong in human society. The nature of water is moving. When water is moving, it is fresh and clean, and when it stops, it becomes stagnant and stale. If the water moves without direction, it will be either wasted or exhausted. If it is dammed up without a plan, it will cause flood and calamity. The ancient Chinese accumulated experience in dealing with the Yellow River, which flooded once a year for thousands of years. Their experience was to dredge the riverbed and to guide the water, based upon the principle of adjusting its excessiveness and insufficiency, to control the rate of its flow. From this experience, they applied the principle of regulating rivers and watercourses to social affairs.

The lower gua is Lake. Water in the lake is rising. Beyond the third line, it will overflow. The upper gua is Water. The nature of water is to flow. When the water reaches the topmost line, it should stop. Otherwise flood and calamity will ensue. The message of the gua is that if there is too much water, one needs to take precautions against its flooding. If there is too little water, one should be concerned about possible drought. In our daily lives, we should strike a balance between excess and insufficiency and walk in the central path.

The host of the gua is the solid line at the fifth place. Only a person of supreme wisdom and one in an honorable place is able to adjust right and wrong and practice the Tao of restriction.

During King Wen's sitting in stillness he realized that after overcoming dispersion, people came together to work in full cooperation and with unity of purpose. It was time to promote restriction—to set limits to one's expenses and bounds on one's behavior. Promoting restraint would bring people and the government success, but painful restriction should not become common practice. The Duke of Zhou narrates different consequences of restriction. If either the government or the people do not observe restraint, it would create unhappiness. Peaceful restriction brings success and invites good fortune. Painful restriction results in misfortune.

(1) Initial Nine. Restricting alternates to Darkness (29)

The bottom line is a yang element at a yang place. One at this place is able to stand out among his fellows. However, during a time of restriction, he understands that it is not yet appropriate for him to do so. So he restrains himself and acts cautiously, not going beyond the courtyard. There is no fault. This line suggests that one should exercise restraint in what one says and be aware of what one is doing.

(2) Second Nine. Restricting alternates to Beginning (3)

The second line is a yang element at a yin place, central but not correct. It is time to go out to do something. But he does not. He thinks that his position is not correct, and he has no correspondent in the upper gua. He restricts himself to the outer courtyard. But he forgets that he is in the central place. He follows the principle dogmatically and loses the chance. Thus the Commentary says that he misses the crucial moment. There is misfortune.

(3) Third Six. Restricting alternates to Needing (5)

The third line is a yin element at a yang place, neither central nor correct. It is at the top of the lower gua, Lake. The water has reached its height, but one at this place knows no bounds. In the end he will lament and sigh. He creates his own reality; there is no one else to blame. Thus, Confucius says in his commentary, "Who should be blamed?"

(4) Fourth Six. Restricting alternates to Joyful (58) ☱

The fourth line is a correct yin element at a yin place. One at this place is gentle and docile. He follows the one at the supreme place, the fifth line, and understands the situation of restriction. So he accepts the restriction without having to make an effort.

(5) Fifth Nine. Restricting alternates to Approaching (19) ☱

The fifth line is at the supreme position, a king's place. He is the one referred to in the Commentary on the Decision where Confucius says, "Passing the danger with joy, carry out restriction in the proper position. From the central and correct place, his advance is without limitation." He accepts the situation of restriction pleasantly. He practices frugality and encourages people to live a thrifty life. Good fortune prevails. Advance will bring esteem.

(6) Top Six. Restricting alternates to Innermost Sincerity (61) ☱

The topmost line has reached the boundary of restriction. Excessive restriction makes one feel pain. Overdoing and being stubborn will bring misfortune. If one at this place realizes the error and will repent, then regret will disappear.

Additional Reference Information for This Gua

Image:	Water above, Lake below
Recite as:	Water in Lake, Restricting
Element:	Water
Structure:	Three yang with three yin
Month:	The seventh month of the lunar calendar, or August
Host of the Gua:	Fifth Nine
Opposite Gua:	Traveling (56) ☶
Inverse Gua:	Dispersing (59) ☴
Mutual Gua:	Nourishing (27) ☶

61

Zhong Fu •
Innermost
Sincerity

Xun • Wind
Dui • Lake

NAME AND STRUCTURE

Zhong means core, center, middle, or to hit the mark. Fu means sincerity, confidence, honesty, reliability, and trustworthiness. Literally, Zhong Fu means to hit the core of sincerity and trustworthiness.

Sequence of the Gua: *When restriction is established, then people will be trustworthy. Thus, after Restriction, Innermost Sincerity follows.*

Wilhelm translates Zhong Fu as Inner Truth, and Blofeld translates it as Inward Confidence and Sincerity. I use Innermost Sincerity.

The name of the gua is made up of two Chinese characters. The ideograph of the first character, zhong, is a picture of an arrow that hits the center and passes through a target. The rectangle represents the target and the vertical stroke, the arrow. Only an arrow passing through the target in the center can strike a balance, without pushing the target to the left or right. The second character, fu, is a picture of a hen hatching her little ones. At the top of the ideograph is a hen's claw, representing a hen. The lower part is a picture of a little one with arms stretching upward. An image of a hen hatching a chick was created to express sincerity and trustworthiness. In hatching chicks, the hen must be faithful to her obligation.

The structure of the gua is Wind ☴ above, Lake ☱ below—an image of the wind blowing over the water. The area above a lake is a wide-open space. When wind fills this space, the space appears empty, though it is full of the wind's energy. Similarly, sincerity comes from the heart and is

470

often more easily felt than seen. In ancient times, common people could not afford to offer big animals to worship the Lord of Heaven. They presented pigs and fishes in the spring and autumn. Because of their inner sincerity and trustworthiness, they were still bestowed blessing. Thus, King Wen says, "Innermost sincerity. Pigs and fishes. Good fortune."

From this gua Confucius gained insight concerning the principle of the Golden Mean. In his Doctrine of the Golden Mean, Confucius says,

> *Under Heaven, only the person possessing the most complete sincer-*
> *ity and trustworthiness is able to fully develop his true nature. If*
> *one is able to fully develop his true nature, he is able to fully develop*
> *the nature of other people. If one is able to fully develop the nature*
> *of other people, he is able to fully develop the nature of all creatures.*
> *In so doing, he is able to be involved in Heaven and Earth's trans-*
> *formational and nourishing functions and become one with Heaven*
> *and Earth.*

Decision on the Gua

Innermost Sincerity.
Pigs and fishes.
Good fortune.
Favorable to cross great rivers.
Favorable to be steadfast and upright.

Commentary on the Decision

Innermost Sincerity.
The yieldings are within,
And the solids obtain the central places.

Joy and humility, with innermost sincerity and trustworthiness.
One is able to transform a country.

Pigs and fishes.
Good fortune.
Innermost sincerity and trustworthiness turn pigs and fishes to
*   blessings.*

Favorable to cross great rivers.

The symbol looks like an empty boat.
Innermost sincerity and trustworthiness are favorable
With steadfastness and uprightness.
It responds to the principle of Heaven.

Commentary on the Symbol

Wind over Lake.
An image of Innermost Sincerity.
In correspondence with this,
The superior person judges criminal cases carefully
And postpones execution.

Yao Text

1. Initial Nine
   With ease and confidence:
   Good fortune.
   Seeking something else:
   No peace.

   With ease and confidence, good fortune.
   His original will does not change.

2. Second Nine
   A crane calling from a hidden place.
   Its young respond.
   "I have good wine.
   You and I share."

   Its young responds
   From the affection of the heart.

3. Third Six
   Confronts an adversary.
   Now beats the drum, now leaves off.
   Now sobs, now sings.

   Now beats the drum, now leaves off.
   The place is not appropriate.

4. Fourth Six
   The moon is nearly full.
   A pair of horses, lost one.
   No fault.

   A pair of horses, loses one.
   He leaves his companion, turning to the above.

5. Fifth Nine
   Innermost sincerity
   Links another, hand in hand.
   No fault.

   Innermost sincerity links another, hand in hand.
   His place is correct and appropriate.

6. Top Nine
   A cock's crow rises to Heaven.
   Being steadfast: misfortune.

   A cock's crow rises to Heaven.
   How can it last long?

SIGNIFICANCE

This gua expounds the principle of sincerity and trustworthiness. The ancient Chinese regarded these as the source of all virtues. Sincerity and trustworthiness draw people close together—they are the root of getting along with people. The structure of the gua is Wind ☴ above, Lake ☱ below. Wind represents the eldest daughter; Lake represents the youngest daughter. In this gua, the eldest and the youngest are in their appropriate positions. They love and trust each other. The nature of each is so harmonious with the other that one is gentle and the other joyous.

The two solid lines at the top represent Heaven, and the two solid lines at the bottom represent Earth. The two yielding lines in the middle represent human beings. Human beings receive nourishment from Heaven and Earth and inherit the nature of sincerity and trustworthiness. This is why Heaven and Earth created us. The broken lines in the middle resemble an open heart, free from prejudice and receptive to the truth. Either would be appropriate as host of the gua. However, since sincerity and trustworthiness need inner strength, the solid line at either the second or fifth place should be the host. The solid line at the fifth place is more suitable, because it is at the supreme position. The Yao Text of this gua is difficult to grasp. Five lines do not contain the name of the gua; only the fifth line does. Thus, there is no direct connection between the theme and the text of the gua.

During King Wen's sitting in stillness he felt happy that after promoting restraint in his country, people became accustomed to restricting their expenses as well as their behavior. They practiced setting limits with sincerity and trustworthiness. In this way, even presenting small offerings still brought good fortune. It was time to make further progress. The Duke of Zhou says that, being sincere and trustworthy, one should be at ease and confident. It should be as natural as a mother crane calling affectionately to her young. One should persist in being sincere and trustworthy. First beating the drum and then stopping is not the proper attitude. Being sincere and trustworthy, one is able to link with others in union. Overstatement is likened to a cock's crow mounting to Heaven; it is not practical and realistic. It only brings misfortune.

(1) Initial Nine. Innermost Sincerity alternates to Dispersing (59)

This line is a yang element at a yang place at the bottom of the gua. One at this place is sincere and trustworthy. The ancients believed that every infant possesses sincerity and trustworthiness. These virtues are part of human nature. All evils derive from negative social influences. On this ground, one at the bottom place must be sincere and trustworthy. If one is able to maintain these virtues, one can be relaxed and confident. There is good fortune. On the other hand, if one is seeking something other than sincerity and trustworthiness, one will not be at ease.

(2) Second Nine. Innermost Sincerity alternates to Increasing (42)

The second line takes the image of a crane calling from a hidden place to expound on the power of sincerity. The second line is the central line of the lower gua, Lake. In the I Ching, Lake also stands for autumn, when cranes call each other as they migrate. Although the second line does not correspond with the fifth line, they respond to each other. Because both are yang elements, they have a bond even if they are not close and cannot see each other; their sincerity and trustworthiness resonate, like cranes responding to each other. "I have good wine. You and I share" exemplifies the merits of sharing joy with one of like mind. The image of wine comes from the result when this line alternates to yin, forming the lower gua Thunder ☳, which is shaped like a wine cup.

(3) Third Six. Innermost Sincerity alternates to Little Accumulation (9) ☴

The third line is next to the fourth line. They are both yin. Thus, the Yao Text says, "Confronts an adversary." The third line is at the highest place of the lower gua, Lake. It responds to the yang element at the topmost place. These two lines have both reached the extreme, and they tend to alternate to their opposites. One at this place is in confusion—first beating the drum, then stopping; first sobbing, then singing. This line says that one should remain sincere and trustworthy to avoid being at a loss.

(4) Fourth Six. Innermost Sincerity alternates to Fulfillment (10) ☴

The fourth line is at a place next to the king. This is the highest position in the court, represented by the full moon. It corresponds to the yang element at the bottom, and the two lines are likened to a pair of horses. However, the one at this place decides to follow the one at the fifth line, because it is more sincere. In this way, it abandons the bottom one, who is less sincere. Thus the Yao Text says, "A pair of horses, lost one," and the commentary says, "He leaves his companion, turning to the above." This is the right thing to do in the situation.

(5) Fifth Nine. Innermost Sincerity alternates to Decreasing (41) ☶

The fifth line is in the supreme place. It is a yang element at a yang place, firm and substantial, and is the host of the gua, representing one who is sincere and trustworthy. The Commentary on the Decision says, "Joy and humility, with innermost sincerity and trustworthiness one is able to transform a country." This line responds with the yang element at the second place, which is also sincere and trustworthy. They link, forming a union, showing the importance of mutual sincerity and trustworthiness in bringing people together. It is unusual for two responding yang lines to form such a bond, but their complete sincerity makes this special relationship possible.

(6) Top Nine. Innermost Sincerity alternates to Restricting (60) ☵

The topmost line reaches the extreme of being sincere and trustworthy. One at this place is overconfident, strutting like a cock crowing; its call rises, but it is stuck on the ground. He cannot take a proper measure of himself. If he remains steadfast in his overconfidence, there will be misfortune. Any statement not stemming from sincerity and trustworthiness is like a cock's crow. It amounts to nothing.

Additional Reference Information for This Gua

Image:	Wind above, Lake below
Recite as:	Wind above Lake, Innermost Sincerity
Element:	Wood
Structure:	Four yang with two yin
Month:	The eleventh month of the lunar calendar, or December
Host of the Gua:	Fifth Nine
Opposite Gua:	Little Exceeding (62)
Inverse Gua:	Innermost Sincerity (61)
Mutual Gua:	Nourishing (27)

62
Xiao Guo ·
Little Exceeding

Zhen • Thunder
Gen • Mountain

NAME AND STRUCTURE

Xiao means small or little. Guo has a variety of meanings: to exceed, to pass, to cross, beyond the limit, after, fault, mistake, and others. The list is long. Wilhelm translates Xiao Guo as Preponderance of the Small. Blofeld translates it as The Small Get By. I use Little Exceeding.

Sequence of the Gua: *When people have sincerity and trustworthiness, surely they will carry it into practice. Thus, after Innermost Sincerity, Little Exceeding follows.*

In King Wen's Decision, Xiao Guo denotes Little Exceeding. When one takes action it is difficult to avoid overdoing it. In the Duke of Zhou's Yao Text, it denotes passing by.

The first ideograph of this gua, xiao, symbolizes little. There are three strokes: one curved to the left, one curved to the right, and one vertically positioned between the other two. It symbolizes an act of dividing. To the ancients, after things are divided, they become little. The second ideograph, guo, consists of two parts. Three curved strokes at the top left represent three footprints going forward. Underneath is the ideograph zhi, which means stop. On the right is the ideograph for guo; its function is to provide the sound of the character. It resembles the side view of a cross-section of a house. Two pillars stand on each side and a beam sits on the pillars. Underneath the beam is a tiny square representing a mouth, symbolizing a person. A person pictured underneath the beam and between the pillars shows that the structure is a house. Above the beam is an extra structure that gives the beam an extra load, symbolizing exceeding.

This gua is the inverse of the preceding one, Innermost Sincerity. Little Exceeding comes from being overly sincere and trustworthy. The structure of the gua is Thunder ☳ above, Mountain ☶ below. The ancients observed that the sound of thunder becomes weak when it is blocked by a mountain. In correspondence with this, they weighed the pros and cons of excess and insufficiency.

The gua itself is thought to resemble a bird. Two solid lines in the middle represent the body. Two yielding lines at the top and two more at the bottom represent the wings. This gua is a continuation of the previous gua, Zhong Fu. Fu is a hen hatching a little one. Now the chick has grown up. For a cock or hen, it is not favorable to fly upward. Flying downward is much easier and safer, and there is a place to rest. For this reason, the Commentary on the Decision says,

> *The flying bird leaves a message:*
> *Not appropriate to ascend,*
> *Appropriate to descend.*
> *Great good fortune!*

Each gua is composed of six lines. If three are yang and three are yin, they are in balance. Yang lines symbolize the strong; yin lines symbolize the weak. In Great Exceeding (28) ䷛, there are four yang lines and two yin lines. In this gua, there are four yin lines and two yang lines; thus, the little and weak exceeds the great and the gua is called Little Exceeding.

Decision

> Little Exceeding.
> Prosperous and smooth.
> Favorable to be steadfast and upright.
> Little affairs can be done,
> Not great affairs.
> A flying bird leaves a message:
> Not appropriate to ascend,
> Appropriate to descend.
> Great good fortune.

Commentary on the Decision

Little Exceeding.
The little ones exceed and proceed.
Favorable to be steadfast and upright
And to act in accord with the time.

The yieldings attain the central places.
There is good fortune in dealing with small affairs.
The solids are neither central nor correct.
Great affairs should not be dealt with.

There is an image of a flying bird.
The flying bird leaves a message:
Not appropriate to ascend,
Appropriate to descend.
Great good fortune!
To ascend is contrary to the situation;
To descend is in accord with the time.

Commentary on the Symbol

Thunder above Mountain.
An image of Little Exceeding.
In correspondence with this,
The superior person weighs the pros and cons of his conduct:
Excessive humility is better than excessive arrogance in behavior.
Excessive sorrow is better than excessive expense in a funeral.
Excessive frugality is better than excessive luxury in spending.

Yao Text

1. Initial Six
   Flying bird soars.
   Misfortune.

   Flying bird soars.
   Misfortune.
   Nothing can be done to avoid the misfortune.

2. Second Six
   Surpass one's grandfather,
   Meet one's grandmother.
   Do not pass superior to one's king;
   Meet one's subject.
   No fault.

   One cannot reach one's lord.
   The minister should not exceed the lord.

3. Third Nine
   Go not too far.
   Guard against this.
   Otherwise one might be injured: misfortune.

   Otherwise one might be injured.
   What a serious misfortune it is.

4. Fourth Nine
   There is no fault.
   Go not too far; meet instead.
   Going forward: adversity.
   Must be on guard.
   Do not act;
   Be perpetually steadfast and upright.

   Not going too far, meeting instead.
   The place is not appropriate.
   Going forward: adversity.
   Must be on guard.
   The situation cannot last long.

5. Fifth Six
   Clouds condense, yet no rain
   At my west side.
   The prince shoots,
   And hits it in the cave.

   Clouds condense, yet no rain.
   The cloud is already high.

6. Top Six
   Not meeting, going too far.

A flying bird falls upon calamity.
Misfortune.
This is what is called calamity and trouble.

Not meeting, going too far.
He is too haughty.

SIGNIFICANCE

Little Exceeding, the name of the gua, is difficult to grasp. The text does not define it clearly. Owing to the variety of meanings of the gua, different scholars hold different views. It is clear that in King Wen's Decision Xiao Guo denotes little exceeding. It is a warning against overdoing it. In the Duke of Zhou's Yao Text, it means passing by. In the Decision, there are two instances where the word "not" is used; the Yao Text uses "no" three times and "not" five times. Negatives occur in every Yao Text, except the first. Obviously, this gua is full of warnings.

King Wen's Decision says, "A flying bird leaves a message: not appropriate to ascend, appropriate to descend." Confucius's commentary reiterates the cautionary message: "To ascend is contrary to the situation; to descend is in accord with the time." Pay attention to this, and be very careful.

The structure of the gua, Thunder ☳ above, Mountain ☶ below, suggests that the sound of thunder is weakened by the blockage of the mountains. This gua displays the principle of weighing the pros and cons of excess and insufficiency. Generally, insufficiency is better than excess. For instance, undereating is better than overeating. When traffic laws limit the speed to fifty-five miles per hour and if one drives forty miles per hour, he loses only his time. If he exceeds the speed limit, he might have an accident or get a ticket. Moreover, King Wen suggested that only little affairs can be exceeded a little, never great affairs.

The host of the gua is the yielding line at the fifth place. In Chinese, the exact meaning of excess is going beyond the middle way. It violates the Doctrine of the Golden Mean. Small Exceeding is a time of transition. During transition, insufficiency is better than excess. Little affairs may be accomplished, but not great affairs.

During King Wen's sitting in stillness he had the insight that after people gained inner sincerity and trustworthiness they tended to overdo things. Experience told him that great exceeding made a ridgepole sag.

He realized that insufficiency was better than excess. One needed to be steadfast and upright to accomplish little affairs; then little affairs would accumulate and become great. A flying bird cannot fly all the time. It is proper to descend at times. The Duke of Zhou gives warning that if one soars too high, like a bird, it will bring misfortune. When meeting someone, one must be on guard to the danger of going too far. If one does not exercise self-restraint, the misfortune will be of one's own doing.

(1) Initial Six. Little Exceeding alternates to Abundance (55) ☰☰

The bottom line is a yin element at a yang place. Its attribute is weakness. It responds to the yang element at the fourth place. She wants to fly—there should be no problem. If she wants to reach what is beyond her grasp, however, it goes beyond little exceeding. If one does not practice restraint, there will be misfortune.

(2) Second Six. Little Exceeding alternates to Long Lasting (32) ☰☰

The second line is a yin element at a yin place, central and correct. In this gua, the yang element at the third place represents a father, and the yang element at the fourth place represents a grandfather. The yin element at the fifth place represents a grandmother. The second line responds with the fifth line. Thus the Yao Text says, "Surpass one's grandfather, meet one's grandmother." The second line responds to the fifth line but they do not correspond—they are both yin. The Yao Text says, "Do not pass superior to one's king; meet his subject." This is in accord with the Decision, "Not appropriate to ascend, appropriate to descend." Although one at this place is not able to reach the ones she wants to meet, she still gets the help she needs from another source.

(3) Third Nine. Little Exceeding alternates to Delight (16) ☰☰

The third line is a yang element at a yang place. It represents a firm and truthful person. He tends to march forward courageously. But the one with whom he corresponds is the topmost yin element, which is weak. One at this place should not go forward, not ascend. He should take extra precautions because the one at the fourth place can harm him.

(4) Fourth Nine. Little Exceeding alternates to Humbleness (15) ☰☰

The fourth line is a yang element at a yin place. One at this place is firm and gentle and does not overdo things. He corresponds to the yin element on the bottom, a little fellow who tends to ascend. Because the one here does not overreact, when they meet, there should be no fault; they complement each other. One must be on guard against overreacting; do not insist on being stubborn forever.

(5) Fifth Six. Little Exceeding alternates to Mutual Influence (31)

The first part of the Yao Text, "Clouds condense, yet no rain," is exactly the same as the Decision for Little Accumulation (9) . The fifth place is the supreme place, yet this is a yin element at a yang place—central but not correct. This one is gentle and magnanimous, she wants to do something for her people, but she is unable to do what she wants, because the time is not ripe. Thus, the Yao Text says, "Clouds condense, yet no rain." She responds to the yin element at the second place and needs its complete support if she is to shoot a bird in a cave. Unfortunately, they are both yin elements and do not correspond. The Yao Text does not mention good fortune or misfortune. The commentary on the Yao Text says, "The cloud is already high"; there is a chance of rain.

(6) Top Six. Little Exceeding alternates to Traveling (56)

The top line and the bottom line are the two wings of the bird. They are both yin. Both of them want to fly, to reach what is beyond their grasp. However, the bottom line is weak; if it does not use restraint, there will be misfortune. This line is at the top of the gua; it already reaches the extreme of Little Exceeding without obstruction. There is misfortune. From a lack of self-knowledge and restraint, she brings the misfortune on herself.

From the insight that the Yao Text of the fifth line of this gua repeats the Decision of Little Accumulation (9) , this gua, Little Exceeding, can be considered a summary of King Wen's experience related to the Lower Canon, the Tao of Humanity. The Decision of Little Accumulation says, "Clouds condense, yet no rain at my west side." It relates that King Wen was imprisoned in You-li prison by the Tyrant of Shang for seven years. King Wen realized that it was time for him to gather his strength and energy to overthrow the tyrant. King Wen's homeland, Zhou, was to the west of You-li. Thus, the Decision says, "no rain at my west side."

It is significant that the text of the Decision of Little Accumulation is repeated in the Yao Text of this gua. King Wen summarized his life experience earnestly, and he tirelessly instructed his descendants and his people that inner sincerity and restraint were the highest principles in life. During the course of his life, King Wen experienced the process of change and development, as layed out in the first gua, Initiating, from a hidden dragon to a flying dragon, from dragons without a chief to a true dragon. As a true dragon, he was the Son of Heaven. His obligation was to manifest the will of Heaven. What is the will of Heaven? It is to realize the wishes of the people. This is what "appropriate to descend" means. Furthermore, the central theme of Little Exceeding is to avoid overdoing things, to walk in the central path. King Wen initiated a brilliant and benevolent government. To undertake such a project is a difficult task, yet to maintain it is even more so. Thus, recalling the most arduous period in King Wen's life, we can summarize what he learned and what his advice would be to future generations:

> Be sincere and truthful,
> Walk in the central path,
> And act in accord with the proper situation and the right time.

After King Wen's son, King Wu, overthrew the Tyrant of Shang, it seemed that his destiny had been fulfilled. However, according to the Tao of I, this was just the moment that it became clear that it was not yet fulfilled.

Additional Reference Information for This Gua

Image:	Thunder above, Mountain below
Recite as:	Thunder above Mountain, Little Exceeding
Element:	Wood
Structure:	Four yin with two yang
Month:	The first month of the lunar calendar, or February
Host of the Gua:	Fifth Six
Opposite Gua:	Innermost Sincerity (61)
Inverse Gua:	Little Exceeding (62)
Mutual Gua:	Great Exceeding (28)

63
Ji Ji • Already Fulfilled

☵ Kan • Water
☲ Li • Fire

NAME AND STRUCTURE

Both Wilhelm and Blofeld translate Ji Ji as After Completion. In this book, Ji Ji is translated as Already Fulfilled. In Chinese, the original meaning of the first Ji is finishing a meal. Later, the meaning was extended to already or already finished. The ancient ideograph of this character inscribed on an oracle bone shows a person kneeling on the right with a food vessel on the left. The ideograph cast on a bronze cauldron from the Zhou dynasty shows the food vessel replaced with an ear of grain and the kneeling person substituted with a person standing by the grain with an open mouth. Originally the second Ji meant to cross a river. The left side of the second ideograph shows water flowing in a riverbed. On the right, there is a boat carrying three persons who are steering. Three people are pulling together to overcome a difficult situation, a picture of people helping each other get past an obstacle. Taken as a whole, the two parts of this ideograph mean to complete a course of action or to fulfill an achievement.

The structure of the gua is Water ☵ above, Fire ☲ below. It is characteristic of water to flow downward, while fire flames upward. The upward and downward movements mutually help each other. In this way, the water is boiled. This image denotes a perfect situation in which everything is right. This gua has a close connection to the eleventh gua, Tai, Advance ䷊, one of the most auspicious gua. The structure of Advance is Earth above, Heaven below. When the second and the fifth lines of Advance interchange, Advance ䷊ alternates to this gua. Here, all yang lines are in yang places, and all yin lines are in yin places. All lines are in equilibrium, and all movements are in the proper order. Thus, the gua represents a condition of balance, harmony, and absolute correctness. It is an ideal situation.

However, sages with profound experience had the insight that this was also a time of climax. Beyond the climax, every perfect condition alternates to its opposite. For this reason, the sages advised extreme caution. They understood that in a perfect situation there is still some imperfection. They purposefully made progress in small steps and achieved moderate success. They remained steadfast and upright. They acted to keep the good fortune at the beginning from becoming disorder in the end.

Already Fulfilled sounds like an auspicious gua, but King Wen's Decision is not terribly auspicious and the Duke of Zhou's Yao Text is filled with warnings. This is essential to the I Ching, showing the wisdom of the ancient Chinese. The delicacy of ancient Chinese wisdom evolved from the experience that only in intricate situations are changes possible. In Ji Ji, everything is too perfect. When people find themselves in perfect situations, when they have achieved their goals, they tend to lose focus and drive. That is why this gua, Already Fulfilled, cannot end the I Ching.

Sequence of the Gua: *Those who exceed others surely are able to fulfill their duty. Thus, after Little Exceeding, Already Fulfilled follows.*

Decision

> Already Fulfilled.
> Even the little,
> Being prosperous and smooth.
> Favorable to be steadfast and upright.
> Beginning: good fortune.
> End: disorder.

Commentary on the Decision

> *Already Fulfilled.*
> *Being prosperous and smooth.*
> *Only in little affairs is there prosperity and smoothness.*
>
> *Favorable to be steadfast and upright.*
> *Because the firm and the yielding are in correct places*
> *And correspondent to their proper ones.*

Beginning: good fortune,
For the yielding is in the central.
End: disorder.
There is no way out.

Commentary on the Symbol

Water over Fire.
An image of Already Fulfilled.
In correspondence with this,
The superior person contemplates the law of waxing and waning
And takes preventive measures against possible decline.

Yao Text

1. Initial Nine
   Dragging his wheels,
   Wetting his tail.
   No fault.

   Dragging his wheels.
   Cautious as this, there should be no fault.

2. Second Six
   Woman loses her ornaments.
   Do not pursue.
   In seven days, regained.

   In seven days, regained.
   It is in the central position.

3. Third Nine
   Emperor Gao Zong attacks the Gui Fang.
   Three years: conquered.
   Petty fellows should not be used.

   After three years he conquered them.
   He was exhausted.

4. Fourth Six
   Caulking the leak,
   There are rags.

All day long
On guard.

All day long on guard,
There is room for doubt.

5. Fifth Nine
The eastern neighbor slaughters an ox,
But does not attain as much blessing as the simple offering of
the western neighbor.

The eastern neighbor slaughters an ox;
Is not as much in accord with the time as the western neighbor
Who attains much blessing,
Because good fortune in great measure comes.

6. Top Six
Immersing one's head.
Adversity.

Immersing one's head: adversity.
How can one endure this for long?

SIGNIFICANCE

This gua outlines the Chinese way of dealing with a perfect situation. Generally, in a situation where everything has been fulfilled, people let the success turn their heads. They want more and more success. Only the ancient sages were aware that a time of perfection is also a time of climax. Beyond that, there will be a decline. The structure of the gua is Water ☵ above, Fire ☲ below. Fire boils water, but when the boiled water spills out of the pot, the fire might be quenched. Thus Confucius says, "In correspondence with this, the superior person contemplates the law of waxing and waning and takes preventive measures against possible decline." And King Wen warns us, "Beginning: good fortune. End: disorder."

The Chinese know that to undertake a project is difficult, but to maintain what has been achieved by oneself or one's forefathers or predecessors is even more so. When an undertaking reaches its climax, one should guide its course to another new achievement. That is why after Already Fulfilled there comes Not Yet Fulfilled. Where there is an ending, there is also a beginning. The ending is not really Already Fulfilled—it is Not

Yet Fulfilled. The host of the gua is the yielding line at the second place. Confucius's Commentary on the Decision says, "Beginning: good fortune, for the yielding is in the central."

During King Wen's sitting in stillness he reflected on the past in light of the present. The rise and decline of the Shang dynasty gave him insight. The Chinese believe that every entity has a predetermined lifespan that cannot be altered. The destiny of the Shang was already fulfilled; it could no longer accomplish great affairs, only little ones. The Duke of Zhou notes that the Shang dynasty had gone through different stages of progress and success. After Emperor Gao Zong conquered the Gui Fang, a tribe in northern China, he eliminated the petty men in his court, which is compared to caulking the leak of a boat with ragged clothes and staying on guard all day long. This ushered in a period of good times. The Shang worked very hard and enjoyed the fruits of their labors. Then the tide turned. They became spoiled by success, which is likened to a woman who is so rich that she does not bother to recover her lost valuables. The whole ruling class of the Shang wallowed in sensual pleasures, as if immersing their heads in water. Danger was not far ahead.

(1) Initial Nine. Already Fulfilled alternates to Hardship (39) ☷☵

The initial line is a yang element at a yang place. It symbolizes a firm and steadfast character. This element corresponds to the yin element at the fourth place which is at the bottom of the upper gua, Water ☵. In the I Ching, Water also represents the wheel of a cart. Lord Zi Chan of the Kingdom of Zheng, during the Spring and Autumn Period (722–480 B.C.) of the Zhou dynasty, helped someone ford a river by cart. He asked his servants to hold the wheels in order to control the cart. This is a warning for one to take precautions at an initial stage of an undertaking. Another story tells that the ancient sage saw a fox crossing a river. The fox was careful and lifted its tail to avoid getting it wet, though the water turned out to be too deep and its tail got wet anyway. The emphasis here is on being careful: one can do no more than take precautions, then accept whatever consequences follow. Thus, Confucius says, "Cautious as this, there should be no fault."

(2) Second Six. Already Fulfilled alternates to Needing (5) ☵☰

The second line is a yin element at a yin place, central and correct. It corresponds to the yang element at the fifth place. Everything seems to be in order. However, as discussed above, in his Commentary on the

Decision Confucius says "Beginning: good fortune . . . end: disorder." The Yao Text says, "Woman loses her ornaments. Do not pursue." Like the woman who is too rich to pursue her valuables, trouble lies ahead. In Chinese, this line is fu (a woman) sang (losing) qi (her) fu (ornaments), wu (don't) zhu (pursue). Here, most English translations translate the second fu as "veil." However, in ancient times, this fu was a simplified form of "ornaments." The mutual gua are Fire over Water. Water also symbolizes a veil, which is where the interpretation of "veil" comes from. In ancient China, a veil was either a covering over a woman's face or the curtain of a carriage. It was ancient custom that when a woman went out, she hid herself in a carriage with curtains. If this line means that the woman loses her veil, she cannot go forward. She has to wait for seven days, representing a period of time, a cycle. However, in the context of this gua, it is more appropriate to translate the second fu as ornaments.

(3) Third Nine. Already Fulfilled alternates to Beginning (3)

This line is a yang element at a yang place. Its attribute is firm and strong. Historical events were employed to describe the situation of this line. Emperor Gao Zong (reigned 1324–1266 B.C.) was a brilliant king of the Shang dynasty. The Gui Fang were the ancestors of the Huns, an ancient people from northern China. Gao Zong conducted a punitive expedition against them, and after three years he conquered them. The emperor bestowed rewards upon those who had great merit, but he did not employ persons with mean character no matter how much they had contributed. This line indicates that approaching success is not easy. One should take preventive measures against possible trouble, on one hand, and carefully take actions to make one's own plans work out, on the other. Confucius says, "After three years he conquered them. He was exhausted." This is a warning never to use force lightly.

(4) Fourth Six. Already Fulfilled alternates to Abolishing the Old (49)

The theme of this gua is crossing a river. The fourth line is about to cross a river. In ancient times when a boat was leaking, padded jackets with ragged cotton were used to plug the leak. The commentary says, "All day long on his guard." Being watchful is the key to avoiding accidents. This line is a yin element correctly positioned at a yin place. Its attribute is being careful and attentive. One at this place should heed what Confucius says in his Commentary on the Symbol, "The superior person contemplates the law of waxing and waning and takes preventive measures against a possible decline."

(5) Fifth Nine. Already Fulfilled alternates to Brilliance Injured (36)

This line is at the supreme position of this gua. A profound analogy gives warning to one in this position. There are two neighbors offering sacrifices at the same time. One slaughters an ox, and the other practices a simple ceremony with utmost sincerity. One who offers a simple sacrifice gains more blessing than one who slaughters an ox.

This line is a yang element at a yang place, central and correct. It symbolizes a person who has achieved his goal. This is the climax of a situation that is fulfilled. One at this place becomes proud and loses enthusiasm to produce achievements. According to the I Ching, east is a yang direction. The solid line at the fifth place is a yang element, representing the eastern neighbor who slaughters an ox for the offering. The yielding line at the second place symbolizes the western neighbor, who is humble, enthusiastic, and productive and can dedicate only his own sincerity to the offering. Spring is not a harvest season—it is not appropriate to slaughter an ox. The essence of offering is truthfulness and sincerity, not material things. Thus, the western neighbor receives more blessing. It is believed that the eastern neighbor refers to the brutal Tyrant of Shang. The western neighbor is King Wen, who was sincere and magnanimous. Before the Zhou dynasty took over the Shang dynasty, King Wen was titled the Lord of the West.

(6) Top Six. Already Fulfilled alternates to Household (37)

This line is at the top of the upper gua, Water, thus the Yao Text says, "Immersing his head." This topmost yin line is at a yin place. One at this place is weak; if one were to take the risk of crossing the river, it would be like a fox immersing its head in the water. How can one endure this for long? There is danger. This line indicates the end of a cycle. When one's initial success has reached the final stage, one should maintain one's success but prepare for a new beginning.

Additional Reference Information for This Gua

Image:	Water above, Fire below
Recite as:	Water over Fire, Already Fulfilled
Element:	Water
Month:	The tenth month of the lunar year, or November
Structure:	Three yang with three yin
Host of the Gua:	Second Six
Opposite Gua:	Not Yet Fulfilled (64)
Inverse Gua:	Not Yet Fulfilled (64)
Mutual Gua:	Not Yet Fulfilled (64)

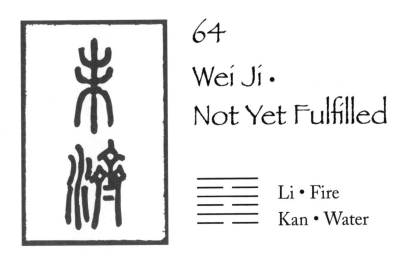

64
Wei Ji •
Not Yet Fulfilled

Li • Fire
Kan • Water

NAME AND STRUCTURE

Both Wilhelm and Blofeld translate this gua as Before Completion. In this translation I give it as Not Yet Fulfilled. This gua is the inverse as well as the opposite of the preceding gua, Already Fulfilled. Wei means not yet, and ji originally meant "cross a river." Later on, the meaning was extended to encompass from here to there, then, or from beginning to end. More recently, it has come to mean to be completed or to be fulfilled. When these two characters are put together, they mean Not Yet Fulfilled.

The ideograph of wei is meticulous—it looks simple, yet its meaning is profound. The stem of the ideograph is a tree, mu. A second curved stroke was added through the tree and thus the ideograph of wei was created. Without the horizontal stroke we have a picture of a tree with its roots growing downward and its branches growing upward. The horizontal stroke represents the ground. The portion of the tree underneath the ground is still alive. It has already grown to its full height (fulfilled its growth), and now it starts a new cycle of growth. The structure of the ideograph supplies a vivid picture of having achieved one's goal, but not yet having been fulfilled. There is a new cycle to come. The meaning of the ideograph of ji, fully explained in the previous gua, signifies crossing a river, from here to there, or from beginning to end.

Sequence of the Gua: *The succession of events never ends. Thus, after Already Fulfilled, at the end, Not Yet Fulfilled follows.*

It is a natural phenomenon that after waxing comes waning; before fullness there was emptiness. Therefore, Already Fulfilled is the end of Not Yet Fulfilled; it is also the beginning of a new cycle of Not Yet Fulfilled. The structure of the gua is Fire ☲ above, Water ☵ below. The nature of fire is flaming upward, and the nature of water is flowing downward. Their actions move in opposite directions and dissociate. This movement signifies a difficult situation.

This gua has a close relationship with the twelfth gua, Hindrance ䷋, which is Heaven above, Earth below. When the positions of the second and fifth lines of Hindrance are interchanged, Hindrance alternates to this gua, Not Yet Fulfilled. Here, all yang lines are at yin places, and all yin lines are at yang places. There is no perfect equilibrium and no absolute correctness, yet there is still balance. That is, all the lines are in a harmonious relationship with one another. This configuration denotes a difficult time, a time of confusion, but there is still a promise of success. It is the beginning of a new cycle, a transition from disorder to order. There is a responsibility for one to bring the disordered situation back to order. Thus Confucius's Commentary on the Symbol says, "The superior person discriminates carefully the nature of things and keeps each of them in its proper position."

Decision

Not Yet Fulfilled.
Prosperous and smooth.
Little fox, almost across the river,
Wets its tail.
Nothing is favorable.

Commentary on the Decision

Not Yet Fulfilled.
There is prosperity and smoothness,
For the yielding attains the central place.

Little fox, almost across the river.
It is not yet past the central line.

Wets its tail. Nothing is favorable.
There is no continuation at the end.

Although all lines are not in their proper place,
Yet the strong and the weak still correspond to each other.

Commentary on the Symbol

Fire over Water.
An image of Not Yet Fulfilled.
In correspondence with this,
The superior person discriminates carefully the nature of things
And keeps each of them in its proper position.

Yao Text

1. Initial Six
   Wetting one's tail.
   Humiliation.

   Wet one's tail.
   Overlook one's limitation.

2. Second Nine
   Dragging one's wheels.
   Being steadfast and upright: good fortune.

   Good fortune of the second nine.
   It is centered and in accord with proper actions.

3. Third Six
   Not yet fulfilled.
   Moving forward: misfortune.
   Favorable to cross great rivers.

   Not yet fulfilled.
   Moving forward: misfortune.
   Its position is not appropriate.

4. Fourth Nine
   Being steadfast and upright: good fortune.
   Regret vanishes.
   Attacks the Gui Fang like thunder.
   Three years:
   Rewards come from a great kingdom.

Being steadfast and upright:
Good fortune.
Regret disappears.
His will is fulfilled.

5. Fifth Six
Being steadfast and upright: good fortune.
No regret.
The light of a superior person,
Being sincere and truthful: good fortune.

The light of the superior person.
Good fortune comes from his diffusion of brightness.

6. Top Nine
Being sincere and truthful
While drinking wine.
No fault.
Immersing one's head,
Being sincere and truthful,
Loses correctness.

Drinking wine and wetting one's head.
One knows no self-control.

SIGNIFICANCE

This gua ends the sixty-four gua and the three hundred and eighty-six yao of the I Ching. But the principle of change continues without end. Events in the universe move forward and alternate in cycles. The stage of Not Yet Fulfilled will gradually reach the stage of Already Fulfilled. The stage of Already Fulfilled is merely the fulfillment of certain events or of a certain stage in a cycle of events. If some occurrences have reached the stage of Already Fulfilled, there are always others that are Not Yet Fulfilled. The stage of Already Fulfilled is also the stage of Not Yet Fulfilled. The stage of Not Yet Fulfilled is the beginning, like the dark before the dawn. The I Ching starts with Qian, the Initiating, and ends with Wei Ji, Not Yet Fulfilled. When the development of events reaches the end of a cycle, Already Fulfilled, then another cycle, Not Yet Fulfilled, begins. In this way, the cycles of change and development repeat endlessly.

This gua, Not Yet Fulfilled, indicates a situation in which disorder

at first takes a dominant position and is eventually replaced by order. This is just the opposite of the preceding gua, Already Fulfilled, which says "Beginning: good fortune. End: disorder." In Not Yet Fulfilled, the yielding line in the outer gua represents the transition from a time of disorder to order. Thus, Confucius's Commentary on the Decision says, "Not Yet Fulfilled. There is prosperity and smoothness, for the yielding attains the central place." The host of the gua is the yielding line at the fifth place. This yielding line is what Confucius refers to in saying that the yielding attains the central place.

A transition from disorder to order is representative of the I Ching as a whole, as well. In the beginning it swings from extreme to extreme, with six yang lines in Initiating changing to six yin lines in Responding, with no balance in between. By the time it reaches the final gua, Already Fulfilled and Not Yet Fulfilled, a perfect state of balance has been achieved, with three yin lines and three yang lines gently alternating back and forth.

During King Wen's sitting in stillness he reflected on the past in light of the present. The destiny of the Shang dynasty had been fulfilled. The destiny of the Zhou was not yet fulfilled. Its situation was like that of the little fox who had almost crossed a river. There was success in store, and nothing was unfavorable. The Duke of Zhou records the rise of the Zhou dynasty. At the beginning it encountered hindrance, likened to dragging one's wheels and getting one's tail wet. King Wen proceeded with utter caution. After the Zhou helped the Shang defeat the Gui Fang, regret disappeared and good fortune reined. Being truthful and faithful in establishing alliances and setting up feudal lords, even while drinking wine, still brought good fortune and no fault.

(1) Initial Six. Not Yet Fulfilled alternates to Diversity (38) ☷

The Yao Text of the initial line and the second line of this gua, Not Yet Fulfilled, share the same subject as the initial two lines of the preceding gua, Already Fulfilled. The initial line, at the bottom of the gua, is like the tail of a fox at the end of its body. This line is a yin element at a yang place, neither central nor correct. Weakness is its attribute. One positioned at the beginning of Not Yet Fulfilled is not able to cross the river, unlike her counterpart in the previous gua. If she tries, her tail might get wet, meaning that if one overlooks one's limitations, one suffers humiliation. Comparing this Yao Text with the initial Yao Text of the previous gua, we can see that there is a fine line between bravely and carefully moving forward and foolishly getting in over one's head.

(2) Second Nine. Not Yet Fulfilled alternates to Proceeding Forward (35)

The second line refers to the time of difficulty before success. It is a yang element at a yin place, central but not correct. Although it corresponds to the yin element at the fifth place, that element is weak. Thus, one at the second place has no choice but to rely on himself. Owing to his central position and strong character, he is able to act correctly and be steadfast and upright, symbolized by dragging one's wheels. Dragging one's wheels means digging in, not parading about and striving to outshine others. In so doing, there is good fortune.

(3) Third Six. Not Yet Fulfilled alternates to Establishing the New (50)

The Yao Text of this line says, "Not yet fulfilled. Moving forward: misfortune. Favorable to cross great rivers." There appears to be a contradiction between the two sentences—one would ask: If proceeding now would bring misfortune, how can it still be favorable to cross the great river? My interpretation would be that one must be *extremely* cautious as one proceeds, because of the structure of the gua.

According to the structure, the third line is positioned between the upper gua and the lower gua; it has reached a turning point. The third line is also at the top of the lower gua, Water. Although Water represents danger, and at this place has already reached the verge of the danger, one is about to leave the area of danger. Moreover, the third line is a yin element at a yang place. It is neither central nor correct and has, in fact, gone beyond the center. One in this position should consider this specific condition; it is better not to take any risky action. She should be extremely cautious; only then will she safely arrive at the other shore.

(4) Fourth Nine. Not Yet Fulfilled alternates to Childhood (4)

The fourth line has moved out of the lower gua, Water/Darkness, into the upper gua, Fire/Brightness. In this situation, one is able to finish one's task. Yet the fourth line is a yang element at a yin place. It is neither central nor correct. This is the regret. Remaining steadfast and upright dissolves regret and invites good fortune. Since this one is in an incorrect place, it suggests that it is difficult for him to remain steadfast and upright. He should make a determined effort to mobilize his strength and spirit, as in attacking the Gui Fang tribe over a long period of time. Only then will he fulfill his will. The message of this gua is that before the success of a venture one should remain steadfast and upright, mobilize his strength and spirit, and make a great and sustained effort to fulfill one's goal.

(5) Fifth Six. Not Yet Fulfilled alternates to Contention (6)

The fifth line is a yin element at a yang place. Although this is the supreme position, it is not appropriate for her. Fortunately, one at this place is gentle and humble and corresponds to the yang element at the second place, who is a powerful supporter. Thus, remaining steadfast and upright will bring good fortune. Moreover, the upper gua is Fire, the Light. The fifth line is in the center of the Light, suggesting that she is able to be bright and virtuous. Thus the Yao Text says that the light of the superior person is sincere and truthful. There is good fortune.

(6) Top Nine. Not Yet Fulfilled alternates to Relief (40)

Here the text employs an analogy to express the meaning of this gua. It says, "Being sincere and truthful while drinking wine. No fault." Here, drinking wine is for enjoyment, not for indulging in sensual pleasures. One at this place has come to the end of an unfulfilled situation, yet sooner or later it will be fulfilled. A wise person pays special attention at the moment just before success is achieved. By understanding that after darkness there will be light, then, while enjoying drinking wine, one still remains steadfast and upright. There is no fault. When success is near at hand, most people get dizzy at the prospect. When one loses self-restraint, one might run into trouble. Thus, Confucius warns: "Drinking wine and wetting one's head. One knows no self-control."

Additional Reference Information for This Gua

Image:	Fire above, Water below
Recite as:	Fire over Water, Not Yet Fulfilled
Element:	Fire
Month:	The eleventh month of the lunar year, or December
Structure:	Three yang with three yin
Host of the Gua:	Fifth Six
Opposite Gua:	Already Fulfilled (63)
Inverse Gua:	Already Fulfilled (63)
Mutual Gua:	Already Fulfilled (63)

A Brief History of the Zhou Dynasty

Many of the references and judgments in the I Ching are based on the events that led up to the founding of the Zhou dynasty in 1066 B.C. To truly understand the I Ching, it is helpful to be familiar with the following background information.

The original Zhou people were an agricultural tribe that lived in the province presently known as Shaanxi in central China. Qi, their leader, taught them how to farm the land. They called him King Millet and revered him as the god of agriculture. They engaged in farming for generation after generation and flourished. Many generations later they were invaded by foreign tribes and their leader, Lord Tan Fu, relocated the tribe to a place called Zhou at the foot of Mount Ji. People from all around brought their families to seek shelter under Lord Tan Fu's magnanimous rule, and Zhou's population greatly increased. Lord Tan Fu abolished the old slave system and reestablished the ancient commune system. The tribe became prosperous and strong, and became known as Tribe Zhou. They built city walls and houses to hold those who came and established counties. Zhou became a state.

Lord Tan Fu was succeeded by his son Ji Li. Under Ji Li, Zhou became very formidable. The king of the Shang dynasty felt threatened and killed Ji Li. After that, Ji Li's son ruled Zhou with extreme humility and caution for fifty years. In his later years he was known as the Western Lord, and posthumously as King Wen.

King Wen ruled Zhou as magnanimously as his grandfather had. He gained influence among all the vassal states. When there was a dispute among the states the rulers would bring it before King Wen; a wise and fair settlement could always be assured. Emperor Yi of the Shang dynasty married off his daughter to King Wen with her niece as consort. King Wen and his wives dressed as plainly as the common people and worked in the field alongside them. He understood the toilsome lives of his people. To replenish his people's productivity and spirit, King Wen abolished the remnants of the slave system and gave land to the people. The initial stages of a feudal system were established. Slaves of the Shang dynasty and neighboring states escaped to Zhou for shelter.

At the time of the Tyrant of Shang, King Wen was summoned to serve at the tyrant's court. He pleaded with the Tyrant to relieve the unbearable burdens of his people several times, but was rejected. Eventually King Wen was imprisoned for seven years, during which time he realized that there was no way to change the tyranny of the Shang dynasty. After he was released King Wen devoted himself to establishing feudal lords, preparing to overthrow the Tyrant of Shang. At the same time, he brought civilization to the outlying uncivilized tribes. In his old age, his influence extended over two thirds of China. The stage was set for the overthrow of the Tyrant.

King Wu, King Wen's eldest son, followed his father's unfulfilled wish by calling two gatherings to form an alliance. Over eight hundred lords came to the first gathering. They urged King Wu to move against the tyrant, but King Wu decided that the time was not right and continued to make preparations for another two years. In the first lunar month of 1066 B.C., King Wu held a ceremony offering sacrifices to the spirit of King Wen and, carrying King Wen's memorial tablet, launched an expedition against the Tyrant of Shang. The eight hundred lords came again with four thousand chariots. After two months the troops captured the capital of Shang. Many soldiers of Shang defected to King Wu's side. The Tyrant was overthrown.

Even after King Wu overthrew the Shang dynasty there was no peace. Internally, the ruling class of the Shang resisted and demanded counter-attack. Externally, there were ninety-nine minor states and six hundred and fifty-two lords to be subdued.

Returning victorious, King Wu selected a place known as Gao to be his capital. He proclaimed himself King Wu, revered his father as King Wen, and appointed his brother, The Duke of Zhou, as Prime Minister. The Zhou dynasty was established. For the first time in Chinese history all of China was united.

In the eighth month of 1066 B.C. King Wu became ill. Two years later he passed away. His son, King Cheng, succeeded him. Because King Cheng was young the Duke of Zhou acted as regent. The slave owners of the Shang, allied with clans in the east, seized the opportunity to rebel. The Duke of Zhou launched a punitive expedition and, after putting down the rebellion, founded an Eastern Capital at a place known as Lo in the province presently called Henan. He established a feoffment system, investing the nobility with hereditary titles and territories. At the same time he established institutions and regulations, composed music, and encouraged social etiquette. Zhou became more prosperous than ever and thrived for centuries.

In 256 B.C. the Zhou dynasty was overthrown by the Chin dynasty. In all, it had passed through thirty-four kings and lasted over eight hundred years.

About the Author

Born in 1921, Master Alfred Huang is a professor of Taoist philosophy, former Dean of Students at Shanghai University, and a third-generation master of Wu-style Tai Chi Chuan, Chi Kung, and Oriental Meditation, with more than 70 years of experience.

His initial teacher of Taoist philosophy and I Ching was his grandfather. In his youth Master Huang did not understand books written in ancient Chinese, so he could not read or access the I Ching directly. His grandfather gave him his first basic instruction on the text, and later on he relied on Richard Wilhelm's excellent English translation. During the Japanese invasion, when all schools in China were closed, he had a private tutor who taught him ancient Chinese, allowing him to understand the deeper meaning behind the original text. It was not until years later, when he met some of China's most eminent masters, most notably Master Yin, that he began to actually enter into the Gate of the I Ching.

In 1957, after proposing some improvements to the Communist Party members' undemocratic working style, he was labeled an ultra-Rightist and sentenced to "House Arrest" for "reeducation" through hard manual labor. Nine years later, at the very beginning of the Cultural Revolution, he was imprisoned and sentenced to death. During his combined 22 years of house arrest and imprisonment, Master Huang meditated on the I Ching and found the strength to survive.

In 1979, China's Supreme Court proclaimed Master Huang innocent. He was released from prison weighing only 80 pounds. He then emigrated to the United States where he discovered that no I Ching existed in English that emphasized the unity of Heaven and humanity and the Tao of Change, as the Chinese text does. *The Complete I Ching* is the result of his desire to bring the authentic Classic of Change to the West.

In *The Complete I Ching*, Master Huang not only emphasizes the unity of Heaven and humanity and the Tao of Change but also, and even more important, he includes translations of the Ten Wings, the commentaries by Confucius that are essential to the I Ching's insights. Previous English translations have either given these commentaries a minor place in the book or have left them out altogether. But the Chinese say that the I Ching needs the Ten Wings to fly, and with the Ten Wings restored to their central place by Master Huang, the I Ching at last flies in English.

Master Huang is also the author of *The Numerology of the I Ching*, *Dragon Flying in the Sky*, *Creating a Better Future*, and *The Complete Tai Chi*. In addition to his writing, in 1981 Master Huang founded New Harmony, a nonprofit organization devoted to the pursuit of total community well-being through the promotion of health and the prevention of illness on the physical, mental, emotional, and spiritual levels. New Harmony is currently based in Maui, Hawaii, where Master Huang has lived since 1987.

At age 89 Master Huang is still healthy and sound, and he has plans for many more I Ching books to come!

Glossary

Accomplished Gua: The six-line gua. It is formed by combining two primary gua. It is the main gua used for divination, indicating one's present situation.

Approached Gua: The gua formed after a moving line in the accomplished gua alternates from yin to yang or yang to yin. It indicates one's future tendency or potential.

Carry: A line "carries" the line above it, as a horse carries a rider. It is considered auspicious for a yin line to carry a yang line, supporting it. Compare *Mount.*

Central: The middle place of the lower or the upper gua, i.e., the second or fifth places. It is considered auspicious.

Correct: A line in an appropriate position. A yang line at the initial, third, or fifth places is correct. A yin line at any of these places is incorrect. A yin line at the second, fourth, or top places is correct. A yang line at any of these places is incorrect. For instance, in ☲ all the lines are correct; in ☷ they are all incorrect.

Correspond: The relationship between places in a gua. The initial and fourth places, the second and fifth places, and the third and top places correspond to each other. See also *Respond.*

Element: By observing the patterns of the natural world and comprehending the never-ending interplay between all things, the ancient Chinese developed a system of five elements to explain the energetic balances that composed the world. These five elements—Water, Fire, Metal, Wood, and Earth—existed in a compact of mutual promotion and restraint within a continuous process of transformation. The original text of the I Ching does not mention the five elements. During the Han dynasty (206 B.C. to A.D. 220) the Symbol and Numerology School of the I Ching began to integrate the gua with the five elements and many other systems. I indicate the element associated with each gua in the Additional Reference Information tables for those who would like to work with this system in their divinations.

Gua: Hexagram or trigram, a six-line or three-line symbol.

Host: A host is the principal yao of a gua, the one on which the divination focuses. In the eight primary gua, the hosts of Heaven ☰, Earth ☷, Water ☵, and Fire ☲ lie in the central place; the hosts of Wind ☴ and Thunder ☳ lie on the bottom; and the hosts of Lake ☱ and Mountain ☶ lie on top.

Each six-yao gua also has a host which represents the central theme of the gua. Being the host of a gua, the yao should be virtuous and appropriate at the right time and the right position. In most cases the host resides at the second or the fifth place, because these two places are central, most favorable in the I Ching. As the fifth place is superior to the second place, it is the most frequent host.

The host of Initiating (1) ☰ is the yang element at the fifth place. Firm, vital, central, and correct, it inherits the pure yang energy from Heaven and is most appropriate to be the host.

The host of Responding (2) ☷ is the yin element at the second place. Yielding, submissive, central, and correct, it inherits the pure yin energy from Earth and deserves the position of a host.

Occasionally a yin element at the fifth place can be the host. Although it is not correct to have a yin element at the fifth place, there are certain gua where this yao clearly represents the central theme. The host of Great Harvest (14) ☲ is the yin element at the fifth place, surrounded by five yang elements that respond to it. The Commentary on the Decision says, "The yielding obtains the honored position, great and central. The upper and the lower respond. So the name of Great Harvest comes." Great Harvest is a well-known auspicious gua.

Certain gua have more than one host. There are two hosts in the third gua, Beginning ☳. Both of Beginning's two yang elements are correct. The initial one represents the beginning of a situation and is thus particularly significant for this gua. The yang element at the fifth, superior place represents the ultimate realization of goals begun in this gua. Both yao are key, and both serve as hosts.

Inner Gua: See *Lower Gua*.

Inverse: When the six lines of a gua are written in reverse order, an inverse gua is obtained. The inverse of ☱ is ☴.

Judgment: Divinations in the I Ching result in judgments of good fortune and misfortune, some conditional, some absolute, but all the result of one's subjective intention and objective action. The I Ching is not a superstitious book; it always puts the responsibility for one's fate solely on one's actions. There are six principal judgments of good fortune and misfortune: adversity, fault, good fortune, humiliation, misfortune, and regret. Obviously, with five negative judgments and only one positive one, bad fortune is much more frequent than good fortune. Because of this, Confucius advised, "think thrice before you act."

> **Adversity:** Adversity is between misfortune and regret; one's situation is difficult and dangerous, but if one is able to be alert and cautious and improve oneself, the outcome can still be good.

> **Fault:** Fault causes hardship and trouble. If one is able to correct one's mistake and amend the fault, the situation can be saved.

> **Good Fortune:** Auspicious. The outlook is good.

> **Humiliation:** Humiliation brings suffering and distress. It also indicates hindrance and annoyance. If one continues one's evil ways and refuses to repent, misfortune will result.

> **Misfortune:** Misfortune may happen suddenly and unexpectedly. It may result from carelessness, negligence, or bad judgment. The outlook is not good.

> **Regret:** Regret often refers to a fault one has made. With this judgment, the situation is salvageable. If one realizes the error in one's ways and decides to correct one's behavior, the outlook can still be good. "Regret vanishes" indicates that repentance rights the situation.

Lower Gua: The lower three-line symbol, also known as the inner gua.

Message Gua: See *Tidal Gua*.

Mount: A line "mounts" the line beneath it, as a rider mounts a horse. It is considered auspicious for a yang line to mount a yin line, governing it. Compare *Carry.*

Moving Line: The line of an accomplished gua that is about to alternate from yang to yin or vice-versa. It also indicates the particular stage of a situation that you are in.

Mutual Gua: The six-line gua formed by the lower mutual gua (the second, third, and fourth lines of the accomplished gua) and the upper mutual gua (the third, fourth, and fifth lines). It gives the hidden meaning of each accomplished gua.

Neighbors: Lines adjacent to one another are called neighbors. If one line is yang and the other yin, they form a close bond called "holding together." It is especially important for the fourth and fifth lines to hold together, because the fifth represents a leader and the fourth represents his minister.

Opposite: When each line of a six-line gua alternates to its opposite, that is, from yin to yang or from yang to yin, an opposite gua is formed. The opposite of ☷ is ☰.

Outer Gua: See *Upper Gua.*

Place: The position of each line. Lines are counted from the bottom to the top, beginning with the "initial" place and counting up to the "top" place. The top place is for a sage or a hermit; someone retired from human affairs. The fifth place is generally the position for a king or a ruler. The fourth place is for a minister or adviser. Because it is close to the ruler, caution is required. The third place is a place of transition—from the inner situation to the outer situation. It is an insecure position. The second place is usually for an official or general. It is a favorable position if one is not directly controlled by the ruler (fifth line) and has interests in common with the ruler. The initial place is for someone who is about to enter or has not yet entered society, or who has little power over a situation for some other reason.

Primary Gua: The three-line gua.

Radical: The root of a Chinese character, generally modified by a second character. For example, each character related to water, such as lake, ocean, tear, soup, etc., has the character for water ☵ on the left side, modified by a second character on the right.

Respond: Complementary lines (yin and yang) at corresponding places *respond* to each other. In the I Ching, opposites attract. If the initial and fourth places, the second and fifth places, or the third and top places are a yin and yang pair, they respond to each other and work well together. For instance, in ䷀ all corresponding lines respond to each other. In ䷁ none do. The responding of the second and fifth lines is most important. See also *Correspond.*

Solar Terms: The Chinese divide the year into twenty-four solar terms, each named for a natural phenomenon that best represents that part of the year. The solar terms are:

Beginning of Spring	Beginning of Autumn
Rain Water	Limit of Heat
Waking of Insects	White Dew
Spring Equinox	Autumnal Equinox
Pure Brightness	Cold Dew
Grain Rain	Frost's Descent
Beginning of Summer	Beginning of Winter
Grain Full	Slight Snow
Grain in Ear	Great Snow
Summer Solstice	Winter Solstice
Slight Heat	Slight Cold
Great Heat	Great Cold

Tidal Gua: The twelve tidal gua, also known as the twelve message gua, are the twelve accomplished gua that represent the waxing and waning of yin and yang energy over the course of a year. Each is associated with a month. See page 182 for a chart of the tidal gua.

Upper Gua: The upper three-line symbol, also known as the outer gua.

Yao: A line of a gua, either yin (yielding, broken) or yang (firm, solid).

Index

CHART OF THE TRIGRAMS AND HEXAGRAMS

Find the point of intersection of your upper and lower trigrams to find the number of your hexagram

Upper Trigram

	Qian Heaven	Zhen Thunder	Kan Water	Gen Mountain	Kun Earth	Xun Wind	Li Fire	Dui Lake
Qian Heaven	1	34	5	26	11	9	14	43
Zhen Thunder	25	51	3	27	24	42	21	17
Kan Water	6	40	29	4	7	59	64	47
Gen Mountain	33	62	39	52	15	53	56	31
Kun Earth	12	16	8	23	2	20	35	45
Xun Wind	44	32	48	18	46	57	50	28
Li Fire	13	55	63	22	36	37	30	49
Dui Lake	10	54	60	41	19	61	38	58

Lower Trigram